Vital Records of the
PROTESTANT DUTCH REFORMED CHURCH
at
Acquackanonk (Passaic, New Jersey)
1727-1816
(INCLUDING SOME BIRTHS 1692-1726)
and
Acquackanonk Reformed Church Graveyard

Transcribed and Indexed by

Arthur C. M. Kelly

Previous Holland Society Collections

Records of:

I. Reformed Dutch Church of Hackensack, N.J.	1891
II. Reformed Dutch Church of Schraalenburgh, N.J.	1891
III. Reformed Dutch Church of New Paltz, N.Y.	1896
IV. Reformed Dutch Church of Bergen, N.J.	1915
V. Domine Henricus Selyns of New York, 1686-7	1916

Note: These books are now out of print, but are available in libraries. Certain of these records and others have been published in Holland Society Year Books

KiNSHiP

60 Cedar Heights Road
Rhinebeck, New York 12572
1992

Ministers who served this church include:

1694-(1723)	Guliam Bertholf
1726-1734	Henricus Coens
1735-1748	Johannes Van Driessen
1752-1773	David Marinus
1774-1816	Henricus Schoonmaker

Abbreviations used in this volume:

b	- born	j.d.	- young daughter, single female
bap	- baptised	j.m.	- young man, single male
Co.	- County	liv	- lives, living
cong	- congregation, community, parish	mar	- married
dau	- daughter	Riv.	- river
d	- died	sn	- son
e	- elected	w	- wife
i	- installed	wid	- widow(er)

Transcribed and indexed by:
Arthur C.M. Kelly
Rhinebeck, New York 12572
June 1, 1977
copyright Arthur C.M. Kelly 1977
ISBN   1-56012-037-1

KĬNSHĬP
60 Cedar Heights Road
Rhinebeck, New York 12572
1977

TABLE OF CONTENTS

PREFACE

The vital records of this church are presented chronologically in this volume with the contents of each section (Baptisms, Marriages, etc) following a columnar format that will be evident from the page headings. They were carefully copied from photostats of the originals and compared with transcripts made previously and now housed in the Holland Society Library. This copy is presumed to be as accurate as the quality of the manuscript would allow. Where the information in the original seemed confusing, footnotes or other notations by the compiler have been included. Cases of illegibility or uncertainty are copied with parenthesis to show that the letter(s) or date(s) enclosed by those parenthesis are questionable. Apparent errors in spelling or dates were copied as found and are followed by a "?". Interpretation is left to the reader.

The Index: See note regarding indexing on page 150.

Page Color Code: White   - transcript of record
                   Blue   - Parent's/Married/General index
                   Yellow - Sponsor's/Other index

A. C. M. K.

Additional copies of this volume, if not available from The Holland Society, can be obtained from the compiler at Rhinebeck, New York.

INTRODUCTION

Soon after the organization of The Holland Society of New York, the attention of its trustees was called to the importance of collecting and publishing the records of the old Dutch churches in the area formerly known as New Netherland. Subsequently the first volume, Records of the Reformed Dutch Churches of Hackensack and Schraalenburgh, New Jersey, appeared in 1891, to be followed by other Dutch church records, either in separate volumes or within the pages of the Year Books of the Holland Society, until 1928.

Now, following a regretable lapse, publication of these records is being resumed with the current volume, Records of the Protestant Dutch Reformed Church at Acquackanonk (Passaic, New Jersey) which includes the baptisms, marriages, members, consistory members, and pew holders of this church from 1726 to 1815 with some obvious omissions due to missing records. Also included is a list of inscriptions from the old Acquackanonk graveyard.

For a period of 30 years (1694-1724) the Acquackanonk and Hackensack churches were served by a joint consistory representing both churches under the pastorate of Domine Guiliam Bertholf. Members, marriages, baptisms and names of consistory members for both churches during this period appear in Records of the Reformed Dutch Churches of Hackensack and Schraalenburgh, New Jersey. Although the Acquackanonk church was organized as early as 1693, its first volume of records as an independent church began in 1726 when the Rev. Henricus Coens became the minister at Acquackanonk exclusively. N.B.

Baptism records of the Fairfield Dutch Reformed Church, first known as Horseneck and later as Gansegat, an adjacent community to Acquackanonk, are included from June 5, 1741 to March 1, 1748, a period when the Rev. Johannes Van Driessen served both of these churches. Additionally, the membership list of the Totowa Dutch Reformed Church, contiguous to Acquackanonk, was recorded in the Acquackanonk records from May 9, 1793 to August 27, 1813 during the time that the Rev. Henricus Schoonmaker was minister of these churches.

A history of the Acquackanonk church by two of its later pastors, the Rev. Ame Vennema and the Rev. Dr. John Gaston, can be found in A History of the Classis of Paramus of the Reformed Church of America 1800-1900, published by the Board of Publications, R.C.A. in 1902.

The contents of this volume were carefully compared with the original records preserved by The Protestant Reformed Dutch Church at Acquackanonk of Passaic, New Jersey and compiled by Arthur C.M. Kelly who was selected for his demonstrated ability in transcribing church records. They amend and supersede previous limited publications that are out of print.

The Holland Society of New York gratefully acknowledges the kind assistance of the Rev. Gordon P. Alexander and cooperation of the church's consistory in permitting the original records to be examined and reproduced here.

June 1, 1977

THE HOLLAND SOCIETY OF NEW YORK
Committee on History and Tradition

*Note: Baptisms #1-174 were probably recorded in 1727 by Rev. Henricus Coens. Where he obtained the information is questionable,- from other church records? from a diary or notebook kept by a previous minister? A history of the church suggests that perhaps they came from Bible entries. However, Bible records normally do not include sponsors so that this possibility seems unlikely. Perhaps the children listed in these first 174 baptisms indicates those that survived at least through 1727. Another confusing item is that these first 174 baptisms are recorded in at least 4 different handwritings although the majority of the information is in the same hand that occurs after Rev. Coens became the minister in 1727.

Baptism year for each item is uncertain but probably occurred in the same year as the birth.

Bap	Parents	Item	Child	Sponsors

Register of children born here at Akquegnonk and baptised since:

Bap	Parents	Item	Child	Sponsors
9.26	Gerrit Hermanusse Annaetje Sip	1	Annaetje b 9.12.1714	Johannes Walings Hillegond Sip
2.18	Same as #1	2	Hermanus b 2.4.1717	Hermannus Gerritse Antje Walings
12.25	Same as #1	3	Lena b 12.3.1720	Arien Sip Gerritje Helmingse
__.__	Same as #1	4	Catarina b 12.8.1722	Johannes Gerritse Margrieta Sip
__.__	Same as #1	5	Janneke b 9.12.1725	Idde Sip Antje Van Wageningen
3.28	Thomas Jurjaense Jannetje Straet	6	Gerrit b 2.6.1692	Geurt Courte Geesje Gerritse
9. 1	Same as #6	7	Jurjaen b 6.12.1693	Jurjaen Tomasse Reykje Harms
11.25	Same as #6	8	Jan b 10.28.1694	Jan Straet Geurtje Harms
5. 4	Same as #6	9	Abram b 4.4.1696	David Hennion Antje Straet
11.16	Same as #6	10	Isaac b 10.28.1697	Christopher Steinmets Gerritje Matteusse
10.23	Same as #6	11	Jacob b 10.9.1699	Aelt Jurjaense Fietje Andriesse
10. 9	Same as #6	12	Geesje b 10.4.1702	Hendrik Gerritse Grietje Straet
10.17	Same as #6	13	Martje b 10.3.1704	Jan Jurjaense Neeltje Gerbrantse
4.13	Same as #6	14	Elisabet b 4.4.1707	Gerrit Post Lea Straet
3. 6	Same as #6	15	Dirck b 1.25.1709	Geurt Juriaens Beletje Dircks
__.__	Gerrit Post Lea Straet	16	Adriaen b 12.18.1705	Jan Straet Katryna Gerrits

Bap	Parents	Item	Child	Sponsors
__.__	Same as #16	17	Geesje b 7.4.1708	Gerrit Stynmets Janneje Straet
__.__	Same as #16	18	Johannes b 8.12.1712	Pieter Van Houte Klaertje Post
__.__	Same as #16	19	Katrina b 11.30.1714	Hannes Post Elisabet Van Houte
__.__	Same as #16	20	Ragel b 3.21.1717	Adriaen Post Elisabet Merselisse
__.__	Same as #16	21	Antje b 8.20.1719	Jan Bon Antje Stynmets
__.__	Same as #16	22	Gerret b 12.12.1721	Peter Post Catrine Beeckman
__.__	Same as #16	23	Leeja b __.__.1723	Gerr't Hendirukse Jannitie Van Houten
__.__	Johannis Post Elisabeth Van Houten	24	Adirean b 6.25.1715	Peter Van Houten Clartie Post
__.__	Same as #24	25	Helmegh b 5.4.1717	Johannes Gerretze Katlintie Van Houten
__.__	Same as #24	26	Catrina b 10.11.1720	Peter Post Catrina Beeckman
__.__	Same as #24	27	Gerret b 9.2.1722	Casparis Stinmets Lena Stynmets
__.__	Same as #24	28	Jannitie b 10.7.1724	Helmigh Van Houter Jannitie Van Houten
__.__	Same as #24	29	Peter b 11.6.1726	Arye Sip Gerretie Van Houten
__.__	Arent Toors Gertruy Spier	30	Francintie b 5.23.1704	Jan Spier Francintie Toors
__.__	Same as #30	31	Johannis b 10.1.1706	Louwerence Toors Marrya Spier
__.__	Same as #30	32	Louwerence b 6.7.1712	Johannis Toors Marytie Toors
__.__	Same as #30	33	Jacob b 1.20.1715	Roelof Van Houten Jannitie Spier
__.__	Same as #30	34	Maritie b 8.23.1718	Cornelus Toors Leeja Spier
__.__	Same as #30	35	Abram b 5.20.1723	Jacob Vrie Landt Antie Toors
2.19	Jan Juriance Neeltie Gerrebrantze	36	Jurie b 1.22.1703	Gerrebrant Classe Ryke Harmse
3.30	Same as #36	37	Marritie b 3.16.1706	Tho's Juriance Maritie Clasen
8. 5	Same as #36	38	Mettie b 7.22.1711	Gerret Jurriance Metie Gerrebrantze

Bap	Parents	Item	Child	Sponsors
6.13	Same as #36	39	Gerrebrant b 6.1.1719	Gerret Gerretze jr Marritia Gerrebrantze
__.__	Cornelus Doremes Rachel Peterze	40	Elisab'th b 7.1.1711	Hessel Peterze Jannitie Van Eels Landt
__.__	Same as #40	41	Jannitie b 11.4.1714	Thom:s Deremes Annika Ackerman
__.__	Same as #40	42	Peter b 8.11.1717	Tho's Oldwater Mettie Peterze
__.__	Same as #40	43	Cornelius b 2.11.1720	Jorys Deremes Maritie Berdan
__.__	Same as #40	44	Maritie b 5.15.1721	Magiel Vree Landt Elsie Peterze
__.__	Same as #40	45	Jenneke b 9.7.1726	Hendreck Deremes Antie Peters
__.__	Jurye Thom:s Altie Van Winkel	46	Thomas b 1.7.1715	Thom's Juriance Antie Van Winkel
__.__	Same as #46	47	Anite b 11.4.1716	Marinus Van Winckle Leeja Van Winckel
__.__	Same as #46	48	Simion b 2.8.1719	Didrick Straat Trintye Buys
__.__	Same as #46	49	Jenneke b 12.25.1720	Simon Van Winckel Jannitie Straat
__.__	Same as #46	50	Abra'm b 9.27.1722	Abr'm Tho:s Elisa'th Peterze
__.__	Same as #46	51	Johannis b 5.7.1725	Jan Tho:s Marritie Thomese
6. 2	Evert Wessels Annatie Reyorse	52	Jannetje b 5.19.1716	Hermanus Gerritse Annaetje Sip
6. 2	Same as #52	53	Lena b 5.20.1718	Joris Reyerse Antje Schouten
11.13	Same as #52	54	Wessel b 10.28.1720	Marten Reyerse Martje Reyerse
2. 1	Same as #52	55	Antje b 1.24.1724	
2. 1	Same as #52	56	Joris b 1.24.1724	
__.__	Cornelis Helmerichs Van Houte Echje Vreland	57	Jannetje b 1.21.1712	Dirk Vreland Catalyntje Van Houte
__.__	Same as #57	58	Johannes b 3.25.1714	Peter Helmerichse Jannetje Vreeland
__.__	Same as #57	59	Helmerich b 4.12.1716	Elias Vreland Gerritje Van Houte
__.__	Same as #57	60	Klaesje b 4.30.1721	Johannes Van Houte Helena Vreeland

Probably recorded in 1727 - see page 1

Bap	Parents	Item	Child	Sponsors
4.13	Same as #57	61	Fietje b 4.8.1725	Roelof Van Houte Fietje Sichels
__.__	Dirk Helmerichse Van Houte Netje Gerbrants	62	Martje b 9.25.1715	Jan Jurjaense Neeltje Gerbrants
__.__	Same as #62	63	Jannetje b 4.19.1717	Jacob Van Houte Janneke Van Houte
__.__	Same as #62	64	Dirk b 12.24.1722	Roelof Van Houte Fitje Sichels
__.__	Same as #62	65	Jacob b 8.22.1724	Peter Helmerichse Klaertje Post
__.__	Isaac Van Der Hoev Elisabet Van Seyl	66	Annaetje b 8.10.1726	Hendrik Valk Antte Dits
3.22	Arye Sip Gerretie Van Houten	67	Annatie b 3.15.1712	Jacob Van Houten Antie Sip
3.18	Same as #67	68	Hellegmek b 3.10.1715/16	Edde Sip Jannike Van Houten
8.25	Same as #67	69	Johannis b 8.17.1718	Johannis Van Winckel Heligond Sip
4.23	Same as #67	70	Jannitie b 4.15.1722	Piter Van Houten Clartie Post
__.__	Johannis Louw Sarah Provoost	71	Maria b 9.23.1726	Josias Ogden Marrya Van Der Poel
4.13	Isaac Kip jr Anna Van Noorstrand	72	Jannetie b 2.1.1725	
__.__	Jacobus Post Maria Kirstien	73	Francoses b 9.3.1724	Frans Post Lena Van Schyven
__.__	Same as #73	74	Jacobus b 6.20.1726	Peter Van Houten Clartie Post
4.18	Gerret Gerretze jr Maritie Gerrebrantze	75	Marritie b 4.17.1715	Didrick Van Hooren Elisab'th Gerretze
1.29	Same as #75	76	Leeja b 1.8.1720	Johannis Niefie Antie Gerretze
10.11	Same as #75	77	Gerrebrant b 9.21.1723	Jan Jurance Neeltie Gerrebrantze
__.__	Dirk Barendse Elisabeth Gerritse	78	Gerrit b 10.1.1706	Peter Helmerigse Klaertje Post
1. 1 1711	Same as #78	79	Geertje b 12.17.1710	Gerrit Gerritse Atje Gerritse
__.__	Same as #78	80	Johannes b 1.12.1717	Johannes Gerritse Margreta Sip
__.__	Same as #78	81	Lea b 6.6.1720	Peter Gerritse Froutje Hesselse
__.__	Same as #78	82	Neesje b 10.22.1723	Johannes Neefje Martje Gerbrandse

Bap	Parents	Item	Child	Sponsors
__.__	Johannis Gerretze Margritie Sip	83	Gerret b 1.29.1714	Peter Gerretze Antie Sip
__.__	Same as #83	84	Johannis b 2.27.1721	Diderick Van Hoorn Lybe Gerretze
__.__	Same as #83	85	Cornel(us) b 7.2.1723	Johannis Van Wincke(l) Hellegond Sip
__.__	Same as #83	86	Jacobus b 4.27.1725	Gerret Harmanes Froutje Hessels
__.__	Roelof Van Houte Fietje (Sich)els	87	Cornelis b 1.16.1715	Peter Van Houte Claertje Post
__.__	Same as #87	88	Johannes b 6.1.1717	Hendrik Sichelse Geertrui Frerikse
__.__	Same as #87	89	Jannetje b 3.19.1719	Arien Sip Gerritse Van Houte
__.__	Same as #87	90	Geertrui b 1.20.1721	Jacob Van Houte Marietje Sichels
__.__	Same as #87	91	Catalyntje b 6.8.1726	Dirk Van Houte Metje Gerbrands
__.__	Jacob Van Houte Marietje Sichels	92	Jannetje b 2.24.1719	Dirk Van Houte Mettje Gerbrands
__.__	Dirk Dey Jannetje Blanshar	93	Thuenis b 10.18.1726	Mother
4.29	Johannes Doremes Elisabeth Akkerman	94	Jannetje b 4.27.1711	Abraham Akkerman Jannetje Van Elsland
1.23	Same as #94	95	Abraham b 1.2.1714	Abraham Akkerman Aeltje Van Laer
6.19	Same as #94	96	Aeltje b 6.3.1718	Andries Hoppe Abigaeltje Akkerman
9.30	Same as #94	97	Cornelis b 9.7.1722	Hendrik Doremes Antje Hesselse
__.__	Peter Gerritse Froutje Hesselse	98	Gerrit b 11.7.1711	Hessel Pieterse Elisabeth Kuiper
__.__	Same as #98	99	Elisabeth b 8.5.1713	Dirk Barendse Elisabeth Gerritse
__.__	Same as #98	100	Hessel b 12.11.1715	Hessel Peterse Helena Bruin
__.__	Same as #98	101	Peter b 3.29.1719	Gerrit Gerritse Martje Gerbrantse
__.__	Same as #98	102	Johannes b 11.14.1721	Johannes Gerritse Elisabeth Hesselse
__.__	Same as #98	103	Neesje b 3.11.1724	Hendrik Doremes Antje Hesselse
__.__	Same as #98	104	Froutje b 2.6.1727	Abraham Thomasse Margreta Sip

Probably recorded in 1727 - see page 1

Bap	Parents	Item	Child	Sponsors
__.__	Adriaen Fran. Post Catharina Sanders	105	Franco(i)s b 2.26.1718	Francois Post Mayke Jacobusse
__.__	Same as #105	106	Alexander b 2.29.1720	Sander Egbertse Magdalena Van Gysen
__.__	Same as #105	107	Peter b 9.6.1722	Egbert Sandersse *(Helena Van) Schyven
__.__	Same as #105	108	Elsje b 4.1.1726	Hendrik Post Catharina Van Winkel
__.__	Dirk Hartman Vreeland Margreta Banta	109	Hartman b 1.24.1704	Klaes Vreland Hester Banta
__.__	Same as #109	110	Rachel b 7.16.1707	Dirk Epke Banta *(Martje Vreeland)
__.__	Same as #109	111	Martje b 4.7.1709	Klaes Vreeland Antje Banta
__.__	Same as #109	112	Hester b 2.25.1712	Johan Dirkse Banta Martje Vreeland
__.__	Same as #109	113	Dirk b 11.16.1715	Enoch Vreeland Sietje Banta
__.__	Same as #109	114	Johannes b 10.12.1719	Jacob Dirkse Banta Raechel Banta
__.__	Same as #109	115	Antje b 7.4.1722	Thomas Frerikse Leea Banta
__.__	Thomas Frerikse Martje Vreeland	116	Hartman b 2.10.1714	Andries Frerikse Fietje Vreeland
__.__	Same as #116	117	Catharina b 9.16.1710	Dirk Hart Vreeland Pirsilla Hooms
__.__	Same as #116	118	Martje b 1.29.1717	Klaes H. Vreeland Martje Frerikse

(female sponsor's surname "Vreeland" crossed out)

Bap	Parents	Item	Child	Sponsors
__.__	Same as #116	119	Frederik b 4.28.1719	Cornelis Van Houte Aegtje Vreeland
__.__	Same as #116	120	Abraham (twin) b *(1.29).1721	Harmen Jur(r)aense Margriet Banta
__.__	Same as #116	121	Isaac (twin) b *(1.29).1721	Gerrit Thomasse Jannetje *(Vreeland)
__.__	Paulus Van Der Beek Catalina Reyerse	122	Catalyna b 10.25.1704	Simon Van Es Hester De Lammeter
__.__	Same as #122	123	Maria b 2.21.1706	Frans Reyerse Janneke Dey
__.__	Same as #122	124	Sara b 12.31.1708	Abraham Bresser Sara Schoute
__.__	Same as #122	125	Elisabeth b 4.7.1711	Hendrik Brackos Debora Berri

* - manuscript destroyed

Bap	Parents	Item	Child	Sponsors
__.__	Roelof Corn. Van Houte Jannetje Spyr	126	Helena b 10.15.1715	Bastiaen Van Gysen Helena Van Gysen
__.__	Same as #126	127	Cornelis b 4.11.1717	Reinier Corn. Van Houten Lea Spyr
__.__	Same as #126	128	Johannes b 11.30.1719	Johannes Spyr Maria Fransen
__.__	Same as #126	129	Jacob b 10.26.1721	Jacob Spyr Gerritje Spyr
__.__	Same as #126	130	Maria b 12.30.1724	Arent Lourense Tours Geertruit Spyr
__.__	Same as #126	131	Henricus b 2.17.1726	Hessel Pieterse Lena Bruin
4.23	Cornelis Westerveld Antje Breant	132	Jurjaen b 3.25.1727	Jurjaen Westerveld Cornelia Stevense
12.21	Stephanus V: Courland Cathalina Staet(es)	133	Olif Stephanus b 11.22.1719	Samuel Bayard Cathalina Phillips
2.30?	Same as #133	134	Johannes b 2.16.1721	Arent Schuyler Anna V: Courland
1.21 1723	Same as #133	135	Cathalina b 12.31.1722	Eduard Smit Tryntje Staets
1.22	Same as #133	136	Phillip b 1.7.1727	Dom. William *(Skin)ner Elisabeth V. Cortland
__.__	Frans Fransisco Harmtje Xanders	137	Jan b 3.5.1719	Alexander Egtbertse Magdalena Van Gysen
__.__	Johannes Fransisco Grietje Beuis	138	* *	Jan Jurjaense Neeltje Gerbrants
4.26	Johannes Jacobse Van Winkel Tietske Banta	139	Hendrik b 3.20.1714	Hendrik Epke Agnietje Helling
__.__	Same as #139	140	Jacob b 3._*.1716	Abraham Vreeland Margrietje Van Winkel
__.__	Same as #139	141	Johannes b 7.3.1719	Jacob B*(anta) Margrietje Banta
3.16 1724	Same as #139	142	A-nietje, twin b 12.16.1723	Hendrik Banta Geertruy Ter Huin
3.16 1724	Same as #139	143	Daniel, twin b 12.16.1723	Jacob Jacobs V. Winkel Grietje Helling
12.17 1726	Same as #139	144	Aeltje b 11.25.1726	Jacob Jacobs V. Winkel Egje Pauwelse
__.__	Alexander Couifer Johanna Kind	145	Alexander b 3.8.1721	Johannes Simons Van Win Leentje Spyr /kel
__.__	Same as #145	146	Elisabeth b 3.4.1724	Abraham Fransisco Elisabeth Steg
__.__	Harmen Jurjaense Marietje Frerikse	147	Jurjaen b 9.12.1710	Jan Jurjaense Brisilla Homs

* - manuscript destroyed

Probably recorded in 1727 - see page 1

Bap	Parents	Item	Child	Sponsors
__.__	Same as #147	148	Frerik b 2.22.1713	Guert Jurjaense Geertruy Frerikse
__.__	Same as #147	149	Abraham b 1.25.1716	Thomas Jurjaense Jannetje Straet
__.__	Same as #147	150	Johannes b 7.21.1718	Thomas Frerikse Martje H. Vreeland
__.__	Harmen Jurjaense Judith Steinmets	151	Christopher b 9.6.1722	Christopher Steinmets Sara Van Nest
__.__	Same as #151	152	Marietje b 9.14.1724	Klaes Gerbrantse Martje Jurjaense
__.__	Hendrik Doremes Antje Hesselse	153	Elisabeth b 2.3.1717	Hessel Peterse Helena Bruin
__.__	Same as #153	154	Jannetje b 2.13.1719 Marietje	Joris Vreeland, J.M. Jorisse Van Elsland
__.__	Same as #153	155	Cornelis b 3.20.1721	Cornelis Doremes Rachel Hesselse
__.__	Same as #153	156	Hessel b 7.10.1723	Peter Gerritse Froutje Hesselse
__.__	Same as #153	157	Annetje b 9.20.(1725)*	Johannes Doremes Elisabeth Akkerman
__.__	Frans Oudwaeter Jannetje Doremes	158	Catharina b 4.10.1718	Thomas Oudwaeter Antje Hesselse
__.__	Same as #158	159	Jannetje b 8.29.1722 Marietje	Hendrik Doremes Jorisse Van Elsland
__.__	Same as #158	160	Marietje b 3.20.1724	Jacob Oudwater Marietje Vreeland, j.d.
__.__	Frans Oudwaeter Johanna *(Sanderson)	161	Thomas b 4.28.1727	Jan Oudwater Aeltje Bruin
__.__	Peter Van Houte Claertje Post	162	Jannetje b 2.16.1704	Adriaen Post Elisabet Marselisse
__.__	Same as #162	163	Adriaen b 8.17.1706	Roelof Van Houte Eegje Vreeland
__.__	Same as #162	164	Helmerich b 12.10.1709	Gerrit Post Lea Straet
__.__	Same as #162	165	Johannes, twin b 3.17.1713	Johannes Post Elisabet Van Houte
__.__	Same as #162	166	Catarina, twin b 3.17.1713	Jacob Van Houte Annetje Steynmets
__.__	Same as #162	167	Gerrit b 9.24.1721	Peter Post Catarina Beekman
__.__	Thomas Doremes Annaeke Akkerman	168	Cornelis b 4.16.1714	Cornelis Doremes Rachel Peterse
__.__	Same as #168	169	Abraham b 8.31.1716	Abraham Akkerman Aeltje Van Laer

* - manuscript destroyed

Bap	Parents	Item	Child	Sponsors
__.__	Same as #168	170	Johannes b 3.29.1719	Johannes Doremes Elisabeth Akkerman
__.__	Same as #168	171	Golyn b 3.20.1722	Golyn Akkerman Sara Akkerman
12.26 1725	Same as #168	172	Aeltje b 12.14.1725	Andries Hoppe Abigael Akkerman
__.__	Abraham Thomasse Elisabeth Hesselse	173	Jannetje b 4.17.1723	Thomas Jurjaense Jannetje Straetmaker
__.__	Same as #173	174	Elisabeth b 11.17.1726	Hessel Pieterse Helena Bruin

----

1727		1727		
6.25	Henricus Coens Belia Provoost	175	Helena b 6.21	David Provoost Catarina Provoost
7.16	father unknown Neeltje Messeker	176	Neeltje b 4.17 illegitimate	Mother
8. 6	Hendrik Bos Maria Stegers	177	Marietje b 7.11	Barend Fransisco Catalina Stegers
8.13	Gerrit Post Fransyntje Petersen	178	Claertje b 8.11	Johannes Petersen Aerjaentje Hui(s)mans
8.13	Jan Uyt Den Bogaerd Margreta Paelding	179	Dirk b 8.7	Roelof Potter Elisabeth Ekker
8.13	Hendrik Van Nes Catharina Jacobusse	180	Hester b 7.21	Johannes Jacobusse Geertruy Beuis
8.27	Johannhs Post Johanna Houwerd	181	Claertje b 8.7	Hendrik Post, j.m. Geesje Post, j.d.
8.27	Thomas Stegh Sietje Bruin	182	Silvester b 8.9	Thomas Stegh Anna Meyers
8.27	Peter Zanderson Margrietje Stegh	183	Silvester b 7.28	Abraham Fransisco Silvester Stegh, j.d.?
8.27	Isaac Kingsland Hanna Kraen	184	Isaac b 7.30	Edmond Kingsland Maria Pinhorn
8.27	Jacob Van Noordstrand Antje Steinmets	185	Christopher b 8.13	Peter Steinmets Mother
9. 3	Johannes Gerritse Margrietje Sip	186	Hendrik b 8.17	Arien Sip Gerritje Van Houte
9. 3	Johannes Brikker Fransyntje Toers	187	Susanna b 8.23	Arent Toers Geertruy Spyr
9.24	Isaac Kip Anna Van Noordstrand	188	Catalina b 8.26	Hessel Peterse Lena Bruin
9.24	Jurjaen Thomasse Aeltje Van Winkel	189	Rachel b 9.4	Simeon Van Winkel Pryntje Van Gysen
10.22	Evert Wessels Antje Reyerse	190	Lucas b 10.21	Elisabeth Reyerse

Bap	Parents	1727-1728 Item	Child	Sponsors
11. 5	Roelof Van Houte Jannetje Spyer	191	Abraham b 10.12	Hendrik Spyer Magdalena Van Gysen
11. 5	Cornelis Toers Sara Akkerman	192	Lourens b 10.26	Arie Toers Anna Immit
11.12	Casparus Tadesse Jannetje Post	193	Fransoos b 9.22	Hendrik Post Annetje Steinmets
11.26	Johannes Tadesse Petertje Van Houte	194	Cathrina b 9.30	Thuenis Van Houte Mother
11.26	Staes Bos Anna Van Winkel	195	Josua b 11.1	Hendrik Bos Lea Van Blerkum
11.26	Elias Smit Cornelia Woortendyk	196	Fransooys b 11.8	Jacob Van Houte Maria Sichelse
12.31	Frans Fransisco Harmtje Xanders	197	Alexander b 11.27	Hendrik Fransisco Laveyntje Koeck
1728 1.14	Hendrik Mendevyl Elisabeth Vreeland	198	Peter b 12.24.1727	Klaes Vreeland Elsje Peterse
2. 4	Cornelis Dreek Maria Toers	199	Jacobus b 1.16	Cornelis Van Houte Egje Vreeland
2. 4	Marten Van Duyn Maria Themouth	200	Elisabeth b 1.2	Jacob Themouth Elisabeth Febers
2. 4	Richard Day Elisabeth Reyke	201	Antje b 12.26.1727	
2.25	Dirk Dey Jannetje Blanshar	202	Janneke b 1.18	Janneke Dey
3.10	Harmen Jurjaense Judith Steinmets	203	Jacob b 2.8	Jacob Tomasse Neeltje Gerbreantse
3.10	Johannes Dideriks Geertruy Van Winkel	204	Jacob b 2.12	Gerrit Dideriks Aeltje Van Wageningen
4. 7	Johannes Doremes Elisabeth Akkerman	205	Elisabeth b 3.13	Mother
4.21	Johannes Reyerse Geertje Hesselse	206	Elisabeth b 4.6	Peter Gerritse Froutje Hesselse
4.22	Gerrit Gerritse jr Martje Gerbrandse	207	Neesje b 4.17	Dirk Van Houte Metje Gerbrandse
5. 3	Hendrik Doremes Antje Hesselse	208	Froutje b 4.20	Andries Frerikse Geertje Klaese Kuiper
5. 5	Cornelis Van Houte Egje Vreeland	209	Cathalina b 4.18	Johannes Post Elisabeth Van Houte
5. 5	Johannes Peterse Adrijaentje Huisman	210	Tryntje b 4.27	Gerrit Post Fransyntje Peterse
5.19	Hendrik Kip Geertruy Van Dyn	211	Gerrit b 4.25	Cornelis Van Dyn Elisabeth Kip
5.19	Golyn Akkerman Rachel Van Voorheesen	212	Abraham b 5.2	Lourens Akkerman Geesje Pauwelse

Bap	Parents	Item	Child	Sponsors
6.10	Johannes Meet Maria Blanshar	213	Jacob b 5.11	Jillis Meet Jannetje Blanshar
6.16	Andries Van Gysen Martje Dirkje	214	Abraham b 5.18	Simeon Van Winkel Prientje Van Gysen
6.16	Gerrit Hendrikse Jannetje Van Houte	215	Hendrik b 5.31	Johannes Post Elisabeth Van Houte
6.30	Marten Berry Maria Rome	216	Maria b 6.6	Willem Rome Sara Turk
7. 7	Johannes Van Gysen Annaetje Westerveld	217	Aeltje b 6.23	Bastyaen Van Gysen Aeltje Blinkerhof
7. 7	Zacharias Ellerton Catryntje Valk	218	Aerjaentje b 6.8	Hendrik Valk Aerjaentje Brouwer
8.18	Gerrit De Boog Marietje Van Der Beek	219	Catalina b 8.17	Paulus Van Der Beek Catalina Reyerse
8.25	Dirk Terhuin Catharina Kip	220	Albert b 8.21	Abraham Huisman Gerrebregt Terhuin
9.15	Abraham Akkerman Hendrikje Hoppe	221	Aeltje b 8.25	Lourens Akkerman Geesje Martese
10.13	Baerent Van Hoorn Rachel Aeltse	222	Aeltje b 9.19	Jurjaen Aeltse Martje Vreeland
10.27	Johannes Neefjes Antje Gerritse	223	Elisabeth b 10.7	Gerrit Van Hoorn Geertje Van Hoorn
10.27	Johannes Van Seil Lena Van Blerkum	224	Sara b 10.6	Isaac Van Seil Sara Key
11.17	Gerbrand Klaeseb Johanna Steynmets	225	Christopher b 11.2	Christopher Steynmets Sara Van Nest
11.24	Gerrit Hermanusse Antje Sip	226	Johannes b 11.18	Michiel Van Winkel Geertruy Van Winkel
11.24	Isaac Van Der Hoev Elisabeth Van Seyl	227	Dortie b 10.30	Jan Jurjaense Neeltje Gerbrants
11.24	Albert Bordan	228	Jan b 11.4	Jan Bordan
12.25	Johannes Steg Hendrikje Huisman	229	Neeltje b 12.2	Thomas Steg Grietje Steg
12.26	Simeon Van Winkel Prientje Van Gysen	230	Janneke b 10.9	Abraham Van Winkel Anna Maria Van Gysen
1729 1. 5	Jan Oudwaeter Aeltje Bruin	231	Tryntje b 11.29.1728	Barend Bruin Antje Bruin
1. 5	Philip Schuyler Hester Kingsland	232	Janneke b 10.26.1728	Hessel Peterse Lena Bruin
1. 5	Johannes Hennion Antje Taelman	233	Antje b 12.5.1728	Gerrit Van Waegening Jannetje Van Houte
1. 5	Thomas Stegh Sietje Bruin	234	Hendrik b 12.9.1728	Abraham Franssoos Elisabeth Stegh

Bap	Parents	1729 Item	Child	Sponsors
1. 5	Cornelis Kip Annaetje Bordan	235	Elisabeth b 12.19.1728	Jacob Kip Helena Bordan
1.26	Dirk Van Seyl Tryntje Van Blerkum	236	Egbert b 9.30.1728	Johannes Van Seyl Helena Van Blerkum
3. 9	Elias Vreeland Lea Aeltse	237	Gerrit b 2.5	Peter Adolf Martje Aeltse
3. 9	Lourens Akkerman Geesje Martense	238	Margrietje b 2.10	Marten Pauwelse Marietje Martense
3.23	Frans Oudwaeter Johanna Xanderse	239	Annaetje b 2.17	Thomas Oudwater Anna Oudwater
3.23	Abraham Gerritse Rachel Hesselse	240	Hendrik b 3.5	Gerret Ger. Van Wagening Martje Gerbrandse
3.30	Peter Tibou Margrietje Reyerse	241	Catrina b 3.1	Willem Traphage Catrina Traphage
4.13	Baerend Fransisco Catalina Stegers	242	Johannes b 3.10	Johannes Fransisco Margrietje Beuis
4.13	Gerrit Van Vorst Sara Van Winkel	243	Waling b 4.5	Johannes Dideriks Geertruy Van Winkel
6. 8	Dirk Vreeland Sietje Banta	244	Klaesje b 4.25	Jacob Banta Rachel Banta
6.15	Paulus Berri Annaetje Suidam	245	Paulus b 5.26	Paulus Van Der Beek Catalina Reyerse
6.15	Jurjaen Thomasse Aeltje Van Winkel	246	Lea b 6.14	Isaac Thomasse Geesje Gerritse
6.27	Abraham Kaljer Hanna Peerker	247	Elisabet b 2.20.1725	Jacob Thomasse Marietje Gerbrandse
6.27	Same as #247	248	Susanna b 9.8.1727	Jan Lodloo Maria Merrel
6.29	Willem Rome Sara Turk	249	Henricus b 6.27	Henricus Coens Belia Provoost
7. 6	Johannes Van Houte Helena Vreeland	250	Helmerich b 6.22	Marten Wenne Jannetje Vreeland
7. 6	Thomas Frerikse Martje Vreeland	251	Jacob b 6.20	Cornelis Brinkerhoff Eghje Vreeland
7.20	Johannes Toers Lea Spyr	252	Rachel b 7.3	Jacob Spyr Egje Van Houte
8. 3	Gerrit Post Fransyntje Peterse	253	Jannetje b 7.15	Casparus Steinmets Rachel Peterse
8. 3	Adriaen Post Tryntje Xanderse	254	Antje b 7.3	Jacobus Post Marietje Christyn
8.10	Johannes Gerritse Margrietje Sip	255	Abraham b 7.26	Gerrit Joh: V: Waegening, Mother /j.m.
8.17	Peter Gerritse Froutje Hesselse	256	Lea, twin b 8.10	Jacob Van Wagening Lea Jurjaense

Bap	Parents	1729 Item	Child	Sponsors
8.17	Same as #256	257	Helena, twin b 8.10	Peter Hesselse Klaesje Hesselse
9.21	Cornelis Toers Sara Akkerman	258	Abraham b 9.1	Thomas Doremes Anneke Akkerman
9.21	Petrus Van Blerkum Rachel Van Seil	259	Johannes b 9.3	Johannes Van Blerkum Jannetje Van Seil
9.21	Staeds Bos Johanna Van Winkel	260	Catrina b 9.4	Josua Bos Willemtje De Groot
9.21	Johannes Post Elisabeth Van Houte	261	Catrina b 9.15	Cornelis Van Houte Egje Vreeland
10. 5	Jacob Thomasse Maria Gerbrandse	262	Catrina b 9.28	Jan Thomasse, j.m. Petertje Post, j.d.
10. 5	Gerrit Van Hoorn Elisabeth Thomasse	263	Dirk b 9.29	Dirk Barendse Elisabeth Gerritse
10.19	Cornelis Westerveld Antje Brieant	264	Grietje b 9.28	Jurjaen Thomasse Aeltje Van Winkel
10.19	Casparus Tades Hendrikje De Grauw	265	Hermannus b 10.2	Parents
10.19	Evert Wesselse Annaetje Reyerse	266	Maria b 10.12	Jacob Van Houte Marietje Sichelse
10.12	Harmen Jurjaense Judith Steynmets	267	Isaac b 9.30	Peter Steynmets Elisabeth Steynmets
10.26	Benjamin Steynmet- Anna Van Stee	268	Sara b 9.20	Christopher Steynmets Sara Van Nest
10.26	Hendrik Van Nes Catryntje Jacobusse	269	Simon b 10.8	Dirk Steger Jannetje Jacobusse
11. 2	Cornelis Van Der Hoef Elisabeth Akkerman	270	Marietje b 9.19	David Akkerman Sara Kolve
11. 2	Arie Toers Anna Immet	271	Antje b 10.18	Johannes Post Elisabeth Van Houte
11. 9	Jacobus Millids Lena Defvenpoort	272	Antje b 7.21	Johannes Millids Antje Millids
11. 9	Daniel Rothan Harmtje Spyr	273	b __.__.1729	Johannes Reyerse Geertje Hesselse
11.23	Paulus Rothan Elisabeth Vosschue	274	Johannes b 10.19	Jan Van Voorheese Elisabeth Van Norden
11.23	Hendrik Mandevyl Elisabeth Vreeland	275	Hendrik b 10.31	Willem Mandevyl Jannetje Bruin
11.23	Johannes Post Johanna Houwerd	276	Maria (twin) b 11.16	Jan Houwerd Maria Kyrstede
11.23	Same as #276	277	Elisabet (twin) b 11.16	Adriaen Van Houte Geertje Van Hoorn
11.30	Johannes Terhuin Geesje Westerveld	278	Alberth b 11.7	Albertus Terhuin Marietje Akkerman

1729-1730

Bap	Parents	Item	Child	Sponsors
11.30	Johannes Brikker Fransyntje Toers	279	Geertruy b 11.13	Jacob Walings Geertruy Brikkers
12. 7	Cornelis Aeltse Geesje Post	280	Lea b 12.1	Gerrit Post Fransyntje Peterse
12.21	Jan Westerveld Fietje Haering	281	Cornelis b 11.29	Cornelis Westerveld Antje Breant
12.21	Hendrik Post Elisabeth Christyn	282	Fransoois b 12.9	Gysbert Van Blerkum Antje Christyn
12.28	Gerrit De Boog Marietje Van Der Beek	283	Elisabeth b 12.23	Johannes De Boog Sara Van Der Beek
1730 1. 4	Jurjaen Aeltse Martje Vreeland	284	Gerrit b 12.30.1729	Hartman D. Vreeland Antje Aeltse
1. 4	Johannes Dedriks Geertruy Van Winkel	285	Geertruy b 12.29.1729	Johannes Walings Hillegond Sip
1. 4	David Lauw. Akkerman Sara Kolve	286	Egbert b 12.15.1729	Cornelis Van Der Hoef Maria Teba
1.11	Johannes Tadesse Pietertje Van Houte	287	Rachel b 12.30.1729	Arie Van Winkel Jannetje Tadesse
1.11	Dirk Dey Jannetje Blanshaer	288	Johannes b 11.7.1729	Johannes Meet Maria Blanshaer
2. 1	Johannes Akkerman Jakomina De Maree	289	Louwrens b 1.2	Egbert Akkerman Elsje Van Der Beek
2.15	Johannes Van Gysen Annaetje Westerveld	290	Roelof b 12.31.1729	Roelof Westerveld Jannetje Westerveld
2.2(5)	Jacobus Post Marietje Christyn	291	Lena b 1.30	Adriaen F: Post Tryntje Xanders
2.25	Jacob Spyr Echje Van Houte	292	Johannes b 2.15	Hendrik Spyr Maria Franse
3. 1	Gerrit Jacobusse Anna Nes	293	Hester b 12.11.1729	Thomas Cadmus Maria Van Deusse
3. 1	Steven Van Seyl Neeltje Messeker	294	Egbert b 12.29.1729	Hendrik Messeker Femmetje Messeker
3. 8	Peter Xanders Margriet Stegh	295	Annetje b 2.12	Alexander Egbertse Tryntje W. Van Winkel
3.15	Jacob Van Der Hoef Elisabeth Stegers	296	Catryntje b 12.23.1729	Harmen Jurjaense Judith Steynmets
3.15	Barend Van Hoorn Rachel Aeltse	297	Dirk b 2.20	Gerrit Van Hoorn Elisabeth Thomasse
3.15	Marinus Van Winkel Geesje Hendriks	298	Annaetje b 2.2-	Jurjaen Thomasse Aeltje Van Winkel
3.22	Simeon Van Winkel Pryntje Van Gysen	299	Helena b 2.24	Henricus Coens Belia Provoost
3.29	Abraham Brouwer Elisabeth Akkerman	300	Xander b 2.24	Uldrik Brouwer Marietje Brouwer

Bap	Parents	1730 Item	Child	Sponsors
3.29	Gysbert Van Der Hoef Margrietje Vreeland	301	Gerrit b 3.14	Gerrit Van Der Hoef Margrietje Jac: Vreeland
5. 3	Peter Jong Antje Smith	302	Hendrik b 3.20	Roelof Hel: Van Houte Fietje Sichelse
5. 3	Isaac De Lamontanje Nelletje Brouwer	303	Isaac b 4.6	Klaes Hartm: Vreeland Elsje Peterse
5. 3	Hendrik Reyke Marta Gould	304	Marietje b 1.11	Johannes Reyke Rachel Van Nes
5.10	Arie Sip Gerretje Van Houte	305	Cornelis b 5.6	Johannes Post Elisabeth Van Houte
5.17	Isaac Kip Antje Van Noordstrant	306	Helena b 5.1	Jacob Kip Mother
5.24	Johannes Perker Jakomina Van Blerkum	307	Johannes b 3.15	Abraham Van Seyl Raechel Van Blerkum
5.24	Thomas Doremes Anneke Akkerman	308	Thomas b 5.9	Jannetje Doremes
5.31	Enog Hartm: Vreeland Jannetje Van Blerkum	309	Michiel b 5.23	Thomas Frerikse Martje Vreeland
6.28	Marte Berri Maria Rome	310	Sara b 5.26	Paulus Berri Sara Van Der Beek
6.28	Samuel Berri Jakomina Van Duyn	311	Catalina b 6.4	Paulus Van Der Beek Catalina Reyerse
6.28	Cornelis Dreek Maria Toers	312	Sara, twin b 5.24	Johannes Toers Sara Akkerman
6.28	Same as #312	313	Francina, twin b 5.24	Elias Jac: Vreeland Margrietje Jac. Vreeland
6.28	Johannes Cavelier Catalina Enderson	314	Johannes b 6.15	Johannes Neefje Antje Van Wageningen
7. 5	Philip Schuiller Hesther Kingsland	315	Johannes b 6.4	Mother
7. 5	Johannes Hennion Antje Taelman	316	Margrietje b 6.17	Gerrit Hendrikse Jannetje P. Van Houte
7.19	Dirk Steger Jannetje Jacobusse	317	Geertruit b 6.23	Roelof Jacobusse Geertruit Beuis
7.19	Joris Bord Antje Van Winkel	318	Helena b 6.29	Andries Frerikse Geertje Cuiper
7.26	Hendrik Bos Marietje Steger	319	Sara b 6.31?	Jacob Van Der Hoev Elisabeth Steger
9. 6	Elias Thomasse Styntje Meet	320	Maria b 8.6	Joris Vreeland Marietje Jor: Van Elsland
9. 6	Jurjie Peterse Antje Hendrikse	321	Margrietje b 8.20	Gerrit Van Wagening Martje Gerbrandse
9.13	Elias Vreeland Marietje Van Hoorn	322	Johannes b 8.30	Dirk Joh: Vreeland Sytje Banta

-16-

Bap	Parents	Item	Child	Sponsors
		1730-1731		
9.13	Frans Reyerse / Janneke Dey	323	Lena b 8.20	Hendrik Gerritse / Margrietje Straetmacker
10. 4	Johannes Reyke / Rachel Van Nes	324	Marietje b 8.23	Peter Reyke / Hester Van Nes
10. 4	Isaac Van Nes / Neeltje Reyke	325	Petrus b 9.2	Peter Reyke / Marietje Messecer
10.11	Johannes Meet / Maria Blanshaer	326	Isaac b 9.13	Dirk Dey / Mother
10.11	Robert Gould / Geertje Van Duyn	327	Marietje b 8.2(1)	Abraham Van Duyn / Geertje Reyerse
10.11	Gerrit Thomasse / Jannetje Vreeland	328	Antje b 9.16	Jacob Thomasse / Marietje Gerbrandse
10.18	Albert Terhuyn / Marietje Martesse	329	Stephanus b 9.18	Sthephanus Terhuyn / Maria De Maree
10.18	Reynier Van Gysen / Metje Vreeland	330	Metje b 9.24	Helmerich R: Van Houten / Catryna Van Gysen
11. 1	Isaac Thomasse / Lea Van Winkel	331	Simon b 10.3	Jurjie Thomasse / Aeltje Van Winkel
11. 8	Jan Berry / Maria Braedberry	332	Willem b 8.31	Jacob Spyr / Elisabeth Braedberry
11.22	Hendrik Doremes / Antje Hesselse	333	Hendrik b 11.15	Joris Doremes / Martje Bordan
12. 6	Jacob Van Noordstrand / Antje Steinmets	334	Johannes b 11.2	Jurje Jans Jurjaense / Elisabeth Steynmets
12. 6	Johannes Vreeland / Metje Jurjaense	335	Johannes b 11.16	Jan Jurjaense / Neeltje Gerbrandse
12. 6	Gerret Van Hoorn / Elisabeth Thomasse	336	Janneke b 11.17	Abraham Thomasse / Catharina Andriesse
12.13	Johannes Reyerse / Geertje Hesselse	337	Helena b 11.25	Joris Reyerse jr / Klaesje Peterse
12.13	Adriaen Post / Martje Thomasse	338	Adriaen b 12.2	Jan Thomasse / Petertje Post
12.25	Baerend Bruin / Annetje Bortens	339	Hendrik b 12.2	Johannes Bruyn / Hillegond Van Gysen
1731 1.17	Staets Bos / Johanna Van Winkel	340	Johanna b 1.1	Arie Van Winkel / Jannetje Tadesse
1.3	Joris Vreeland / Elsje Meed	341	Johannes b 1.13	Peter Meed / Marietje Joris Van Elsland
2.14	Thomas Stheg / Sietje Bruin	342	Rebekka b 1.13	Johannes Bruin / Lydia Day
2.28	Nicolaes Joons / Elisabeth Bruyn	343	Susanna b 11.21.1730	Hendrik Brackos / Maria Verplank
3. 4	Jan Gould / Martha Aesben	344	Robert b 1.17.1706	

Bap	Parents	1731 Item	Child	Sponsors
3. 4	Jurje Thomasse Aeltje Van Winkel	345	Abraham b 2.12	Abraham Thomasse Cathrina Andriesse
3. 7	Marte Van Duyn Maria Themout	346	Abraham b 1.25	Abraham Van Duyn Geertje Reyerse
3.28	Jacob Scheerman Neeltje Messecor	347	Antje b 2.19	Jacob *(Thomasse) Maria Gerbrandse
3.28	Isaac Van Der Hoef Elisabeth *(___er) Van Seyl	348	Maria b 3.6	Abraham Van Der Hoef Maria Van Seyl
4. 4	Gerret Van Vorst Sara Van Winkel	349	Waling b 3.20	Egbert Xanders Tryntje Wa: Van Winkel
4. 4	Johannes Gerritse Margrietje Sip	350	Hermanus b 3.14	Gerret Van Wagening Martje Gerbrandse
4. 4	Gerbrant Klaesse Johanna Steynmets	351	Martje b 3.8	Jurje Jans Jurjaense Elisabeth Steynmets
4.25	Johannes Reyke Fransina Valk	352	Sara b 9.13.1730	Mother
4.25	Jacob Thomasse Marietje Gerbrandse	353	Harpert b 4.16	Marselis Post Petertje Gerbrandse
5.16	Jacobus Akkerman Dirkje Van Gysen	354	Lourens b 2.24	Andries Van Gysen Martje Dirkse
5.30	Johannes Kyrstede Sietje Bruin	355	Dyna b 5.8	Abraham Hennion Anna Kyrstede
__.__	Johannes Neefje Antje Gerritse	356	Jacobus b 6.14	Jacob H: Van Houten Maria Sichelse
8.2(9)	Hendrik Post Elisabeth Christyn	357	Helena b 8.8	Jacobus Post Maria Christyn
8.29	Barnard Mollen Klaesje Andriesse	358	Jacobus b 8.13	Johannes Cavillier Catalina Andriesse
8.29	Cornelis Aeltse Geesje Post	359		Adriaen G: Post Raechel Harte
9.12	Gerret Post Fransina Peterse	360		Petrus Peterse Lea Peterse
9.12	Hendrik Mandevyl Elisabeth Vreland	361	Elsje b 8.25	Hartman K: Vreeland Maria Brouwer
9.12	Johannes Bruin Femmetje Messecer	362	Johannes b 8.15	Hendrik Messecer Sara Bruin
9.26	Abraham Gerritse Rachel Pieterse	363	Neesje b 9.13	Gerret Joh: Van Wagening Klaesje Peterse
9.26	Johannes Post Elisabeth Van Houte	364	Johannes b 9.2	Jacob Van Houte Maria Sichelse
10.10	Gerret Hendrikse Jannetje Van Houte	365	Klaertje b 9.29	Adriaen Van Houte Cathrina Van Houte
10.28	Derk Van Gysen Helena Marselisse	366	Johannes b 9.23	Basteaen Van Gysen Heltje Blinkerhof

* - manuscript destroyed

1731-1732

Bap	Parents	Item	Child	Sponsors
10.31	Abraham Van Seyl Rachel Van Blerkum	367	Eechje b 9.26	Johannes Neefje Eechje Neefje
11.14	Jilles Meet Jannetje Bruin	368	Johannes b 10.16	Elias Thammis Styntje Meet
11.28	Helmerich Van Houte Catharina Van Gysen	369	Echje b 10.29	Jacob Spyr Echje Van Houten
11.28	Jacob Van Der Hoef Elisabeth Steger	370	Elisabeth b 11.1	Barend Fransiska Cathalina Steger
12. 5	Casparus Tadesse Hendrikje De Grauw	371	Elisabeth b 11.3	Cornelis De Grauw Geertruid Riddenars
12.12	Barend Van Hoorn Rachel Aeltse	372	Elisabeth b 11.18	Cornelis Aeltse Geesje Post
12.12	Johannes Brikker Fransina Toers	373	Hester b 11.12	Johannes Toers Grietje Vreeland
1732 1.30	Marten Berry Maria Rome	374	Henricus b 12.4.1731	Henricus Brakhos Maria Verplank
1.30	Gerrit De Boog Maria Van Der Beek	375	Paulus b 1.2(1)	Paulus Van Der Beek Catalina Reyerse
2. 6	Joris Bord Antje Van Winkel	376	Arie b 1.14	Arie Van Winkel Jannetje Tadisse
2.13	Isaac Brouwer Rachel De Maree	377	Niclaes b 1.1	Klaes Vreeland Elsje Peterse
3.12	Daniel Hennion Lena Andriessen	378	Prisilla b 2.2	Abraham Thomasse Geertje K: Kuiper
3.12	Peter Gerritse Froutje Peterse	379	Gerretje *	* *
4. 2	Gerrit Gerritse Martje Gerbrandse	380	Metje b 3.2	Jurjaen Peterse Antje Hendrikse
4. 9	Jan Oudwaeter Aeltje Bruin	381	Tryntje b 3.12	Barend Bruin Annetje Bortens
4. 9	Petrus Van Blerkum Raechel Van Seyl	382	Egbert b 2.14	Isaac Van Der Hoef Lea Van Seyl
4. 9	Joris Vreeland Elsje Meet	383	Johannes b 2.16	Peter Meet Maria Jor: Van Elsland
4.16	Isaac Van Nes Neeltje Reyke	384	Hester b 2.8	Evert Van Nes Hester De Lameter
4.23	Steven Van Seyl Neeltje Messeker	385	Harmen b 2.14	Frans Koek Sara Franse
4.30	Johannes F: Post Johanna Houwerd	386	Maeyke b 3.21	Johannes Gerritse Post Antje Van Nieuwkerk
5. 7	Robert Gould Geertje Van Duyn	387	Johannes b 3.25	Samuel Berry Jakomina Van Duyn
5.28	Dirk Dey Jannetje Blansjaer	388	Dirk b 5.14	Thuenis Spyr Maria Spyr

* - manuscript destroyed

Bap	Parents	Item	Child	Sponsors
6. 4	Jellis Mendevyl Lea Bruin	389	Magdalena b 3.16	Hendrik Bruyn Margriet Lacomba
6.18	*(Hartman Vreeland) Lea Peterse	390	Peter b 6.9	Paulus Peterse Rachel Vreeland
6.25	Marte Van Duyn Maria Themouth	391	Elisabeth b 5.25	Thomas Stegh Zeytje Bruyn

(parent's names "Peter Sanders & Maregriet Stegh" written in)

7. 2	Jan Ludlouw Susanna Braedberry	392	Jacobus b 6.16	Fredrick Themout Scharlotte Miller

(parent·s names "Marte Van Duyn & Maria Themout" written in)

7. 2	Harmen Jurjaense Judith Steinmets	393	Jan b 6.11	Richard Braedberry Maria Merrel

(parent's names "John Ludlow & Susanna Braedberry" written in)
Note: Sponsors for #391-393 appear to have been written in at
the same time that the Parent's names were changed.

7.10	Harmen Jurjanse Judith Steynmets	394	Sara b 6.30	Jacob Van Noorstrandt Antje Steynmets
7.30	Jacobus Post Maria Chrystien	395	Jannetje b 6.11	Hendrick Post Elizabeth Chrystien

1734
12. 8	Harmen Jurjanse Judith Stymets	396	Gerrit b 11.3	Johannes Stymets Marytje Stymets

1735
__.__	Jurrje Jansze Elizabeth Jansze	397	Sara b 2.7	Joh's Thymetz Sara Van Nest
12.18	Philip Schuyler Hesther Schuyler	398	Casparus	Arend Schuyler Johanna Schuyler
12.18	Jacob Ouwdwater Martyntie Ouwdwater	399	Sara	Jacob Kip Lena Kip
12.18	Onphe Devenpoort Elizabeth Devenpoort	400	Nathaneel	Net Parreleman Atje Parreleman
12.18	Paulus Berry Antje Berry	401	Sammuel	Sammuel Berry Jacumyntje Berry

1738
1. 8	Lucas Reyerszen Elizabeth Reyerszen	402	Mary b 11.12.1737	Joh's Reyerszen Geertje Reyerszen
8.27	Johannes Van Driessen Margaretha Van Driessen	403	Catharina b 8.15	Gerrit Van Wageningen Antje Van Wageningen

1739
12.26	Same as #403	404	Maria b 12.24, 6 a.m.	Johannes Walingszen Hillegond Walingszen

1741
9. 6	Same as #403	405	Rachel b 8.30, 7 p.m.	Joh's Wanshaar Christina Wanshaar
6. 5	Simon V. Winckel Geertruy V. Winckel	406	Marynus	John Franscisco Lena Van Der Coek
6. 5	Elias Kind Rachel Kind	407	Johannes, twin	Gysbert V. Der Hoef Laydi Day

* - manuscript destroyed

At Penfold?

Bap	Parents	Item	Child	Sponsors
6. 5	Same as #407	408	Hendrik, twin	Gysbert V. Der Hoef / Laydi Day
6. 5	Jacob Kind / Angnetha Kind	409	Cornelia	Simeon V. Winckel / Geertruy V. Winckel
6. 5	Ones Rabbelin / Rebecka Rabbelin	410	Catharina	Hendrik Bos / Maria Bos
6. 5	Lucas Bras / Lena Bras	411	Hendrikus	Ryck Rycke / Willempie Rycke
9.17	Isaak Rycke / Lena Rycke	412	Johannes	Isaak Van Nes / Neeltje Van Nes
9.17	Ab. Rycke / Sophyja Rycke	413	Abraham	Ab. Steeger / Femmetje Steeger
9.17	Alexand'r Van Winckel / Antje Van Winckel	414	Wyntje	Barend Franscisco / Cath: Steeger
9.17	Frederick Mauritzs / Jannetje Mauritzs	415	Judic	Isaak Mauritzs / Jesyntje Mauritzs
9.17	John Deavenpoort / Maria Deavenpoort	416	Abraham	Nicolaas Hosk / Jannetje Wessels
9.17	Machiel V. Der Hoef / Tryntje V. Der Hoef	417	Rachel	Jacob Spier / Neeltje Courte
9.17	Lucas Bras / Lena Bras	418	Willempie	Ryck Rycke / Catryntje Rycke
1742 4.27	Peter Moeritszen / Maria Moeritszen	419	Jacob	Jacob Moeritszen / Sintje Moeritszen
4.27	Coenradus Bos / Mareytje Bos	420	Isaak	Hendrikus Bos / Marretje Bos
6.17	Barend Franscisco / Cathal: Franscisco	421	Cathalyntje	Hendrik Rixz / Catharina Rixz
7.20	Steven Van Zeyl / Neeltje Van Zeyl	422	Abraham	Ab: Messeker / Mareytje Messeker
7.20	Jacob Spier / Neeltje Spier	423	Frans	Hendrik Spier / Sara Spier
1745 9.11	Joh's Messeker / Cath. Messeker	424	Everth	Joh's Rycke / Franscyntie Rycke
9.11	Isaak V. Der Hoef / Elizbth V. Der Hoef	425	Feytie	Hend'k Mouristzen / Elizabth Mouristzen
9.11	Joh's Franscisco / Annatie Franscisco	426	Franscoys	Jan Franscisco / Lyde Day
9.11	Coenradus Bos / Maria Bos	427	Jan	Jacob Pier / Sara Bos
9.11	Alexander Pietersen / Mareytie Pietersen	428	Echberth	Mett Philips / Rachel Van Zeyl
1747 2.15	Elias Kind / Rachel Ellenthorn	429	Mally	Symon Kind / Mareytje Kind

1747-1750

Bap	Parents	Item	Child	Sponsors
2.15	Symon Kind Mareytje Kind	430	Elias	Elias Kind Rachel Ellenthon
2.15	Hend'k Rycke Martha Rycke	431	Martha	Joh's Rycke Elizabeth Ryke
2.15	Alexand'r Pieterssen Maria Pieterssen	432	Lea	Frans Coock Lena Cook
2.15	Lodewyck Messeker Lena Messeker	433	Dirk	Coenraed Boss Mally V. Blerkum
2.15	Simeon Van Winckel Geertruy V. Winckel	434	Geertruy	Ma(___) V. Der Cook Cornelia V. D. Cook
3. 4	Echtb't Pieterssen Sara Pieterssen	435	Hendrikus	Hendrikus Boss Maria Boss
3. 4	Ab: Rycke Maria Ryke	436	Anneke	Joh's Steeger Anneke Steeger
1748 2. 7	Ab: Rycke Feytie Rycke	437	Willem	Ryck Rycke Fryntie Rycke
2.21	Thenis Pier Antie Pier	438	Susanna	Abrah Pier Elizabeth Miller
2.21	Hend'k Rixs Elsie Rixs	439	Saartie	Ab: Rycke Cath: Rycke
2.21	Matth's Philips Lydia Philips	440	Maria	Sander Pieterssen Maria Pieterssen
2.21	Yllis Mandeviel Lea Mandeviel	441	Sytie	Joh's Kiersteet Sytie Kiersteed
3.20	John Vincent Elizab'th Vincent	442	Mareytie	Joh's Echtberssen Mareytie Eghtberszen
3.20	Coenraat Boss Mareytie Boss	443	Mareytie	Joh's Van Driessen, Mar: Boss /pastor
3.20	Fredk: Mauritsz Jannetie Maurits	444	Synte	Izaak Mauritsz Janneke Maurits
3.20	Isaak Mauritszen Mareytie Mauritsz	445	Mareytie	Fred'k Mauritszen Jannetie Mauritszen
5. 1	Alexander V: Winckel Antie Van Winckel	446	Jacob	Hans Kiersteed Sytie Kiersteed
1749 3. 5	Johannes Brouwer Sara Blekwil	447	Gerret b 1.24	Stoffel Van Reype Metje Brouwer
3. 5	Johannes Van Houte Jannete Doremes	448	Hendrik	Hendrik Van Ale
3. 5	Jurri Evens	449	Jannete	Magiel Van Wikkel
3. 5	Antone Van Blerkum	450	Jan	Jan Van Blerkum
10. 1	Waling Van Winkel Janneti Van Houte	451	Hillegont b 9.25	Johannes Van Winkel Eva Kip
1750 ─.─	Johannes Van Horen	452	Tomes b 12.31.1749	Isaak Kadmus

Bap	Parents	Item	Child	Sponsors
__.__	Teunis Van Reype	453	Sara b 11.30.1749	Dirck Dey
1.16	Willem Van Blerkum Frenaa (C)amin(go)er	454	Jacob	Geysbert Van Blerkum Aenter Cirstien
1.16	Corneles Van Houte	455	Ragel b 12.26.1749	Pieter Hesselse
2. 9	Helmegh (G.) Van Houjte Janneke	456	Corneles	Johannes Van Houte Jannete
3.18	Jacob Van Wageninge Rachel Van Winkele (this entry found at end of 1756 baptisms)	457	Annatje b 2.15	Abraham Van Winkel Annatje Van Winkel
4.16	Manes Van Wagenen Geertruy Van Houjte	458	Roelof b 3.17	Johannes Van Houjte Lybeti
6.24	Johannes Vrelant Feyte	459	Margrita b 5.3	Tuenes (Spier) Lena
3. 5	Caspares Zab(r)iski Catrina V: Wagenen (this baptism inserted above #461 with no year indicated)	460	Antje b 2.13	Gerret Van Wagenen Antje Baldwin
9. 2	Caspares Zabriski Catrina V. Wag.	461	Joost b 9.1	Joost Zabris. Carstyn
9. 2	Robbert V. Houte (Elisabet) Post	462	Adrijaan b (8).1	Helmus V. Houte Ante Va(nnite)
9. 2	Nicolaes Jones	463	Nicolaes	Gerrebrand V. Hout
__.__	Abraham (S)teger	464	Johannes	
11. 3	Johannes Sip Annati V. Winkel	465	Adrijaan	Helmegh Sip Jannete
11. 4	Johannes V. Vegte	466	Fryntje	Luykes Wesselse Lena Kip
11. 9	Johannes d'Vasseni	467		Dirk Vrelandt
1751 3. 3	Abraham V. Winkel Jakemynte	468	Jakob b 1.9	Johannes Bekli Katryn V. Winkel
11.16	Jores Smit	469	Elisabet b 7.16.1748	Tade Van Eyderstyn Eliesabet (N)uks
11.16	Same as #469	470	Pieter	Pieter Nuks and wife
11.16	Gerret Post	471	Jacob b 10.12	Isack Kadmus and wife
11.16	Daved Marines Annatie De Booys	472	Daved	Caspares Zabruski Katrynte Van Wagening
1752 11.12	Joost Cog	473	Joost b __.__.1752	Abraham Toerse Beeletje Toers
11.12	Abraham Van Giese	474	Andries b 10.20	Andries Van Giese Marritje Van Giese

Bap	Parents	Item	Child	Sponsors
11.19	Abraham Powelse Marytje Van Rype	475	Dirrick b 11.5	Enoch Powelse Jannetje Powelse
11.19	Isaac Ryke Annathie Ekbertse (appears as though father's surname was changed from "Rype")	476	Petrus b __.__.1752	Cornelus Doremis and wife
11.23	Abraham Pier Catrina Pier	477	Susanna b 8.28	Abraham Pier Susanna Ryke
11.23	Johannis Massaker	478	Antje b 9.9.1751	Niclaes Ryke Rebecca Bruyn
11.23	Johannis Bruyn Femmetje	479	Jacob b 9.15	Jacob Boss Marritje Boss
11.23	Ryk Ryke Catrina	480	Willem b 11.9.1751	Jacob Sisco Antje Millags
11.23	Niclaes Ryke Marritje	481	Johannis b 9.25	Johannis Ryke Francyntje Ryke
11.23	Samuell Johnson Janneke Devenpoort	482	Marytje b __.__.1752	Johannes Kook Marritje Kool
11.26	Johannis Van Hoorn Marretje	483	Neesje b 11.11	Hendrik Zaboiski Elizabet Van Hoorn
11.26	Hendrik Gerritse Catrina Powelse	484	Johanis b 11.9	Isaac Huysman Grietje Akerman
12. 7	Joseph Wood Lea	485	Ezechiel	
12. 7	Abraham Messeker Annatje	486	Johannis (twin)	Johannes Coerte Catrina Coerte
12. 7	Same as #486	487	Catrina (twin)	Dirrik Bos Marytje Bos
12. 7	Michiel Kook Cornelia	488	Hester	Simon Vaness Catlyntje Vaness
12. 7	Lodewyk Messeker Lena	489	Johannis	Johannis Bruyn Femmetje Bruyn
12.10	Mercelius Post Annatje	490	Annetje b 11.30	Gerrebrand Van Houte Jannetje Sip
12.17	Jacobus Post Metje	491	Neesje	Gerrebrand Van Wagening Neesje Van Wagening
12.24	Frans Post Catlyntje Van Houte	492	Jacobus	Jacobus Post and wife
12.24	Johannes Van Houte Lybetje Van Rype	493	Elizabet	Helmech Van Houte and wife
12.24	Abraham Deremis Magdalena Van Houte	494	Martyntje	Johanis Van Houte Martyntje Bartholf
1753 1.15	Johannis Devosne Hester Vreeland	495	Marya b 12.9.1752	Dirrik Vreeland Maragritje Vreeland

Bap	Parents	1753 Item	Child	Sponsors
1.21	Casparus Zaboiski Catrina Van Wagening	496	Christientje b 1.3	Arent Schuylder Helena Van Wageninge
1.21	Jacobus Smit Janneke Boss	497	Catrina	Johanis Van Winkel Jennike Van Vorst
1.26	Hendrick Van Wageninge Annathje Van Winkele	498	Gerret b 1.14	Abraham Van Wagening Maragritje Van Wagening
2. 4	Hartman Vreeland Lea Vreeland	499	Catrina b 1.18	Petrus Powelse Annatje Powelse
2.18	Abraham Gerrebrandse Maria Gerrebrandse	500	Jurrie b 1.26	Petrus Gerrebrandse Elizabeth Gerrebrandse
2.27	Abraham Van Rype Elizabet Van Rype	501	John b 2.12	John Ludlo Susanna Ludlo
4.15	Gerrebrand Jurryanse Fytje Jurryanse	502	Gerret b 4.6	Johannis Van Winkel Jenneke Van Winkel
4.15	Johannis (D:) Vreeland	503	Anna b 3.29	Elyas Vreeland Cristiena Vreeland
4.29	Johannis Jeraleman Elizabeth Reyerse	504	Joris b 4.7	Joris Reyerse Blandina Reyerse
5. 6	Pieter Post Grietje	505	Maragrita b 4.12	Jacob Van Houte Jenneke Van Houte
6.10	Abraham Cadmus Lea Cadmus	506	Marritje b 6.1	Hartman Cadmus Lea Cadmus
6.10	James Collard mother deceased	507	Jurrie b 5.13	Gerrebrand Juryanse Fytje Van Vorst
6.10	Hessel Gerritse Catrina	508	Johannis b 5.27	Jacob Van Winkele Vroutje Van Winkele
6.23	Johannis Stynmets Catrina Post	509	Johannis b 6.6	Johannis Post Antje Post
7. 1	Phillip Berry Lena Degrauw	510	Richard b 6.2	John Berry Marytje Berry
7.22	Hendrik Veltman Anna Sandvoort	511	Jacoba b 6.28	D: Marinus Anna Dubois
7.22	Abraham Ryke Marrytje Rex	512	Wyntje b 6.18	Hendrik Ryke Wyntje Ryke
7.29	Abraham Van Der Hoef Sara Boss	513	Hendrick b 6.30	Hendrich Boss Dina Kierstede
8.19	Johannis Reyerse Maria Wesselse	514	Evert (twin) b 7.26	Hessel Brouwer Lena Wesselse
8.19	Same as #514	515	Marthen (twin) b 7.26	Marthen Reyerse Antje Van Rype
9.30	Joris Smit Catrina Smit	516	Cornelia b 8.11	Cristoffel Nix Catrina Ydestyn
9.30	Jacobus Spier Neeltje Coerte	517	Gerrit b 9.12	Gerrit Spier Saertje Van Rype

Bap	Parents	Item	Child	Sponsors
9.30	Petrus Jacobusse / Lea Van Rype	518	Antje / b 8.25	Johannis Van Winkele / Jannetje Van Rype
9.30	Waling Van Winkele / Jannetje Van Houte	519	Waling / b 9.22	Hessel Pieterse / Antje Post
11.17	Johannis Egbertse / Marytje Doremis	520	Cornelus / b 10.25	Cornelus Doremis / Elsje Egbertse
11.18	Thade Van Eydestyn / Elizabet Nix	521	Catrintje / b 10.29	Marinus Van Winkele / Pietertje Van Eydestyn
11.25	Cristoffel Van Rype / Metje Brower	522	Harmen	Johannis Van Rype / Saertje Van Rype
12.16	Robbert Van Houte / Elizabeth Post	523	Cornelus / b 11.20	Johannis Van Houte / Lybetje Van Rype
12.16	Helmich Post / Francyntje Toers	524	Jannetje / b 12.1	Hessel Van Wagening / Jannetje Post
12.23	Rev. David Marinus / Anna Dubois	525	Johannis / b 12.4	Johannis Wanshair / Christina Wanshair
12.25	Johannis Van Winkele / Eva Kip	526	Isaac	Nicasie Kip / Elizabeth Kip
1754 1.20	Tade Van Eydestyn / Catrina Wynand	527	Jannetje / b 12.21.1753	Joris Stynmets / Claerte Stynmets
2.17	Jan Van Vechten / Antje Post	528	Lea	Cornelus Aalsen / Geesje Post
3.10	Gerret Van Houte / Jannetje Kip	529	Helmich / b 2.9	Helmich Van Houte / Eva Rattan
3.17	Abraham Pouwelse / Marytje Van Rype	530	Fytje / b 2.2	Isaac Pouwelse / Catrina Niewkerk
	(female sponsor's surname "Jurryanse" crossed out)			
3.17	Pieter Gerrebrandse / Elizabeth Gerritse	531	Marritje / b 2.3	Geurt Gerrebrandse / Leentje Gerritse
3.17	Jurrie Evertse / Elizabeth Evertse	532	Marytje	Jacob Everse / Martha Portie
3.24	Jacob Van Wageningen / Rachel Van Winkele	533	Maragrietje / b 3.9	Hermanus Van Wageninge / Geertruy Van Houte
4. 7	Pieter De Garmo / Maragrietje Valk	534		Isaac Van Giesen / Catrina De Garmo
4.21	Johannis De Garmo / Lucretia Streeh	535	Johannis / b 4.7	Waling Egbertse / Majeke Spier
4.21	Thomas Van Rype / Neeltje Vreeland	536	Isaac / b 3.31	Isaac Van Rype / Lea Van Winkele
4.21	Helmich Van Houte / Catrina Van Giesen	537	Geertruy / b 3.19	Hermanus Van Wageninge / Geertruy Van Houte
5. 5	Cornelus Doremus / Elsje Egbertse	538	Pieter / b 4.7	Pieter Doremus / Elizabeth Harvey

Bap	Parents	1754 Item	Child	Sponsors
5.19	Jacob Van Houte Jennike Van Rype	539	Marritje b 4.13	Pieter Post Maragrietje Westervelt
5.19	Hessel Vreland Elizabeth Stilwell	540	Elizabeth b 4.2	Jurrie Van Rype Sarah Van Rype
5.19	Jan Van Rype Marritje Van Houte	541	Gerrit b 5.2	Gerrit Van Rype Jannetje Vreeland
6. 2	Hermanus Van Bosse Abigael Forbess	542	Marytje 5.12	Johannis Cadmus Fytje Cadmus
6. 9	Adriaen Post Annatje Post	543	Catrina b 5.22	Mercelus Post Annetje Sip
6. 9	Dirrick Dye Sarah Tours	544	Marytje b 5.15	Hartman Vreland Marritje Vreland
6.30	Isaac Van Rype Catrina Van Rype	545	Harme b 6.17	Jacob Van Rype Sarah Van Rype
7.14	Helmich Jeralemarn Rachel Cadmus	546	Rachel b 6.18	Abraham Cadmus Geertje Cadmus
7.14	Helmich Van Houte Jennicke Van Rype	547	Catlyntje b 7.4	Abraham Van Giese Jannitje Van Houte
8. 4	Abraham Toers Belitje Provoot	548	Sem b 7.19	Sem Provoot Marytje Provoot
8.11	Gerrebrand Jurryanse Fytje Van Vorst	549	Gerrit b 7.27	Johannis Van Winkel Jennike Van Vorst
9.29	Pieter Meed Jennike Van Winkele	550	Maria b 8.15	Jan Meed Grietje Slot
10. 6	Joris Stynmets Claertje Van Eydestyn	551	Hendrickje b 8.12	Gerrit Stynmets Pietertje Toers
10. 6	Lucas Wesselse Annatje Van Driese	552	Annatje b 9.24	Wessel Wesselse Blandina Ryerse
10. 6	Jacob Van Winkel Helegond Bruyn	553	Johannis b 9.6	Hendrik Van Winkele Maritje Gerritse
10.15	Dirrick Van Der Haen Metje Gerrebrandse	554	Catrina b 10.1	Hendrick Koejeman Marritje Koejeman
10.27	Jan Amerman Eva Ouke	555	Annathje b 10.4	Anthonie Van Blerkom Maria Ryerse
11.10	Elias Vreleland Catlynte Smith	556	Pieter b 10.24	Pieter Jacobusse Lea Van Rype
11.17	Adrijaen J. Post Hendrickje Akkerman	557	Pieter b 11.1	Johanis J. Post Catrina Stynmets
12. 8	Teunis Spier Catlyntje Ouke	558	Marytje b 11.19	Benjamin Spier Marytje Spier
12. 8	Jacobus Smith Jannitje Boss	559	Staats b 11.17	Staats Boss Annatje Boss
12. 8	Frans Post Catlyntje Van Houte	560	Fytje b 10.19	Hermanus Van Wagening Geertruy Van Wagening

1754-1755

Bap	Parents	Item	Child	Sponsors
12. 8	Jacobus Post Metje Van Wageninge	561	Jacobia	Johannis J. Post Helena Post
12.25	Hendrick G. Van Wagening Annatje Van Winkele	562	Marinis b 12.19	Jacob Van Wagening Rachel Van Wageninge
12.25	Jacob Van Winkele Vrowtje Van Wageninge	563	Pieter	Hessel Van Wageninge Catrina Bonn
1755				
1. 5	Johannis Ryerse Maria Wesselse	564	Johannis b 12.4.1754	John Degraw Lena Ryerse
2. 2	Abraham Van Rype Elizabeth Broadberry	565	Phillip b 1.8	John Lodlo Marytje Berry
2. 2	unknown Catrina Van Vorst	566	Catrina b 12.23.1754	Gerrebrand Jurryanse Fytje Van Vorst
3. 9	Johannis Brouwer Sarah Blackwil	567	Ariaentje b 2.9	Adriaen A: Post Geertje Vreeland
3.16	Johannis Jeraleman Elizabeth Ryerse	568	Geertje b 2.23	Joris Ryerse Blandina Ryerse
3.30	Abraham Van Giesen Marytje Van Vorst	569	Gerrit b 2.20	Gerrebrand Van Rype Fythje Van Rype
4.12	Johannis Cadmus Fytje Van Houte	570	Andries b 3.20	Johanis Sikkelse Catrina Cadmus
4.12	Jacob Toers Catlyntje Kip	571	Arend b 3.16	Joost Cogh Marytje Toers
4.13	Gerrebrand Gerrebrandse Catrina Pier	572	Gerrebrand b 3.21	Hartman Vreland Marritje Gerrebrands
5.18	Johanis E. Vreland Jennike Post	573	Elias b 4.13	Thomas Van Rype Neeltje Vreeland
5.18	Cornelus Gerritse Claesje Pieterse	574	Claesje b 4.13	Hendrick Gerritse Catrina Pieterse
5.18	Johanis D. Vreeland Fytje Vreeland	575	Anna b 4.17	Hartman Vreeland Lea Pieterse
6. 8	Anthony Van Blercom Marritje Ryerse	576	Marthen b 5.12	Marthen Ryerse Antje Van Rype
6.22	Michiel D: Vreeland Aaltje Van Giese	577	Johannis b 5.31	John Devosne Hester Vreeland
6.22	Johannis Van Hoorn Maritje Cadmus	578	Jacob b 6.5	Abraham Cadmus Lea Van Winkele
7. 6	Johannis A. Van Winkele Jennike Van Vorst	579	Arie b 7.21	Michiel Van Winkel Sietje Van Hoorn
7.20	Hendrick Kip Jannetje Bantha	580	Agnitje b 6.25	Gerrit Kip Cornelia Bantha
8. 3	Josua Boss Elizabeth Van Eydestyn	581	Staats b 7.9	Staats Boss Hannah Van Winkele
7.20	Simeon Van Rype Maragrietje Pieterse	582	Lea	Cornelus Doremus Annatje Van Rype

Bap	Parents	1755-1756 Item	Child	Sponsors
8. 3	John Knolin Elizabeth Bennet	583	John b 7.15	
8.10	Cornelus E. Vreeland Maragrietje Van Winkele	584	Marinis b 7.21	Michiel Vreeland Jannetje Van Winkele
8.10	Gerrit Van Rype Hellena Post	585	Marytje b 7.8	Dirrick Van Rype Jannitje Post
9. 7	Johanis Degraw Helena Ryerse	586	Dirrick b 8.19	Albert Terhuen Marytje Terhuen
11.16	Abraham Van Rype Catrina Winne	587	Lea b 10.3	John Winne Rachel Kip
11.16	Manus Van Eytestyn Catrina Boss	588	Casparus b 10.25	Casparus Van Ydestyn Hendrickje Degraw
11.16	Gerrebrand Van Houte Jannetje Sip	589	Adriaen b 10.9	Mercelus Post Annatje Sip
11.16	Jacob Steg Antje Vreeland	590	Johannis b 10.22	Johannis D. Vreeland Fytje Vreeland
11.30	William Ennis Lea Douchee	591	Maragrieta b 11.19	Pieter De Gromo Maragrita Valk
11.30	Jacobus Spier Neeltje Koerte	592	Marytje b 10.25	
12.14	Hermanus Van Wagening Geertruy Van Houte	593	Johannis	Frans Post Catlyntje Van Houte
12.25	Helmich Van Houte Eva Ratan	594	Helmich	Gerrit Van Houte Jannitje Kip
12.25	Abraham Gerrebrandse Marritje Vreeland	595	Dirrick b 12.8	Dirrick Vreeland Elizabeth Van Der Hoef
1756 1.11	Johannis Devoseni Hester Vreeland	596	Maragrietje b 11.24.1755	Johannis Vreeland Jennike Post
2. 8	Johannis G: Van Winkele Eva Kip	597	Geertje b 2.4	Gerrit Van Wagening Saertje Van Winkele
2. 8	Abraham Van Winkele Jacomyntje Van Niewkek	598	Simeon b 12.22.1755	Jacob Van Winkel Vrowtje Van Wagening
2.22	Johannis Spier Lea Smith	599	Francois b 1.23	Elyas Vreeland Catlyntje Smit
3.21	Joris Cadmus Jannetje Vreeland	600	Michiel b 12.3.1756?	Johannis Cadmus Fytje Van Houte
4.19	Jacobus Post Metje Van Wagening	601	Metje	Gerrit Van Wageninge Marritje Van Wageninge

(The name "Cristyntje" placed in Birth Date column - may indicate twins with no birth date given)

| 4.25 | Tade J: Van Eydesteyn
Elizabeth Nix | 602 | Christyna
b 4.10 | Pieter Nix
Cornelia Degraw |
| 5.16 | Rev. David Marinus
Anna Dubois | 603 | Ezechiel
b 5.3 | Waling Van Winkele
Jannitje Van Houte |

Bap	Parents	1756 Item	Child	Sponsors
5.16	Cornelus Van Vorst Antje Toers	604	Arie b 4.26	Helmich Post Francyntje Toers
5.16	Waling Van Vorst Catrina Van Eydestyn	605	Gerrit b 4.30	Gerrebrand Van Rype Fytje Van Vorst
5.16	Johannis Van Rype Hester Stynmetz	606	Marytje b 4.19	Pieter Stynmets Marytje Stynmets
5.22	Theunes Dey Hester Dey	607	Anna b 5.10	Jan Varik Jannitie Varek
__.__	Thomes Jones Lisabeth Jones	608	Willem	Nicklaes Joens Marritie Joens

(#607-608 found on a page with 1735 baptisms)

Bap	Parents	Item	Child	Sponsors
5.27	Adrijaen A. Post Geertje Vreeland	609	Adrijaen b 5.13	Johannis Vreeland Jennike Post
5.27	Michiel Vreeland Jannitje Van Winkele	610	Geesje b 5.13	Cornelus Vreeland Maragreta Van Winkele
5.27	Mercelus Post Annatje Sip	611	Adrijaen b 5.23	Dirrick Van Rype Claesje Vreeland
6. 6	Cristoffel Van Oostrand Sarah Van Oostrand	612	Jannitje b 5.13	Jacob Van Oostrand Jannitje Van Oostrand
7. 4	Casparus Van Winkele Lidia Van Winkele	613	Gideon b 5.27	Johannis Van Winkele Jennicke Van Vorst
7. 4	Cornelus Van Giese Jannike Doremis	614	Metje b 6.10	Johannis Egbetse Marytje Deremis
7.18	Thomas Van Rype Saertje Van Rype	615	Johannis b 7.4	Adrijaen Post Marritje Van Houte
7.18	Johannis E. Vreeland Antje Van Blerkom	616	Jannitje b 6.18	Hartman Vreeland Jannitje Van Oostrand
7.18	Tade Van Eydestyn Catrina Wynant	617	Lena b 7.17	Joris Burd Antje Van Winkele
7.18	Petrus Van Ess Hendrica Pier	618	Neeltje b 6.28	Isaac Van Ess Neeltje Van Ess
8. 1	Cornelus Jeraleman Marytje Cadmus	619	Maragretie b 5.30	Evert Van Zyl Hendrikje Verwy
8. 1	Johannis Post Antje Huysman	620	Jan b 7.15	Jan Huysman Marytje Huysman
8. 1	Gerrit Van Houte Jannitje Kip	621	Anna b 7.8	Jacob Toers Catlyntje Kip
10.10	Waling Egbertse Marritje Spier	622	Waling b 8.19	
10.24	Jacobus Smit Jannitje Boss	623	Hanna b 9.16	Hermanus Van Eydesteyn Catrina Boss
10.24	Jacob Van Houte Lena Kip	624	Anna b 10.1	Petrus Pieterse Anna Kip
10.24	Helmich Post Francyntje Toers	625	Feytje b 10.2	Johannis Vreeland Fytje Vreeland

Bap	Parents	Item	Child	Sponsors
12. 5	James Collard Geertruy Didirks	626	Johannis b 11.6	Johannis G: Van Winkel Eva Kip
12. 5	Frans Post Catlyntje Van Houte	627	Roelif b 11.10	Robbert Van Houte Elizebeth Post
12.12	Wessel Wesselse Sarah Post	628	Adrijaen b 11.21	Johannis Spier Lea Post
1757 1. 9	Jacob Van Wageninge Rachel Van Winkel	629	Geesje b 12.21.1756	Michiel Vreeland Jannitje Van Winkel
2. 6	Isaac Van Rype Catrina Van Rype	630	Marytje b 2.2	Harp Van Rype Geertje Gerrebrands
2. 6	Cristoffel Nix Sarah Hennion	631	Catrina b 1.2	Teunis Van Eydestyn Catrina Nix
2. 6	Jacobus Slot Fytje Jeffers	632	Petrus b 1.20	Gerrit Spier Sarah Spier
2. 6	Hartman Vreeland Marritje Gerrebrandse	633	Belitje b 1.5	Gerrit Vreeland Belitje Vreeland
2. 6	Dirrik Dye Sarah Toers	634	Dirrik b 1.6	Jacob Van Winke Vrowetje Van Wagening
2. 6	Abraham Deremis Lena Van Houte	635	Lena b 1.9	Thomas Deremis Aaltje Ackerman
3. 6	Gerrebrand Jurryanse Fytje Van Vorst	636	Sarah b 2.24	Waling Van Vorst Catrina (P.) Van Eydestyn
5.29	Cornelus Doremis Else Egberts	637	Johannis b 5.6	Abraham Brooks Jannitje Doremis
6.26	Joris Stynmetz Claeryje Van Eydestyn	638	Elizabeth b 5.22	Jurrie Jurryanse Elizabeth Stynmetz
7. 9	Jurrie Evertse Elizabeth Pottum	639	Elizabeth b 5.14	Marinis Van Winkel Marytje Everse
7.24	Michiel J. Vreeland Aaltje Van Giese	640	Zietje b 7.5	Dirrick Vreeland Maragrietje Vreeland
7.24	Elias Vreeland Catlyntje Smith	641	Abraham b 7.8	Abraham Smith Lena Jacobusse
10. 2	Waling Van Winkel Jannitje Van Houte	642	Marytje b 9.11	Helmich Sip Jannety Van Houte
10. 2	Joost Cogg Marytje Toers	643	Arent b 8.31	Gerrit Post Elizabeth Toers
10. 2	Gerrit Van Rype Leentje Post	644	Gerrit b 9.14	Johannis Post Maragriete Van Rype
10. 2	Abraham Van Giesen Maria Van Vorst	645	Sarah b 9.6	Cornelus Van Vorst Antje Toers
10.16	Frans Post Maragritje Van Wagening	646	Jannietje b 10.9	Hendrik Van Wagening Antje Van Winkel
10.16	Jan Tho's Van Rype Marritje Van Houte	647	Adrijaen b 9.19	Helmich Van Houte Antje Post

Bap	Parents	Item	Child	Sponsors
11.19	Marinis Van Rype Catrina Cogg	648	Lea b 9.26	Thomas Van Rype Neelje Vreeland
11.19	 Antje Nix	649	Annatje Van Winkel b 10.30	Tade Van Ydestyn Pietertje Van Houte
11.20	Johannis Egbertze Marytje Doremis	650	Petrus b 10.28	Waling Egbertze Maritje Spier
11.20	Peter De Garmo Maragrietje Valk	651	Isaac b 9.11	Johannis Van Winkel Jannitje Van Rype
12. 4	Johannis E. Vreeland Antje Van Blerkom	652	Janitje b 11.7	Hendrikus Van Blerkom Lybetje Cowenoven
1758 1.15	Adrijaen Post Geertje Vreeland	653	Michiel b 1.13	Michiel Vreeland Maria Vreeland
1.29	Thomas Van Rype Sarah Van Rype	654	Harmen b 1.21	Jacob Van Rype Marytje Van Rype
2.12	Helmich Van Houte Eva Rattan	655	Paulus b 1.16	Thomas Steg Hester Rattan
2.12	Johannis D: Vreeland Fytje Vreeland	656	Rachel b 1.12	Gerrit Van Rype Leena Post
2.12	Daniel Van Winkel Sarah Brass	657	Antje b 1.8	Johannis Van Winkel Jannitje Van Rype
2.26	Johannis Cadmus Fytje Van Houte	658	Geertje b 2.4	Joh: Cornelisse Van Houte Jannitje Doremis
3.26	Barent Spier Immetje Bond	659	Abraham	Hendrick Spier Catlyntje Spier
3.26	John Harris Elizabeth Kip	660	Isaac b 3.8	Isaac Cadmus Antje Kip
3.27	Gerrit Vreeland Maragrita Vreeland	661	Neeltje b 2.13	Michiel Vreeland Maria Vreeland
4. 9	Michiel Van Winkel Sietje Van Hoorn	662	Lucas b 3.12	Pieter Demoree Aaltuje Van Hoorn
4.23	Johannis Spier Lea Spier	663	Sarah b 3.26	Waling Egbertze Marritje Spier
4.23	Abraham Van Winkel Jaccomyntje Nieukerk	664	Helena b 2.28	Abraham Cadmus Lea Van Winkel
5.28	Jan Pier Dirrickje Spier	665	Jacob b 5.7	Teunis Pier Christina Van Cent
5.28	Gerret Van Rype Fytje Van Winkel	666	Abraham b 5.16	Cornelus Van Rype Annatje Van Winkel
9.10	Jacob Stegg Antje Vreeland	667	Antje b 8.17	Hessel Pieterse Lena Dey
9.17	Johannis H: Van Rype Hester Stynmetz	668	Harmen b 8.31	Abraham Van Rype Maragrietje Koejeman
9.17	Cornelus Van Giesen Jeneke Doremis	669	Jannetje b 8.17	

	1758-1759		
<u>Bap</u>	<u>Parents</u>	<u>Item</u> <u>Child</u>	<u>Sponsors</u>
10.22	Gerrit Van Houte Jannitje Kip	670 Johannis b 9.23	Jacob Van Houte Helena Kip
10.22	David Marinus Anna Dubois	671 Maragreta b 10.7	Gerrit Van Wagening Sarah Van Winkel
11.12	Tade Van Eydestyn Elizabeth Nix	672 Rachel b 10.9	Teunis Van Eydestyn Annatje Nix
11.19	Jacobus Post Metje Van Wageninge	673 Gerrit	Frans Post Catlyna Van Houte
11.19	Gerrit Post Antje Stynmetz	674 Gerrit b 11.6	Jan Van Vechte Antje Post
12. 3	Cristoffel Van Oostrand Sarah Van Oostrand	675 Jacob b 11.5	Johannis Van Oostrand Arrijaentje Van Oostrand
12.10	Dirrick Van Rype Claasje Vreeland	676 Pietertje b 11.16	Helmich Post Lybetje Post
<u>1759</u> 1.28	Abraham Toers Belitje Brevoot	677 Jacob b 1.11	Jacob Toers Catlyntje Kip
1.14	Cornelus Jeraleman Marytje Cadmus	678 Thomas b 10.11.1758	Helmich Jeraleman Rachel Cadmus
1.14	Cornelus Van Vorst Antje Toers	679 Gerrit b 11.21.1758	Gerrebrand Jurryanse Fytje Van Vorst
2. 4	Jacobus Slot Fytje Jeffers	680 Hester b 1.17	Jan Pier Dirrikje Spier
2. 4	Johannis Jeralemon Elizabeth Ryerse	681 Blandina b 12.31.1758	Thomas Cadmus Cornelia Jeralemon
2.25	James Collard Geertje Didirks	682 Annatje b 2.1	Gerret Van Wageninge Saartje Van Winkel
3.25	Johannis Toers Agnitje Van Winkel	683 Daniel b 3.10	Daniel Van Winkel Sarah Brass
3.30	Jacob Van Wageninge Rachel Van Winkel	684 Helena b 3.18	Gerrit Van Rype Fytje Van Winkel
4. 8	Marinis Van Rype Catrina Cogg	685 Lea b 3.24	Casparus Cogg Maria Cogg
4. 8	Abraham Gerrebrandtz Marritje Vreeland	686 Gerrebrand b 3.5	Claas Gerrebrandz Marytje Clarkson
4.29	Hendrick G. Van Wagening Annatje Van Winkel	687 Johannis b 3.12	Cornelus Gerritse Claasje Pieterse
5.13	Gerret Van Der Hoef Cristina Weever	688 Maragrita b 4.15	Michiel Vreeland jr Maria Vreeland
5.27	Luycas Wesselse Annatje Van Driese	689 Johannis b 4.20	Hessel Brower Helena Wesselse
5.27	Johannis Van Winkel Eva Kip	690 Catrina b 5.16	Gerrebrand Gerrebrandse Wyntje Van Winkel
6. 3	Johannis Devoe Aaltje Jacobusse	691 Arryaentje b 2.7	Johannis Jeralemon Elizabeth Ryerse

1759-1760

Bap	Parents	Item	Child	Sponsors
8.(11)	Hessel Vreeland Elizabeth Stilwill	692	Hartman b 7.1	Hendrick Van Houte Aaltje Jacobusse
8.26	Richard North Coat Marytje Kerk	693	Johannis b 5.29	John Cackefer Jenny Turner
9. 2	Adryaan A. Post Geertje Vreeland	694	Marritje b 8.12	Thomas Post Lybetje Post
9. 2	Johannis Sip Annatje Van Winkele	695	Cornelus b 8.23	Waling Van Winkel Jannitje Van Houte
9. 9	Gerret G: Van Wageninge Rachel Westervelt	696	Antje b 8.13	Pieter Post Grietje Westervelt
9. 9	Tade Van Eydestyn Catrina Wynant	697	Casparus b 7.3	Joris Stagg Antje Van Eydestyn
9. 9	Jacob Vreland Antje Post	698	Elyas b 8.23	Pieter Post Neesje Van Wageninge
9.16	Thomas Van Rype Sarah Van Rype	699	Marritje b 8.28	Jacob Van Rype Marya Van Rype
10.28	Jacob Van Houte Jennike Van Rype	700	Lea b 9.24	Gerrebrand Van Houte Jannitje Sip
11. 4	Abraham Brower Antje Nix	701	David b 10.7	David Brower Jannitje Hertje
11.11	Barent Spier Immitje Bond	702	Pieter b 10.21	Isaac Van Giese Marytje Hoppe
12.23	Helmich Van Houte Jennike Van Rype	703	Catrina b 12.4	Hartman Vreeland Marritje Gerrebrandz
1760				
1.13	Teunis Spier Catlyntje Ouke	704	Johannis b 12.22.1759	Johannis Vreeland Fytje Vreeland
1.13	Gerrit Van Rype Helena Post	705	Maragrieta	Jacobus Post Metje Van Wagening
1.13	Johannis Van Rype Marragrietje Van Rype	706	Cornelus b 12.13.1759	Gerrit Van Rype Fytje Van Winkel
2.17	Jan Pier Dirrickje Spier	707	Cornelus b 1.17	Cornelus Spier Fytje Jacobusse
2.23	Adryaen Post Jannitje Van Vechte	708	Gerrit b 2.4	Hartman Vreeland Jennike Van Oostrand
2.24	Jacobus Spier Neeltje Koerte	709	Hendrick b 1.17	Willem Ennis Lea Dec(ker)
3.16	Hessel Van Wagening Catrina Bon	710	Hessel b 1.25	Gerrebrant Van Wagening Helena Van Wageninge
5. 4	Jacob Van Houte Helena Kip	711	Johannis	Johannis Van Houten Hester Jacobusse
5. 4	Johannis Vreeland Fytje Vreeland	712	Zophia	Jacob Vreeland Antje Post
6. 8	Elyas Vreeland Catlyntje Smith	713	Gerret b 5.24	Abraham Ryke Aaltje Smith

Bap	Parents	1760-1761 Item	Child	Sponsors
6. 8	John Harris Elizabeth Kip	714	Johannis b 5.24	Petrus Peterse Annatje Kip
7.13	Abraham Van Giesen Jannitje Santfort	715	Rynier b 5.10	Isaac Van Giese Metje Van Giesen
7.20	Gerret Van Rype Fytje Van Winkel	716	Cornelus b 6.29	Johannis Van Rype Maragrieta Van Rype
7.20	Robbert Drummund Jannitje Vreeland	717	Marytje b 6.27	Dirrick Van Rype Claasje Vreeland
7.27	Jacobus Slott Fytje Jeffers	718	Johannis b 7.16	Hermanus Van Wagening Geertruy Van Houten
8.17	Jan Van Vechten Antje Post	719	Benjamin b 7.18	Johannis Post Catrina Bigley
9.12	Dirrick Van Der Haan Metje Gerrebrandse	720	Meyndert b 9.9	Jan Thomasse Marritje Van Houte
9. 7	Hendrick Jacobusse Sarah Stynmetz	721	Pieter b 8.16	Pieter Stynmetz Marytje Brower
__.__	Gerret Van Houte Jannetje Kip	722	Claertje b 9.7	Hendrick Traphage Claartje Hoppe
10.12	John Jeralemon Elizabeth Ryersen	723	Teunies b 9.2	Jacob S. Van Winkele Vrowtje Gerretse
10.12	Isaac Van Rype Catrina Van Rype	724	Jacobus b 9.22	Gerret Van Rype Marytje Van Rype
10.12	Jacobus Sichlers Marya Willis	725	Marya b 8.14	Abraham Van Giese Marya Van Vorst
12. 7	Willem Van Blerkom Frena Cammegaren	726	Hendrick b 11.1	Hendricus Van Blerkom Elizabeth Cowenoven
1761 1.11	Thomas Van Rype Sarah Van Rype	727	Judic b 12.14.1760	Cristoffel Van Rype Metje Brower
1.25	Gerret Van Der Hoef Cristina Wever	728	Hendrik b 11.26.1760	Hendrik Van Der Hoef Sarah Franscisco
2.15	Frans Post Maragriet Van Wagening	729	Hendrik b 1.28	Hendrik Post Elizabeth Cristien
3. 8	Helmich Post Francyntje Toers	730	Cornelus b 2.21	Cornelus Bantha Agnietje Bogert
3. 8	Tade Van Eydestyn Elizabeth Nix	731	Johannes b 2.6	Enoch Vreland Catrina Oudwater
5. 3	Waling Van Vorst Catrina Van Eydelstyn	732	Sarah b 4.14	Harmanus Van Eydelstyn Catrina Boss
5.17	Joris Ryerse Antje Hennion	733	Geertje b 4.19	Dirrik Ryerse Helena Ryerse
5.17	Abraham Brower Antje Nix	734	Annatje b 3.30	Pieter Nix Cornelia Degraw
5.31	Jacob Stagg Antje Vreland	735	Jacob b 4.23	Pieter Vreland Maragrietje Stagg

Bap	Parents	1761 Item	Child	Sponsors
6. 7	Samuell Stives Rachel Van Winkel	736	Simeon b 5.4	Gideon Van Winkel Lidia Van Winkel
6.21	Cornelus Post Marritje Cadmus	737	Johannis b 6.9	Jacob Gerretse Catrina Post
7.12	Waling Van Winkel Jannetje Van Houte	738	Helmich b 6.22	Cornelus Van Vorst Antje Toers
7.12	Tades Van Eydelstyn Catrina Wynant	739	Joris b 6.17	Joris Wynant Sarah Van Rype
7.12	Pieter Post Neesje Gerresse	740	Johannis b 6.26	Cornelus Post Marritje Cadmus
7.19	Johannis Sikkelse Helena Post	741	Elizabet b 6.20	Hendrik Post Elizabet Cristien
10.28	Gerret Vreeland Maragrietje Vreland	742	Michiel b 9.21	Jacob Vreland Jannitje Van Rype
8. 3	Abraham Gerrebrandse Marritje Vreland	743	Gerret b 5.23	Gerret Vreland Marretje Stynmetz
8. 9	Cornelus Van Giese Jennike Doremis	744	Fytje b 7.19	Isaac Van Giesen Metje Van Giese
8. 9	Jan Berdan Catrina Van Hoorn	745	Antje b 7.19	Dirrik Berdan Antje Van Winkel
8.30	Adriaen A. Post Jannetje Van Vechten	746	Mercelus b 8.6	Johannis Post Catrina Bigly
9.27	Thades Van Winkel Theodosiah Earl	747	Theodorus b 8.26	Marinis Van Winkel Marytje Evertse
9.27	Johanis E. Vreland Antje Van Blerkom	748	Marritje b 8.26	Cornelus Vreland Maragrietje Van Winkel
9.27	Dirrik Van Rype Claesje Vreland	749	Elias b 9.1	Johanis Vreland Jennike Post
9.27	Johanis Van Winkel Eva Kip	750	Antje b 9.15	Jan Kip Jannitje Van Voorheesen
10.25	Daniel Van Winkel Sarah Brass	751	Johannis b 9.29	Johanis Toers Agnietje Van Winkel
11. 1	Jacob Van Rype Fytje Jacobusse	752	Harmen b 9.19	Pieter Jacobusse Lea Van Rype
11.15	Abraham Van Giesen Jannitje Sandvoord	753	Pieter b 9.11	Pieter De Garmo Grietje Valk
12.13	Jacobus Brower Elizabeth Degraw	754	Catrina b 11.20	Johanis Brower Catrina Brower
12.27	Christoffel Van Oorstrand Sarah Van Oorstrand	755	Anna b 11.29	Petrus Poulusse Anna Kip
9.21	Gerret Van Houten Jannetje Kip	756	Claartje b 9.7	Hendrick Traphagen Claartje Hoppen
11.29	Adriaan Post jr Geertje Vreeland	757	Michael b 10.14	Michael Vreland Marytje Vreland

Bap 1762	Parents	1762 Item	Child	Sponsors
1. 1	Arie Boss Hillegond Van Vorst	758	Sarah b 12.6.1761	Johanis Van Winkel Jennike Van Vorst
1.25	Anthony Van Blerkum Marretje Ryerse (baptism year listed as "1761")	759	Anthony b 12.13.1760	Hessel Doremus Geesje Westerveld
1.16	David Marinus Anna Dubois	760	Gerret Wynkoop b 12.10.1761	Petrus Poulusse Annatje Kip
9.24	Cornelius Doremus Elsje Egbertse	761	Gerret b 9.3	Cornelius Van Giesen Jenneke Doramus
5. 2	Martinus Schoonmaker Maria Basret	762	Sarah b 3.18	Johannis Wanshair Helena Schoonmaker
1. 3	Johannes Van Rypen Maragrieta Van Rypen	763	Jurrie b 12.17.1761	Gerret Van Rypen Helena Post
1. 3	Johannes Spier Lea Smith	764	Cornelia b 12.12.1761	Jacob Smith Elisabeth Brouwer
2.14	Jan Pier Dirckje Spier	765	Johannes b 1.19	Johannes Spier Lea Post
3. 7	Anthony Pichstoon Antje Kip	766	Daniel b 2.5	Theunis Spier Catalyntje Ouke
3.14	Helmich Van Houten Jenneke Van Rypen	767	Jannetje b 2.11	Dirck Dey Sarah Toers
3.28	Christophel Van Rypen Metje Brouwer	768	Ariaantje b 1.31	Jacob Smith Elisabeth Brouwer
4. 4	Pieter Jacobusse Lea Van Rypen	769	Gerret b 2.26	Hendrick Van Winkel Marretje Van Rypen
4.18	Jacobus Sickler Marytje Willes	770	Fytje b 2.24	Isaac Bruyn Fytje Willes
5.23	William Willer Elsje Philips	771	Petrus b 3.3	John Cockefer Jannetje Torner
8.22	Barent Spier Immetje Bant	772	Theunis b 8.1	Theunis Spier Catalyntje Ouke
8.22	Michael E. Vreeland Jannetje Van Winkel	773	Michael b 8.1	Pieter Gerretse Catharina Van Winkel
9. 5	John Jeraalman Elizabeth Reyerse	774	Nicholaas	Dirck Jeraalman Antje Jeraalman
10. 3	John Willes Rachel Doremus	775	Abraham b 9.7	Isaac Bruyn Fytje Willes
10.17	Abraham Van Giesen Marytje Van Vorst	776	Gerret b 9.2	Gerrebrand Jurrianse Fytje Van Vorst
10.17	Jacob Toers Catalyntje Kip	777	Anna b 9.17	Jacob Van Houten Lena Kip
10.17	Hendrick Gerretse Antje Van Winkel	778	Abraham b 9.26	Cornelius Vreeland Maragrieta Van Winkel
10.31	Robert Drummond Jannetje Vreeland	779	Robert b 9.30	Hendrick Spier Marytje Drummond

Bap	Parents	Item	Child	Sponsors
12.19	Michael D. Vreeland Aaltje Van Giesen	780	Hendrickje b 11.19	Dirck Van Rypen Claasje Vreeland
1763 1. 2	Gerret Van Rypen Fytje Van Winkel	781	Gerret b 12.4.1762	Johannes Post Catharina Bickly
1.30	Christ-phel Nix Sarah Hennion	782	Grietje b 1.1	Pieter Nix Cornelia Degraauw
2.13	Jacobus Slott Tyntje Jeffers	783	David b 12.26.1762	Abraham Van Giesen Marytje Van Vorst
2.19	Jacob Van Winkelen Hillegont Bruyn	784	Hendrick b 1.11	Johannes Van Winkel Jannetje Van Rypen
2.20	Helmich Van Houten Eva Ratan	785	Johannes b 1.30	Johannis Ratan Cathalyntje Spier
4.17	Johannes Sickelse Lena Post	786	Geertruy b 3.25	Cornelius Van Wagenen Catharina Sickelse
5.12	Theunis Jeraalman Maria Varck	787	Maragrita b 4.2	
5.15	Hermanus Degraaw Jenneke Van Eydestyn	788	Catharina b 4.16	Hermanus Van Eydestyn Catharina Boss
5.15	Thomas Cadmus Pietertje Cadmus	789	Johannes b 4.8	Thomas Cadmus Cornelia Jeraalman
5.15	Johannes Koningh Marytje Spier	790	Arent b 4.6	Sarah Jacobusse
5.15	Gerret Van Houten Jannetje Kip	791	Gerret b 4.11	Dirck Van Houten Metje Van Houten
5.29	Thade Van Eydestyn Elizabeth Nix	792	Annaetje b 5.8	Johannes Nix Rachel Van Eydestyn
6. 5	Gerret Brass Antje Johnson	793	Catharina b 5.15	Hendrick Outwater Catharina Brass
6.26	Abraham Post Maragriatje Kogh	794	Johannes b 6.5	Johannes Post Catharina Bigley
7. 3	Jacob Spier Lea Koeyeman	795	Jacob b 5.25	Abraham Van Rypen Maragrita Koejeman
7.24	Simeon Van Rypen Maragrita Pieterse	796	Christina b 7.7	Pieter Vreland Lea Doremus
8.21	Gerret J. Van Rypen Lena Post	797	Marretje b 8.5	Johannes Van Rypen Maragrietje Steck
9.11	Jacob Van Houten Lena Kip	798	Isaac b 9.1	Isaac Cadmus Sarah Kip
10.23	Adriaan Post jr Geertje Vreland	799	Elizabeth b 9.27	Michael Vreeland Jannetje Ryerse
10.23	John Mackerthy Abigail Van Bussen	800	Abigail b 10.10	Hermanus Van Bussen Abigail Forbosch
10.23	Daniel Van Winkel Sarah Brass	801	Marytje b 9.27	Hendrick Outwater Catharina Brass

-38-

1763-1764

Bap	Parents	Item	Child	Sponsors
10.23	Hendrick Hallem Catharina Meyers	802	Johannes b 9.26	Johannes Gerrebrantse Sarah Gerrebrantse
11.13	Abraham Van Giesen Jannetje Sandfordt	803	Maria b 7.17	William Sandfordt Maria Sandfordt
11.13	Helmich Jeraalman Rachel Cadmus	804	Johannes b 9.27	Johannes Cadmus Aaltje Van Winkel
11.27	Pieter Vreeland Lea Doremus	805	Cornelius b 11.2	Cornelius Doremus Annaatje Van Rypen
11.27	Johannes Koejeman Antje Van Winkel	806	Rachel b 11.5	Abraham Van Winkel Jacomyntje Nieuwkerck
1764 1.22	Wessel Wesselse Sarah Post	807	Annaatje	Hessel Brouwer Lena Wesselse
4. 1	Johannes E. Vreeland Antje Van Blerkum	808	Lena b 2.27	Hendrick Van Blerkum Annaatje Van Winkel
4.23	Thade Van Eydestyn Catharina Wynants	809	Franscois b 11.22.1763	Hermanus Degrauw Jenneke Van Eydestyn
5. 6	Jan Pier Dirckje Spier	810	Cornelius b 1.19	Cornelius Spier Fytje Jacobusse
7. 1	Gerret Spier Tryntje Doremus	811	Johannes b 5.1	Cornelius Doremus Elsje Egtbertse
7. 1	Cornelius Post Marretje Cadmus	812	Hartman b 6.21	Johannes Van Hoorn Marretje Cadmus
7.15	Waling Van Vorst Catharina Van Eydestyn	813	Gerret b 6.22	Johannes Van Winkel Jenneke Van Vorst
7.22	Jan Berdan Catharina Van Hoorn	814	Johannes b 6.27	Johannes Van Hoorn Marretje Cadmus
7.29	Dirck Van Rypen Claasje Vreeland	815	Marytje b 7.11	Johannes Vreland Jenneke Post
8. 5	James Sigler Maria Willes	816	Johannes b 6.13	Pieter De Gromoo Margrietje Valck
9.16	Cornelius Van Vorst Antje Toers	817	Annaatje b 8.25	Pieter Van Houten Annaatje Post
9.23	Johannes Spier Magdalena Van Dyck	818	Elisabeth b 8.25	Willem Koningh Egje Sickelse
10.14	Johannes Van Rypen Maragrita Van Rypen	819	Johannes b 9.15	Johannes Post Catharina Bigly
10.21	Arie Bos Hilegont Vab Vorst	820	Casparus b 10.7	Hermanus Van Eydestyn Catharina Boss
10.14	Dirck Van Der Haan Metje Gerrebrantse	821	Tryntje b 9.18	Hendrick Koejeman Marretje Gerrebranse
10.27	unknown Pryntje Van Winkel	822	Joseph b 7.14	Abraham Van Winkel Antje Van Winkel
10.28	Christophel Van Rypen Metje Brouwer	823	Gerret b 9.4	Christophel Jurrianse Annaatje Brouwer

Bap	Parents	Item	Child	Sponsors
10.28	Daniel Van Winkel Sarah Brass	824	Marytje b 10.8	Hendrick Outwater Catharina Brass
12.23	John Jeraalman Elisabeth Ryerse	825	Elizabeth b 12.3	Michael Vreland Jannetje Ryerse
12.23	Johannes Brouwer Aaltje Smith	826	Abram b 11.22	Abraham Smith Lena Jacobusse
1765 1.27	Robert Drummond Jannetje Vreeland	827	Marytje b 1.1	Dirck Van Rypen Claasje Vreeland
2.17	Abraham Van Giesen Marytje Van Vorst	828	Fytje b 12.24.1764	Isaac Van Giesen Metje Van Giesen
2.17	Hendrick Franscisko Hillegont Bruyn	829	Hillegont b 1.18	Johannes Bruyn Marytje Spier
3.17	Johannes Van Winkel Eva Kip	830	Antje b 2.6	Gerret Van Rypen Geertje Gerrebrantse
3.17	Johannes Gerrebrantse Sarah Stymets	831	Gerrebrand b 2.7	Christophel Stymets Jannetje Stymets
3.31	Gerrebrand Gerrebrantse Catharina Pier	832	Cornelius b 2.18	Cornelius Gerrebrantse Jannetje Pier
3.31	Harp Van Rypen Maragrita Berry	833	Jacobus b 2.25	Gerrebrand Gerrebrantse Wyntje Van Winkel
4.21	Hendrick Outwater Catharina Brass	834	Tryntje b 3.20	Enoch Poulusse Tryntje Outwater
4.21	Josua Boss Elizabeth Van Eydestyn	835	Johanna b 3.8	Gerret Degraauw Annaatje Boss
4.21	Theunis Jeraalman Maria Vaarik	836	Abraham b 3.21	
4.21	Jacob Van Rypen Fytje Jacobusse	837	Helena b 3.19	Hendrick Jacobusse Catharina Jacobusse
5.19	Archabald Thomson Elisabeth Stryker	838	Jannetje b 5.10	Jannetje Van Der Beek
4.28	Joris Doremus Elizabeth Titsoort	839	Joris b 3.27	
5.19	Dirck Vreland Fytje Van Wagenen	840	Dirck b 4.15	Michael Vreeland Aaltje Van Giesen
5.26	John White Elsje Vreland	841	 b 5.7	Dirck Vreland Aaltje Van Giesen
8.18	Abraham Boss Rachel Van Dyck	842	Johannes b 7.23	Helmich Van Houten Mally Van Dyck
8.25	Gerret Van Houten Jannetje Kip	843	Jannetje b 7.18	Paulus Pieterse Antje Cadmus
10.13	Cornelius Van Rypen Maragrita Vreland	844	Sietje b 9.16	Dirck Vreland Fytje Van Wagene
10.13	Hendrick Van Blerkum Annaatje Van Winkel	845	Johannes b 9.10	Jan Van Blerkum Vrouwtje Kip

Bap	Parents	Item	Child	Sponsors
11.17	Christophel Gerrebrantse Aaltje Jacobusse	846	Johannes b 10.11	Jurre Gerrebrantse Marretje Gerrebrantse
11.17	Thomas Van Rypen Sarah Van Rypen	847	Sarah b 9.8	Helmich Van Rypen Metje Van Rypen
11.24	Adriaan Van Rypen Rachel Koejeman	848	Cornelius b 10.27	Hendrick Koejeman Marretje Gerrebrantse
12. 1	Marynus Van Rypen Catharina Cogh	849	Casparus b 11.10	Cornelius Doremus Annaatje Van Rypen
1766				
1. 5	Gerret Van Rypen Fytje Van Winkel	850	Cornelius, twin b 12.5.1765	Adriaan Van Rypen Rachel Koejeman
1. 5	Same as #850	851	Marytje, twin b 12.5.1765	Hendrick Van Blerkum Elisabeth Van Winkel
1.19	Johannes Koejeman Antje Van Winkel	852	Johannis b 12.6.1765	Hendrick Koejeman Marretje Gerrebrantse
1.26	Abraham Berry Annaatje Outwater	853	Marytje b 12.29.1765	Harp Van Rypen Maragrietje Berry
2. 2	Johannes Spier Metje Van Giesen	854	Reynier b 11.17.1765	Cornelius Van Giesen Jenneke Doremus
2. 2	Johannes E. Vreland Antje Van Blerkum	855	Johannes b 12.29.1765	
2. 9	Claas Gerrebrantse Marytje Maurusse	856	Pieter b 12.31.1765	Pieter Gerrebrantse Elizabeth Van Wagenen
3. 1	Gerret Van Der Hoef Christina Wever	857	Abraham b 11.26.1765	Abraham Kool Elizabeth Devenpoort
3. 2	Joseph Godwin Ruth Morgen	858	Joseph b 12.18.1765	
3.16	Michael Vreeland Jannetje Van Winkel	859	Johannes b 2.16	Machiel Vreeland Aaltje Van Giesen
3.16	Adriaan Post jr Geertje Vreeland	860	Jenneke	Adriaan Post Jannetje Van Veghten
3.30	Theunis Van Eydestyn Aaltje Van Winkel	861	Sietje b 3.2	Michael Van Winkel Sietje Van Hoorn
4. 6	Gerret Spier Tryntje Doremus	862	Rachel b 3.3	Cornelius Doremus Elsje Egtbertse
4.13	Nicolaas Gerrebrantse Marytje Klercken	863	Christophel b 2.24	Christophel Gerrebrantse Aaltje Jacobusse
5.18	Thade Van Winkel Theodosie Erl	864	Jenneke b 4.6	Johannes Van Winkel Jenneke Van Vorst
5.18	Thade Van Eydestyn Elizabeth Nix	865	Petrus b 4.7	Hermanus Degrauw Jenneke Van Eydestyn
5.25	Abraham Van Rypen Catharina Van Winkel	866	Helena b 4.20	Hendrick Van Wagenen Antje Van Winkel
5.25	Sacharias Kerck Sarah Spier	867	Hendrick b 4.10	Jacob Spier Lea Koejeman

Bap	Parents	Item	Child	Sponsors
9.14	David Retan Catharina Bord	868	Antje b 8.15	Marynus Van Winkel Marytje Everse
9.21	Dirck Van Rypen Elisabeth Meet	869	Johannes	Johannes Van Rypen Maragrieta Van Rypen
9.28	Elias Kogh Jacomyntje Viel	870	Catharina b 9.2	Marynus Van Rypen Catharina Kogh
10.19	Hendrick Post jr Jannetje Vreeland	871	Hendrick b 9.21	Hendrick Post Elizabeth Christien
10.19	Abraham Post Maragrieta Cogh	872	Maria b 9.17	Joost Kogh Marytje Toers
11. 2	Gerret Toers Maragrieta Van Winkel	873	Maragrieta b 9.20	Jacob Van Winkel Hillegont Bruyn
11. 2	Jacob Philips Elizabeth Cockefer	874	Antje b 6.26	Thomas Sigler Maragrita Ferren
11.30	Dirck Van Rypen Claasje Vreeland	875	Lybetje b 11.8	Dirck Van Rypen Catharina Van Rypen
11.30	Dirck Vreeland Fytje Van Wagenen	876	Hermanus b 10.27	Hermanus Van Wagenen Geertruy Van Houten
12. 7	Joris Brinckerhoff Lena Banta	877	Hendrick b 11.14	Jacobus Brinckerhoff Aaltje Didericks
12.21	Gerret Degrauw Sara Van Eydestyn	878	Hendrickje b 11.30	Josua Boss Elizabeth Van Eydestyn
1767				
1. 4	Daniel Van Winkel Sarah Brass	879	Sietje b 12.5.1766	Johannes Toers Angonietje Van Winkel
1.11	Jacob Vreeland Antje Post	880	Elizabeth b 12.17.1766	Cornelius Post Anna Maria Cogh
1.11	Johannes Van Winkel Gerretje Sip	881	Jannetje b 12.12.1766	Adriaan Sip Metje Sip
1.18	Jan Pier Dirckje Spier	882	Petrus b 12.16.1766	Petrus Van Nes Hendricka Pier
1.25	Michael Vreeland Gerretje Van Houten	883	Marretje b 12.31.1766	Hartman Vreeland Marretje Gerrebrantse
1.25	Thomas Van Rypen Sarah Van Rypen	884	Catharina b 12.8.1766	Helmich Van Rypen Catharina Van Rypen
2. 1	Dirck Van Der Haan Metje Gerrebrantse	885	Cornelius b 12.8.1766	Christophel Stymets Tryntje Koejeman
2. 1	Thade Van Eydestyn Catharina Wynants	886	Catharina b 12.22.1766	Marynus Van Winkel Marytje Everse
2.15	Pieter Van Houten Annaetje Post	887	Gerret b 12.30.1766	Arie Post Elizabeth Post
2.15	 Helena Spier	888	Abraham b 12.30.1766	Theunis Spier Cathalyntje Ouke
2.22	Gerret Vreland Maragrieta Vreland	889	Marretje b 12.11.1766	Paulus Huston Jenneke Van Winkel

Bap	Parents	1767 Item	Child	Sponsors
3.15	Jacobus Sigler Marytje Willes	890	Thomas b 11.4.1766	Johannes Spier Metje Van Giesen
3.15	Hendrick Hallem Catharina Meyers	891	Maria b 2.1	Willem Willer Marytje Van Winkel
3.15	Christophel Van Rypen Annaetje Brouwer	892	Jurrie b 2.8	Joris Wynants Sara Van Rypen
3.15	Theunis Jeraalman Maria Varick	893	Jacobus b 2.1	
3.22	Abraham Van Giesen Jannetje Sandfort	894	Isaac b 2.13	Egbert Egbertse Marytje Doremus
3.22	Isaac Van Rypen Catharina Van Rypen	895	Catharina b 3.12	Thomas Van Rypen Maragrieta Berry
3.29	Arie Boss Hillegont Van Vorst	896	Annaatje b 2.21	Cornelius Van Vorst Antje Toers
3.29	Samuel McNies Neeltje Stegg	897	Nencey b 2.7	Jan Vreland Margrietje Vreeland
4.19	Thomas Doremus Sarah Sandfort	898	Marytje b 3.2	Willem Santfort Elisabeth Santfort
4.19	Adriaan Sip Gerretje Sip	899	Jannetje b 3.16	Johannes Van Winkel Gerretje Sip
4.19	Johannes Van Rypen Maragrietje Van Rypen	900	Gerret	Cornelius Van Rypen Maragrietje Vreland
5. 3	Johannes Koningh Mallie Morris	901	Stephen b 4.2	Hendrick Koningh Marytje Corby
5. 3	Archebald Thomson Elizabeth Stryker	902	Jacobus b 3.24	
5. 3	Johannes Spier Magdalena Van Dyck	903	Petrus b 2.22	Johannes Winne Annetje Jeraalman
5.24	Hermanus De Grauw Jenneke Van Eydestyn	904	Franscois b 4.19	Josua Boss Elizabeth Van Eydestyn
6. 7	Anthony Wouters Marytje Koejeman	905	Marretje b 4.12	Hendrick Koejeman Marretje Gerrebrantse
6. 7	Johannes A. Post Fytje Neefjes	906	Marretje	Adriaan Post jr Geertje Vreeland
8.16	Thomas Cadmus Pietertje Cadmus	907	Cornelia b 7.17	Abraham Spier Marytje Cadmus
8.16	Hendrick Van Sisco Hillegont Bruyn	908	Margrietje b 7.11	Rynier Bruyn Marytje Jeraalman
9. 6	Abraham Van Giesen Marytje Van Vorst	909	Hillegont b 6.16	Arie Boss Hillegont Van Vorst
10.11	Daniel Retan Margrietje Stegg	910	Jacob b 9.6	Johannes Van Rypen Catharina Post
11. 1	Johannes Spier Metje Van Giesen	911	Rynier b 9.21	

Bap	Parents	Item	Child	Sponsors
11.15	Johannes Gerrebrantse Jannetje Davidse	912	Elisabeth b 9.26	Jurrie Gerbrantse Elizabeth Gerrebrantse
11.15	Gerret Van Rypen Geertje Gerrebrantse	913	Jacob b 11.2	Jacob Van Winkelen Willemyntje Van Winkel
11.15	Hendrick Van Blerkum Annaatje Van Winkel	914	Abraham b 9.14	Geret Van Rypen Fytje Van Winkel
12. 6	David Brouwer Areaantje Stymets	915	Marytje b 11.8	Pieter Stymets Marytje Brouwer
12. 6	Johannes Ryke Lea Ryke	916	Lena b 10.22	Theunis Pier Elizabeth Smith
12. 6	Johannes Brouwer Aaltje Smith	917	Johannes b 11.8	Petrus Jacobusse Lea Van Rypen
12.20	Johannes Van Winkel Eva Kip	918	Isaac b 12.7	Nicasie Kip Margrietje Romeyn
12.25	Gerret Van Houten Jannetje Kip	919	Sarah b 10.29	Pieter Gerretse Marretje Cadmus
1768 1.17	Yilles Mandeviel Christina Huysman	920	Johannes b 12.3.1767	Jan Huysman Jenneke Huysman
1.31	Dirck Jacobusse Sarah Steger	921	Maria b 12.16.1767	Jacobus Jacobusse Marytje Steger
2.21	Robert Drummond Jannetje Vreeland	922	Sarah b 1.25	John Ludlow Lea Post
3. 6	Adriaan Post jr Geertje Vreeland	923	Marretje	Johannes Post Fytje Neefjee
3.27	Jacob Jacobusse Sarah Jacobusse	924	Johannes b 1.3	Adriaan Jacobusse Polly Van Rypen
4. 3	Isaac Van Giesen Marytje Van Sent	925	Ephraim b 2.24	Johannes Spier Metje Van Giesen
4. 3	John White Elsje Vreeland	926	William b 2.22	Claas Vreeland Claasje Vreeland
4. 3	Adriaan Van Rypen Rachel Koejeman	927	Marretje b 2.18	Arie Post Catharina Van Rypen
4. 3	Elias Cogh Jacomyntje Viel	928	Catharina	Cornelius Post Anna Maria Cogh
4.17	Wessel Weselse Sarah Post	929	Catharina b 3.23	Jacob Wesselse Annaatje Wesselse
5. 1	Gerret Spier Tryntje Doremus	930	Sarah b 3.19	Johannes Spier Metje Van Giesen
5. 1	Roelif Vreeland Aalje Doremus	931	Abraham b 4.11	Abraham Doremus Lena Van Houten
5. 1	Johannes Ryerse Metje Van Houten	932	Jenneke	Dirck Van Houten Elizabeth Van Winkel
5. 8	Abraham Boss Rachel Van Dyck	933	Maria b 4.23	Johannes Van Hoorn Marretje Cadmus

Bap	Parents	1768 Item	Child	Sponsors
5.22	Cornelius Neefjes Aaltje Van Giesen	934	Marretje	Marcelus Van Giesen Catharina Van Rypen
5.29	David Morris Geertruy Jacobusse	935	Maragrieta b 3.12	Johannes Kidnie Rachel Spier
5.29	Gerret J. Van Rypen Lena Post	936	Jannetje b 5.7	Frans Post Cathalyntje Van Houten
7. 5	Jacob Van Houten Lena Mourusse	937	Lena b 5.8	Gerret Van Houten Jannetje Kip
7.10	Cornelius Van Rypen Margrietje Vreeland	938	Rachel	Gerret Van Rypen Fytje Van Winkel
7.10	Johannes E. Vreeland Antje Van Blerkum	939	Marretje b 4.23	
__.__	Johannes Cockefer Jannetje Torner	940		Geurt Gerrebrantse Neesje Van Wagenen
8.21	Hendrick Spier Margrietje Vreeland	941	Theunis b 7.27	Theunis Spier Cathalyntje Ouke
8.28	Thomas Doremus Rachel Spier	942	Franscois b 8.14	Cornelius Spier Susanna Van Sent
8.28	Pieter Vreeland Lea Doremus	943	Dirck, twin b 7.26	Hendrick Spier Margrietje Vrelandt
8.28	Same as #943	944	Annaatje, twin b 7.26	(Hendrick Spier) Annaatje Van Rypen
9. 4	Sacharias Kerck Sarah Spier	945	Johannes b 8.12	Waling Egtbertse Marretje Spier
9.11	Roeleph Jacobusse Franscina Ryke	946	Aaltje b 8.25	Hendrick Jacobusse Sarah Ryke
10. 9	Arie Post Catharina Post	947	Rachel b 9.11	Cornelius Van Rypen Maragrietje Vreeland
10. 9	Samuel McNies Neeltje Stegg	948	Margrietje b 9.6	Cornelius Van Houten Antje Vreeland
10.23	Machiel E. Vreeland Jannetje Van Winkel	949	David b 9.20	Hendrick Van Wagenen Antje Van Winkel
10.23	Daniel Retan Maragrietje Segg	950	Antje b 9.2(2)	Gerret Van Rypen Helena Post
10.30	Hendrick Koningh Marretje Corby	951	Henricus b 9.24	
10.30	Jacob Van Rypen Fytje Jacobusse	952	Johannes b 9.12	Jacobus Jacobusse Jannetje Jacobusse
11.13	Hendrick Outwater Catharina Brass	953	Sarah b 10.7	Daniel Van Winkel Sarah Brass
11.13	Isaac Paulusse Rachel Van Nes	954	Annaatje b 10.25	Hendrick Jacobusse Annaatje Van Nes
11.13	Christophel Stymets Tryntje Koejeman	955	Hendrick b 10.2	Hendrick Koejeman Marretje Gerrebrantse

Bap	Parents	Item	Child	Sponsors
11.27	Johannes Van Rypen Catharina Post	956	Marretje b 11.2	Gerret Van Rypen Helena Post
12. 4	Johannes Lambart Areaantje Mandeviel	957	Jannetje b 10.6	Johannes Van Wagenen Geertje Ryerse
12.18	Johannes Van Giesen Metje Van Houten	958	Antje b 11.10	Dirck Houten Gerretje Post
12.18	Joseph Godwin Elizabeth Griffisis	959	Nathanael b 11.13	Nathanael Godwin Antje Dobbs
12.18	Enoch Jo. Vreeland Cornelia Kip	960	Annaatje	Hermanus Van Wagenen Geertruy Van Houten
12.25	Johannes Van Rypen Aaltje Van Rypen	961	Johannes b 12.4	Helmich Van Rypen Metje Van Rypen
12.26	Jan Koejeman Antje Van Winkel	962	Abraham b 12.4	
1769				
1.22	Pieter Gerretse Priscilla Cadmus	963	Gerret	Hendrick Gerretse Antje Van Winkel
1.29	Abraham Godwin Aaltje Van Houten	964	Dirck	Dirck Van Houten Elizabeth Van Winkel
2. 5	Theunis Jeraalman Maria Varick	965	Anna	
2.19	Thade Van Eydestyn Catharina Wynants	966	Polly b 12.24.1768	Cornelius Van Vorst Antje Toers
2.19	Gerret Degraau Sarah Van Eydestyn	967	Geertje b 1.23	Hermanus Van Eydestyn Catharina Boss
2.19	Joseph Godwin Ruth Morgen	968	John b 2.3	Henry Godwin Mary Butters
4.16	Barent Spier Sarah Spier	969	Theunis b 3.12	Theunis Spier Cathalyntje Ouke
5.14	Abraham Van Giesen Jannetje Sandfort	970	Cornelius b 4.2	Alpheus Gerretse Elizabeth Sandfort
5.14	Jan Jurrianse Elizabeth Post	971	Gerrebrand b 4.27	Jan Vreeland Neeltje Jurrianse
5.14	Christophel Jurreanse Annaatje Brouwer	972	Hessel b 4.12	Gerret Van Rypen Geertje Gerrebranse
6. 4	Jan Outwater Hendrickje Lezier	973	Jacob b 5.1	Jacob Outwater Martyntje Bartholf
6.11	Johannes Spier Magdalena Van Dyck	974	Magdalena b 4.24	Theunis Jeraalman Maria Varick
6.18	Myndert Gerebrantse Elisabeth Post	975	Annaatje b 5.25	Helmich Post Gerretje Post
6.18	Jacobus Sigler Marytje Willes	976	Abraham b 4.18	Isaac Van Giesen Marytje Van Sent
7. 2	Barent Everse Jenneke Spier	977	Benjamin b 6.4	Hendrick Spier Margrietje Vrelandt

Bap	Parents	Item	Child	Sponsors
7. 2	Thomas Dey Abigail Lewis	978	Sarah b 5.18	John Dey Polly Day
7. 9	Theunis Van Eydestyn Antje Van Winkel	979	Johannes b 6.26	Thade Van Eydestyn Annaatje Boss
7.16	Johannes Vreeland Annaatje Vreeland	980	Aaltje b 6.21	Machiel Vreeland Aaltje Van Giesen
7.23	Johannes Kidnie Rachel Spier	981	Jacob b 6.1	Hendrick Spier Franscyntje Cadmus
7.30	Joris Ryerse Tammesyn Van Bosekerk	982	Johannes b 7.3	Johannes Ryerse Lena Ryerse
8. 6	Joris Doremus Maragrietje Westervelt	983	Margrietje b 7.8	
9.24	Waling Van Vorst Catharina Van Eydestyn	984	Casparus b 9.3	Cornelius Degraauw Cornelia Van Eydestyn
10. 1	David Morris Geertruy Jacobusse	985	John b 8.28	Thomas Jacobusse Sarah Spier
10.22	Johannes Gerrebrantse Sarah Stymets	986	Jores b 9.19	Christophel Van Noortstrand Annaatje Stymets
10.22	Pieter Simmons Rachel Kip	987	Susanna b 8.8	Hendrick G. Gerretse Antje Van Winkel
11.26	Petrus Kadmus Blandina Kip	988	Petrus b 10.31	Abraham Spier Annaatje Spier
12. 3	Hendrick Doremus Egje Van Houten	989	Roeliph b 11.8	Roeliph Van Houten Annaatje Kip
12.17	Nicholaas Gerrebrantse Marytje Mourusse	990	Dirck b 10.15	Dirck Mourusse Rachel Debou
1770 1.14	Johannes Gerrebrantse Jannetje Davidse	991	Jurrie b 10.10.1769	Jurrie Gerrebrantse Elisabeth Gerrebrantse
1.14	Johannes Gerretse Geertje Ryerse	992	Johannes b 11.12.1769	Geurt Gerrebrantse Neesje Gerretse
1.21	David Retan Catharina Bord	993	Elizabeth b 12.22.1769	Pieter Van Houten Annaatje Post
1.28	Johannes Spier Martha Coeld	994	Thomas b 11.2.1769	Thomas Spier Lena Spier
1.28	Hendrick Hallem Catharina Meyers	995	Pieter b 12.22.1769	Peter Ryker Nencey Godwin
1.28	John Leuwis Pietertje Jeraalman	996	William b 1.2	Jacobus Jeraalman Marytje Jeraalman
1.28	Nicholaas Vreeland Elisabeth Van Schyve	997	Vrouwtje b 12.26.1769	Jan Jurrianse Elizabeth Post
2. 4	Johannes E. Vreeland Antje Van Blerkum	998	Enoch b 11.25.1769	
3. 4	Thomas Duvaal Antje Ennis	999	William b 2.3	William Ennis Lea Cha

Bap	Parents	1770 Item	Child	Sponsors
4. 1	Anthony Pickstoon Antje Kip	1000	Isaac b 2.21	Jacob Toers Cathalyntje Kip
3.18	Matheus Shitterlen Jannetje Corbie	1001	Jannetje b 2.12	Gerret Van Rypen Geertje Gerrebrantse
7. 8	Isaac Van Giesen Marytje Van Sent	1002	Lidea b 5.14	Cornelius Van Giesen Jenneke Doremus
7. 8	Johannes Spier Metje Van Giesen	1003	Metje b 4.22	Elias Spier Elisabeth Sandfort
7.15	Johannes Brouwer Aaltje Smith (this entry crossed out)	1004	Petrus b 6.3	Petrus Jacobusse Lea Van Rypen
7. 8	Same as #1004	1005	Gerret b 6.21	Gerret Jacobusse Aaltje Jacobusse
7. 8	Hendrick Post Jennetje Vreland	1006	Hartman b 6.15	Hartman Vreland Marretje Gerrebrantse
7. 8	Cornelius Post Anna Maria Cogh	1007	Gerret b 6.10	Jacob Vreland Antje Post
5.20	Archebald Thomson Elisabeth Stryker	1008	Pieter b 4.26	
6.24	Jan Kip Elizabeth Van Voorhees	1009	Lucas b 5.7	
6.24	Dirck Van Rypen Claasje Vreeland	1010	Jannetje b 5.25	Robert Drummond Jannetje Vreland
9.24	Jillis Mandeviel Christina Huysman	1011	Seytje b 9.22.1769	Johannes Mandeviel Claasje Madeviel
7.15	Dirck Jacobusse Sarah Steeger	1012	Petrus b 6.3	Petrus Jacobusse Lea Van Rypen
7.22	Michael H. Vreeland Gerretje Van Houten	1013	Hartman b 6.25	Cornelius Van Houten Metje Van Houten
8. 5	Pieter Kip Willenmyntje Van Winkel	1014	Hendrick b 7.14	Enoch Jo. Vreeland Cornelia Kip
8.19	Dirck Cadmus Jannetje Evertse	1015	Lea b 7.16	Cornelius Post Anna Maria Cogh
8.19	Jacob Van Rypen Fytje Jacobusse	1016	Thomas b 7.12	Gerret Van Rypen Geertje Jurrianse
9.30	Moses Terp Hannah Schidmoor	1017	Abigail b 9.6	
9.30	Barent Spier Sarah Spier	1018	Geertruy b 9.2	Hendrick Gerretse Antje Van Winkel
10.14	Hendrick Koningh Maria Corby	1019	Maria b 9.28	
10.21	Jan Jurrianse Franscyntje Mourusse	1020	Jannetje b 10.3	Pieter Jacobusse Lea Van Rypen
10.21	Johanes Van Giesen Metje Van Houten	1021	Leena	Cornelius Neefius Aaltje Van Giesen

Bap	Parents	Item	Child	Sponsors
10.21	Willem Van Bussen Lena Spier	1022	Cathalyntje b 9.26	Hendrick Spier Annaatje Spier
10.28	Jan Van Giesen Jannetje Nieuw-Kerck	1023	Rachel b 10.1	Rachel Nieuw-Kerck
11.18	Christophel Jurrianse Annaatje Brouwer	1024	Elizabeth b 10.24	Jan Jurrianse Franscynte Mourusse
11.18	Arie Boss Hillegont Van Vorst	1025	Gerret b 10.21	Cornelius Van Vorst Antje Toers
12. 2	Abraham Boss Rachel Van Dyck	1026	Thomas b 11.1	Dirck Cadmus Jannetje Evertse
12.16	Dirck Van Houten Marytje Van Rypen	1027	Gerrebrand b 11.2	Michael Vreeland Gerretje Van Houten
12.16	Jacob Vreeland Antje Post	1028	Johannes b 11.14	Johannes Vreeland Margrietje Vreeland
12.25	Abraham Vreeland Lea Vreeland	1029	Maragrietje	Marynus Vreeland Jannetje Vreeland
12.30	Daniel Retan Margrietje Stegg	1030	Saartje b 12.7	Abraham Retan Saartje Van Gelder
1771 1. 6	David Brouwer Ariaantje Stymets	1031	David b 12.11.1770	
1.13	Helmich Post Metje Van Rypen	1032	Marcelus b 12.13.1770	Johannes Van Rypen Aaltje Van Rypen
2. 3	Gerret Spier Tryntje Doremus	1033	Lea b 12.6.1770	Waling Egtbertse Marretje Spier
2. 3	Abraham Van Giesen Jannetje Sandfort	1034	Thomas b 11.12.1770	Cornelius Van Giesen Jenneke Doremus
2. 3	Sacharias Kerck Sarah Spier	1035	Leentje b 1.7	Johannes Jacobusse Leentje Spier
2.24	Gerret Brouwer Jannetje Hopper	1036	Antje b 1.30	Christophel Jurrianse Annaatje Brouwer
2.24	Joris Doremus Margrietje Westerveld	1037	Jan b 2.4	
3.24	John Lam Marytje Van Winkel	1038	David b 12.15.1770	John (H)aal Annaatje (H)aal
4. 1	Cornelius Van Rypen Margrietje Vreeland	1039	Margrietje b 3.5	
4. 7	John White Elsje Vreeland	1040	Margrietje b 3.13	
4.21	Enoch Vreeland Lea Van Winkel	1041	Jacomyntje b 3.24	
4.28	Johannes Vreeland Efje Terhune	1042	Benjamin b 3.14	Isaac Vreeland Tryntje Vreeland
5. 5	Jacob Berdan Sarah Van Imburgh	1043	Geertje b 4.8	Jan Berdan Catharina Van Hoorn

Bap	Parents	1771-1772 Item	Child	Sponsors
5.12	Enoch Vreeland Catharina Outwater	1044	Annaatje b 4.21	Hendrick Valck Marytje Outwater
5.12	John Koejeman Antje Van Winkel	1045	Sarah b 4.16	
5.20	Matheus Shitterlem Jannetje Corby	1046	Michael b 4.18	John Corby Rhode Parker
5.26	Johannes Isaac Ryke Lea Ryke	1047	Sarah b 4.20	Joost Stegg Elisabeth Low
6. 2	Johannes Vreeland Annaatje Vreeland	1048	Lea b 5.5	Cornelius Degraauw Catharina Vreeland
6.16	Marynus Van Rypen Elizabeth Luthem	1049	Isaac b 5.26	Elias Cogh Jacomyntje Viel
6.16	Nicholaas Vreeland Elisabeth Van Schyven	1050	Hessel b 5.15	Jacob Toers Cathalyntje Kip
6.16	Roeliph Vreeland Aaltje Doremus	1051	Anneke b 5.24	Pieter Vreeland Marytje Doremus
7.21	Adriaan Post jr Geertje Vreeland	1052	Thomas	Jacob Vreeland Antje Post
8. 4	Jacobus Sigler Marytje Willes	1053	Sylvester b 7.2	John Koningh Lea Van Giesen
9.22	Abraham Godwin Aaltje Van Houten	1054	Antje	
9.29	Charles Slate Fullwood Fytje Boskerck	1055	Elizabeth b 8.29	Jan Kip Elizabeth Van Voorhees
10.27	Johannes Van Giesen Metje Van Houten	1056	Helena b 10.3	Roelof Van Houten Catharina Van Rypen
11.10	John Winters Sallie Steeb	1057	Pollie b 10.16	Johannes Vreeland Catharina Easterly
11.30	Michael E. Vreland Jannetje Van Winkel	1058	Jannetje b 11.2	
12.22	Dirck Van Rypen Claasje Vreeland	1059	Jannetje	Robert Drummond Jannetje Vreeland
1772 1.12	Cornelius Degraau Catharina Vreeland	1060	Hartman b 12.14.1771	Casparus Degraau Jannetje Degraau
1.12	Theunis Jeraalman Maria Varick	1061	Sarah b 12.14.1771	
1.12	Hendrick Post Jannetje Vreeland	1062	Elizabeth b 12.17.1771	Michael Vreeland Gerretje Van Houten
1.19	Johannes Van Rypen Aaltje Van Rypen	1063	Thomas b 12.20.1771	Abraham Van Rypen Catharina Van Winkel
1.19	Johannes A. Post Fytje Neefius	1064	Cathalyntje	Thomas Post Maria Vreeland
1.19	Cornelius Van Houten Metje Van Houten	1065	Roelef	Michael Vreeland Gerretje Van Houten

Bap	Parents	1772 Item	Child	Sponsors
2. 2	Rynier Blancher Marretje Cadmus	1066	Sarah b 1.6	John Van Bussem Antje Cadmus
2.16	Thomas Doremus Sarah Sandfort	1067	Jannetje b 1.14	John Dey Jennetje Doremus
2.16	Jacob Van Houten Lena Mourusse	1068	Jannetje b 7.10.1771	Hendrick Van Houten Aalje Jacobusse
3. 1	Philip Van Bussen Elizabeth Post	1069	Pieter b 1.31	Pieter Post Neesje Van Wagenen
3. 8	Samuel Gould Jenneke Van Sent	1070	Benjamin b 1.18	Isaac Van Giesen Marytje Van Sent
3. 8	Helmich Post Metje Van Rypen	1071	Jenneke	Johannes Van Rypen Aaltje Van Rypen
4. 5	David Retan Catharina Bord	1072	Jannetje b 3.10	Paulus Retan Jannetje Bord
4.19	Hessel Ryerse Doretje Erl	1073	Johannes b 3.21	Michael Vreeland Jannetje Ryerse
4.26	Hendrick Doremus Catharina Terhune	1074	Annaatje b 4.9	Cornelius Doremus Annaatje Van Rypen
5. 3	Elias Spier Lena Jacobusse	1075	Lea b 3.17	Gerret Spier Tryntje Doremus
4.20	Hendrick Hallem Catharina Meyers	1076	Paulus b 2.15	Coenradus Hasenfloeg and wife
5.10	Hendrick Gerretse jr Hillegont Van Winkel	1077	Catharina b 4.7	Hendrick Gerretse Catharina Ackerman
5.24	Egbert Egbertse Rachel Van Giesen	1078	Johannes b 4.27	Waling Egbertse Marytje Spier
6. 7	Jacobus Jeraalman Rachel Kingsland	1079	Maragrietje b 5.20	Hendrick Jeraalman Annaatje Jeraalman
6. 7	Pieter Ryke Marytje Steeger	1080	Anneke b 5.6	Isaac Ryke Anneke Ryke
6.28	Johannes Van Winkel Gerretje Sip	1081	Waling b 6.6	Hendrick Van Wagenen Hillegont Van Winkel
7. 5	Gerret Degraau Sarah Van Eydestyn	1082	Cornelius b 6.13	Theunis Van Eydestyn Aaltje Van Winkel
7.26	Hendrick Steeger Marytje Ryke	1083	Abraham b 6.23	Abraham Van Giesen Tryntje Spier
7.26	Barent Spier Sarah Spier	1084	Geertruy b 6.30	Isaac Montanje Annetje Spier
8.16	Rynier Spier Anomie Schidmoor	1085	Samuel b 7.22	Samuel Schidmoor Claasje Vreeland
8.30	Nicholaas Gerrebrantse Marytje Mourusse	1086	Elizabeth b 7.8	Pieter Gerrebrantse Elisabeth Van Wagenen
8.30	Edward Billington Marytje Gerrebrantse	1087	John b 7.2	John Cockefer Jannetje Torner

		1772-1773		
Bap	Parents	Item	Child	Sponsors
9.20	John Cockefer Jannetje Torner	1088	Frederick Dason b 8.10	Frederick Dason Molly Killy
9.26	Elias Smith Sarah Kock	1089	Jacob b 8.21	Thomas Dodd Elizabeth Smith
9.20	Jacob Van Winkel Annaatje Van Noodstrand	1090	Johannes b 9.1	Pieter Kip Willemyntje Van Winkel
9.27	Jan Pier Dirckje Spier	1091	Marytje b 9.5	Brandt Jacobusse Gerretje Spier
9.27	Johannes Gerretse Geertje Ryerse	1092	Antje b 8.20	Gerrebrand Gerretse Lena Gerretse
9.27	Mourus Mourusse Tryntje Jacobusse	1093	Lena b 8.28	Jacobus Jacobusse Jannetje Jacobusse
10. 4	Jurrie Gerrebrantse Hendrickje Stymets	1094	Claartje b 9.8	Joris Stymets Claartje Van Eydestyn
10.11	Hendrick Van Nes Rachel Sandfort	1095	Evert b 9.24	Simeon Van Nes Engeltje Van Nes
10.11	Enoch Vreeland Lea Van Winkel	1096	Cornelius b 9.2	
10.25	Gerret Van Rypen Lena Post	1097	Jacobus b 9.25	Hendrick Gerretse Catharina Van Houten
11. 8	Johannes Van Winkel Eva Kip	1098	Eva b 10.11	Waling Van Winkel Jannetje Van Houten
12. 6	Moses Terp Annaatje Schidmoor	1099	Nathanael b 11.8	
12.13	Waling Van Vorst Catharina Van Eydastyn	1100	Hendrick b 11.17	Josua Boss Elizabeth Van Eydestyn
12.25	Christophel Jurrianse Annaatje Brouwer	1101	Gerret b 11.27	Gerret Brouwer Jannetje Hoppen
1773				
1. 1	Walter Degr-auw Metje Sip	1102	Gerret b 12.5.1772	John Wanshaar Helena Schoonmaker
1. 1	Matheus Shitterlin Jannetje Corby	1103	Martha b 12.5.1772	Cornelius Van Vorst Antje Toers
1. 3	Jacobus Jeraalman Rachel Spier	1104	Cornelius b 11.24	John Jeraalman Marytje Devoursne
1.17	Johannes Gerrebrantse Jannetje Davids	1105	Jannetje	Pieter Gerrebrantse Elsje Gerrebrantse
1.17	Daniel Retan Margrietje Stegg	1106	Maragrietje	John Stegg Antje Stegg
1.24	Abraham Van Giesen Jannetje Sandfort	1107	John b 10.17.1772	Rynier Van Giesen Maragrietje Spier
1.24	John Koejeman Antje Van Winkel	1108	Jacomyntje b 12.21.1772	Jacob Van Winkel Sarah Van Winkel
3.21	Nicholaas Gerrebrantse Marytje Kockefer	1109	Feebie b 1.31	Zebedeus Kockefer Abigail Kockefer

Bap	Parents	1773-1774 Item	Child	Sponsors
3.21	Johannes Spier Metje Van Giesen	1110	Cornelius b 1.24	Cornelius Van Giesen Jenneke Doremus
4. 4	Frans Koningh Marytje Koejeman	1111	Marretje b 2.16	Christophel Stymets Tryntje Koejeman
4.11	Marynus Van Rypen Elisabeth Luthen	1112	Harme b 2.18	Joris Doremus Sarah Luthen
4.11	Hendrick Spier Geesje Everse	1113	Lena b 3.11	Abraham Spier Marytje Everse
4.25	Jan Van Giesen Jannetje Nieuwkerck	1114	Paulus b 3.16	Jan Kip Elizabeth Van Voorhees
5.16	Johannes Brouwer Aaltje Smith	1115	Elias b 4.11	Elias Smith Marytje Jacobusse
5.30	Jacob Van Rypen Lea Post	1116	Antje	Adriaan Post Cathalyntje Van Houten
6.13	Jan Spier Antje Jacobusse	1117	Jannetje b 5.10	Pieter Jacobusse Lea Van Rypen
7. 4	Arie Boss Hillegont Van Vorst	1118	Gerret b 6.18	Cornelius Van Vorst Antje Toers
8.15	Anthony Pickstoon Antje Kip	1119	Richard b 7.25	Richard Pickstoon Pryntje Van Winkel
9.19	Hendrick Van Houten Marytje Van Rypen	1120	Johannes b 8.29	Johannes Van Houten Jannetje Doremus

END OF VOLUME I

1774

Bap	Parents	Item	Child	Sponsors
4.10	Christophel Stymets Jannetje Degraauw	1121	Jenneke b 3.17	Casparus Stymets Jannetje Stymets
4.16	Johannes E. Vreland Antje Van Blerkom	1122	Henricus b 2.24	
4.17	Stephanus Reyder Geertje Zabriskie	1123	Antje b 4.3	Wilhelmus Reyder Styntje Zabriskie
6.26	Adriaan J. Post Cathalyntje Van Houten	1124	Helmich b 5.18	Cornelius Van Houten Antje Hennion
8.14	Isaac Van Giesen Marytje Van Sent	1125	Reynier b 7.20	Egbert Egbertse Rachel Van Giesen
8.14	Gerret Spier Tryntje Doremus	1126	Johannes b 7.17	Egbert Doremus Geesje Jacobusse
8.14	David Retan Catharina Bord	1127	Johannes b 7.25	Rynier Blancher Marretje Cadmus
8.21	Teunis Jeraalman Maria Varick	1128	Joannes b 7.17	
9. 4	Joris Smith Annaatje Van Winkel	1129	Gideon b 8.17	Arie Van Winkel Catharina Van Winkel
9.25	Robert Drummond Jannetje Vreeland	1130	Elias b 9.1	Johannes Vreeland Jenneke Post
10. 9	Johannes Gerrebrantse Sara Stymets	1131	Johannes b 9.14	Abraham Van Giesen Elizabeth Gerrebrantse

Bap	Parents	Item	Child	Sponsors
10. 9	Hendrick Jeraalman Marytje Poel	1132	Johannes b 9.11	Gerrit Wouterse Maragrietje Jeraalman
10.16	Enoch Vreland Lea Van Winkel	1133	Abraham b 9.25	Abraham Van Winkel Lena Van Winkel
10.16	Rev. Henricus Schoonmaker Salome Goetschius	1134	Helena b 9.26	John Wanshair Helena Schoonmaker
10.23	Michael E. Vreland Jannetje Van Winkel	1135	Johannes	Adriaan Sip Gerritje Sip
10.30	Jacob Van Winkele Annaetje Van Noorstrand	1136	Jacob b 10.17	Johannes Sip Geertje Van Winkel
11.27	Rynier Blancher Marretje Cadmus	1137	Maria b 10.21	Johannes Van Hoorn Marretje Cadmus
12.11	Nicholaus Gerrebrantse Marytje Cockefer	1138	Marretje b 11.13	Pieter Gerrebrantse Marretje Gerrebrantse
12.11	Dirck Van Rypen Elizabeth Van Houten	1139	Jenneke b 11.18	Abraham Van Houten Annaetje Wesselse
1775				
1. 8	Hendrick Doremus Catharina Terhune	1140	Cornelius b 12.19.1774	Pieter Vreland Lea Doremus
1.22	Hendrick Van Wagenen Hillegont Van Winkel	1141	Jannetje b 12.19.1774	Waling Van Winkel Marytje Van Winkel
1.29	Hendrick Post Jannetje Vreeland	1142	Beeletje b 1.1	Jacobus Post Beletje Vreland
2. 5	Gerret Van Wagenen Catharina Van Bussen	1143	Annaetje b 1.13	Philip Van Bussen Elizabeth Post
2. 5	Barent Spier Sara Spier	1144	Barent b 1.16	Hendrick Spier Geesje Evertse
2.19	Nicholaus Vreeland Elizabeth Van Schyven	1145	Joannes b 1.14	Abraham Post Maragrietje Kogh
3.26	Johannes Vreeland Gouda Easterly	1146	Jacob b 2.23	
3.27	Hermanus Van Bussen Annaatje Spier	1147	Abigail b 3.5	Hermanus Van Bussen Maragrieta Van Bussen
3.31	James Barclay Maria Barclay	1148	Maria b 3.19	Thomas Duncan Catharina Van Cortland Elizabeth Byard
4. 2	Ezechiel Campbell Hannah King	1149	Jacobus b 3.10	John Dow Rachel King
4. 9	Christophel Jurreanse Annaatje Brouwer	1150	Neeltje b 3.13	Jurre Calyer Polly Toeder
4. 9	Jan Jurrianse jr Elizabeth Post	1151	Adriaan b 3.15	Egtbart Post Sara Stuyversant
4.16	Gerret De Grauw Sarah Van Eydestyn	1152	Geertje b 3.24	Casparus Van Eydestyn Geertje Degrauw
6. 8	Yilles Mandeviel Christina Huysman	1153	Rachel b 5.14	Hendrick Spier Fytje Poulusse

| | | 1775 | |
Bap	Parents	Item	Child	Sponsors
4.30	Cornelius Egtbertse Maragrita Spier	1154	Rachel b 3.29	Egtbert Egtbertse Rachel Van Giesen
6. 5	Johannes Van Rypen Catharina Post	1155	Elizabeth b 3.16	Jan Jurreanse Elizabeth Post
6. 8	Abraham Gerrebrantse Maragrieta Kingsland	1156	Theunis b 5.15	Gerrebrand Gerrebrantse Catharina Pier
6.15	Adriaan Sip Gerretje Sip	1157	Joannes b 6.6	Johannis Sip Geertje Van Winkel
6.25	Christophel Gerrebrantse Aalje Jacobusse	1158	Lena b 5.23	Johannis Gerrebrantse Marretje Jacobusse
7.16	Marynus Van Rypen Elizabeth Luthen	1159	Antje b 6.23	Jan Van Der Beek Jannetje Luthen
7.16	Moses Terp Henne Schidmoor	1160	Benjamin b 6.6	
7.30	David Archibald Annaetje Van Houten	1161	Lena b 6.18	Paulus Paulusse Neeltje Jurreanse
7.30	Thomas Jacobusse Sarah Thoers	1162	Arie b 7.12	Jacob Jacobusse Sara Jacobusse
8.20	Enoch Vreelandt Catharina Outwater	1163	Rachel b 7.27	Isaac Vreeland Tryntje Vreeland
8.20	Abraham Spier Immetje Wouterse	1164	Helena b 7.19	Johannes Spier Magdalena Van Dyck
8.27	John Van Giesen Jannetje Nieuwkerck	1165	Joannes b 7.23	Matheus Nieuwkerck Geertje Kogh
8.27	Johannes Stegg Marytje Spier	1166	Cathalyntje b 7.3	Theunis Spier Cathalyntje Ouke
9.10	Barent Retan Annaatje Van Rypen	1167	Geesje b 8.12	Arie Post Catharina Van Rypen
10. 1	Walter Degrauw Metje Sip	1168	Helmich b 9.3	
10. 1	Jacob Van Rypen Fytje Jacobusse	1169	Hendrick b 9.3	Hendrick Jacobusse Feytje Poulusse
10. 8	Johannes Spier Metje Van Giesen	1170	Gerret b 8.26	Gerrit Spier Tryntje Doremus
10. 8	Gerret Van Rypen Fytje Van Winkel	1171	Rachel	
10.29	Thomas Duncan Margrita Van Beverhoud	1172	Johannes Van Beverhoud b 9.29	Mary Burk Johannes Pannet James Barclay
11. 5	Cornelius Van Houten Lena Van Houten	1173	Helmich b 10.18	Johannis Van Houten Mary Berry
11.12	John Vreelandt Jannetje Spier	1174	Sophia	Johannes Vreelandt Fytje Vreelandt
11.19	Cornelius H. Vreelandt Elizabeth Vreelandt	1175	Marretje b 10.12	Hendrick Post Jannetje Vreeland

Bap	Parents	Item	Child	Sponsors
12.24	Hendrick Spier Geesje Everse	1176	Cathalyntje b 11.16	John Stegg Jannetje Spier
12.31	Charles Slate Fulwood Sophia Van Boskerck	1177	John b 12.6	John Van Boskerck Catharina Van Winkel
1776 1. 1	Elias Kogb Jacomyntje Viel	1178	Elizabeth b 11.30.1775	Christiaan Diderick Elizabeth Viel
1. 1	Pieter Simmons Rachel Kip	1179	Rachel	Cornelius Van Rypen Maragrieta Vreeland
2.11	Jan Banta Lena Bord	1180	Arie b 1.19	Arie Banta Lena Westervelt
3. 3	Arie Van Winkel Maragrietje Van Wagenen	1181	Jacob b 1.7	Jacob Van Wagenen Annaatje Van Wagenen
3. 3	Helmich Post Metje Van Rypen	1182	Adriaan, twin b 1.26	Adriaan Post Gerretje Post
3. 3	Same as #1182	1183	Johannis, twin b 1.26	Dirck Van Rypen Elizabeth Van Houten
3.10	Mammerduke Ackerman Lena Van Eydestyn	1184	Caty b 2.13	Christophel Van Eydestyn Annaatje Steymets
3.17	Johannes Koningh Annaatje Ecke	1185	Dirck b 2.27	Dirck Vreeland Fytje Van Wagenen
3.31	Johannes Brouwer Aaltje Smith	1186	Jenneke b 2.3	Johannis El. Vreeland Jenneke Post
4. 8	Johannis Goetschius Annaatje Deeter	1187	Hendrick b 2.7	Hendrick Zabriskie Elizabeth Goetschius
4. 8	David Marinus jr Egje Cadmus	1188	Johannis b 3.10	John Marinus Catharina Post
4. 8	Hermanus Van Bussen Annaatje Spier	1189		Philip Van Bussen Elizabeth Post
5.26	Samuel Huddenut Hester Drummond	1190	Sarah b 4.22	
6.19	Thomas Duvaal Antje Ennis	1191	Jacobus b 4.30	Jacobus Ennis Maragrieta Ennis
6.30	Robert Keeter Jannetje Hopper	1192	Samuel b 5.21	Matheus Hopper Aaltje Jacobs
7.21	Beekman Van Buuren Elizabeth Gilbertse	1193	Pieter	
7.21	Anthony Van Blerkum Annaatje Kool	1194	Henricus b 7.2	Barent Kool Cornelia Van De Waters
7.21	Arie Boss Hillegont Van Vorst	1195	Annaatje b 7.2	Thade Van Eydestyn Annaatje Boss
7.28	Matheus Everse Lena Mourusse	1196	Jacob b 6.18	Hendrick Mourusse Aaltje Mourusse
8.25	Thomas Doremus Sara Sandfort	1197	Lena b 7.17	Abraham Doremus Lena Van Houten

Bap	Parents	1776-1777 Item	Child	Sponsors
8.25	Gerret Stymets Marretje Jurreanse	1198	Catharina b 7.22	Jan Jurreanse Franscyntje Mourusse
12.14	Paulus Paulusse Neeltje Jurrianse	1199	Annaatje b 11.17	Aardt Huysman Elizabeth Marschalk
1777 1.12	John Spier Antje Jacobusse	1200	Jacobus b 11.27.1776	Rynier Spier Naomie Schidmoor
2. 2	Enoch Vreeland Lea Van Winkel	1201	Simeon b 10.24.1776	
2.16	William Van Bussen Lena Spier	1202	Sara b 1.21	John Vreeland Jannetje Spier
3. 2	Gerret Brouwer Jannetje Hopper	1203	Antje b 1.21	
3. 9	Hendrick Van Houten Marytje Van Rypen	1204	Lena b 2.17	Gerret Van Rypen Maragrieta Van Rypen
4. 6	Gerret Van De Wales Maria Crolius	1205	Maria b 1.20	Johannis Crolius _____ Clerkson
4. 6	Johannes Ryke Annaatje Wesselse	1206	Adriaan b 1.3	
4.27	Johannes Spier Aaltje Ryke	1207	Sara b 3.23	Frans Spier Sara Spier
5.11	Gerret Spier Maragrieta Ennis	1208	Jacobus b 3.__	
5.18	Abraham Cadmus Cathalyntje Van Wagenen	1209	Thomas b 4.26	Johannes Van Hoorn Marretje Cadmus
6. 1	Rev. Henricus Schoonmaker Salome Goeschius	1210	Jacob b 5.11	Jacob Van Saan Hester Goetschius
7. 2	Hendrick Kingsland Annaatje Haal	1211	Elizabeth b 12.10.1776	Isaac Kingsland Elizabeth Haal
7.27	Pieter Luthen Annaatje Van Blerkom	1212	Petrus b 7.6	Alberdt Van Voorhees Marretje Doremus
8.10	Johannes Van Winkel Maria Canada	1213	Catharina b 6.9	
8.10	John Cusaart Sara Schidmoor	1214	Samuel b 5.19	
8.10	Cornelius Post Anna Maria Cogh	1215	Cornelius b 7.9	Elias Kogh Jacomyntje Viel
8.17	Gerardus Deforeestes Rachel Kingsland	1216	Selley b 8.17	Aaron Kingsland Jinne Kingsland
8.24	Johannes Vreeland Annaatje Vreland	1217	Michael b 7.24	John Devoursne Sietje Van Winkel
8.31	Thomas Jacobusse Sara Toers	1218	Franscyntje b 7.23	Jacobus Jacobusse Rachel Jeraalman
9. 7	Jacob Berdan Sara Van Imburgh	1219	Lea b 8.23	Jan Berdan Hendrikje Van Dien

Bap	Parents	Item	Child	Sponsors
9. 7	John Sandfoort Susanna (mother's surname "(__d__) Van Eydestyn" crossed out)	1220	Antje b 8.21	Thade Van Eydestyn Annaatje Boss
9.22	Adolph Waldrom Catharina Phoenix	1221	Elizabeth b 9.3	
10. 5	John Stegg Marytje Spier	1222	Antje b 8.23	
10. 5	John Borres Jannetje Post	1223	Johannes b 8.31	Cornelius Van Houten Antje Hennion
10. 5	Adriaan J. Post Cathalyntje Van Houten	1224	Antje b 9.1	Jacob Van Rypen Lea Post
11. 2	Abraham Gerrebrantse Maragrieta Kingsland	1225	Maragrieta b 10.4	John Kingsland Catharina Gerrebrantse
11. 9	John Vreeland Jannetje Spier	1226	Johannes b 10.5	Hendrick Spier Geesje Everse
10. 5	Gerret Spier Tryntje Doremus	1227	Cornelius	Egbert Doremus Geesje Jacobusse
9. 7	David Archabald Annaatje Van Houten	1228	Jannetje b 8.23	Matheus Evertse Lena Mourusse
9.21	Johannes Koningh Lea Van Giesen	1229	Johannes b 8.15	
10.26	John Hopper Fytje Doremus	1230	Andries b 9.28	Gerret Hopper Antje Zabriskie
9.21	Johannes Gerretse Geertje Ryerse	1231	Gerret, twin b 8.22	Gerret Van Wagenen Fytje Westerveld
9.21	Same as #1231	1232	Jacob, twin b 8.22	Joh's Gerretse Marytje Zabriskie
9.28	John Van Rypen Lea Winne	1233	Elizabeth b 9.1	Abraham Van Rypen Antje Post
9.28	Thomas Van Hoorn Maragrita Devoursne	1234	Johannes b 9.8	Jan Berdan Cathrina Van Hoorn
9.28	Gerret G. Van Rypen Lea Simmons	1235	Gerret b 9.4	Marynus Van Wagenen Marytje Van Rypen
11.30	Jacob Van Rypen Fytje Jacobusse	1236	Dirck b 11.5	Johannes Spier Lea Post
11.23	Nicholaus Gerrebrantse Marytje Cockefeer	1237	Jannetje b 10.5	Johannes Gerrebrantse Jannetje Deves
11.30	Gerret H. Van Wagenen Catharina Van Bussen	1238	Abigail b 10.25	Hermanus Van Bussen Elizabeth Hammelton
12. 7	Michael H. Vreeland Gerretje Van Houten	1239	Cornelius b 11.10	Hendrick Post Jannetje Vreeland
12.28	Hendrick Ferdon Jannetje Archabald	1240	Annaatje b 10.30	Annaatje Van Houten
1778 1.16	William Kingsland Mary Richard	1241	Richard b 11.29.1776	James Lesley Maragrietje Kingsland

Bap	Parents	1778 Item	Child	Sponsors
1.16	Johannis Van Rypen Catharina Post	1242	Catharina b 10.23.1777	Frans Post Maragrietje Van Rypen
1.18	Johannes Vreeland Gouda Easterly	1243	Gouda b 11.21.1777	
1.25	Hendrick Jacobusse jr Hester Van Nes	1244	Jannetje b 1.1	Jan Jacobusse Jannetje Jacobusse
2. 8	Johannes Sip Geertje Van Winkel	1245	Annaatje b 1.4	Catharina Van Winkel
2. 8	John Davorsne Sietje Van Winkel	1246	Thomas b 1.1	Petrus Jacobusse Lea Van Rypen
3. 1	William Nixon Catharina Degrauw	1247	Walter b 1.25	
3.29	Cornelius Egbertse Maragrieta Spier	1248	Jacob b 2.24	Jacob Spier Lea Spier
4.12	Gerret Roorbach Frances Helme	1249	Sophia b 3.6	Arthur Helme Catharina Wendel
9.13	Elias Nexen Maria Waldrom	1250	Susanna b 8.13	
8. 6	William Nexen Catharina Degrauw	1251	Elias b 7.7.1780?	(baptism year listed as "1770")
4.12	Moses Terp Annaatje Schidmoor	1252	Annaatje b 3.4	
4.19	Pieter Winne Sarah Spier	1253	Hendrick b 3.1	Hendrick Bruyn Rachel Burger
4.19	Rynier Blancher Marretje Cadmus	1254	Anna b 3.12	Paulus Paulusse Neelje Jurrianse
4.19	Johannes Gerrebrantse Jannetje Davids	1255	Johannes b 2.19	Claas Gerrebrantse Marytje Cockefer
4.26	Gerret Abeel Maria Byvanck	1256	Petrus b 3.30	
4.26	Christophel Gerrebrantse Aalje Jacobusse	1257	Gerret b 3.1	Johannes Gerrebrantse Sarah Stymets
5. 3	Marynus Van Rypen Elizabeth Luthen	1258	Johannes b 4.6	Harme Luthen Antje Zabriskie
5. 3	David Koning Catharina Van Winkel	1259	Gideon b 2.28	
5.10	Thomas Cadmus Pietertje Cadmus	1260	Petrus b 3.26	Petrus Cadmus Blandina Kip
5.24	Dirck Van Rypen Elizabeth Van Houten	1261	Marretje b 4.24	Adriaan Van Rypen Metje Van Rypen
6. 1	Edmund Leslie Maria Kingsland	1262	Maragrieta b 5.24.1777	James Leslie Maragrita Kingsland
6. 8	John Van Brerkum Catharina Van Rypen	1263	Dirck b 5.17	Elias Vreeland Pietertje Van Rypen

Bap	Parents	Item	Child	Sponsors
6. 8	Philip Van Bussen Elizabeth Post	1264	 b 5.2	Jacob Vreeland Antje Post
6. 8	Jacob Van Rypen Lea Post	1265	Johannes	Abraham Post Margrietje Cogh
6.14	Isaac Van Giesen Marytje Van Sent	1266	Lidea b 5.24	Cornelius Egbertse Margrietje Spier
6.21	Micha Gillam Christina Cogh	1267	Maria b 6.8	Abraham Post Margrietje Cogh
7.19	Hendrick Steeger Aaltje Jacobusse	1268	Johannes b 7.2	Roeliph Jacobusse Jannetje Meet
7.19	Thomas Doremus Sarah Sandfort	1269	William b 6.7	Thomas Sandfort Dirckje Spier
7.19	Hermanus Van Bussen Annaatje Spier	1270		Hendrick Spier Geesje Everse
7.26	Dirck Cadmus Jannetje Everse	1271	Dirck b 6.7	Samuel Toers Antje Toers
8. 9	Cornelius Edeson Dorcas Friebos	1272	Neeltje b 6.14	
8.23	Johannes Van Rypen Aaltje Van Rypen	1273	Marretje b 7.23	Adriaan Van Rypen Marytje Van Winkel
9. 6	Johannes Gerrebrantse Sarah Stymets	1274	Claartje b 8.9	Christophel Gerrebrantse Aaltje Jacobusse
9.13	Johannes Ratan Cathalyntje Spier	1275	Abraham b 8.10	David Ratan Catharina Bord
10.18	Isaac Montanje Annetje Spier	1276	Susanna b 9.11	
11. 8	Jurrie Gerrebrantse Hendrickje Stymets	1277	Judick b 10.10	Johannes Gerrebrantse Jannetje Stymets
11. 8	Matheus Everse Lena Mourusse	1278	Judick b 10.10	Johannes Vreeland Judick Mourusse
11.15	Jacob Smith Fytje Post	1279	Cathalyntje b 10.9	Roeliph Post Jannetje Post
11.29	Christophel Jurrianse Annaatje Brouwer	1280	Jan b 10.29	
11.29	Cornelius Degrauw Catharina Vreeland	1281	Lea b 10.19	
12.20	Jan Jurrianse Franscyntje Mourusse	1282	Elizabeth b 11.14	Christophel Jurrianse Annaatje Brouwer
1779 1.17	Dirck Pickstoon Aaltje Mourusse	1283	Hendrick b 12.5.1778	Matheus Everse Lena Mourusse
1.17	Samuel Fleming Maria T. Pearson	1284	Theresia b 11.5.1778	
2. 7	Cornelius Van Dien Sarah Luthen	1285	Antje b 1.15	Jan Van Der Beek Jannetje Luthen

Bap	Parents	1779 Item	Child	Sponsors
2.14	Helmich Post Metje Van Rypen	1286	Helmich b 1.19	
3.21	Dirck Van Hoorn Maragrietje Terhune	1287	Catharina b 2.28	Jan Berdan Catharina Van Hoorn
3.28	Hendrick Wesselse Jannetje Degrauw	1288	Lea b 2.25	Abraham Van Houten Annaatje Wesselse
4.11	Barent Spier Sarah Spier	1289	Barent b 3.20	
4.25	Joris Wynants Sarah Jurrianse	1290	Elizabeth b 2.21	Christophel Jurrianse Annaatje Brouwer
5. 2	Johannes Cusaart Sarah Schidmoor	1291	Johannes b 3.5	
5. 9	Johannes Koejeman Antje Van Winkel	1292	Jacob b 4.5	Jacob Spier Lea Koejeman
5.23	Roelef Jacobusse Jannetje Meet	1293	Marytje b 4.24	Arie Meet Hester Jacobusse
5. 2	Dirck Berry Antje Vreeland	1294	Marytje b 3.2	Harp Van Rypen Margrietje Berry
5. 2	Pieter Vreeland Lea Doremus	1295	Pieter	Hendrick Doremus Catharina Terhune
6.20	Walter Degrauw Metje Sip	1296	Dirck b 5.18	
6.27	Hendrick Herris Neesje Van Hoorn	1297	Johannes b 6.16	Thomas Van Hoorn Margrietje Devoursne
6.27	Gerrebrand Gerrebrandse Junes Sigler	1298	Margrietje b 5.13	Abraham Gerrebrantse Margrietje Kingsland
7. 4	Cornelius Vreeland Elizabeth Vreeland	1299	Johannes b 6.7	Gerret Westerveld Beletje Vreeland
7.25	Joseph Devoe Aaltje Outwater	1300	Hendrick b 6.28	Hendrick Outwater Catharina Brass
8. 8	John Van Der Hoef Maria Linsie	1301	Jacob b 6.28	Cornelius Van Vorst Annaatje Outwater
8. 8	Adolph Brass Maragrietje Van Der Hoef	1302	Thomas b 6.21	
8. 8	Johannes Bruyn Pietertje Winne	1303	Fytje b 7.3	Isaac Bruyn Fytje Willes
8. 8	Johannes A. Post Fytje Neefjes	1304	Jenneke	Elias Vreeland Elizabeth Post
8.15	Caleb Haal Catharina Boss	1305	Sarah b 4.25	Abraham Boss Sarah Boss
8.15	Jacob Vreeland Sarah Jacobusse	1306	Johannes b 7.26	Johannes Spier Metje Van Giesen
9.12	Hendrick Kingsland Annaatje Haal	1307	Margrietje b 8.16	Johannes Haal Hester Northcoat

Bap	Parents	Item	Child	Sponsors
9.19	Johannes Jeraalman Marytje Devoursne	1308	Marytje b 8.24	Johannes Devoursne Sietje Van Winkel
10. 3	Gerret Spier Marretje Ennis	1309	Jacobus b 9.5	Pieter De Garmo Marytje Van Rypen
10. 3	Thomas Duvaal Antje Ennis	1310	Joseph b 8.29	
10. 3	Gerret G. Van Rypen Lea Simmons	1311	Pieter b 9.4	Frans Post Margrietje Van Rypen
10. 3	Enoch C. Vreeland Lea Van Winkel	1312	Margrietje b 8.31	
10.24	Cornelius Edeson Dorcas Edeson	1313	Cornelius b 9.19	
10.31	Jan Verwye Catharina Snyder	1314	Laurence b 8.25	Johannes Van Schyve Vrouwtje Verwye
12. 9	Johannes S. Van Winkel Maria Caneda	1315	Sarah b 11.11	
12.19	Johannes Spier Antje Jacobusse	1316	Petrus b 11.11	Paulus Huston Jannetje Van Winkel
1780 1.16	John Borres Jannetje Post	1317	Hester b 11.15.1779	Hendrick F. Post Elisabeth Sickelse
1.28	Johannes Bighlie Franscyntje Claasse	1318	Antje, twin b 1.22	
1.28	Same as #1318	1319	Syntje, twin b 1.22	
1.30	Rev. Henricus Schoonmaker Salome Goetschius	1320	Maria b 1.1	Thomas Post Maria Vreland
1.30	Hendrick Spier Geesje Everse	1321	Johannes b 1.11	William Van Bussen Lena Spier
2. 6	Francois Van Winkel Susanna Forrester	1322	Abraham b 12.26.1779	Johannes Sip jr Geertje Van Winkel
3.19	Paulus Paulusse Neeltje Jurrianse	1323	Sarah b 2.17	Jan Vreeland Sarah Jurrianse
3.19	Hendrick Van Houten Marytje Van Rypen	1324	Jannetje	Cornelius Van Houten Lena Van Houten
3.19	Cornelus Degrauw Catharina Vreeland	1325	Geertruy	
3.26	Uldrick Van Rypen Anneke Doremus	1326	Christophel b 2.7	Harme Van Rypen Marytje Van Rypen
3.26	Johannes Gerretse Geertje Ryerse	1327	Gerret b 2.18	
4. 9	Hendrick Gerretse jr Hillegont Van Winkel	1328	Johannes b 3.2	Johannes Van Winkel Gerretje Sip
4.16	Matheus Ackerman Marretje Van Houten	1329	Provedence b 1.15	Abraham Ackerman Susanna Messeker

1779-1780

Bap	Parents	1780 Item	Child	Sponsors
4.23	John Stegg Marytje Spier	1330	Jacob b 3.31	Barent Spier Sarah Spier
4.31?	Marynus Van Rypen Elisabeth Luthen	1331	Cornelius b 4.4	Hendrick Doremus Catharina Terhune
4.31?	Marynus Gerretse Annaatje Lisk	1332	Hendrick b 4.8	John Gerretse Annaatje Gerretse
5.15	Hendrick Spier Jannetje Van Giesen	1333	Jenneke b 4.17	Cornelius Van Giesen Jenneke Doremus
5.15	Abraham Boss Rachel Van Dyck	1334	Abraham b 4.15	
5.15	John Van Rypen Lea Winne	1335	Antje b 4.23	Hendrick Ratan Antje Jeraalman
5.21	Arie Van Winkel Maragrietje Van Wagenen	1336	Johannes b 4.30	Lucas Van Winkel Lena Van Wagenen
5.28	Jacobus Sigler Marytje Willes	1337	Jacobus, twin b 5.9	Cornelius Van Giesen Jenneke Doremus
5.28	Same as #1337	1338	Catharina, twin b 5.9	Hendrick Spier Jannetje Van Giesen
6.25	Daniel Folkonier Rachel Ryke	1339	Catharina b 5.21	Cornelius Broocks Marretje Ryke
7. 9	Cornelius Van Rypen Elizabeth Vreeland	1340	Marretje b 6.2	Cornelius Van Rypen Beletje Vreelandt
7.16	Aarent Cogh Antje Ackerman	1341	Joseph b 6.10	Micha Gillam Christina Cogh
7.21	John Van Buren Catharina Vreeland	1342	John b 6.2	
7.23	Jacobus Linckfoot Christina Van Rypen	1343	Johannes b 4.18	Adriaan Jacobusse Marytje Van Rypen
8.13	Arie Boss Hillegont Van Vorst	1344	Johannes b 7.14	Paulus Paulusse Neeltje Jurrianse
9.17	Abraham Steeger Grietje Meet	1345	Saartje b 8.3	Christophel Seeger Sarah Ryke
10. 8	Pieter Gerretse Priscilla Cadmus	1346	Jannetje b 7.16	John Gerretse Margrietje Van Rypen
10.22	Johannes Sip jr Geertje Van Winkel	1347	Johannes b 9.18	
10.22	Enoch Jo. Vreeland Jenneke Marselusse	1348	Joris b 9.27	Dirck Vreeland Fytje Van Wagenen
11.12	Egbert Egbertse Rachel Van Giesen	1349	Jenneke b 10.2	Cornelius Van Giesen Jenneke Doremus
11.19	Elias Cogh Willemyntje Viel	1350	Maria b 10.23	Jacob Cogh Maria Laroe
11.26	Hendrick Post Jannetje Vreeland	1351	Lena b 11.1	

Bap	Parents	1780-1781 Item	Child	Sponsors
11.26	Adriaan J. Post Cathalyntje Van Houten	1352	Helmich b 10.25	Cornelius Van Houten Antje Hennion
12.17	Elias Spier Lena Jacobusse	1353	Aaltje b 11.18	Roelef Jacobusse Jannetje Meet
12.24	Thomas Van Hoorn Maragrietje Devoursne	1354	Dirck b 11.27	Dirck Van Hoorn Margrietje Terhune
12.24	Abraham Spier Metje Van Giesen	1355	Lea b 11.20	Jacob Spier Lea Koejeman
10.31	Nicholaas Gerrebrantse Marytje Mourusse	1356	Gerret b 10.10	

Bap	Parents	Item	Child	Sponsors
1.21	Christophel Steeger Sarah Ryke	1357	Tryntje b 12.8.1780	Pieter Ryke Marytje Steeger
1.28	John Degrauw Marytje Berry	1358	Lena b 12.10.1780	Dirck Degrauw Lena Berry
2.18	Philip Van Bussen Elisabeth Post	1359	Abigail b 1.4	Gerret H. Gerretse Catharina Van Bussen
2.18	Hendrick Wesselse Jannetje Degrauw	1360	Casparus b 1.9	Waling Van Vorst Geertje Degrauw
3. 4	Anthony Cadmus Jannetje Vreeland	1361	Jilles b 1.8	Marynus Vreeland Geesje Vreeland
3.25	Adolph Brass Margrietje Van Der Hoef	1362	Catharina b 1.1	Egbert Rix Catharina Outwater
3.25	Jacob D. Berdan Sarah Van Imburgh	1363	Dirck b 2.22	Jan Berdan Catharina Van Hoorn
4. 1	Matheus Evertse Lena Mourusse	1364	Fytje b 2.7	
4. 1	Walter Degrauw Metje Sip	1365	Johannes b 2.18	
4. 1	Johannes Dow Margrietje Willes	1366	Margrietje b 2.8	Jacobus Dow Angonietje Dow
4.15	Harme Van Rypen Marretje Van Rypen	1367	Sarah b 3.4	
4.22	Thomas Sigler Judick Van Rypen	1368	Thomas b 2.22	Gerrebrand Gerrebrantse Junis Sigler
4.29	Abraham Vreeland Annaatje Moor	1369	Elias b 3.8	Pieter Vreeland Claasje Vreeland
5.13	John Davis Sarah Jacobusse	1370	Stephanus b 1.19	Johannes Gerrebrantse Jannetje Davis
6. 3	Rynier Blancher Marretje Cadmus	1371	Susanna b 4.29	Hendrick Harris Neesje Van Hoorn
6.17	Jacob Pier Cathalyntje Everse	1372	John b 5.19	Johannes Pier Dirckje Spier
6.24	John Cusaart Sara Schidmoor	1373	Anthony b 1.4	

Bap	Parents	1781 Item	Child	Sponsors
7.15	father unknown Jannetje Van Winkel	1374	John Vreeland b 5.16	Marynus Van Winkel Aaltje Van Winkel
7.29	Adriaan Sip Gerretje Sip	1375	Annaatje b 6.6	
8. 5	Thomas Doremus Sarah Sandfort	1376	Abraham b 6.22	Abraham Doremus Lena Van Houten
8. 5	Helmich Post Metje Van Rypen	1377	Annaatje, twin b 6.30	Dirck Sip Pietertje Van Rypen
8. 5	Same as #1377	1378	Marretje, twin b 6.30	
8.29	Cornelius Van Houten Lena Van Houten	1379	Jannetje b 7.29	Hendrick Van Houten Marytje Van Rypen
8.26	Hendrick Steeger Marytje Boss	1380	Aaltje b 7.26	Elias Spier Lena Jacobusse
9. 2	Uldrick Brouwer Anneke Doremus	1381	Thomas b 7.7	Gulyn Doremus Aaltje Doremus
9. 2	Joost Stegg Elisabeth Louw	1382	Elizabeth b 6.24	Thomas Sandfort Dirckje Spier
9. 2	Hendrick Cadmus Maragrietje Wouterse	1383	Leentje b 7.26	Rynier Bruyn Marytje Jeraalman
9.16	Mourus Mourusse Wyntje Ryke	1384	Catharina b 2.25	Daniel Folkonier Rachel Ryke
9.23	Jacob Van Rypen Fytje Jacobusse	1385	Judick b 8.11	Adriaan Jacobusse Marytje Van Rypen
10.14	Moses Terp Annaatje Schidmoor	1386	Lidea b 9.12	
10.14	Anthony Pickstoon Antje Kip	1387	Annaatje b 9.3	Paulus Paulusse Fytje Jurrianse
10.21	Lucas Van Winkel Lena Van Wagenen	1388	Rachel b 9.15	Arie Van Winkel Margrietje Van Wagenen
10.28	Gerret Spier Maragrietje Ennis	1389	Lea b 10.7	
11. 4	Isaac Kingsland Hilletje Franscisco	1390	Hendrick b 10.7	Anthony Brouwn Elizabeth Franscisco
11.11	Dirck Jacobusse Lena Spier	1391	Lena b 10.11	Hendrick Jacobusse Sarah Stymetz
11.15	Abraham Masselaar Elizabeth Haal	1392	Annaetje b 8.1	
11.25	Thomas Duvaal Antje Ennis	1393	John b 10.9	Theunis Jeraalman Maria Varick
11.25	Roelof Jacobusse Jannetje Meet	1394	Adriaan b 8.30	Jacob Vreeland Sarah Jacobusse
12. 9	Dirck Van Hoorn Maragrietje Terhune	1395	Elizabeth b 11.17	Hendrick Doremus Catharina Terhune

Bap	Parents	1781-1782 Item	Child	Sponsors
12.23	Caleb Johson Hester Van Sendt	1396	Annaetje b 3.10	
12.30	Francois Van Winkele Susanna Forester	1397	John Forester b 11.6	Susanna Preston
12.30	William Post Jerusah Smith	1398	Mary b 7.30	
12.30	Gerrebrand Gerrebrantse Eunice Sigler	1399	Margrietje b 11.21	Samuel Sigler Judick Van Rypen
1782 1.13	Jacobus Jeraalman Marytje Kingsland	1400	Antje b 11.3.1781	Hendrick Ratan Marytje Jeraalman
1.13	Marynus Gerretse Annaatje Lisk	1401	Johannes b 12.14.1781	Marcelus Post Jenneke Ouke
1.20	Hendrick Spier Jannentje Van Giesen	1402	Jacob b 12.22.1781	Jacob Spier Lea Spier
1.27	Christophel Jurrianse Annaatje Brouwer	1403	Annaatje b 12.12.1781	
2. 7	Arie Koningh Catharina McKray	1404	Henricus b 11.6.1781	Maragritje Roosevelt
2.24	Johannes S. Van Winkel Maria Caneda	1405	Benjamin b 1.22.1781	
2.24	Rynier Spier Anomie Schidmoor	1406	Maria b 1.25	Jan Spier Antje Jacobusse
2.24	Enoch C. Vreeland Lea Van Winkel	1407	Helena b 1.23	
2.24	John Goetscheus Catharina Butler	1408	Jannetje b 1.12	Casparus Van Eydesty~ Geertje Degrauw
2.24	Johannes Vreeland Annatje Spier	1409	Michael b 1.12	Hermanus Spier Annaatje Vreeland
3.17	Dirck Berry Antje Vreeland	1410	Antje b 12.16.1781	Johannes Vreeland Antje Van Blerkum
3.24	Johannes Van Houten Marytje Doremus	1411	Aaltje b 2.25	Roelof Vreeland Aaltje Doremus
3.24	John Personet Lena Doremus	1412	Sarah b 2.11	
3.24	Marynus Van Rypen Elisabeth Luthen	1413	Gerret b 2.5	Adriaan J. Post Cathalyntje Van Houten
3.31	Jacob Van Winkel Annaatje Van Noorstrand	1414	Jannetje b 3.6	
4. 7	Yilles Mandeviel Christina Huysman	1415	Hester b 1.21	Simeon Van Winkel Elsje Huston
4.14	Johannes Gerrebrantse Marretje Gerrebrantse	1416	Pieter b 3.10	Christiaan Interest Vrouwtje Gerrebrantse
4.21	Arie Post Catharina Van Rypen	1417	Abraham b 3.22	Elias Vreland Annaatje Post

Bap	Parents	1782 Item	Child	Sponsors
4.28	Thomas Bruyn Annaatje Hooghteling	1418	Johannes b 3.31	John Drummond Elisabeth Bruyn
5. 5	Cornelius Egbertse Margrietje Spier	1419	Lea b 4.7	Abraham Spier Metje Van Giesen
5.19	Isaac Van Giesen Marytje Van Sent	1420	Elizabeth b 4.20	
5.19	Johannes Vreeland Gouda Easterly	1421	Catharina b 4.11	
5.26	Jurie Kiesler Jannetje Jacobusse	1422	Johannes b 5.6	Hendrick Steeger Maria Boss
6. 2	Matheus Ackerman Marretje Van Houten	1423	Matheus b 5.5	Dirck Van Houten Rachel Van Eydestyn
6. 2	Frans Outwater Charity Cockefer	1424	Sarah b 5.8	Nicholaas Gerrebrantse Marytje Cockefer
6. 2	John Cockefer Naomie Honeysoet	1425	Alexander b 4.4	John Cockefer Jannetje Torner
6. 2	Christophel Gerrebrantse Aaltje Jacobusse	1426	Christophel b 10.3.1780	Johannes Gerrebrantse Rebecca Linckfoot
6. 2	John Van Buren Catharina Vreeland	1427	Elizabeth b 4.18	Engelbert Cammena Elisabeth Van Buren
6.17	William Garven Catharina Kingsland	1428	Maria b 11.11.1781	
7.21	Jan Verwye Tryntje Snyder	1429	Elisabeth b 6.5	Gerret Van Rypen Geertje Gerrebrantse
7.21	Cornelius Van Der Hoef Maragrita Keyser	1430	Matheus b 12.16.1781	Matheus Van Der Hoef Elizabeth Bennet
7.28	Gerardus Deforeestes Rachel Kingsland	1431	Anna b 3.29	
7.28	John Borres Jannetje Post	1432	Hendrick b 12.26.1781	
7.28	Edmund Taylor Catharina Bensen	1433	Susanna Forrester b 4.16	
7.28	John Sandfort Susanna Welstead	1434	John b 6.24	Arie Van Winkel Maragrietje Van Wagenen
7.28	Daniel Folkonier Rachel Ryke	1435	Abraham b 5.25	
8.11	Johannes Winne Elizabeth Corse	1436	Johannes b 7.11	Johannes Koningh Jannetje Koningh
9.15	Anthony Bruyn Elisabeth Franscisco	1437	Catharina b 8.6	Jacobus Bruyn Sara Smith
9.15	Abraham Gerrebrantse Margrietje Kingsland	1438	Johannes b 8.5	
9.15	Frans Koningh Marytje Koejeman	1439	Maria b 5.27	

Bap	Parents	Item	Child	Sponsors
9.15	Hendrick Harris Neesje Van Hoorn	1440	Marretje b 8.9	
9.22	Christophel Van Noorstrand Annaatje Stymets	1441	Johannes b 8.22	Jan Vreeland Sarah Jurrianse
9.29	Pieter Kip Willemyntje Van Winkel	1442	Catharina b 9.2	Helmich Van Winkel Antje Van Winkel
10.20	William Kingsland Grietje Jeraalman	1443	Maria b 9.2	Rynier Brown Maria Jeraalman
10.20	Johannes Ryker Annaatje Wesselse	1444	Abraham b 9.9	Abraham Spier Hendrickje Vreeland
10.20	Jan Spier Antje Jacobusse	1445	Gerret b 9.27	Gerret Spier Margrietje Ennis
10.27	Gerret Abeel Maria Byvanck	1446	Abraham b 9.30	
11. 3	Zacharias Snyder Margrietje Fiere	1447	David b 10.28	Walingh Van Winkel Marytje Van Winkel
11. 3	John Vreeland Jannetje Spier	1448	Theunis b 9.22	
11. 3	John Van Rypen Lea Winne	1449	Abraham b 9.15	Abraham Van Rypen Neesje Van Wagenen
11. 3	Barent Spier Sarah Spier	1450	Sarah b 9.22	
12. 1	Harme Van Rypen Lea Spier	1451	Jacob b 10.29	Hendrick Spier Jannetje Van Giesen
12. 8	Walter Degrauw Metje Sip	1452	Jannetje b 11.3	
12.15	Johannes Sip jr Geertje Van Winkel	1453	Catharina b 11.8	Adriaan Sip Antje Van Winkel
12.22	Jacobus Sigler Marytje Willes	1454	Isaac b 12.1	
12.29	Frans Spier Catharina Gerrebrantse	1455	Jannetje b 11.2	Gerrebrant Gerrebrantse Catharina Pier
1783 1. 1	Gerret H. Gerretse Catharina Van Bussen	1456	Annaatje b 12.1.1782	Hendrick H. Gerretse Hillegont Van Winkel
1.19	Matheus Everse Lena Mourusse	1457	Aaltje b 12.15.1782	Dirck Pickstoon Aaltje Mourusse
1.19	father unknown Catharina Bord	1458	Isaac b 11.21.1782	Jan Banta Lena Bord
1.19	Hendrick Spier Geesje Everse	1459	Margrietje b 12.26.1782	Hendrick Wesselse Jannetje Degrauw
1.19	Johannes Jeraalman Marytje Devoursne	1460	Margrietje b 12.21.1782	Johannes Van Winkel Marytje Jeraalman
1.26	Johannes Tyse Marytje Jonck	1461	Pieter b 12.31.1782	Theodorus Van Winkel Annaatje Van Eydestyn

Bap	Parents	1783 Item	Child	Sponsors
1.26	Gerret H. Gerretse Catharina Van Bussen	1462	Annaatje b 12.11.1782	Hendrick H. Gerretse Hillegont Van Winkel
2. 2	Hendrick Van Houten Marytje Van Rypen	1463	Marretje b 12.20.1782	
2. 2	John Dow Margeret Willes	1464	George Willes b 1.2	John Brown Nancey Willes
2. 9	Jan Jurrianse Franscyntje Mourusse	1465		Dirck Pickstoon Aaltje Mourusse
2. 9	Jacobus Ennis Jannetje Hopper	1466	Johannes b 1.6	Gerret Van Rypen Geertje Gerrebrantse
2.12	Gerrit Spier Tryntje Doremus	1467	Catharina b 1.7	Frans Spier Catharina Gerrebrantse
2.12	Samuel Sigler Judick Van Rypen	1468	John b 1.12	
3.16	Daniel Thoers Marytje Jacobusse	1469	Johannes b 2.14	
3.23	Jacob Van Rypen Abigail Laroe	1470		Cornelius Van Rypen Elizabeth Vreland
6. 1	Nickolaas Gerrebrantse Marytje Cockefer	1471	Elizabeth b 4.27	John Cockefer Naomie Honeysoot
6. 1	Johannes S. Van Winkel Maria Caneda	1472	Marytje b 4.5	
6. 1	Hendrick F. Post Jannetje Van Houten	1473	Margrietje b 3.21	Adriaan J. Post Cathalyntje Van Houten
6. 9	David Secor Bridged Forguson	1474	David b 7.20.1778	
6. 9	Same as #1474	1475	John b 8.25.1780	
6. 9	Same as #1474	1476	Martha b 9.21.1782	
6.15	Casparus Degrauw Lena Jurrianse	1477	Hermanus b 5.7	Gerret Van Rypen Geertje Gerrebrantse
6.15	John Stegg Marytje Spier	1478	Theunis b 5.25	Johannes Spier Antje McKnies
6.22	Christophel Steeger Sarah Ryke	1479	Johannes b 5.23	
6.29	Abraham Vreeland Lea Vreeland	1480	Elias b 4.28	
6.29	Jacob Oof Neeltje Vreeland	1481	Gerret	
8.31	Isaac Van Giesen Pryntje Cadmus	1482	Rynier b 7.15	Abraham Huysman Marytje Van Winkel
8.31	Jacob Van Noorstrand Geertje Degrauw	1483	Christophel b 8.15	Casparus Van Eydestyn Jannetje V. Noorstrand

Bap	Parents	Item	Child	Sponsors
9.28	John Schidmoor Catharina Degrauw	1484	Annaatje b 8.20	Franscois Degrauw Sarah Van Vorst
10. 5	Christiaan Interest Vrouwtje Gerrebrantse	1485	Pieter b 8.19	Thomas Cockefer Catharina Cockefer
10. 5	Helmich Post Metje Van Rypen	1486	Gerret b 8.26	
10.13	John Read Catharina Livingston	1487	Anna Livingston b 8.11	
10.26	Aarent Cogh Antje Ackerman	1488	Annaatje b 9.16	Jacobus Van Gelder Jannetje Ackerman
10.26	Theodorus Van Winkel Annaatje Van Eydestyn	1489	Elizabeth b 9.13	
11. 2	Jacob Ryke Sietje Vreeland	1490	Michael b 10.12	Johannes Devoursne Annaatje Vreeland
11.16	Adolph Brass Margrietje Van Der Hoef	1491	Jacobus b 10.2	
11.16	Jacob A. Van Winkel Jenneke Van Winkel	1492	Simeon b 9.26	
11.16	Cornelius Degrauw Catharina Vreeland	1493	Hermanus	
11.30	Uldrick Van Rypen Anneke Doremus	1494	Aaltje b 10.8	Thomas Doremus Sarah Sandfort
11.30	Rynier Spier Anomie	1495	Jacobus, twin b 10.23	
11.30	Same as #1495	1496	Johannes, twin b 10.23	
1784 1. 4	Hendrick Doremus Catharina Terhune	1497	Albert	
1. 4	Jacob Van Houten Rachel Ackerman	1498	Gerret b 12.12.1783	Matheus Ackerman Marretje Van Houten
1.11	Hendrick Thysse Fytje Vreeland	1499	Leentje b 10.27.1783	
1.11	Hendrick Doremus Margrietje VanWinkel	1500	Susanna b 11.18.1783	Hendrick Doremus Catharina Terhune
1.11	father unknown Annatje Smith	1501	Johannes Post	Arie Boss
1.11	Dirck Van Der Hoef Sarah Thommas	1502	Sarah b 11.19.1783	Hendrick Van Der Hoef Rachel Kierstede
1.25	Enoch C. Vreeland Lea Van Winkel	1503	Johannes b 12.7.1783	
2. 1	Cornelius H. Vreeland Elisabeth Vreeland	1504	Hartman b 12.11.1783	Michael Vreeland Gerretje Van Houten
2. 1	Hendrick Kool Abigail Mackerty	1505	Johannes b 12.25.1783	John Mackerty Elisabeth Van Bussen

Bap	Parents	1784 Item	Child	Sponsors
2. 1	Waling Van Winkel Pietertje Van Rypen	1506	Waling b 12.30.1783	Hendrick H. Gerretse Hillegont Van Winkel
2.15	William Kingsland Elizabeth Demsey	1507	Marget b 5.18.1783	William Kingsland Isabel Kingsland
2.15	Cornelius Van Rypen Elizabeth Vreeland	1508	Cornelius b 1.9	
2.22	Johannes Post Catharina Van Houten	1509	Adriaan b 1.21	Hessel Pieterse Fytje Van Houten
2.22	John Vreeland	1510	John b 1.26	Pieter Vreland
3.21	John Goetschius Catharina Butler	1511	Hester b 1.30	
4.11	Jacobus Jeraalman Rachel Spier	1512	Lea b 2.20	
4.18	Memmerduke Ackerman Lena Van Eydestyn	1513	Mar(ia) b 3.19	Casparus Van Eydestyn Sarah Van Vorst
4.11	Gerret Spier Margrietje Ennis	1514	William b 3.23	Jan Spier Antje Jacobusse
5. 2	Hendrick Spier Jannetje Van Giesen	1515	Cornelius b 4.4	Egbert Egbertse Rachel Van Giesen
5.15	John Van Buren Catharina Vreland	1516	Beekman b 4.8	Beekman Van Buren Agnus Van Buren
5.16	Hendrick Harris Neesje Van Hoorn	1517	Isaac b 4.26	Rynier Blancher Marretje Cadmus
5.23	Cornelius Sip Marytje Van Rypen	1518	Claasje b 4.24	Waling Van Winkel Pietertje Van Rypen
5.30	John Personet Lena Doremus	1519	Jannetje	
7.28	Marynus Van Rypen Elizabeth Luthin	1520	Simeon b 7.11	Rev. Henricus Schoonmaker Salome Goetschius
5.30	father deceased Catharina Kingsland	1521	Charles James b 4.28	Jacobus Jeraalman Marytje Kingsland
5.30	John Cockefer Naomie Honeysoet	1522	Michael b 3.28	Thomas Cockefer Marytje Honeysoet
5.31	Matheus Ackerman Marretje Van Houten	1523	Jannetje b 4.12	
__.__	father unknown Maria Roos	1524	Charles Slate Fulwood b 4.22	
6.17	Gerrebrand Gerrebrantse Fytje Poulusse	1525	Marretje b 5.21	Nicholaas Gerrebrantse Marytje Cockefer
6.27	John Bruyn Margrietje Sigler	1526	Hendrick b 5.20	Theunis Bruyn Marytje Bruyn
6.27	Abraham Boss Rachel Van Dyck	1527	Rachel b 5.20	

Bap	Parents	1784-1785 Item	Child	Sponsors
7. 4	Johannes A. Post Fytje Neefius	1528	Cornelius b 7.3	Margrietje Nefius
7. 8	John Gerretse Antje Toers	1529	Annaatje b 6.11	Elias Vreeland Elizabeth Vreeland
8. 8	Elias Vreeland Elisabeth Post	1530	Polly b 7.10	Thomas Post Tryntje Vreeland
8. 8	Helmich Van Winkel Marretje Post	1531	Waling b 7.2	Waling Van Winkel Pietertje Van Rypen
9. 5	William Kingsland Maragrita Jeraalman	1532	Elizabeth b 7.14	Henry Kingsland Annaatje Kingsland
9. 5	Thomas Brooks Susanna Laurier	1533	Selley b 7.16	
9. 5	Lucas Van Winkelen Lena Van Wagenen	1534	Sietje b 8.7	David Van Bussen Sietje Van Eydestyn
9. 5	Cornelius Van Houten Helena Van Houten	1535	Hendrick (twin) b 7.29	Jannetje Hennion
9. 5	Same as #1535	1536	Pieter (twin) b 7.29	

(Numbers 1535-1536 may be one child, "Hendrick Pieter")

Bap	Parents	Item	Child	Sponsors
9.19	Gerret Joh. Gerretse Margrietje C. Gerretse	1537	Marretje b 9.3	
10. 3	John Perrot Rachel Koejeman	1538	Annaatje b 9.1	John Koejeman Antje Van Winkel
10.10	Pieter Gerrebrantse Annaatje Gerrebrantse	1539	Jurrie b 9.19	Nicholaas Gerrebrantse Marytje Cockefer
10.17	Waling Egbertse Sarah Steeger	1540	Maria b 9.1	Hendrick Steeger Maria Ryke
10.17	Paulus Paulusse Neeltje Jurrianse	1541	Jenneke b 9.17	Arie Boss Hillegont Van Vorst
10.31	John Tucker Annaatje Cockefer	1542	Pheben b 9.20	Nicholaas Gerrebrantse Marytje Kockefer
11. 7	John Van Rypen Lea Winne	1543	Johannes b 9.28	
11.21	Casparus Degrauw Lena Jurrianse	1544	Annaatje b 9.19	Christophel Jurrianse Annaatje Brouwer
12.12	Elias Smith Sarah Koeck	1545	Elias b 10.8	Cornelius Spier Annaatje Stymets
12.12	Moses Terp Annaatje Schidmoor	1546	Sarah b 10.30	
12.26	Dirck Vreeland Fytje Van Wagenen	1547	Roelof b 11.23	Roelof V. Wagenen Sarah Jurrianse
1785 1.11	Henry Duplacey Anna Butler	1548	John b 1.9	John Emans Hester Emans

Bap	Parents	1785 Item	Child	Sponsors
1.16	Dirck Van Hoorn Margrietje Terhune	1549	Margrietje b 12.20.1784	Thomas Van Hoorn Margrietje Devoursne
1.16	Matheus Everse Lena Mourusse	1550	Aaltje b 11.19.1784	Dirck Pickstoon Aaltje Mourusse
1.16	Elias Spier Lena Jacobusse	1551	 b 12.11.1784	Rynier Spier Metje Spier
2.27	Jacob Spier Rebecca Linkfoot	1552	Jacob b 1.31	Cornelius Egbertse Margrietje Egbertse
2.27	Pieter Vreeland Margrietje Demsey	1553	Marcus b 2.3	
2.27	Helmich Post Metje Van Rypen	1554	Cornelius b 2.4	
3.13	David Blair Beletje Vreeland	1555	Marretje b 2.7	Michael Vreeland Gerretje Van Houten
3.20	Jacob Ryke Sietje Vreeland	1556	Tryntje b 2.24	Christophel Steeger Sarah Ryke
3.20	Cornelius Van Giesen Sophia Sigler	1557	Rynier b 2.28	Cornelius Van Giesen Jenneke Doremus
4.17	Theodorus Van Winkel Annaatje Van Eydestyn	1558	Theodosie b 3.25	Franscois Van Eydestyn Antje Thyse
4.17	Joris Van Eydestyn Lena Van Rypen	1559	Catharina b 3.4	Jacob Vreeland Catharina Van Winkel
4.17	John Stegg Marytje Spier	1560	Dirck b 3.1	Cornelius Van Houten Antje Hennion
4.17	Cornelius Van Rypen Marretje Gerretse	1561	Gerret b 4.1	Gerret Gerretse
5. 1	Johannes J. Vreeland Gouda Easterly	1562	Maria b 3.29	
6.26	Abraham Huysman Maria Terhune	1563	Elizabeth b 5.23	Roeliph Terhune Elisabeth Brauveld
6.26	Johannes Thyse Marytje Jongh	1564	Catharina b 4.13	
6.26	Jacob Van Winkel Jenneke Van Winkel	1565	Lena b 5.8	
7.17	Pieter Kip Wilemyntje Van Winkel	1566	Johannes b 6.20	
7.31	Johannes Cor. Post Cornelia Cadmus	1567	Johannes b 7.7	Andries Cadmus Pryntje Doremus
7.31	Daniel Folkonier Rachel Ryke	1568	Jacob b 6.21	
7.31	Cornelius Vreeland Elizabeth Vreeland	1569	Hartman b 7.4	
8.14	Johannes Terhune Sarah Vreeland	1570	Enoch b 7.21	Cornelius Terhune Tryntje Vreeland

Bap	Parents	Item	Child	Sponsors
8.14	Gerret Wouterse Gerretje Post	1571	Annaatje b 7.8	Adriaan M. Post Annaatje Post
8.28	Franscois Van Eydestyn Antje Thyse	1572	Catharina b 8.5	Isaac Van Houten Annaatje Boss
8.28	Johannes Spier Antje Jacobusse	1573	Thomas b 7.30	Gerret Jacobusse Marytje Coerte
9.25	Philip Van Bussen Elizabeth Post	1574	Andrew Brestead b 8.31	Hermanus Van Bussen Wyntje Terp
9.25	Hendrick F. Post Jannetje Van Houten	1575	Jenneke b 8.14	Dirck Van Houten Elisabeth Van Houten
10. 2	John Brown Margrietje Sigler	1576	Eunice b 8.28	Gerrebrand Gerrebrantse Hester Brown
10.23	David Van Bussen Sietje Van Eydestyn	1577	Hermanus b 9.11	
11. 6	Johannes Sip jr Geertje Van Winkel	1578	Adriaan b 10.9	Cornelius Sip Marytje Van Rypen
11.20	John Berry Sietje Van Rypen	1579	Maragrietje b 10.20	Dirck Vreeland Fytje Van Wagenen
11.20	John Schidmoor Catharina Degrauw	1580	Annaatje b 10.25	Cornelius Degrauw Catharina Vreeland
12. 4	Gerret G. Van Rypen Lea Simmons	1581	Rachel b 10.16	
12.21	Samuel Seely Patience Morrell	1582	Charles Blanchard b 8.24	Rynier Blanchard Marretje Cadmus
12.25	Jan Jurrianse Franscyntje Mourusse	1583	Jan b 11.5	
12.25	Memmerduke Ackerman Lena Van Eydestyn	1584	Jannetje b 11.23	Thade Van Eydestyn Jannetje Van Eydestyn
12.25	Lucas Wesselse Margarita Booth	1585	John b 11.24	
12.26	Waling Van Winkel Pietertje Van Rypen	1586	Claasje b 11.25	
1786 1. 8	Casparus Van Eydestyn Annaatje Post	1587	Catharina b 12.10.1785	Gerret Van Vorst Sarah Van Vorst
1.15	Andrias Cadmus Pryntje Doremus	1588	Fytje b 12.13.1785	
1.21	Pieter Terhune Jenneke Van Winkel	1589	Albert b 12.26.1785	Dirck Terhune Maria Berry
2. 5	Jacobus Ennis Jannetje Hopper	1590	Maria b 9.13.1785	Gerrit Spier Maragrietje Ennis
2.12	Thomas Van Hoorn Maragrietje Devorsne	1591	Jacob b 1.20	
2.19	John Parrot Rachel Koejeman	1592	Thomas b 10.7.1785	Abraham Koejeman Lena Van Winkel

Bap	Parents	1786 Item	Child	Sponsors
2.19	Hendrick Doremus Catharina Terhune	1593	Hessel b 1.14	Cornelius Doremus Annaatje Vreeland
3. 5	Abraham Mourusse Hester Mandeviel	1594	Jacob b 1.27	Jacob Spier Rebecka Linckfoot
3. 5	John Van Eydestyn Maria Wieler	1595	Elizabeth b 1.2	Dirck Van Houten Rachel Van Eydestyn
3.12	Cornelius Van Rypen Elizabeth Vreland	1596	Jannetje b 1.19	Michael Vreeland Gerritje Van Houten
3.19	Arie Post Catharina Van Rypen	1597	Adriaan	Elias Vreland Maragrietje Post
3.21	John Gerritse Antje Toers	1598	Cathalyntje b 2.15	
4. 6	Daniel Kemper Elizabeth Marius	1599	Sylvester Marius b 2.5	
4. 9	Christophel Steeger Sara Ryker	1600	Femmetje b 3.11	Rynier Spier Naomie Schidmoor
4. 9	Barent Spier Sarah Spier	1601	Annetje b 2.27	
4. 9	Isaac Van Giesen Marytje Van Sent	1602	Metje b 2.22	
4.13	John Koejeman Antje Van Winkel	1603	Lea b 3.5	
4.16	John Personet Lena Doremus	1604	Joseph b 3.5	
4.30	Nicholaas Gerrebrantse Marytje Kocjefer	1605	Annaatje b 3.24	John Tucker Annaatje Kockjefer
5. 7	Micha Gillam Christina Kogh	1606	Joseph	
5.28	Arent Kogh Antje Ackerman	1607	David b 4.18	John Westerveld Maragrietje Ackerman
6. 4	Jacob Van Winkel Annaetje Van Noorstrand	1608	Isaac b 4.30	Isaac Van Winkel Eva Van Winkel
6.11	Gerrit Spier Maragrietje Ennis	1609	Neeltje b 5.13	
6.18	Johannis Helm Marytje Roo(s)	1610	Hendrick b 5.26	Hendrick Helm Marytje Helm
7. 9	John Van Buren Catharina Vreland	1611	Rachel b 5.20	Pieter Vreland, & Lea /wife
7. 9	Cornelius Pier Antje Vrelandt	1612	Johannes b 5.17	Pieter Pier Antje Jacobusse
7.24	Abraham Messelaar Annaatje Kemble	1613	Peggy b 6.1	Matheus Valentine Perrow Elizabeth Hall
8. 6	Abraham Bogert Antje Gerretse	1614	Rachel b 6.25	Gerrit Gerritse Maria Ryerse

		1786-1787		
<u>Bap</u>	<u>Parents</u>	<u>Item</u>	<u>Child</u>	<u>Sponsors</u>
8. 6	Hendrick Herris Neesje Van Hoorn	1615	Jacob b 7.20	Jan Berdan Catharina Van Hoorn
8. 6	Enoch Vreelandt Lea Van Winkel	1616	Pryntje b 6.29	
8.13	Nicasie Van Blerkum Catharina Post	1617	Catharina b 7.15	Cornelius Van Houten Antje Hennion
8.27	Hendrick Spier Metje Vrelandt	1618	Jacobus b 7.27	
8.27	Gerrit Egbertse Rachel Spier	1619	Marretje	Elias Spier Lena Jacobusse
10. 1	Pieter Van Giesen Sarah Spier	1620	Pally b 8.26	Gerrit Egbertse Rachel Spier
10. 1	Gerrit Lansingh Dallie	1621	Catharina b 8.20	
10. 1	Cornelius Hoppen Catharina Terhune	1622	Catharina b 9.10	
10.22	Johannis Ryke Annaetje Wesselse	1623	Joannes b 9.11	John Jorcks Ariaantje Smith
10.22	Helmich V. Winkel Marretje Post	1624	Geertje b 9.28	Adrian Post Geertje Vreland
10.22	Johannis Bilju Maria Bel	1625	Maragrietje b 10.4	Jacob D. Berdan Catharina Bilju
11.19	Albert Ackerman Antje Van Winkel	1626	Jannetje b 10.29	Isaac Van Winkel Jannetje Kip
11.26	Christofel Jurrianse Annaetje Brouwer	1627	Gerrit b 9.28	Jacobus Ennis Jannetje Hoppen
11.26	Adriaan M. Post Elizabeth Van Rypen	1628	Claasje b 11.4	Waling Van Winkel Pietertje Van Rypen
12. 3	Roelof Post Marretje Post	1629	Francois b 11.7	Hendrick Gerritse Cathalyntje Van Houten
12.17	Johannes Van Wagenen Rachel Trophagen	1630	Gerret b 11.13	Gerret Van Wagenen Fytje Westervelt
12.17	Michael Post Jannetje Ackerman	1631	Adriaan	Adriaan Post Geertje Vreeland
<u>1787</u> 1.20	William Agnew Margaret Brant	1632	Brant b 12.31.1786	
1.28	John Furguson Nellie McLean	1633	Barbarie b 4.19.1786	
3. 6	Marynus Van Rypen Elizabth Luthen	1634	Thomas b 2.11	Thomas Post Tryntje Vreland
6.21	Johannis Gerrebrantse Jannetje Vreeland	1635	Jannetje	Dirck Paulusse Annaatje Gerrebrantse
7. 1	David Secorn Bridget Furgeson	1636	Catharina b 6.9	Johannis J. Vreland Gouda Easterly

Bap	Parents	1787 Item	Child	Sponsors
7. 8	Richard Ludlow Elizabeth Van Kampe	1637	Catharina b 6.9	
7.22	Cornelius Van Rypen Marretje Gerritse	1638	Cornelius b 6.21	Jurrie Van Rypen Marretje Vreland
7.22	John Van Rypen Lea Winne	1639	Philip b 6.16	
7.22	Michael Vreland Gerritje Van Houten	1640	Jannetje b 6.30	
7.29	Johannis Post Maria Bradfort	1641	Abraham b 7.2	Abraham Post Maragrietje Kogg
8. 5	Thomas Kockefer Mary Handerschut	1642	John b 6.27	John Cockefer Jannetje C-ckefer
8.19	Thomas Bruyn Annaetje Hoogteeling	1643	 b 7.15	
9. 2	Jacob Ryker Sietje Vreland	1644	Aaltje b 8.4	Johannis Vreland Annatje Spier
9.16	Lucas Van Winkel Lena Van Wagenen	1645	Lena b 8.19	Jacobus Terhune Lena Van Dyck
9.16	John Parrot Rachel Koejeman	1646	Lea b 6.18	
9.30	John Terhune Sarah Vreland	1647	 b 8.28	Thomas Vreland Annaetje Vreland
10.14	Elias Vreland Marritje Post	1648	Antje b 9.21	Casparus Post Elizabeth Vreland
10.14	Simeon Van Winkel Antje Marselusse	1649	Johannis b __.__.1787	Pieter Marselusse Jannetje Van Winkel
10.28	Johannes C. Post Cornelia Cadmus	1650	Cornelius b 10.4	Cornelis Cadmus Jannetje Van Rypen
10.28	John Browen Margaret Sigler	1651	Hendrick b 8.19	
11.18	Isaac Vreland Myntje Romyn	1652	Abraham b 10.26	Thomas Post Tryntje Vreland
11.22	William Kingsland Maragrita Jeraalman	1653	John Jeraalman b 10.15	John Jordan Annaatje Kingh
11.25	Paulus Paulussen Neeltje Gerrebrantse	1654	Elizabeth b 11.1	Elias J. Vreland Elizabeth Post
11.25	John Vreland Jannetje Spier	1655	Teunis b 10.29	Hendrick Doremus Tryntje Terhune
11.25	Hendrick Spier Geesje Everse	1656	Matheus b 10.12	Johannis Spier
11.25	Cornelius Van Giesen Sophia Sigler	1657	Jacobus b 10.23	Jacobus Sigler Maria Sigler
11.25	David Blair Beletje Vreland	1658	Henry b 11.1	

Bap	Parents	Item	Child	Sponsors
12. 1	John A. Ackerman Elizabeth Dierman	1659	Petrus b 10.28	Petrus Ackerman Grietje Dierman
12. 9	Dirck Paulusson Annaatje Gerrebrantse	1660	Rachel b 9.19	Gerrebrand Gerrebrantse Fytje Paulusson
12. 9	Cornelius Shipard Marretje Ryker	1661	Polly b 10.24	Albert Ryker Catharina Hurley
12.16	John Gerritse Antje Toers	1662	Hendrick b 10.27	Abraham Gerritse Fytje Gerritse
12.16	Uldrick Van Rypen Anneke Doremus	1663	Johannes b 10.6	
1788 1. 1	Jacob Van Noorstrand Geertje Degrauw	1664	Sarah b 12.10.1787	Gerrebrand Gerrebrantse Sarah Van Noostrand
1. 1	Adriaan Van Rypen Sarah Ackerman	1665	Abraham b 9.14.1787	Jonathan Snyder Pettie Ackerman
1.13	Dirck Van Hoorn Maragrita Terhune	1666	Johannes b 12.20.1787	Hendrick Herris Neesje Van Hoorn
1.13	Moses Terp Hanna Schidmoor	1667	Samuel b 11.8.1787	
1.13	Jurrie Everson Neelje Montanje	1668	Elizabeth b 11.19.1787	Theodorus Van Winkel Annaatje Van Eydestyn
1.20	Casparus Van Eydestyn Annaatje Post	1669	Elizabeth b 12.23.1787	Casparus Van Vorst Jannetje Kip
1.20	Isaac J. Van Houten Annaatje Boss	1670	Lena b 12.26.1787	Rynier Blanchard Marretje Cadmus
1.27	John Goetschius Catharina Butler	1671	Tryntje b 1.1	Elizabeth Messeker
2. 8	John Marinus Catharina Post	1672	David	
2.10	Philip Berry Eva Van Winkel	1673	Johannes b 12.26.1787	Johannes Sip Geertje Van Winkele
2.10	Piete- Kip Myntje Van Winkel	1674	Jannetje b 1.20	Hendrick Kip Jannetje Kip
2.17	Cornelius Sip Maria Van Rypen	1675	Annaatje b 1.17	Adriaan Sip Geertje Sip
2.24	Jacobus Ennis Jannetje Hoppen	1676	Jannetje b 1.1	Hendrick Spier Metje Vreland
2.24	Isaac Ryker Santje Pier	1677	Maria b 1.25	
2.24	Petrus Ryker Martha Corby	1678	Rhoda b 1.12	
3. 2	John Schidmoor Tryntje Degrauw	1679	Hermanus b 2.4	
3. 2	David Van Bussen Sietje Van Eydestyn	1680	Teunis b 2.10	

Bap	Parents	1788 Item	Child	Sponsors
4.13	Pieter Terhune Jenneke Van Winkel	1681	Theodorus b 3.14	Theodorus Van Winkel Annaatje Van Eydestyn
4.13	Memmerduck Ackerman Lena Van Eydestyn	1682	John b 3.15	
4.13	Johannis Spier Antje Jacobusse	1683	Hendrick b 3.12	Hendrick Spier Metje Vreland
4.13	Andries Cadmus Pryntje Doremus	1684	Hendrick b 3.10	Cornelius Doremus Styntje Van Rypen
4.13	Jacob Van Rypen Fytje Jacobusse	1685	Isaac b 10.26	Cornelius Spier Annaatje Stymets
4.13	Same as #1685	1686	Jacob b 10.26.1787	Hendrick Jacobusse Fytje Paulusson
5. 4	Jacob En. Vreland Marritje Vreland	1687	Enoch b 4.5	Enoch Vreland Jannetje Kip
5. 4	Abraham Ryker Annaatje Ennis	1688	Sarah b 3.29	Albert Ryker Catharina Horley
5.18	Cornelius Cadmus Jannetje Van Rypen	1689	Johannes b 4.4	Johannes Post Cornelia Cadmus
5.18	Nicholaus Gerrebrantse Maria Cockefeer	1690	Annaatje b 3.22	Gerrebrant Gerrebrantse Fytje Poulusson
5.18	John Bruyn Cathalyntje	1691	Hendrick b 4.9	Isaac Vreland Jannetje Bruyn
5.18	Joseph Passe Tryntje Pengman	1692	William b 2.3	
5.18	Daniel Folkonier Rachel Ryker	1693	Johannis b 4.23	Dirck Vreland Jannetje Van Rypen
6. 8	James D. Christie Geertje Degrauw	1694	Jenneke b 10.21.1785	
6. 8	Same as #1694	1695	Lena b 5.1	Casparus Degrauw Lena Jurrianse
6.29	Rynier Van Giesen Altje Van Rypen	1696	Catharina b 5.4	
6.29	Abraham Mauerse Hester Mandeviel	1697	Tryntje b 5.29	
7. 6	Johannes Van Rypen Jannetje Van Noorstrand	1698	Saartje b 5.30	
7. 6	John T. Van Eydestyn Maria Miller	1699	Angenietje b 6.27	
7. 6	Jacob Van Winkele Jenneke Van Winkele	1700	Jenneke b 6.9	
8. 3	Gerret Van Vorst Elizabeth Bilju	1701	Jacob b 7.17	Jacob Berdan Catharina Bilju
9.14	Teunus Bruin Saartje Outwater	1702	Maria b 8.25	Hendrick Jeraalman Maria Spier

Bap	Parents	1788-1789 Item	Child	Sponsors
9.14	Abraham Koejeman Myntje Vreland	1703	Johannes b 6.19	
9.21	John Van Blerkom Antje Jacobusse	1704	Brandt b 8.20	
9.21	John Kidnie Rachel Spier	1705	Annaatje b 8.19	
9.21	Arie King Tryntje Corre	1706	Annaatje b 8.19	
9.21	Thomas Beekhorn Lena Kierstede	1707	Jannetje b 10.25.1788?	
9.21	Arie Canceljie Jannetje Liense	1708	Catharina b 6.1	
9.25	Abraham Willis Catharina Post	1709	Pieter b 9.3	
9.28	John Berry Sietje Van Rypen	1710	Philip b 9.4	Philip Berry Efje Van Winkel
10. 5	Cornelius Doremus Styntje Van Rypen	1711	Maragrietje b 8.24	
10.12	Harmen Van Rypen Lea Spier	1712	Marritje b 9.17	
10.26	Jurrie Kiesler Jannetje Jacobusse	1713	John b 9.9	
11. 2	Christophel Steger Sarah Rit	1714	Anneke b 10.8	
11. 2	Gerret Van Der Hoef Syntje Doremus	1715	Sarah b 10.10	Cornelius Gerrebrantse Lena Spier
11. 2	Rynier Blancher Marritje Cadmus	1716	Isaac b 9.21	
11. 9	John Ludlow Elizabeth Vreland	1717	Richard b 9.13	
11. 9	Francois Degraauw Jacob Van Noorstrand?	1718	Hermanus b 10.9	Geertje Degrauw
12.14	John Stagg Maria Spier	1719	Maria b 11.17	Abraham Van Rypen Maria Tysen
12.21	Johannes Brouwer Grietje Wyt	1720	Elizabeth b 11.18	William Wyt Altje Jacobusse
12.22	Jacobus Van Winkele Maragrietje Toers	1721	Annetje b 10.24	Hendrick Van Winkele Hillegond Bruyn
12.25	Jonathan Snyder Pettie Ackerman	1722	Praffie b 11.24	Samuel Spier Maria Snyder
12.26	Hendrick Spier Mettje Vreland	1723	Jacob b 12.1	
1789 1. 4	Adriaan M. Post Elizabeth Van Rypen	1724	Marcelus b 12.12.1788	Gerret Wouterse Gerretje Post

Bap	Parents	1789 Item	Child	Sponsors
1.11	Egbert Egbertse Rachel Van Giesen	1725	Maria b 12.1.1788	Cornelius Egbertse Margrietje Spier
1.18	Egbert Ricks Grietje Spier	1726	Maria b 11.12.1788	Pieter Ryker Maria Spier
1.25	John Spier Elizabeth Terhune	1727	Teunis b 12.28.1788	Hendrick Spier Geesje Everse
1.25	Jacob Pier Cathalyntje Everse	1728	Lena b 11.12.1788	
1.28	Hendrick Doremus Tryntje Terhune	1729	Tryntje b 12.20.1788	Dirck Terhune Maria Berry
2. 1	Matheus Van Noorstrand Maria Phillips	1730	Jenneke b 12.30.1788	
2. 1	Thomas Dod Maria Hellim	1731	John b 12.29.1788	Rynier Spier Anneke Spier
2.15	Cornelius Degrauw Tryntje Vreland	1732	Tryntje b 12.27.1788	
2.22	Jacob Toers Maria Post	1733	Abraham b 2.1	Adrian Post Marritje Post
3. 1	Hendrick Van Houten Maria Van Rypen	1734	Gerret b 2.2	
3. 1	Pieter Gerrebrantse Annatje Gerrebrantse	1735	Christophel b 1.20	Jacob Gerrebrantse Marretje Gerrebrantse
3. 1	Gerrebrand Gerrebrandse Tytje Paulusse	1736	Annaetje b 12.24.1788	Isaac Paulusse Annaatje Paulusse
3. 1	Pieter Ackerman Annaetje Vreland	1737	Lea b 1.18	Pieter Vreland Lea Doremus
3.15	William McLean Hester Jeraalman	1738	Johannes b 2.5	John Jeraalman Maria Devorsne
3.15	Gerret Spier Grietje Ennis	1739	Pieter b 2.9	
3.22	Abraham Berry Tryntje Outwater	1740	Hendrick b 3.3	Hendrick Outwater Tryntje Brass
3.22	William Agnew Magaret Brant	1741	Joseph Brant b 12.21.1789?	
3.22	Hendrickje Bilju	1742	Catharina b 3.2	Jacob Berdan Catharina Bilju
4.12	Helmich Van Winkele Marritje Post	1743	Jannetje b 3.19	Hendrick Gerritse Hillgond Van Winkel
4.19	Adriaan J. Sip Lea Van Rypen	1744	Isaac b 3.19	
5. 3	Franscois Van Eydestyn Antje Tysen	1745	Thade b 4.10	Thade V. Eydestyn Saartje Degrau
5.17	Roeliph Post Marritje Post	1746	Johannis b 4.16	Johannis Spier Lea Spier

Bap	Parents	1789 Item	Child	Sponsors
5.17	Jacob Spier Rebecka Linckfoot	1747	Lea b 4.18	Thomas Linckfoot Jenneke V. Rypen
5.17	Johannes Gerrebrantse Jannetje Vreland	1748	Aaltje b 3.11	
5.17	Helmich Van Giesen Sarah V. Noorstrand	1749	Elizabeth b 4.25	
5.24	Gerrit Spier Tryntje Doremus	1750	Catharina b 4.8	Cornelius Egbertse Maragrietje Spier
5.24	Frans Spier Catharina Gerbrantse	1751	Sarah b 4.20	Adrian P. Post Sarah Spier
5.24	Hendrick Jacobusse Hester Van Nes	1752	Jan b 4.28	
5.24	Petrus Ryker Martha Corby	1753	Antje b 5.10	
5.24	Philip Van Rypen Jannetje Sip	1754	Abraham b 5.14	
5.30	Pieter Aljie Elizabeth Mauersen	1755	Maragrieta b 5.1	
5.30	John Van Rypen Hendrickje V. Rypen	1756	John b 4.25	John M: Vreeland Anna Vreland
5.30	Theodorus Van Winkel Annatje V. Eydestyn	1757	Jenneke b 5.1	Pieter Terhune Jenneke V. Winkel
6.14	Samuel Sigler Judick V. Rypen	1758	Moses b 5.21	
6.21	Helmich Post Metje Post	1759	Hendrick b 5.20	
6.21	Phillip Berry Eva V. Winkel	1760	Catharina b 5.25	
6.21	John Toers Maragritje Kip	1761	Gerrit b 5.27	Gerret Toers Maragritje Tours
6.21	Pieter H. Gerritse Eva Romyn	1762	Geertje b 4.30	Jacob Vreland Geertje V. Winkel
6.14	Johannes Post Jutje Neefje	1763	Elizabeth b 6.4	
7.14	Adriaan J. Post Maritje Post	1764	Jannetje b 6.15	
8.19	Enoch Vreland Lea Van Winkel	1765	Saartje b 6.12	
7.26	Jilles Mandeviel Christina Huysman	1766	Abraham b 5.23	Pieter De Garmo Abigail Shiers
7.26	John Hopkins Aaltje Doremus	1767	Elizabeth b 6.2	
8. 1	Dirck Boss Antje Stegg	1768	Cornelius b 5.10	

-82-

Bap	Parents	1789 Item	Child	Sponsors
8. 1	Thomas Doremus Margrietje V. Der Hoef	1769	Dirck b 4.14	Diena Van Der Hoef
8. 1	Michael Sandvordt Sarah Boss	1770	Sarah b 10.6.1788	
8. 9	Johannes Gerritse Maragrietje Van Rypen	1771	Elizabeth b 7.16	John Westerveld Antje Van Rypen
8.16	Jacob Ryker Sietje Vreland	1772	Maria b 7.12	John Vreland Henckje Vreland
8.16	Cornelius Van Rypen Elizabeth Vreland	1773	Catharina b 7.5	
8.16	John Parrot Rachel Koejeman	1774	Johannis b 3.28	
8.23	Joris Cadmus Efje Fielding	1775	Grietje b 7.19	Cornelius Cadmus Jannetje Van Rypen
8.23	Casparus Degrauw Lena Jurrianse	1776	Christofel b 7.25	Jurrie Jurrianse Elizabeth Jurrianse
8.26	Nathanael Canfield Annaatje Koningh	1777	Matheus b 7.27	
9. 6	Jacob Van Rypen Altje Vreland	1778	Johannes b 8.11	
9. 6	Jan Jurrianse Syntje Mauerse	1779	Hendrick b 8.3	
9.13	Isaac Van Giesen Maria Van Sendt	1780	Maria b 8.15	
9.13	Hendrick Van Der Hoef Rachel Kierstede	1781	Sarah b 8.17	Roelif V. Wagenen Saartje Jurrianse
9.20	Johannes Kierstede Lena Ryker	1782	Arie b 8.23	Arie Kierstede Sarah Ryker
9.20	Albert Ryker Catharina Hurley	1783	Petrus b 8.20	Abraham Ryker Annaatje Ennis
9.20	Cornelius Shiphard Maria Ryker	1784	Samuel b 8.23	Samuel Shiphard
9.30	John Jordan Maragrieta Scisco	1785	Henry b 9.7	
11.23	Hermanus Van Bussen Annaatje Spier	1786	Cathalyntje b 11.9	
11.29	Gerrit G. Van Rypen Lea Simmons	1787	Maragrietje b 10.8	John Simmons Susanna Simmons
12. 3	William Kingsland Margarieta Jeraalman	1788	Maragrietje b 9.23	Abraham Berger Hillitje Bruyn
12.13	Jacobus Jeraalman Maria Kingsland	1789	James b 10.22	
12.13	Klaas Vreland Elizabeth Van Schyve	1790	Pieter b 12.4	Waling Van Vorst Annaetje Post

Bap	Parents	1789-1790 Item	Child	Sponsors
9.20	Hendrick Kierstede Catharina Van Houten	1791	Lena b 7.25	
10.18	Samuel Gould Lena Jacobusse	1792	Saartje b 8.25	
10.18	Daniel Pier Grietje Doremus	1793	David b 6.15	
10.25	Barent Spier Saartje Spier	1794	Abraham b 10.4	
10.25	Joseph Passe Catharina Penman	1795	Jonathan b 8.11	
11.15	John Vreland Annaatje Spier	1796	Abraham b 9.22	Abraham Spier Emmica Wouters
11.15	Gerrit Van Vorst Maria Van Eydestyn	1797	Catharina b 10.17	Casparus V. Eydestyn Sarah Van Vorst
11.15	John Bruyn Pietertje Winne	1798	Anthony b 10.26	John Bruyn Pietertje Gerrebrantse
11.15	Dirck Paulusse Annaatje Gerrebrantse	1799	Isaac b 8.25	Isaac Paulusse
12. 6	George V. Eydestyn Geesje Vreland	1800	Lena b 10.__	
12. 6	Elias Vreland Margrietje Post	1801	Adrian b 11.8	Adrian Post Geertje Vreland
12.25	Stephen King Mary Sandvort	1802	Neeltje b 10.31	
12.27	John Berry Sietje Van Rypen	1803	Cornelius b 12.3	Cornelius Van Rypen Elizabeth Vreland
11.29	Dirck Berger Maria Boerum	1804	Rebecka b 9.8	
1790 1. 1	Jurry V. Rypen Antje Vreland	1805	Simeon b 12.2.1789	
1. 1	Albert Rit Geertje Hellem	1806	Samuel b 12.8.1789	
1. 1	Cornelius V. Rypen Marritje Gerritse	1807	Gerrebrant b 12.7.1789	Gerrit Gerritse Vrouwtje Gerritse
1. 3	Jacob Smith Fytje Post	1808	Uldrick b 11.15.1789	Uldrick Uldrickse Arriaantje Smith
1. 3	John V. Rypen Lea Winne	1809	Maria b 12.12.1789	
1.10	Dirck Cadmus Altje Keen	1810	Abraham b 10.31.1789	Abaham Cadmus Maria Keen
1.10	Arent Koning Styntje Wouterse	1811	Grietje b 11.11.1789	
1.10	Myndert Koejeman Catharina Bruyn	1812	Johannis b 12.16.1789	

Bap	Parents	1790 Item	Child	Sponsors
1.24	John King Rachel Bruyn	1813	Hendrick b 12.27.1789	Rynier Bruyn and wife
1.31	John Spier Maragrietje Jeraalman	1814	Annaetje b 12.20.1789	
2. 1	John Goetschius Catharina Butler	1815	Jacobus	
2.14	Casparus Van Rypen Antje Ackerman	1816	Catharina b 1.24	
2.21	Cornelius Vreland Elizabeth Vreland	1817	Michael b 1.31	Cornelius V. Rypen Elizabeth Vreland
2.21	David Blair Beletje Vreland	1818	Hartman b 1.26	
2.28	John Ackerman Elizabeth Dierman	1819	John b 1.7	
3. 7	Daniel Folkonier Rachel Ryker	1820	Joseph b 2.4	
3.28	John Cadmus Phebe Cadmus	1821	Abraham b 8.29.1789	
3.28	Rynier Spier Maria Jacobusse	1822	Johannes b 1.30	
3.28	Waling Egbertse Sara Stager	1823	Johannes b 1.9	
3.28	John Sigler Sietje Mandeviel	1824	Lea b 2.5	
3.28	John W. King Magdalena Spier	1825	William b 2.15	
4. 4	Lucas Van Winkel Helena V. Wagenen	1826	Rachel b 2.21	Arie V. Winkel Grietje V. Wagenen
4. 4	Cornelius V. Der Beek Hilletje Van Giesen	1827	Abraham b 3.13	Abraham V. Der Beek Maria V. Giesen
4. 4	John Pasnit Lena Doremus	1828	Abraham b 1.31	Abraham Doremus
4.25	Gerrebrand Gerrebrandse Tryntje Paulusse	1829	Tryntje b 2.26	Isaac Paulusse Tryntje Paulusse
4.25	Hendrick Roome Geertruy Van Houten	1830	Aaltje b 5.4.1789	
4.25	Abraham Ryker Annaetje Ennis	1831	Catharina b 3.22	
4.30	Hendrick Maurusse Tryntje Alje	1832	Susanna b 2.27	
5. 4	Pieter Terhune Janneke V. Winkel	1833	Dirck b 4.13	Dirck V. Hoorn Margrietje Terhune
5.16	John Vreland Jannetje Spier	1834	Elias b 4.16	Elias J. Vreland Elizabeth Post

Bap	Parents	1790 Item	Child	Sponsors
5.16	Isaac Kingsland (H)yle Kingsland	1835	Hyle b 4.7	Abraham Franscisco Sarah Franscisco
6.13	_____ Jacobussen Jamyme Williams	1836	Aaron Morris b 5.4	
6.20	Thomas Sigler Lea Spier	1837	Lena b 5.7	
6.27	Johannes Rothan Elizabeth Lake	1838	Susanna b 6.1	
6.27	Teunis Bruyn Saartje Outwater	1839	Hendrick b 5.__	Pieter Brass Maria Snyder
6.27	Johannes Meyer Maria Ecker	1840	Sarah b 6.2	
7.11	Isaac Vreland Maragrietje Vreland	1841	Helena b 6.22	Thomas Vreland Helena Schoonmaker
7.18	Jacob Bruyn Engeltje Van Es	1842	Tryntje b 3.29	Johannes Sindel Tryntje Van Der Hoef
7.25	Gerret Van Vorst Elizabeth Bilju	1843	Gerret b 6.26	
8.22	Abraham Vreland Catharina Easterly	1844	Marragrietje b 1.19	
8.22	Abraham Maurussen Hester Mandeviel	1845	Johannes b 7.10	
8.22	Jacobus V. Winkel Margrietje Van Winkel	1846	Jacob b 6.11	
8.31	Jesse Gould Elizabeth Coljer	1847	Susanna b 7.21	
9.12	Jacobus Jacobusse Tryntje Gerrebrantse	1848	Johannes b 6.24	
9.12	father unknown Sarah Boss	1849	Johannis Smith b 7.29	Cornelius Van Vorst Annaetje Outwater
9.12	Casparus Van Eydestyn Annaetje Post	1850	Hermanus b 8.7	Jacob Van Oostrand Geertje Degrauw
9.12	John Drummond Antje Post	1851	John b 8.10	Abraham Post Margrietje Kogh
9.19	Philip V. Rypen Jannetje Sip	1852	Annatje b 8.22	Cornelius Sip Maria Van Rypen
9.26	Jacob Stagg Maria Endress	1853	John b 8.8	John Spier Elisabeth Post
9.26	Benjamin Sharow Maria Aljee	1854	Elizabeth b 8.26	
10. 3	Jeremiah Evertse Neeltje Montanje	1855	Tryntje b 9.17	Hendrick Brinckerhoff Annaatje Sandfort
10. 3	Johannes Courten Antje Macknes	1856	Margrietje b 9.5	Margrietje Macknes

Bap	Parents	1790-1791 Item	Child	Sponsors
10. 3	Johannes Post Marretje Neefje	1857	Cornelius b 8.30	Jacob V. Winkel Cathalyntje Neefje
10.24	Gerbrand Gerbrandse Fytje Paulusse	1858	Jannetje b 8.4	Jacob Gerbrandsen Jannetje Paulussen
10.24	Johannes Post Maria Pervoo	1859	Johanes b 9.26	Johannes Pervoo Grietje Van Hoorn
10.24	Same as #1859	1860	Margrietje b 9.26	John Zabriskie Grietje Pervoo
10.31	Marynus Van Rypen Elizabeth Luthen	1861	Catharina b 10.2	
10.31	Waling V. Winkel Pietertje Van Rypen	1862	Jannetje b 10.5	Helmich Van Winkel Marretje Post
10.31	Ulrich Van Rypen Anneke Doremus	1863	Gerret b 9.6	
11.14	 Fytje Neefje	1864	Roelif b 9.30	
11.14	William Mills Antje Ennis	1865	Antje b 10.19	William Devaal Antje Devenpoort
11.15	Arendt King Arriaantje Vreeland	1866	Johannes b 9.26	John King
11.21	Teunis Beekhorn Sietje Kierstede	1867	Petrus b 6.1	Elizabeth Kierstede
11.21	Abraham Steeger Margrietje Meet	1868	Phebe b 11.1	Hendrick Steeger Maria V. Rypen
12.19	Abraham Berry Tryntje Outwater	1869	Tryntje b 11.3	Hendrick Outwater Tryntje Outwater
12.25	Cornelius Van De Haan Grietje Post	1870	Tryntje b 10.6	Gerret V. Rypen Jannetje Winne
1791 1. 1	Matheus V. Oostrand Mary Phillips	1871	Annaetje b 10.21.1790	
1. 1	Isaac Ryker Susanna Pier	1872	Isaac b 9.21.1790	
1. 9	David Crane Hilletje Crane	1873	John b 8.31.1790	
1.17	John Van Bussen Antje Cadmus	1874	Margrietje b 11.28.1790	John Macarty Rachel V. Rypen
1.17	Adriaan M. Post Elizabeth V. Rypen	1875	Annaatje b 12.16.1790	Richard Vreland Annatje Post
1.24	Moses Terp Hannah Schidmoor	1876	Naomie b 11.6.1790	
1.30	David Van Bussen Sietje V. Eydestyn	1877	Aaltje b 1.7	
1.30	Hendrick Laroe Annaetje Ackerman	1878	Johannes b 12.29.1790	John Spier Elizabeth Post

Bap	Parents	1791 Item	Child	Sponsors
2. 6	John Van Wagenen Rachel Traphagen	1879	Jacobus b 12.31.1790	William Traphagen Martyntje Westervelt
2.13	Philip Berry Eva Van Winkel	1880	Eva b 1.18	
2.13	John Schidmoor Tryntje Degrauw	1881	Samuel b 1.6	Rynier Spier Naomie Schidmoor
2.13	Joseph Waldrom Leentje Ryerse	1882	Marritje b 12.24.1790	
2.13	John Marcelusse Jannetje Van Rypen	1883	Claasje b 12.(4).1790	
2.20	Johannes J. Post Fytje Ryker	1884	Johannes b 1.31	Gerrit Post Cathalyntje Post
2.20	Jurrie Kiesler Jannetje Jacobusse	1885	Geertruy b 10.28.1790	
2.20	Jonathan Snyder Patty Ackerman	1886	Isaac b 1.29	Isaac Post Catharina Snyder
2.20	John Ludlow Elizabeth Vreland	1887	Jacob b 1.1	
3.13	Matheus Sp-er Cathalyntje Van Bussen	1888	Barent b 2.22	Barent Spier Saartje Spier
3.27	John Holm Maria Roos	1889	Catharina b 2.24	
4. 3	John Parrot Rachel Koejeman	1890	Rachel b 1.25	
4.10	Jacob En. Vreland Maritje Vreland	1891	Cornelia b 3.4	Hendrick Kip jr Catharina Gerritse
4.10	Hendrick Boss Annaatje Kierstede	1892	Johannis b 3.11	
4.10	Abraham Koejeman Myntje Vreland	1893	Rachel b 2.3	
4.17	Hermanus Spier Maria Dow	1894	Elizabeth b 2.18	Francois Van Winkel Elizabeth Dow
4.17	Ephraim Van Giesen Abigail Sigler	1895	Joseph b 3.13	Isaac Van Giesen Maria Van Sent
4.17	John Vreland Sarah Ellen	1896	Abraham b 2.20	Abraham Vreland Rachel Ackerman
4.24	Hendrick H. Jeraalman Hellitje Bruyn	1897	Maria b 2.23	Hendrick Jeraalman Rachel Bruyn
4.24	Isaac Corby Hendrickje Ackerman	1898	John b 9.11.1790	John Corby
5. 8	Casparus Boss Sarah Blanchard	1899	Arie b 4.7	Arie V. Winkel Maragrietje Van Wagene
5. 8	John Simmons Metje Jones	1900	Pieter b 4.8	Pieter P. Simmons Susanna Simmons

Bap	Parents	1791 Item	Child	Sponsors
5.22	Christophel Steger Sarah Ryker	1901	Cornel(ius) b 4.15	
5.22	Michael H. Vreland Lena Romyn	1902	Johannis b 4.22	Isaac Vreland Myntje Romyn
5.22	John Kidnie Rachel Spier	1903	Abraham b 3.10	
5.28	Johnnes Brouwer Grietje Wite	1904	Elsje b 4.14	Abraham Brouwer Fytje Jacobusse
5.28	Cornelius Van Giesen Sophia Sigler	1905	Cornelius b 3.8	Egbert Egbertse Rachel Van Giesen
5.28	Benjamin N(or)ned Hannah Fearchild	1906	Maria b 3.17	
6.12	Robert Glass Sarah Banta	1907	Hendrick b 4.10	Hartman Post Annaatje Sandvoort
6.12	Harmen Van Rypen Lea Spier	1908	Rachel b 5.2	
6.12	Albert Ryker Catharina Hurley	1909	Abraham b 4.18	
6.12	Arie King Catharina Cray	1910	Catharina b 5.22	
6.26	James Christie Geertje Degraau	1911	Daniel b 6.1	
7.10	Helmich Post	1912	Elizabeth b 6.4	
7.17	Gerrebrand Van Houten Jannetje Gerritse	1913	Maria b 6.14	
7.17	Egbert Doremus Geesje Jacobusse	1914	Cornelius b 6.6	Harme V. Rype Grietje Jacobusse
10. 2	Roelif Post Maritje Post	1915	Catlyntje b 8.28	Cathalyntje Post
10. 2	Adriaan J. Sip Lea Van Rypen	1916	Annaetje b 9.5	
10.23	Pieter H. Gerritse Eva Romyn	1917	Joannes b 8.24	Johanis Gerritse Maria Zabriskie
10.23	Johannes Westerveld Lea Pervoo	1918	Elizabeth b 9.11	Antje Westerveld
10.23	Johannis Gerritse Antje V. Winkel	1919	Johannis b 12.7.1790	
10.30	Gerrit Gerritse Grietje Gerritse	1920	Marritje b 9.27	
10.30	Casparus Degrauw Lena Jurrianse	1921	Jenneke b 9.25	
10.30	Johannis Mandeviel Marritje Gerbrantse	1922	Abigail b 9.26	Nicholas Gerbrantse Maria Cockefer

Bap	Parents	1791 Item	Child	Sponsors
10.30	Rynier Van Giesen Aaltje Van Rypen	1923	Rachel b 9.21	
11. 6	Jacob Van Nes Elizabeth Con(s)olie	1924	Isaac b 9.18	
11.13	John Stagg Maria Spier	1925	Neelje b 10.7	John Vreland Jannetje Spier
11.13	Theodorus V. Winkel Annaetje V. Eydestyn	1926	Rachel b 10.2	Dirck V: Houten Rachel V. Eydestyn
11.13	Jacob V. Winkel Jannetje V. Winkel	1927	Jacob b 8.18	Ab-aham V. Winkel Myntje V. Newkerk
7.17	Andries Cadmus Pryntje Doremus	1928	Margrietje b 6.30	
__.__	Gerbrand Jurrianse Lena Kerck	1929	Johannis b 7.19	Pieter Paulusse Fytje Paulusse
7.24	Fransois Van Eydestyn Antje Tysen	1930	Johannis b 6.4	Pieter Van Eydestyn Maria Tysen
7.24	Gerret Spier Grietje Ennis	1931	Marritje b 6.29	Gerret Jacobusse Maria Koerten
7.24	Dirck Bergen Maria Boerum	1932	Gerrit b 6.25	
7.31	Andries Cadmus Pryntje Doremus	1933	Maragrietje b 6.30	
8.21	Pieter Ellen Maria Drummond	1934	Abraham b 7.25	
8.21	Jacob Ryker Catharina Ryker	1935	Sarah b 7.8	
8.21	Abraham Van Rypen Doratie Westerveld	1936	Teunis b 7.22	Teunis Spier Lena Spier
8.21	Gerrebrand Jurrianse Lena Kerck	1937	Johannis b 7.19	Pieter Paulusse Sophya Paulusse
8.21	Johannes Post Cornelia Cadmus	1938	Andries b 7.26	
9.18	Cornelius Cadmus Jannetje Van Rypen	1939	Gerret b 8.10	Jacob Ackerman Efje Cadmus
9.18	Nichlaas Jeraalman Hester Bruyn	1940	Maria b 8.12	Hendrick Jeraalman Maria Jeraalman
10.30	Pieter Ellen Marytje Drummond	1941	Abraham b 7.25	
__.__	Jacob Ryker Tryntje Van Rype	1942	Sarah b 7.8	
__.__	Abram V. Rypen Doretie Westerveld	1943	Teunis b 7.22	Teunis Spier Lena Spier
11.13	Jacob Toers Maria Post	1944	Jacob b 10.12	John Drummond Antje Post

Bap	Parents	Item	Child	Sponsors
11.13	Isaac Van Ess Marcy Consolie	1945	Evert b 5.13	
11.20	Dirck Van Houten Rachel Post	1946	Abraham b 10.12	
11.20	Jacob Kidny Catharina Jacobusse	1947	Hester Jacobusse b 10.22	Hendrick Jacobusse Hester Jacobusse
11.20	 Hester Jeraalman	1948	William b 10.21	John Jeraalman Maria Devorsnie
11.20	John Toers Elizabeth Rethan	1949	Abraham b 10.18	Samuel Toers Bregje Van Blerkom
11.27	Enoch C. Vreland Lea Van Winkele	1950	Jannetje b 9.11	Jannetje Vreland
11.27	Hendrick Pules Sarah Bomen	1951	Sarah b 10.9	John Pules Sarah Hen
11.27	Richard Ludlow Elizabeth Van Campen	1952	Susanna b 9.26	
12.11	Hendrick P. Kip Catharina Gerritse	1953	Pieter b 11.5	Pieter Kip Myntje Van Winkel
12.11	Gerrit G. Gerritse Marritje Doremus	1954	Gerrit b 11.5	
12.11	Albert Wright Geertje Hellem	1955	William b 11.23	William Wright Tryntje Myer
12.25	John Goetschius Catharina Butler	1956	Abraham b 8.18	
12.25	John T. Spier Elizabeth Terhune	1957	Maria b 11.22	William _____ Maria Demarest
12.25	Elias Yorks Rachel Ryker	1958	Grietje b 11.17	Arriaantje Smith
12.25	Richard Paulusse Annaatje Gerbrantse	1959	John b 10.9	John V. Winkel Jannetje Paulusse
1792 1. 1	Philip Van Bussen Elizabeth Post	1960	Philip b 11.25.1791	
1. 1	John Mackerty Rachel Van Rypen	1961	Margrietje b 12.10.1791	Cornelius Van Rypen
1. 1	Daniel Schoonmaker Elizabeth Post	1962	Johannis b 12.8.1791	Johannes Post Catharina Van Houten
1. 8	Cornelius Hellem Lea Cadmus	1963	Samuel b 12.16.1791	Robert Glass Sarah Banta
1. 8	Johannes Gerritse Grietje Van Rypen	1964	Simeon b 12.9.1791	
1. 8	John Bruyn Pietertje Winne	1965	Samuel b 11.28.1791	Samuel Rutan
1. 8	Roelef Van Houten Antje Berdan	1966	Albert b 11.11.1791	

Bap	Parents	1792 Item	Child	Sponsors
1. 8	Jacob Spier Rebecka Spier	1967	Christiantje b 11.11.1791	Hermanus Lineford Maria Lineford
1. 8	Hendrick Van Der Hoef Rachel Van Der Hoef	1968	Margrietje b 10.12.1791	Arent Kierstede Maragrietje Kierstede
1.15	Cornelius Doremus Styntje Van Rypen	1969	Antje b 11.10.1791	
1.22	Jacobus Jacobusse Dina Kierstede	1970	Cornelius b 9.30.1791	Michael Van Der Hoef Rachel Kierstede
1.22	William Ryersen Lena Kock	1971	Maria b 11.21.1791	
1.22	Barent Symenson Jannetje Jones	1972	Elizabeth b 12.3.1791	
1.22	Abraham Ryker Annaetje Ennis	1973	Dirck b 11.24.1791	
1.22	John Jacobusse Grietje Mandeviel	1974	Elizabeth b 11.1.1791	
1.22	William Kingsland Margrietje Kingsland	1975	William b 11.19.1791	John Pake Antje Van Winkel
1.29	Hendrick Messeker Elizabeth Messeker	1976	Elizabeth b 11.25.1791	Elizabeth Messeker
1.29	David Cairns Elizabeth V. Voorhees	1977	Pieter b 12.28.1791	John Cairns Hendrickje Stagg
1.29	Jurrie Van Rypen Neeltje Van Hoorn	1978	Gerrit b 10.16.1791	
1.29	Petrus Ryker Martha Corbie	1979	Maria b 12.21.1791	
1.29	Albert Rix Grietje Spier	1980	Jannetje b 11.7.1791	
1.29	Hendrick Spier Elizabeth Laurence	1981	Maria b 8.5.1791	
1.29	Albert Zabriskie Aaltje Van Orden	1982	John b 12.24.1791	
1.29	John Paslet Lena Doremus	1983	Lidia b 11.17.1791	
1.29	Frans Spier Tryntje Gerbrantse	1984	Elias b 12.1.1791	Elias Spier Lena Jacobusse
2. 5	John Doremus Margrietje Van Rypen	1985	Gerrit b 12.27.1791	Cornelius Cadmus Jannetje Van Rypen
5.27	John Winne Elizabeth Coorson	1986	Maria b 4.24	
2.19	Jacob Spier Grietje Fredrickse	1987	Tryntje b 1.26	Jacob Vreland Tryntje Fredrickse
2.19	Gerret Van Wagenen Helena Schoonmaker	1988	Helena b 1.30	

Bap	Parents	1792 Item	Child	Sponsors
2.19	Johannis Toers Maragrieje Kip	1989	Hendrick b 1.29	Hendrick Rutan Syntje Toers
2.19	Michael Van Eydestyn Antje Banta	1990	Teunis b 1.19	Joris Banta Elizabeth Van Eydestyn
2.19	Cornelius Doremus Lena Mandeviel	1991	Angonietje b 12.28.1791	
2.19	Petrus Ackerman Grietje Doremus	1992	William b 1.30	William Dierman Grietje Doremus
2.19	Johannes Post Sarah Bertholf	1993	Rachel b 1.24	
2.19	Stephen King Polly Sandvoort	1994	Mary b 12.25.1791	
2.19	Dirck Boss Antje Stagg	1995	Neelje b 1.30	John Courten McNish
2.26	Cornelius Shipard Maria Ryker	1996	Abraham b 1.13	
2.26	Isaac Kranck Jannetje Van Houten	1997	Elizabeth b 12.3.1791	Abraham Kranck Jannetje Van Orden
3. 4	John Van Rypen Hendrickje Vreland	1998	Thomas b 2.26	Harper Van Rypen Grietje Berry
3.11	James Van Buren Lettice Dawn	1999	Lettice	
3.11	Hendrick J. Spier Metje Vreland	2000	Johannes b 2.3	
3.25	Jurrie Van Rypen Antje Vreland	2001	Nicholaus b 1.17	
3.25	William Agnew Margrietje Brand	2002	David b 2.16	
4. 8	Arie Post Maria Stagg	2003	Jannetje b 2.19	Jacobus Ackerman Cathalyntje Post
4. 8	John Van Rypen Sarah Romeyn	2004	John b 2.15	Cornelius V. Rypen Marretje Gerritse
4. 8	Abraham Brouwer Fytje Jacobusse	2005	Rachel b 2.2	Teunis Spier Rachel Mandeviel
4. 8	Teunis Spier Fytje Schermerhoorn	2006	Annaatje b 2.15	
4. 8	Joseph Passey _____ Pegman	2007	Maria b 2.20	John Michel Maria Kingsland
4. 8	Hendrick Doremus Tryntje Terhuin	2008	Lea b 2.26	Pieter Vreland Lea Doremus
4.15	Johannis Sip jr Geertje Van Winkel	2009	Eva b 3.19	
4.15	Dirck Van Houten Mallie V. Rypen	2010	Gerretje b 3.8	

Bap	Parents	1792 Item	Child	Sponsors
4.15	Cornelius Meyer Martyntje Terhune	2011	Susanna b 3.28	
4.15	Hessel Reyerse Catharina Van Vegten	2012	Catharina b 3.17	
4.22	Jacobus Jeraalman Maria Kingsland	2013	Charles b 2.13	
4.22	Gerret Nefius Margretje Gerritse	2014	John b 3.25	John Nefius Catharina Post
4.25	Harmen V. Rypen Margrietje Jacobusse	2015	Jacob b 3.10	
4.29	Helmich Van Winkel Marretje Post	2016	Elizabeth b 4.7	Elias Vreland Elizabeth Post
5.13	Hendrick Spier Jannetje Van Giesen	2017	Elizabeth b 4.6	
5.13	Abraham Vreland Annaatje Moore	2018	Natje b 10.12.1791	John Moore Catharina Kiesler
5.13	John V. Rypen Lea Winne	2019	Pietertje b 4.4	
5.13	Jacob V. Rypen Abigail Laroe	2020	Teunis b 3.23	Abraham Willis Catharina Post
5.20	Helmich Masseker Fytje Ryker	2021	Pieter b 12.25.1791	
5.20	Gerrit Vreland Rachel Moor	2022	Sally b 10.5.1791	Cornelius Moor Sally Mease
6. 3	John King Rachel Bruyn	2023	Maria b 5.12	
6. 3	David Demaree Martyntje Mandeviel	2024	John b 2.12	John Mandeviel Maria Haalenbeck
6.17	Fransois Degraauw Antje Degrauw	2025	Jenneke b 4.29	Cornelius Degrauw Catharina Vreland
6.17	Teunis Bruyn Saartje Outwater	2026	Johannis b 5.20	Hendrick Oudwater Tryntje Paulusse
6.24	Pieter Gerbrantse Catharina Gerritse	2027	Pieter b 5.6	Pieter Gerritse Eva Romyn
6.24	Christian Supaner Pally Simenson	2028	Isaac b 5.7	Pieter Doremus Hennah Norred
6.24	David Blair Beletje Vreland	2029	Peggy b 6.4	
6.24	Hermanus P. Van Bussen Sophia Gerritse	2030	Elizabeth b 5.31	
6.24	Myndert Koejeman Catharina Bruin	2031	Pieter Lukas b 5.4	
7. 1	Teunis Berdan Aalje V. Blerkom	2032	Margrieta b 6.10	

Bap	Parents	1792 Item	Child	Sponsors
7. 1	Arie Kirris Anneke Vreland	2033	Johannes b 6.5	
7. 8	John Ackerman Elizabeth Dierman	2034	Lidea b 5.27	
7.15	Albert Ackerman Antje V. Winkel	2035	Johannes b 6.14	
7.15	Pieter Egbertse Maria Van Giesen	2036	Rachel b 5.11	Gerret Egbertse Rachel Spier
7.15	John Messeker Elizabeth Ryker	2037	Hendrick b 6.18	Hendrick Messeker Sarah Messeker
7.22	Jacob En. Vreland Marretje Vreland	2038	Antje b 6.16	
7.29	Casparus Zabriskie Jannetje Kip	2039	Geertje b 6.26	
8.12	John Westerveld Antje Van Rypen	2040	Margrietje b 7.23	Johannis Gerritse Grietje V. Rypen
8.12	Fransis Spier Elisabeth Miller	2041	Johannis b 7.4	Abraham Low Grietje Spier
8.12	Pieter Dey Lena Board	2042	Hester Schuyler b 7.17	Hendrick Post Hester Dey
8.19	Barent Spier Saartje Spier	2043	Isaac b 7.14	
8.19	Hendrick F. Post Jannetje V. Houten	2044	Elizabeth b 7.16	
8.19	Isaac Pier Maria Post	2045	Hester b 7.24	
9. 9	John Moor Catharina Kiesler	2046	John b 8.2	John Pier Lena Vreland
9.16	Joris Banta Elizabeth V. Eydestyn	2047	Lena b 7.29	Robert Glas Sarah Banta
9.16	Abraham Berry Tryntje Oudwater	2048	Maria b 8.15	John J. Berry Claasje Vreland
9.16	Jeremiah Evertse Nellie Montanje	2049	Hannah b 7.29	Hendrick Brinckerhoff Hennah Sandfoord
9.16	Pieter Terhune Jenneke Van Winkel	2050	Johannes b 7.31	Jacobus Terhune Lena Maclachlin
9.16	Daniel Folkonier Rachel Ryker	2051	Cornelius b 8.17	
9.16	Cornelius Van Der Haan Margrietje Post	2052	Martinus b 8.6	
9.16	John Koerten Antje Mackniss	2053	Neeltje b 8.30	
9.16	John J. Drummond Antje Post	2054	Abraham b 8.20	

Bap	Parents	1792 Item	Child	Sponsors
9.16	Abraham Maurusse Hester Mandeviel	2055	Margrietje b 7.22	
10. 7	Johannis Steger Lena Spier	2056	Immetje b 9.28	Abraham Spier Immetje Wouterse
9.23	Gerret Van Rypen Jannetje Winne	2057	Cornelius b 8.30	
9.23	Abraham King Elizabeth Spier	2058	Annetje b 8.14	
9.23	Manus Bosch Saartje Steger	2059	Aaltje b 8.6	Jacob Ryker Maria Steger
9.30	Isaac Vreland Grietje Vreland	2060	Enoch b 9.5	Benjamin Vreland Rachel Vreland
9.30	Bryant Chays Anna Duvaal	2061	William b 8.19	William Duvaal Polly Duvaal
10. 4	Ephraim Van Giesen Abigail Sigler	2062	Maria b 9.9	Pieter De Garmo Abigail Shiers
10.14	Matheus Everse Jannetje Post	2063	Johannes b 9.12	
10.14	Pieter Ellen Marytje Drummond	2064	Robert b 9.17	
10.21	John Van Eydestyn Maria Miller	2065	Thomas b 8.10	Gerrit Van Vorst Maria V. Eydestyn
10.21	Hessel Hennion Tryntje Brouwer	2066	Teunis b 9.9	Teunis Hennion Rachel Ackerman
10.21	Cornelius Marcelisse Maria Post	2067	Catharina b 9.28	Daniel Schoonmaker Elisabeth Post
10.28	Johannis Boss Lena Rix	2068	John b 7.11	
10.28	John B. Spier Elizabeth Post	2069	Barent b 9.18	Barent Spier Geertje Spier
10.28	John Parrot Rachel Koejeman	2070	Jacob	Jacob Koejeman Jacomyntje Koejeman
11. 4	John King Lena Spier	2071	Helena b 9.28	
11. 4	John Sigler Sietje Mandeviel	2072	Maria b 9.8	
11.18	Jacobus Spier Rachel King	2073	Geertje b 10.6	
11.18	Johannis Mandeviel Eva Jacobusse	2074	Hester b 10.23	
11.18	Petrus Jacobusse Rachel Egbertse	2075	Dirck b 9.29	
12. 2	Jacob Van Winkel Annaatje Boss	2076	Abraham	Abraham Boss Rachel Van Dyck

		1792-1793		
Bap	Parents	Item	Child	Sponsors
12. 9	Jacobus Van Houten Maria Banta	2077	Jacob b 11.24	Cornelius Post Jannetje Van Houten
12. 9	John Cairns Hendrikje Stagg	2078	Margritje	Cornelius Stagg Margrietje Banta
12.13	Johannes Ja. Vreland Jannetje Van Wagenen	2079	Annaatje b 11.18	Gerret V. Wagenen Jannetje V. Winkel
1793 1. 6	Jacobus Jacobusse Tryntje Gerbrantse	2080	Tryintje b 10.7.1792	
1. 6	Gerrebrand Gerrebrandse Fytje Pailusse	2081	Trintje b 11.9.1792	
1.20	Hendrick Bruyn Lea Vreland	2082	Annaatje b 12.13.1792	Abraham Scisco Seitje Vreland
1.20	Isaac V. Houten Annaatje Boss	2083	Henricus	Joost Cogh Hendrickje Boss
3. 7	Waling Van Winkel Pietertje Van Rypen	2084	Fytje b 1.26	Adriaan Post Elizabeth Van Rypen
3. 7	John J. Vreland Jannetje Spier	2085	Hendrick b 1.19	John Stagg Maria Spier
3.10	Gerret Van Rypen Lea Simmons	2086	Pally b 1.11	Pieter P. Simmons Pally Simmons
3.24	Teunis Spier Rachel Mandeviel	2087	Maragrietje b 2.17	Cornelius Degrauw Tryntje Vreland
3.24	Adriaen Van Rypen Cathalyntje Spier	2088	John b 2.12	John Strowsberry Maragrietje Van Rype
3.24	Samuel Durje Antje Kingsland	2089	Maria b 1.29	
3.31	Pieter Van Eydestyn Maria Tyse	2090	Pieter b 3.10	Fransois Van Eydestyn Antje Tyse
3.31	Thomas Sigler Lea Spier	2091	Maria b 2.13	
4. 7	Jacobus Young Tryntje Mandeviel	2092	Rachel b 1.7	
4.10	Elias Smith Sarah Koek	2093	Abraham b 3.17	Joseph Koek Elizabeth Smith
4.14	Hendrick P. Kip Catharina Gerritse	2094	Hilletje b 3.19	
4.14	Jacobus Jacobusse Jamime Williams	2095	Geertruy b 1.22	
5. 5	Maurus Maurusse Wyntje Ryker	2096	Polly b 2.12	
5. 5	Johannes Egtbertse Lea Winne	2097	Abraham b 2.26	
5.19	Michael Vreland Lena Romyn	2098	Nicholaes b 4.6	

Bap	Parents	1793 Item	Child	Sponsors
5.19	Robert Glass Sarah Banta	2099	Lena b 4.1	Joris Banta Elizabeth Eydestyn
5.19	Cornelius Van Giesen Sophia Sigler	2100	Isaac b 3.28	Abraham Sigler Hester Sigler
5.19	Johannis Van Giesen Maragrietje Macknes	2101	Maria b 3.25	Jacob Mackniss Annaetje Ennis
5.19	Daniel Blauvelt Grietje Pervoo	2102	Isaac b 4.5	
5.19	Jacob Stagg Maria Endress	21-3	Suke b 2.24	Tyna Stagg
5.19	Obadja Forse Elizabeth Van Houten	2104	Maragrietje b 4.24	
5.19	Jacob Snyder Peggy Van Blerkom	2105	Johannis b 5.6	
5.26	Pieter Karney Elenor Young	2106	Peter b 4.6	James Quin Ester Eman
5.26	Stephen Laurence Agnes Robbertson	2107	John Eman b 4.14	John Eman
5.26	Christopher Garrick Rachel Wallen	2108	Polly b 2.14.1790	Michae- Flin Mary Connors
5.26	Same as #2108	2109	Peter b 12.22.1793?	Same as #2108
6. 9	Jurian Jurrianse Elizabeth Van Blerkom	2110	Christofel b 5.9	Christofel Jurianse Annaetje Brouwer
6.17	Hendrick Laroe Annaatje Ackkerman	2111	Maragrietje b 5.11	
6.23	Gerrebrand Gerrebrandse	2112	Sarah	Joris Gerrebrandse Annaetje Gerrebrantse
6.23	Jacob Van Winkel Jenneke Van Winkele	2113	Myntje b 4.19	
6.23	Hendrick Post Hester Dey	2114	Johannis b 5.12	
7. 7	Abraham Koejeman Myntje Vreland	2115	Antje b 4.26	
7. 7	Albert Ryker Catharina Hurley	2116	Maria b 6.8	Abraham Brass Annatje Bilju
7. 7	John Van Imburgh Polly Jeraalman	2117	Hendrick b 5.8	Hendrick Jeraalman Maragrietje Jeraalman
7.14	Gerrit Vreland Rachel Moor	2118	Cathalyntje b 5.6	Jacob Ryker Cornelia Vreland
7.14	Rynier Van Giesen Aaltje Van Rypen	2119	Aaltje b 5.3	
7.14	John Spier Antje Jacobusse	2120	Lena b 5.22	

Bap	Parents	1793 Item	Child	Sponsors
7.14	Isaac Corbie Henkje Ackerman	2121	Trusthim b 10.4.1792	
7.14	Moses Cancklin Catharina Ryker	2122	Joseph b 5.26	
8. 4	Jacobus Van Rypen Aaltje Vreland	2123	Maragrietje b 7.4	
8. 4	Hendrick Van Es Marytje Doremus	2124	Polly b 7.1	
8. 4	John Brouwer Grietje Wright	2125	Aaltje b 7.8	Jenneke Brouwer
8.18	David Davis Lea Messeker	2126	Lodewyck	Lodewyck Messeker Saartje Spier
8.18	Arie King Caty Crea	2127	William b 7.17	
8.18	Arent King Jannetje Vreland	2128	Immetje b 7.5	
8.18	Jurrie Van Rypen Ante Vreland	2129	Stephen b 7.20	
8.18	Marynus Gerritse Annaatje Lisk	2130	Tryntje b 7.24	
9. 8	Adriaan M. Post Elizabeth Van Rypen	2131	Dirck b 8.20	
9.29	Dirick Van Hoorn Maragrietje Terhune	2132	Johannis b 9.10	Hendrick Harris Neesje Van Hoorn
9.29	Pieter Alje Elizabeth Maurusse	2133	Maria b 7.16	
9.29	Arie Kierstede Jannetje Van Rypen	2134	Jinny b 8.17	Pieter Pier Marretje Van Rypen
9.29	Nicholas Jeraalman Hester Bruyn	2135	Hendrick b 8.10	Hendrick Jeraalman
9.29	Jacob Ryker Tryntje Van Rypen	2136	Johannis b 9.8	Johannis Ryker
10. 6	Jacob Van Der Back Maria Van Busson	2137	Hermanus b 8.30	Rynier Blancher Elisabeth Van Busson
10. 6	John Van Wagenen Rachel Trophagen	2138	Fytje b 9.7	Gerret Van Wagenen Fytje Westerveld
10. 6	Hartman Post Nency Jackson	2139	Hendrick b 9.11	
10.20	Hendrick Van Es Elizabeth Mandeviel	2140	Roelif b 9.25	
11.10	Johannes Post Fytje Ryker	2141	Elizabeth b 9.17	Elias Vreland Elizabeth Post
11.10	Daniel Schoonmaker Elizabeth Post	2142	Catharina b 10.22	Cornelius Post Maria Post

Bap	Parents	1793-1794 Item Child	Sponsors
11.10	Jonathan Snyder Petty Ackerman	2143 Grietje b 9.20	
11.24	John Scidmoor Catharina Degrauw	2144 Jenneke b 10.19	James Christie Geertje Degrauw
11.24	Philip Berry Eva Van Winkel	2145 Philip b 10.18	Catharina Van Winkel
11.24	Arie V. Winkele Grietje Van Wagenen	2146 Maria b 10.17	John Gerritse Antje Toers
11.24	Daniel Sigler Jannetje Paululse	2147 Thomas b 9.5	Pieter De Germo Abigail Siers
11.24	Hendrick Boss Annatje Kierstede	2148 Cornelius b 10.23	
12.15	Jacob Van Rypen Jannetje Van Winkel	2149 Gerret b 11.12	Gerret Van Rypen Geertje Gerrebrantse
12.15	(Ch)ristofer Stager Saartje Ryker	2150 Petrus b 10.24	
12.15	John Holm Maria Boss	2151 Pieter b 10.24	Pieter Holm Catharina Tiepel
12.15	(G)eorge Ennis Susanna Brouwer	2152 Pieter b 10.9	Pieter Ennis Neeltje Stagg
12.21	John Goetschius Catharina Butler	2153 Elizabeth	
12.22	Fransois (V.) Eydestyn Antje Tysen	2154 Fransois b 11.11	
12.26	Jacob Van Rypen Marretje Vreland	2155 Gerritje b 11.27	Michael Vreland
12.29	John Spier Maragrietje Jeraalman	2156 Maragrietje b 11.4	
12.29	John Maccarty Rachel Van Rypen	2157 Ebbie b 11.28	William Van Houten Ebbie Gerritse
	(male sponsor's surname "Van Bossum" crossed out)		
12.29	(G)erret Van Vorst Maria Van Eydestyn	2158 Annaatje b 11.28	
1794 1.12	(M)atheus (S)pier Cathalyntje Van Bussen	2159 Lena b 12.23.1793	
1.12	(De)rrick (Pa)ulusse Annaatje Gerrebrantse	2160 Hendrick b 12.2.1793	Abraham Scisco Lena Gerrebrantse
1.26	Adriaan Post Marritje Post	2161 Johannes b 12.25.1793	Hartman M. Vreland Thyna Post
1.26	(J)ohn M. Vreland Anne Spier	2162 Anne b 12.12.1793	
2. 2	(J)ohn J. Van Winkel Elizabeth Brinkerhoff	2163 Benjamin Vanderlinden b 12.29.1793	

Bap	Parents	1794 Item	Child	Sponsors
2. 2	(J)ohn Ludlow Elizabeth Vreland	2164	John b 12.13.1793	
2. 2	_____ (J)acobussen Dina Kierstede	2165	Jacobus b 11.21.1793	
2. 2	(G)errit Spier Maragrieta Ennis	2166	Johannes b 12.14.1793	
2.16	(Ca)sparus (D)egrauw Lena Jurrianse	2167	Gerret b 1.5	Jacob Van Noorstrand Geertje Degrauw
2.16	(T)homas Boss Elizabeth Case	2168	Maria b 1.26	Jenny Ouke
3. 9	Adries Cadmus Pryntje Doremus	2169	Johannes b 2.3	
3. 9	Jacobus Van Winkel Grietje Toers	2170	Sietje b 1.15	
3. 9	Abraham Spier Metje Van Giesen	2171	Rachel b 2.3	
3.23	John Devorsne Polly Bennet	2172	Maria b 2.26	Hendrick Van Winkel Marretje Van Winkel
3.30	Cornelius Van Houten Helena Van Houten	2173	Helena b 2.21	
3.30	William Van Giesen Elizabeth Spier	2174	Fytje b 10.3.1793	
3.30	Benjamin Norwood Annaetje Fearchild	2175	Rachel b 2.5	
4.13	John Bruyn Pietertje Winne	2176	Lena b 2.19	
4.20	Theodorus Van Winkel Annaatje Van Eydestyn	2177	Annaatje b 3.8	
4.20	John Stagg Maria Spier	2178	John b 3.31	
4.20	Teunis Bruyn Saartje Outwater	2179	Abraham b 4.4	Cornelius Jeraalman Hester Jeralman
4.20	Laurence Van Orden Hendrickje Bilju	2180	Johannes b 4.1	
4.27	Gulyn Ackerman Catharina Verver	2181	Aaltje b 2.25	Cornelius Doremus Elizabeth Doremus
5. 4	Harmen Van Rypen Lea Spier	2182	Maragrietje b 4.3	
5. 4	Hendrick Spier Jannetje Van Giesen	2183	Isaac b 3.24	
5. 4	Elias Yorks Rachel Ryker	2184	Grietje Dubois b 4.12	
5.18	Adriaan J. Sip Lea Van Rypen	2185	Adriaan b 4.9	Philip Van Rypen Jannetje Sip

Bap	Parents	1794 Item	Child	Sponsors
6. 9	William Hunter Elenor Carter	2186	Herout b 4.20	
6.15	Roelif Post Marretje Post	2187	Jacobus b 5.6	
6.15	Ephraim Van Giesen Abigail Sigler	2188	Maragrietje b 5.11	
6.15	John Berry Elizabeth Erl	2189	Abraham b 5.16	
6.15	Johannes Post Cornelia Cadmus	2190	Fytje b 5.17	Casparus Post Geertje Cadmus
6.15	Cornelius Van Rypen Vroutje Gerretse	2191	Elizabeth b 5.9	
6.15	Gerret Jacobusse Annaatje Jacobusse	2192	Isaac b 3.31	
6.15	Abraham Ryker Annaatje Ennis	2193	Antje b 5.12	Jacob Willer Caty Ennis
6.15	John Sindel Grietje Kierstede	2194	Christophel b 5.(11)	Thomas Sindel Jenny Frederikse
6.15	Frans Spier Catharina Gerbrandse	2195	Gerret b 5.2	
6.15	Cornelius Gerbrandse Maria Ryker	2196	Gerbrand b 4.25	
6.15	Thomas Linkfoot Sarah Sigler	2197	Trientje b 4.21	Trientje Linkfoot
6.15	Hartman Vreland Catlyntje Post	2198	Gerritje b 5.23	
6.15	Joseph Van Winkel Lea Woud	2199	Pryntje b 4.24	
6.22	Pieter Gerbrandse Catharina Gerritse	2200	Catharina b 5.13	_____ Jacobusse Catharina Gerbrandse
6.22	Cornelius Shepherd Maria Ryker	2201	Catharina b 4.4	John Butler Elizabeth Maurusse
7.13	John Brown Sarah Koejeman	2202	Antje b 5.28	
7.13	Jacob D. Berdan Catharina Bilju	2203	Johannes	
8. 9	William J. Kingsland Marragrietje Jeraalman	2204	Rachel b 7.5	
8.17	Johannes Ruthan Elizabeth Lake	2205	Catharina b 7.19	
8.17	Hendrick J. Spier Metje Vreland	2206	Geertje b 6.11	
8.24	Daniel Folkonier Rachel Ryker	2207	Fytje b 7.16	

Bap	Parents	1794 Item	Child	Sponsors
9.12	Cornelius Post Jannetje Van Houten	2208	Aaltje b 5.28	Jurrie Snyder Sarah Van Houten
9.14	John Simmons Metty Jones	2209	John b 7.21	
9.14	Hermanus Van Bussen Fytje Gerritse	2210	Jannetje b 8.18	
9.14	Peter Allen Maria Drummond	2211	Elias b 8.27	Elias Vreland Elizabeth Post
9.14	Abraham Berry Tryntje Outwater	2212	Abraham b 8.25	
9.14	Pieter Gerrebrandse Annaatje Gerrebrandse	2213	Maria b 7.6	Gerrebrand Gerrebrandse Elizabeth Messelaar
9.14	Jacob Spier Rebecka Lenkford	2214	Maragrietje b 7.24	
9.14	John Parrot Rachel Koejeman	2215	Abraham b 6.15	
9.28	Aaron King Eva Messeker	2216	Maria b 8.22	
9.28	Hendrick Jeraalman Haly Brown	2217	Rynier b 8.21	Rynier Bruyn Polly Jeraalman
10. 5	Abraham Van Rypen Dorotie Westerveld	2218	Johannes b 9.9	
10. 5	Matheus Everse Jenneke Post	2219	Johannes b 8.21	Johannes Brown Judie Everse
10. 5	 Grietje Post	2220	Rachel b 9.5	
10.19	Helmich Van Winkel Marretje Post	2221	Adriaan b 10.1	Michael Post Jannetje Ackerman
10.19	Hermanus Brass Antje Eler	2222	Maragrita b 8.19	
10.19	Gerrebrand Gerrebrandse Fytje Paulusse	2223	Fytje b 9.4	Paulus Paulusse Lena Gerbrandse
10.19	John B. Spier Elizabeth Post	2224	Hendrick b 9.18	Cathalyntje Spier
11. 9	Johannes Egtbertse Lea Winne	2225	Cornelius b 9.18	Rynier Van Giesen Elizabeth Van Rypen
11. 9	John Koerten Antje Macknesh	2226	John b 9.__	Peter De Germo Abigail Sears
11. 9	Barent Simonson _____ Jones	2227	Maria b 9.5	
11.16	Gerret Gerritse Marretje Doremus	2228	Rachel b 10.15	
11.16	Sylvester Van Buren Anna Douty	2229	Maria b 9.30	Peter Van Buren

Bap	Parents	Item	Child	Sponsors
11.16	Michael Van Eydestyn Antje Banta	2230	John b 10.14	Arie Banta Sarah Banta
11.30	Johannes T. Spier Elizabeth Terhune	2231	Albert b 11.2	Albert Terhune Antje Snyder
11.30	David Van Bussen Sietje Van Eydestyn	2232	David b 11.8	
11.30	Abraham Kranck Selly Brown	2233	Catharina b 10.13	
11.30	Christian Suppener Polly Symeson	2234	Abraham b 9.13	Jacob Van Der Hoef Marretje Nieuwkerk
12. 7	Jacob En. Vreland Marretje Vreland	2235	John b 10.30	Jacob Van Rypen Jannetje Van Winkel
12.21	Hendrick F. Post Jannetje Van Houten	2236	Hendrick b 10.23	John Van Houten Marretje Van Rypen
1795				
1.11	Cornelius Cadmus Jannetje Van Rypen	2237	David b 12.14.1794	David Marinus Dirckje Ackerman
1.25	Albert Terhune Antje Snyder	2238	Maria b 1.1	Maria Demarest
1.25	Abraham Maurusse Hester Mandeviel	2239	Cornelius b 12.15.1794	
2. 1	John Van Rypen Lea Winne	2240	Neesje b 1.4	
2.15	Thomas Snyder Polly Eden	2241	Lucas b 1.9	
3. 8	Jeremia Everson Neeltje Montanje	2242	Johannes b 2.17	John Everson
3. 8	Daniel Schoonmaker Elizabeth Post	2243	Henricus b 2.15	Rev. Henricus Schoonmaker Selly Goetschius
3.22	Gerrit Vreland Maragrietje Van Rypen	2244	Abraham b 3.1	Gerrit C. Post Margrietje Vreland
3.22	Nicholas Ryker Annaetje Gerbrantse	2245	Johannis b 2.31?	
3.22	Cornelius Vreland Elizabeth Vreland	2246	Jacob b 2.17	Hartman Vreland Catlyntje Post
3.29	Johannes Post Fytje Ryker	2247	Elias b 12.20.1794	Elias J. Vreland Elizabeth Post
3.29	Philip Berry Eva Van Winkel	2248	Eva b 3.10	
3.29	Stephanus Bartholf Jannetje Post	2249	Jacobus b 10.1.1794	Jacobus Post Metje Gerritse
4.28	Johannis D. Messeker Margrietje Messeker	2250	John b 4.19	
4.12	Abraham Sigler Phebe Gerbrantse	2251	Isaac b 2.4	

Bap	Parents	1795 Item	Child	Sponsors
4.12	Gerrit Egbertse Rachel Egbertse	2252	Selly b 2.3	
4.19	John Keeler Polly Snyder	2253	Peggy b 3.22	
5. 3	Cornelius Meyer Martyntje Terhune	2254	Antje b 4.3	Gerret Post Margrietje Vreland
5. 3	Thomas Sigler Lea Spier	2255	Catharina b 3.5	
5.10	(Ja)cob (_____)oss Maria Messeker	2256	Margrietje b 4.10	
5.17	(____)ois (____)uw Antje Degrauw	2257	Cornelius b 4.16	Jannetje Degrauw
5.17	George Van Eydestyn Jenneke Degrauw	2258	Johannis b 4.5	Francois Van Eydestyn Antje Tysen
5.17	Pieter Jacobusse Rachel Egberse	2259	Grietje b 3.17	Cornelius Egbertse Grietje Spier
5.17	Daniel Sigler Jinne Paulusse	2260	Isaac b 3.12	Richard Paulusse Annaatje Gerbrantse
5.17	Johannes Stagg Cornelia Van Blercum	2261	John b 4.24	Cornelius Stagg Margrietje Banta
5.25	Joris Banta Elizabeth Van Eydestyn	2262	John b 4.22	Same as #2261
5.25	John Van Eydestyn Maria Miller	2263	Pieter b 4.1	Isaac Van Rypen Elizabeth Witlock
6.14	Roelif Van Wagenen Saartje Yurrianse	2264	Hermanus b 5.8	Hermanus Vreland Fytje Van Wagenen
6.21	Gerrit Van Houten Cornelia Van Ess	2265	Michael b 5.__	
7. 5	Casparus Van Rypen Antje Ackerman	2266	Laurence b 5.26	Laurence Ackerman Annaatje Peeck
7. 5	Philip Van Rypen Jannetje Sip	2267	Abraham b 6.7	Dirck Van Houten Mally Van Rypen
8. 2	Dirck Gerbrantse Annatje Ennis	2268	Lea b 7.1	Pieter Gerbrantsse Lybetje Gerbrantse
8. 2	Hartman Degrauw Jannetje Vreland	2269	Cornelius b 7.12	
8.16	Jacob Van Rypen Annaatje Van Rypen	2270	Thomas b 7.1	
8.22	Pieter Van Eydestyn Maria Tysen	2271	John b 8.1	
8.22	Andrias Snyder Rachel Ackerman	2272	Margrietje b 8.9	Cornelius Stagg Margrietje Banta
9. 6	Isaac Vreland Margrietje Vreland	2273	Catharina b 8.15	Hendrick Hoppen Tryntje Vreland

Bap	Parents	Item	Child	Sponsors
9. 6	Rynier Van Giesen Aaltje Van Rypen	2274	Maria b 6.28	
9. 6	Casparus C. Post Fytje Paulusse	2275	Johannis b 8.10	
9. 6	Hartman Post Nancy Jackson	2276	Hendrick b 8.18	
9.27	Hendrick Post Hester Dey	2277	Benjamin b 8.3	
1796				
2.25	Jurrie Van Rypen Antje Vreland	2278	Antje b 1.26	Nicholas Vreland Nency Bassetti
3.17	Johannes Ja. Vreland Jannetje Van Wagenen	2279	Johannis b 1.3	
3.27	Cornelius Jeraalman Neeltje Jurrianse	2280	Jacobus b 3.9	
4.24	John Edgerly Hanna Baker	2281	George William Scriber b 4.2	
(4).28	Jacob J. Van Winkel Annaatje Boss	2282	Jacobus b 4.17	
5.15	William Hunter Elenor Carter	2283	William b 1.31	
5.15	William Dicky Hester Ellison	2284	Mary b 7.9.1795	

END OF VOLUME II

Bap	Parents	Item	Child	Sponsors
1795				
9.13	John Van Giesen Margrietje Mackniss	2285	Neeltje b 6.20	
10.18	Cornelius Kent Antje Stagg	2286	Maria b 9.28	Polly Simmons
10.18	Jacob G. Van Rypen Jannetje Van Winkel	2287	Geertje b 9.3	Jacob Van Winkel Elsje Kip
10.25	Roeliph Doremus Annaatje Doremus	2288	Eggje b 9.15	
10.25	Teunis Hennion Rachel Ackerman	2289	Gerrit b 9.11	
10.25	Adriaan Van Rypen Cathalyntje Spier	2290	Hendrick b 9.8	
10.25	John Spier Abigail Van Bussen	2291	William b 9.11	Selly Van Bussen
11. 8	James Christie Geertje Degrauw	2292	Jacob b 10.11	
11. 8	John Ryerse Antje Van Alen	2293	John b 9.20	
11.15	Pieter Pier Selly Messker	2294	Dirckje b 10.25	Hendrick Messeker Jamyme Ryker

Bap	Parents	Item	Child	Sponsors
11.15	Thomas Bosch Elizabeth Keersie	2295	John b 10.9	
11.29	Isaac Van Giesen Lea Spier	2296	Catharina b 10.1	Gerrit Egbertse Rachel Spier
12.20	Albert Ryker Catharina Hurley	2297	John b 11.30	
12.20	Gerrit Van Vorst Elizabeth Bilju	2298	John b 11.18	Annaatje Bilju
1796 1.10	Elias Ja. Vreland Margrietje Post	2299	Geertje	Helmich Van Winkel Marretje Post
1.24	William Van Giesen Elisabeth Spier	2300	Abraham b 11.27.1795	
1.24	Cornelius Van Giesen Charity Collyer	2301	Jinny b 11.10.1795	
1.24	Abraham Willis Tryntje Post	2302	James b 12.7.1795	
2.14	Pieter Van Orden Amy Boss	2303	Jannetje b 1.26	Abraham Macfish Jannetje Van Blercum
2.21	Enoch C. Vreland Lea Van Winkel	2304	Margrietje b 11.14.1795	
3. 6	John Vreland Jannetje Spier	2305	Cathalyntje b 2.3	Johannis Spier Elizabeth Terhune
3. 6	Hendrick Laroe Antje Ackerman	2306	Maria b 2.3	Michael Gilliam Christina Kogh
3. 6	Jacobus J. Post Jinny Van Giesen	2307	Hessel Pieterse b 1.28	Johannis Post Fytje Van Houten
3. 6	Obediah Forse Elizabeth Van Houten	2308	Catharina b 1.26	
3.13	Casparus Degrauw Lena Jurrianse	2309	Geertje b 2.1	James Christie
3.27	Ephraim Van Giesen Abigail Van Giesen	2310	Thomas b 1.20	
3.27	Hendrick Spier Jannetje Van Giesen	2311	Lea b 2.17	Johannis Egbertse Lea Winne
4.20	John Sigler Sietje Mandeviel	2312	Rachel b 1.7	
4.20	Cornelius Gerbrantse Maria Ryker	2313	Pieter b 1.14	
4.17	Pieter Terhune Jenneke Van Winkel	2314	Johannis b 2.5	Jacobus Terhune Lena McLaclin
4.17	Kemmena Van Buren Rebecka Ennis	2315	Jinny b 2.21	James Van Buren Blandina Ryerse
4.24	James Van Buren Lettice Dunn	2316	George b 2.18	

Bap	Parents	1796 Item	Child	Sponsors
5.16	Abraham Koejeman Myntje Vreland	2317	Leya b 1.__	
4.28	Jacob Van Winkel Annaatje Boss	2318	Jacobus b 4.17	
5.22	Jacob Ryker Tryntje Van Rypen	2319	Tryntje b 4.4	Annaatje Ryker
5.29	John Vreland Sarah Ellin	2320	Pieter b 4.21	Pieter Vreland Lea Childs
6.12	Franscois Van Eydestyn Antje Tysen	2321	Antje b 5.22	
6.26	Abraham S. Van Imburgh Elizabeth Jurrianse	2322	Simeon b 5.24	
6.26	Hendrick Boss Annaatje Kierstede	2323	Abraham b 5.27	
7.10	Cornelius Van Rypen Marretje Gerritse	2324	Abraham b 6.19	Abraham Bogert Antje Gerritse
7.17	John Kerck Hester Jeraalman	2325	Maria b 4.2	
7.17	Cornelius Jeralman Jannetje Jurrianse	2326	John b 6.24	John Jeralman Marya Devorsne
7.17	Daniel Bensen Rachel Doremus	2327	Rebecka b 6.8	
7.17	Adriann M. Post Elizabeth Van Rype	2328	Adriaan b 6.24	
7.23	Samuel Reading Sarah Govenier	2329	Rachel Vanderbeeck b 3.15	Isaac Van Der Beeck Rachel Ryerse
7.24	John Goetschius Catharina Butler	2330	Selly b 5.8	
7.31	Henry Compton Elenor Coyle	2331	Henry b 7.7	
8. 7	John Kiesler Polly Snyder	2332	John b 7.7	
8.21	Jacob Van Winkel Annaatje Van Noorstrand	2333	Hendrick Van Stee b 7.12	
9.18	John Scidmoor Catharina Degrauw	2334	Sarah b 8.10	
9.18	Abraham F. Post Polly Zabriskie	2335	Rachel b 7.16	
9.25	Johannes Mandeviel Maria Gerrebrantse	2336	Yillis b 8.26	
10.23	Michael H. Vreland Lena Romeyn	2337	Betje b 9.20	
10.23	Harmen Linkford Aaltje Mandeviel	2338	Lena b 9.4	Hendrick Mandeviel Lena Jacobusse

1796-1797

Bap	Parents	Item	Child	Sponsors
10.23	Abraham Sigler Pheben Gerrebrandse	2339	Jinnie b 8.13	
10.30	Theodorus Van Winkel Annaatje Van Eydestyn	2340	Thina b 9.30	
11. 6	Moses Kanclen Catharina Ryker	2341	Rachel b 9.20	
11.20	Gerrit Spier Grietje Ennis	2342	Neeltje b 10.9	
11.27	Jonathan Snyder Pettie Ackerman	2343	Jonathan Matheus b 11.9	Matheus Ackerman Marretje Van Houten
11.27	Cornelius Vreland Dorothie Van Der Hoef	2344	Annaatje b 9.27	Pieter Ackerman Annaatje Vreland
12. 4	Dirck Paulusse Annaatje Gerrebrandse	2345	Lena b 9.13	
12.26	James Christie Annaatje Helms	2346	Samuel b 11.9	
12.26	George Van Eydestyn Jenneke Degraauw	2347	Lea b 11.26	Cornelius Degrauw Catharina Vreland
12.26	Casparus Boss Sarah Blanchard	2348	Maria b 10.30	

1797

Bap	Parents	Item	Child	Sponsors
1. 1	Johannes C. Post Cornelia Cadmus	2349	Maragrietje b 11.18.1796	Gerret Post Maragrietje Vreland
1. 1	Petrus Brouwer Rachel Van Der Bach	2350	Maria b 11.8.1796	Gerret Gerritse Maria Ryerse
1. 1	John Parrot Rachel Koejeman	2351	Maria b 5.28.1796	
1.22	Gerrit Gerritse Marritje Doremus	2352	Marragrietje b 1.1	
1.22	Johannes Egtbertse Lea Winne	2353	Hillegond b 11.20.1796	Elizabeth Van Rypen
2. 5	Daniel Fielding Angonietje Huysman	2354	Hendrick b 1.1	Thomas Vreland Margrietje Fielding
2. 5	Hartman Vreland Cathalyntje Post	2355	Fytje b 1.12	
2. 5	Jacobus Jacobusse Tryntje Gerrebrandse	2356	Aaltje b 12.22.1796	
2. 5	Pieter Gerrebrandse Tryntje Gerritse	2357	Pieter b 11.24.1796	
2. 5	Jacobus Stagg Lidia Schoonmaker	2358	Helena b 1.10	Johannis Wanshair Helena Schoonmaker
2.12	Andries Cadmus Pryntje Doremus	2359	Geertje b 1.3	John Doremus Geertje Doremus
2.26	Gerrit Post Marritje Van Rypen	2360	Dirck b 12.6.1796	

Bap	Parents	1797 Item	Child	Sponsors
2.26	Yurrie Yurrianse Elizabeth Van Blerkum	2361	Jurrie b 12.21.1796	John Jeraalman Polly Devorsne
2.26	John Deeths Gouda Vreland	2362	John George b 1.16	
2.26	Pieter A. Gerrebrantse Annaatje Gerrebrandse	2363	Elizabeth b 1.16	Jacob Gerrebrandse Elizabeth Gerrebrandse
3. 5	Jacob Berdan Catharina Bilju	2364	Johannes b 2.15	
3. 5	John Ludlam Catharina Ackerman	2365	Annaatje b 1.3	
3.26	John Hogen Lillies Doty	2366	Susanna b 2.1	
3.26	John Van Rypen Lea Winne	2367	Neesje b 2.21	
3.26	Hermanus Van Bussen Fytje Gerritse	2368	Philip b 2.25	Pieter Van Bussen Abigail Van Busen
3.26	Jacob Vreland Pheben Wells	2369	Johannis b 2.14	
3.26	Annaatje Haal	2370	Jabez b 12.19.1794	
3.30	Abraham Van Blerkum Vrouwtje Van Blerkum	2371	Frans b 3.7	
4.16	Isaac Van Winkel Helena Schoonmaker	2372	Johannes Wanshair b 3.4	Johannes Wanshair Helena Schoonmaker
4.16	Jacob En. Vreland Marretje Vreland	2373	Annaatje b 2.27	
4.16	Matheus Spier Cathalyntje Van Bussen	2374	William b 3.9	
4.23	Pieter Allen Marytje Drummond	2375	Jacobus b 3.19	Isaac Vreland Maragrietje Vreland
4.30	Jerimia Evertse Neelje Montanje	2376	Benjamin b 3.15	Benjamin Evertse
4.30	Pieter Pier Selly Messeker	2377	Dirckje b 4.11	
5.14	Lucas Van Winkele Helena Van Wagenen	2378	Jacobus b 3.26	Susanna Helm
5.28	Daniel Folkonier Rachel Ryker	2379	Isaac b 4.15	
7. 2	Daniel Schoomaker Elizabeth Post	2380	Helena b 6.12	Isaac Van Winkel Maria Schoonmaker
7. 2	Cornelius Westervelt Polly Simmons	2381	Elizabeth b 6.3	Margrietje Westervelt
7. 2	Jacobus Van Winkel Margrietje Toers	2382	Lena b 5.7	

Bap	Parents	1797 Item	Child	Sponsors
7. 2	Johannis Bruyn Saartje Koejeman	2383	Johannis b 4.3	
7. 2	John Ludlow Elizabeth Vreland	2384	Gabriel	
7. 2	Jacomyntje Koejeman	2385	Lena b 5.3	
7. 2	Annaatje Haal	2386	Benjamin b 5.14	
7. 9	Gerrebrand Gerrebrandse Fytje Paulusse	2387	Elsje b 5.16	Johannis Gerrebrandse Elsje Gerrebrandse
7.16	William Shippy Catharina Eller	2388	Elizabeth b 4.1.1796	
7.16	Pieter Folkonier Abigail Young	2389	Isaac b 3.31	
7.23	Joost Pickston Elizabeth Wood	2390	Richard b 6.21	Richard Pickston
7.23	Casparus Van Rypen Antje Ackerman	2391	Annaatje b 6.27	Lawrence Ackerman Annaatje Peeck
8.13	John Van Eydestyn Mary Miller	2392	Margrietje b 5.27	John Vreland jr Margrietje Van Bussen
8.13	Pieter Van Eydestyn Maria Tysen	2393	Catharina b 7.18	
8.30	Jacobus Post jr Rachel Alje	2394	David b 2.17	Cornelius Van Houten Lena Houten
9. 3	Robert Glass Sarah Banta	2395	Elizabeth b 6.11	Michael Van Eydestyn Antje Banta
9. 3	Nicholaas Ryker Annaatje Gerrebrandse	2396	Abraham b 7.26	Abraham Van Giesen Elizabeth Gerbrandse
9.10	Helmich Van Winkel Marratje Post	2397	Johannis b 8.17	
9.10	Jacob Spier Rebecka Linckford	2398	Maria (twin) b 8.27	Hendrick Stymets Maria Linckford
9.10	Same as #2398	2399	Johannis (twin) b 8.27	Same as #2398
9.10	Richard Gerrebrandse Annaatje Ennis	2400	Marytje b 7.10	Nicholaas Gerbrandse Maria Gerbrandse
9.17	Rem Onderdonck Geesje Rethan	2401	Annaatje b 8.17	
9.24	Johannis Spier Elizabeth Terhune	2402	Cathalyntje b 8.27	
9.24	Jacob Zabriskie Lea Berdan	2403	Sarah b 9.2	Jacob Berdan Catharina Bilju
10.15	Jacob Van Rypen Jannetje Van Winkel	2404	Elsje b 9.8	

Bap	Parents	1797-1798 Item	Child	Sponsors
10.15	Thomas Sindal Catharina Kierstede	2405	Cathalyntje b 9.14	Arie Jacobusse Sarah Jacobusse
11. 5	Hartman Post Nency Jackson	2406	Pieter b 10.2	
11. 5	John Van Winkele Elizabeth Brinckerhoff	2407	Annaatje b 9.27	
11. 5	Cornelius Van Giesen Charity Caljer	2408	Jamyma b 8.3	
11.12	Jacobus Van Rypen Aaltje Vreland	2409	Annaatje b 10.2	
12. 3	Abraham Linckford Maria Van Rypen	2410	Grietje b 10.18	
12. 3	Pieter Van Giesen Sarah Spier	2411	Grietje b 9.24	Cornelius Egtbertse Grietje Spier
12.17	Gerrit Van Houten Cornelia Van Ess	2412	Gerrit b 11.12	
12.24	Abraham Ryker Hanna Ennis	2413	Abraham b 10.11	
12.31	Pieter Ackerman Annaatje Vreland	2414	Jacobus b 12.12	Jacobus Ackerman
1798 1.13	Johannis Stagg Cornelia Van Blerkum	2415	Jacobus b 12.23.1797	Jacobus Stagg Lidia Schoonmaker
1.13	Cornelius Jeraalman Neeltje Jurrianse	2416	Annaatje b 12.3.1797	Christofel Jurianse Annaatje Brouwer
2. 8	Abraham Brouwe- Hendrickje Gerrebrandse	2417	Tryntje b 12.3.1797	
2.18	Stephen Terhune Lidia Romyn	2418	Guliaam b 1.23	Ench Jo. Vreland Marretje Bertholf
2.18	Gerret Jacobusse Maria Coerten	2419	Petrus b 1.2	John Spier Antje Jacobusse
2.18	Albert Ryker Catharina Horley	2420	Nellie b 12.17.1797	
2.25	Isaac Van Houten Annaatje Boss	2421	Elizabeth b 1.22	Staats Boss Geertje Degrauw
3.18	Teunus Berdan Aaltje Van Blerkom	2422	Antje b 1.22	
3.18	Thomas Linckford Sarah Sigler	2423	Johannis b 1.5	
3.18	Adriaan Van Rypen Cathalyntje Spier	2424	Gerrit b 1.25	
3.18	Hendrick Doremus Catharina Terhune	2425	Margrietje b 1.3	
3.18	Jacob Toers Maria Post	2426	Johannis b 2.11	

Bap	Parents	1798 Item	Child	Sponsors
3.18	Jacob Van Rypen Annaatje Van Rypen	2427	Cornelius Spier b 1.14	Cornelius Spier Annaatje Stymets
4.15	Abraham Snyder Maria Kiesler	2428	Sacharias b 3.20	Sacharias Snyder Margrietje Fear
4.15	Pieter Doremus Lena Berry	2429	Hendrick b 3.10	
4.15	Elizabeth Kiese	2430	Jinne Post b 1.26	
4.15	Gerrebrand Bruyn Catharina Van Der Hoef	2431	Rachel b 3.7	Johannis Van Rypen Rachel Van Rypen
4.23	John Van Giesen Margrietje Macness	2432	Isaac b 2.13	
5. 8	Hartman Degrauw Jannetje Vreland	2433	Marynus b 3.4	
5.20	Hendrick Laroe Antje Ackerman	2434	Jannetje b 4.25	
5.27	William Dickey Hester Ellizon	2435	William b 4.14	
6.17	Matheus Van Noorstrand Polly Phillips	2436	John Ludlow b 3.28	
6.24	Hermanus Van Bussen Belitje Post	2437	Annaatje b 5.28	
6.24	Jacobus Post Jannetje Van Giesen	2438	Catharina b 5.26	Robbert Post Jannetje Post
7.15	Jacob Vreland Aalje	2439	Rachel b 4.29	Abraham Vreland Rachel Ackerman
7.15	Gerrebrand Van Houten Jannetje Gerritse	2440	Hillegont b 6.24	
7.29	Cornelius Vreland Santje Helms	2441	Samuel b 6.18	Jacob Koejeman Rachel Gerbrandse
7.29	Albert Ackerman Antje Van Winkel	2442	Isaac b 7.3	
8. 5	Gerrit Van Wagenen Helena Schoonmaker	2443	Cornelius b 7.8	
8.13	Hendrick H. Post Jannetje Van Houten	2444	Jannetje b 8.7	Hendrick Post Ester Dey
8.15	Richard Broun Peggy Smelliger	2445	Rebecka b 9.26.1797	
8.26	James Christie Annaatje Helm	2446	Geertje b 7.17	Cornelius Helm Lea Cadmus
8.26	Hendrick Spier Jannetje Van Giesen	2447	Fytje b 7.4	
9.16	John Kiesler Polly Snyder	2448	Hermanus b 7.22	

Bap	Parents	1798-1799 Item	Child	Sponsors
9.27	Pieter Terhune Jenneke Van Winkel	2449	Maria b 8.12	Johannis Spier Elizabeth Terhune
9.27	Casparus Degrauw Lena Jurrianse	2450	Lena b 8.23	
9.31?	William Simmons Jane Young	2451	William Henry b 8.20	Cornelius Westervelt Polly Simmons
10.21	Samuel Spier Polly Sigler	2452	Rynier b 8.14	
10.21	Isaac Vreland Margrietje Vreland	2453	Enoch b 9.20	Rachel Vreland
11. 4	Henry Compton Eleanor Coyle	2454	Thomas b 8.29	
11.11	John Ennis Maria Steger	2455	Antje b 10.11	Hendrick Van Vorst Sarah Steger
11.11	Gerret Post Marretje Van Rypen	2456	Jenneke b 10.13	Elias Vreland Elizabeth Post
12. 9	Daniel Schoonmaker Elizabeth Post	2457	Jacobus b 11.4	Jacobus Post Jinny Van Giesen
12. 9	Jacob Vreland Pheben Wells	2458	Maria b 11.2	
12.23	Johannis Post Elizabeth Ackerman	2459	Johannis b 9.27	Joost Kogg Bos
12.25	Pieter Folkonier Abigail Young	2460	Rachel b 9.28	
12.25	Kammena Van Buren Rebecka Ennis	2461	Henry b 10.18	Peggy Ennis
12.30	Marcelus Post Judy Evertse	2462	Helmich b 12.1	
1799 1. 1	Gilbert Lake Lena Brouwer	2463	Majeke b 10.9.1798	
1. 1	George Van Eydestyn Jenneke Degrauw	2464	Lena b 11.27.1798	Abraham Vreland Lena Degrauw
1.13	John Van Houten Antje Post	2465	Cornelius b 12.9.1798	
1.20	John Deets Gouda Vreland	2466	Martinus Easterly b 11.25.1798	
2. 3	Adriaan M. Post Elizabeth Van Rypen	2467	Elias b 12.30.1798	
2. 3	Jacob Koejeman Rachel Gerbrandse	2468	John b 12.25.1798	
2. 3	Thomas Van Hoorn Elizabeth Ruthan	2469	Joris b 1.7	Nicasie Van Blerkom Jannetje Bord
2. 3	Cornelius Meyer Martyntje Terhune	2470	Cornelius b 1.7	

Bap	Parents	1799 Item	Child	Sponsors
2.24	Thomas Devorsne Susanna Folkonier	2471	Johannis b 1.12	Michael Vreland Sietje Vreland
2.24	Cornelius Vreland Dorothie Van Der Hoef	2472	Lea b 12.23.1798	Lea Doremus
3. 3	Johannis Van Houten Selly Van Bussen	2473	William b 2.5	
3. 3	Daniel Pickston Elizabeth Wood	2474	Abraham (twin) b 1.21	Abraham Vreland Lea Degrauw
3. 3	Same as #2474	2475	Helmich (twin) b 1.21	Same as #2474
3.17	Daniel Fielding Angonietje Huysman	2476	Maria b 2.17	Michael Terhune
3.17	Hendrick Spier Metje Vreland	2477	Neeltje b 2.2	
3.24	Pieter Paulusse Jannetje Van Houte	2478	Dirck b 2.17	
4. 7	Jacob En. Vreland Marretje Vreland	2479	Henricus b 3.6	
4.21	John Locy Antje Van Rypen	2480	Jacob b 3.16	Casparus Van Rypen Antje Ackerman
4.21	Casparus Post Fytje Paulusse	2481	Neeltje b 3.22	
4.21	Jacob Van Winkel Annatje Boss	2482	John b 3.12	John Deets Gouda Vreland
4.24	Abraham Koejeman Myntje Vreland	2483	Sarah b 10.6.1798	
4.24	Jurrie Van Rypen Elizabeth Van Blerkom	2484	Annaatje b 3.25	John Jurrianse Annaatje Jurrianse
5. 1	Joseph Billings Maria Schoonmaker	2485	Helena b 12.28.1798	
5. 2	Gerrit Spier Maragrietje Ennis	2486	Neeltje b 4.10	
5. 5	Joris Banta Elizabeth Van Eydestyn	2487	Annaatje b 4.8	Dirck Banta Maria Stagg
5. 5	Johannis Egtbertse Lea Winne	2488	Rachel b 3.27	
5. 5	Elias Yorks Rachel Ryker	2489	John b 3.31	
5. 9	John Mac Carty Elizabeth Post	2490	John b 4.29	
5.13	Joseph Peasy Catharina Pingman	2491	Sarah b 3.4	
6. 2	Pieter Eller Marytje Drummond	2492	Dirck b 4.1	

Bap	Parents	1799 Item	Child	Sponsors
6. 2	Jeremia Evertse Neeltje Montanje	2493	Hendrick b 4.13	Jacobus Brinkerhof Cornelia Kip
6. 9	Matheus Evertse Jenneke Post	2494	Matheus b 4.25	
6.23	Johannis Post Cornelia Cadmus	2495	Egje b 5.24	
6.30	Helmich Van Giesen Sarah Van Noorstrand	2496	Annaatje b 5.31	Robert Van Houten Lena Van Giesen
6.30	Abraham Van Rypen Dorothie Westervelt	2497	Elizabeth b 6.4	
6.30	Abraham Brouwer Hendrickje Gerbrandse	2498	Jacob b 4.22	
6.30	Jurrie Jurrianse Catharina Van Hoorn	2499	Margrietje b 6.12	
6.30	Pieter Van Buren Catharina Attredge	2500	Sellet	
7.14	Casparus Boss Selly Blanchard	2501	Rynier b 6.17	Rynier Blanchard Elizabeth Van Bussen
7.21	Pieter Pier Selly Messeker	2502	Johannis b 6.17	
8.25	Isaac Ackerman Syntje Post	2503	David b 7.8	Cornelius Cadmus Jannetje Van Rypen
8.25	Philip Van Rypen Jannetje Sip	2504	Adriaan b 8.2	Adriaan Sip Lea Van Rypen
9.14	Roelif Post Marretje Post	2505	Fytje b 8.21	Gerrit Post Marretje Van Rypen
9.14	Hartman Vreland Thyna Post	2506	Tryntje b 8.11	
9.14	Johannis Westervelt Maria Van Boskerck	2507	Catharina b 8.9	John Osborn Thyna Van Boskerck
9.22	Harmanus Van Bussen Fytje Gerritse	2508	Pieter b 7.30	
9.22	Gerrit Van Houten Cornelia Van Ess	2509	Pieter b 8.16	
9.29	John Vreland Jannetje Spier	2510	Elias b 8.23	
9.29	Encrease Gould Eggy Helme	2511	Sally b 8.10	
10. 6	_____ Gerritse Marritje Doremus	2512	Hendrick b 8.30	
10. 6	Jacob Ssmith Cathalyntje Berry	2513	Sally b 8.18	
10.13	Abraham Spier Martha Van Giesen	2514	Johannes b 9.10	Cornelius Egbertse Margrietje Spier

Bap	Parents	Item	Child	Sponsors
10.27	Albert Ryker Catharina Hurly	2515	Anna b 9.10	
11. 3	Gerrebrand Gerrebrandse Sietje Evertse	2516	Abraham Van Giesen b 9.26	Abraham Van Giesen Elizabeth Gerrebrandse
11.17	Matheus Spier Cathalyntje Van Bussen	2517	Sarah b 10.5	
12. 8	Cornelius Jeralman Neeltje Yurrianse	2518	Christofel b 9.29	
12. 8	Jacobus Stegg Lidaja Schoonmaker	2519	Henricus Schoonmaker b 11.16	Hendrick Schoonmaker Susanna Smith
1800 1. 5	Jacob Van Ryper Annaatje Van Ryper	2520	Cornelius b 11.6.1799	Cornelius Spier Annaatje Stymets
1. 5	John Van Rypen Lea Winne	2521	Margrietje b 12.6.1799	
1.16	Andrias Cadmus Pryntje Doremus	2522	Priscilla b 12.19.1799	
2.16	Hermanus Van Bussen Beletje Post	2523	Hendrick b 1.6	
2.16	Daniel Fielding Angonietje Huysman	2524	Maria b 1.18	
2.16	John Jurianse Elizabeth Van Hoorn	2525	Margrietje b 1.21	Dirck Van Hoorn Margrietje Terhune
2.23	Mathew Bouwden Martha Corby	2526	Mathew b 9.6.1799	
3.30	Teunis Gerrebrantse Jannetje Spier	2527	John b 1.3	John Spier Antje Jacobusse
3. 2	Gerrit Van Vorst Polly Van Eydestyn	2528	Cornelius b 12.14.1799	
3.30	John Scidmore Triyntje Degrauw	2529	John b 2.18	Trintje Brass
3.30	John Kiesler Polly Snyder	2530	Zacharias b 2.15	
3.30	Benjamin Forse Annaatje Haal	2531	John b 3.4	
4.13	Samuel Spier Maria Siglar	2532	James b 3.2	
4.20	Michael Ortley Catharina Spery	2533	William b 3.3	
5. 4	Jacob Van Rypen Jannetje Van Winkel	2534	Jacob b 3.28	
5. 4	Pieter Westervelt Cathalyntje Westervelt	2535	John b 4.15	
5. 4	Philip Berry Eva Van Winkel	2536	Isaac b 4.4	

Bap	Parents	1800 Item	Child	Sponsors
5. 4	John Van Winkel Tiesje Vreland	2537	Anatje b 3.29	
5. 4	John Perrit Rachel Koejeman	2538	Simeon b 4.17	
5.18	Hartman Post Nency Jackson	2539	Maria b 4.16	
5.18	Teunis Berdan Aaltje Van Blerkom	2540	Johannis b 3.6	
5.22	John Ludlow Elizabeth Vreland	2541	Hanmore b 4.__	
6. 1	Casparus Van Vorst Margrietje Van Boskerk	2542	Catharina b 4.12	Hendrick Van Vorst Geertje Degrauw
6. 1	Abraham Ryker Annaatje Ryker	2543	Maria b 3.10	
6. 1	Isaac Van Winkele Hester Van Giesen	2544	Helena b 5.12	
7. 2	 Neeltje Vreland	2545	Lena b 6.21	Gerrit Post Maragrietje Vreland
7.13	Jacob D. Berdan Catharina Bilju	2546	Gerrit b 6.18	
7.13	Cornelius Van Blerkom Maria Doremus	2547	Petrus b 6.3	
7.13	James Christie Annaatje Hellem	2548	Catharina b 6.14	
7.13	Hendrick H. Post Jannetje Van Houten	2549	Cornelius b 6.25	Cornelius V. Houten Helena V. Houten
7.13	Michiel Van Eydestyn Antje Banta	2550	Helena b 6.20	
7.20	Guliam Hopper Annaatje Stagg	2551	Annaatje b 6.15	
7.27	Michael Vreland Lena Romyn	2552	Cornelius b 6.17	
7.27	Robert Glass Sarah Banta	2553	John b 7.1	
7.27	Helmich V. Houten Lena Van Blerkom	2554	Tryntje b 7.3	
8. 3	Peter Ackerman Lea Vreland	2555	Cornelius b 6.26	Cornelius Vreland Dority V. Der Hoef
8. 3	Abraham Vreland Lea Degrauw	2556	Cornelius b 7.17	
8.17	Hartman Degrauw Jannetje Vreland	2557	John b 6.29	Geertje Degrauw
8.17	Pieter Van Eytestyn Maria Tysen	2558	John b 7.23	

Bap	Parents	1800 Item	Child	Sponsors
8.24	John Spier Elizabeth Terhune	2559	John b 7.25	
8.24	John Van Hoorn Margrietje Van Bussen	2560	Margrietje b 7.25	Dirck V. Hoorn Polly Whitlock
8.24	Jacob Brinckerhoff Abigail V. Bussen	2561	Lena b 7.28	
9. 7	Johannes Van Houten Sally Van Bussen	2562	William b 8.21	
9. 7	Adriaan Van Ryper Cathalyntje Spier	2563	Johannes b 8.6	
9. 7	Gerrit Vreland Margrieta Van Ryper	2564	Cornelius b 8.4	
9.14	Cornelius Westervelt Polly Simmons	2565	Pieter b 8.24	Elizabeth Simmons
10. 5	Cornelius Vreland Santje Hellem	2566	Lea b 8.31	Jacob Evertse Lea Vreland
10. 5	Abraham Peeck Tryntje Brass	2567	Lena b 8.30	John Peeck Antje Van Winkel
10. 5	Gerrebrand A. Gerbrantse Fytje Paulusse	2568	Geertruy b 9.5	
10. 5	Jacob Koejeman Rachel Gerrebrantse	2569	Stephen b 8.21	
10. 5	John Van Winkele Elizabeth Brinckerhoff	2570	Jacob b 9.8	
10.26	Jacob Toers Maria Post	2571	Samuel b 9.12	Samuel Toers Annatje Kogh
10.26	Hendrick Printice Margrieta Kingsland	2572	Matheus b 9.23	
10.26	Thomas Van Hoorn Elizabeth Rutham	2573	Joris b 10.6	
11. 9	Hendrick Pickston Marritje Post	2574	Aaltje b 10.5	Richard Pickston Aaltje Mourusse
11. 9	Thomas Cadmus Margrietje Doremus	2575	Abraham b 10.5	Gerrit Gerritse Margrietje Doremus
11. 9	Helmich Van Winkel Marritje Post	2576	Michael b 10.13	Elias Vreland Margrietje Post
11.10	Nathanael Billings Maria Schoonmaker	2577	Polly b 10.17	
11.16	Jacobus Post Jinne Van Giesen	2578	Fytje b 10.19	
11.30	Cornelius Jeraalman Jannetje Jurrianse	2579	Syntje b 9.5	John Jurrianse Syntje Maurusse
11.30	Thomas Devorsne Susanna Folkonier	2580	Daniel b 10.4	

Bap	Parents		Item	Child	Sponsors
		1800-1801			
12.21	Rachel E. Vreland		2581	Richard b 9.14	Cornelius Bogert Peggy Vreland
12.25	Arie Post Maria Stagg		2582	Abraham b 11.14	Cornelius Stagg Margrietje Banta
12.25	Abraham Snyder Polly Kiesler		2583	Polly b 11.7	
1801 1. 1	Waling Van Winkel Jannetje Post		2584	Cornelius b 12.1.1800	Cornelius Van Winkel Annaetje Van Rypen
1.18	Cornelius Myer Martyntje Terhune		2585	Lea b 12.22.1800	
1.18	Benjamin Vreland Elizabeth Van Winkel		2586	John b 12.3.1800	Isaac Vreland Jinny Bruyn
2. 1	Jacob J. Vreland Pheby Walls		2587	James b 12.11.1800	
2. 1	John Van Buren Antje Vreland		2588	James b 10.12.1800	
2. 8	Gerrit Van Wagenen Helena Schoonmaker		2589	Fytje b 12.17.1800	Gerrit P. Van Wagenen Fytje Westerveld
2. 8	Hendrick Labach Thyna Spier		2590	Hendrick b 1.9	Jacob Stegg Sarah Spier
3. 1	Pieter Van Bussum Annaatje Paulusse		2591	Elizabeth b 1.14	
3.16	Cornelius Van Rypen Marretje Gerritse		2592	Rachel b 3.6	
3.16	Daniel Schoonmaker Elizabeth Post		2593	Elizabeth b 2.15	Peter Terhune Elizabeth Whitlock
3.22	Cornelius Doremus Marritje Vreland		2594	Maria b 1.25	Cornelius Vreland Elizabeth Vreland
4. 5	Casparus Degrauw Lena Jurrianse		2595	Cornelius b 3.5	
4. 5	George Van Eydestyn Jenneke Degrauw		2596	Cornelius b 3.10	
4. 6	John Ennis Maria Steger		2597	Abraham b 1.9	Lena Steger
5.10	Jacobus Van Winkel Margrietje Toers		2598	Margrietje b 3.23	
5.10	Peter Simmons Margrietje Westervelt		2599	Rachel b 3.3	
5.17	Gerrit Post Marritje Van Rypen		2600	Johannis b 4.4	
5.25	Johannes H. Post Elizabeth Ackerman		2601	Selly b 3.23	
6.14	Abraham Koejeman Myntje Vreland		2602	Myntje b 3.17	

Bap	Parents	1801 Item	Child	Sponsors
6.20	Pieter Terhune Jenneke Van Winkel	2603	Jenneke b 5.21	Dirck Terhune Annaatje Van Voorhees
6.21	Johannes H. Post Geertje Degrauw	2604	Helmich b 5.28	
6.21	John Stagg Antje Blancher	2605	Rynier Blancher b 5.24	Elizabeth Van Bussen
7.12	Jacob Van Winkel Annaatje Boss	2606	Josua b 6.20	Joris Banta Elizabeth Van Eydestyn
7.12	Camena Van Buren Rebecca Ennis	2607	James b 5.4	Antje Vreland
7.12	Gerrit Pier Jenneke Brouwer	2608	Johannes b 6.12	
8. 2	Adriaan Sip Lea Van Rypen	2609	Cornelius b 6.27	Johannes Sip Geertje Van Winkel
8. 2	Jacobus Brinckerhof Elizabeth Jurrianse	2610	Antje b 7.4	Lena Brinkerhof
8.16	Gerrebrand Jurrianse Lena Kerck	2611	Gerrit b 7.12	Gilbert Van Enburgh Polly Kerck
8.16	Elias Yorks Rachel Ryker	2612	Ulrick b 6.23	
8.16	Thomas Brass Polly Doremus	2613	Antje b 7.13	Hillitje Doremus
8.16	Hendrick Spier Metje Vreland	2614	Hendrick b 7.9	John Spier Antje Jacobusse
8.23	Jerimia Evertson Neeltje Montanje	2615	Benjamin b 7.25	
9. 6	Dirck Van Hoorn Polly Whitlock	2616	Maragrietje b 8.1	Thomas Van Hoorn Elizabeth Ruthan
9. 6	Albert Ryker Catharina Hurly	2617	Catharina b 7.10	
9. 6	Cornelius Vreland Dorithy Van Der Hoef	2618	Rachel b 8.2	John Vreland Lea Ackerman
9.13	Pieter Ellen Maria Drummond	2619	Sally b 8.13	
9.13	Gerrit Van Houten Cornelia Van Ess	2620	Cornelia b 8.6	
9.27	Matheus Pier Antje Moore	2621	Jacob b 8.18	
10. 4	Theodorus Van Winkel Annaetje Van Eydestyn	2622	Pieter b 8.21	
10. 4	Casparus Van Rypen Antje Ackerman	2623	Marynus, twin b 9.4	Abraham Vreland Rachel Ackerman
10. 4	Same as #2623	2624	Rachel, twin b 9.4	Claartje Hoghoort

Bap	Parents	Item	Child	Sponsors
10. 4	Jacob E. Vreeland Marritje Vreland	2625	Jannetje b 8.25	
10.18	Hendrick Van Vorst Antje Pickston	2626	Catharina b 9.17	Casparus Van Vorst Margrietje Boskerck
11. 8	Jurrie Jurrianse Tryntje Van Hoorn	2627	John b 10.7	
11. 8	Isaac Ackerman Syntje Post	2628	Johannes b 9.21	
11.15	Cornelius Jeraalman Neeltje Jurrianse	2629	Margrietje b 9.7	
11.15	John Parrot Rachel Koejeman	2630	Pieter b 7.15	
11.15	Abraham Hopper Elizabeth V. Hoorn	2631	Geesje b 10.9	Andrias V. Hoorn Maria Stagg
12. 6	John H. Gerritse Polly Vreland	2632	Hillegont b 11.6	Hendrick (P.) Kip Catharina Gerritse
12.20	Jerimea Boskerck Antje Gerritse	2633	Johannis b 10.30	
12.20	Samuel Spier Maria Sigler	2634	Maria b 11.18	
12.25	Gerrebrand Gerrebrantse Sytje Everson	*2635	Matheus b 11.27	
12.25	Gerrit Gerritse Marritje Doremus	*2636	Cornelius b 11.24	
12.25	Marcelus Post Judick Everson	*2637	Lena b 11.23	
12.25	Joseph Van Winkel Lidea Wood	*2638	Egbert b 9.29	
1802				
1. 1	Hendrick Kip Claasje Sip	2639	Cornelius b 12.1.1801	Cornelius Sip Maria Van Rype
1.10	Henricus J. Vreland Lea Terhune	2640	Antje b 12.13.1801	
1.10	Daniel Fielding Angonietje Huysman	2641	Abraham b 12.23.1801	Jacobus Huysman Tiesje Terhune
1.17	Isaac Van Winkel Hester Van Giesen	2642	Elizabeth b 12.10.1801	Jacobus Post Jinne Van Giesen
1.17	Hermanus Van Bussen Fytje Gerritse	2643	Neesje b 11.28.1801	
1.17	Johannis Post Fytje Ryker	2644	Abraham b 12.12.1801	Marritje Van Rypen
1.31	Johannis Van Houten Selly Van Bussen	2645	Lena b 1.5	Johannis Van Hoorn
1.31	Teunis Berdan Altje Van Blerkom	2646	Pieter b 12.30.1801	

* - bap year for #2635-38 listed as "1802" but birth year listed as "1801"

Bap	Parents	Item	Child	Sponsors
		1802		
2. 7	Roeliph Doremus Annaatje Doremus	2647	David b 1.7	
2.21	Richard Ennis Jinne Doremus	2648	Nelly b 1.1	
2.21	John Jurrianse Elizabeth Van Hoorn	2649	Annaatje b 1.15	Christopel Jurrianse Annaatje Brouwer
2.21	Jacob Koejeman Rachel Gerrebrantse	2650	Stephen b 1.7	
2.28	John Loosie Antje Van Rypen	2651	Marynus b 1.__	
3.14	Isaac Alje Anna Ryerse	2652	Anna b 2.3	
3.14	Hermanus Brass Antje Eller	2653	Angonietje b 2.14	Angonietje Ellis
3.14	Jacobus Van Rypen Aaltje Vreland	2654	John b 2.7	Harp Van Rypen Margrietje Berry
3.14	Jacobus Stagg Lidea Schoonmaker	2655	Margrietje b 2.9	Cornelius Stagg Margrietje Banta
3.21	Hendrick Post Jannetje Van Houten	2656	Hendrick b 2.28	
3.21	Abraham Vreland Le(y)a Degrauw	2657	Lea b 2.21	Johannis Vreland Pryntje Vreland
4. 4	Benjamin Vreland Elizabeth Van Winkel	2658	Isaac b 3.4	
5. 2	David Blair Belitje Vreland	2659	Robert b 3.3	
5.30	Adriaan Van Rypen Cathalyntje Spier	2660	Johannis b 5.8	
6. 7	Cornelius A. Post Selly Spier	2661	Arie b 5.10	Anna Spier
6. 7	Andrias Cadmus Tyna Doremus	2662	Jannetje b 4.28	Cornelius Cadmus Jannetje Van Rypen
6. 7	Adriaan Post Elizabeth Van Rypen	2663	Helmich b 5.10	
6. 7	Jacobus Van Winkel Jannetje Van Winkel	2664	Jacob b 5.6	
6. 7	Adriaan Van Houten Thyna Van Winkel	2665	Cornelius b 5.12	Cornelius V. Winkel Annatje V. Rypen
6.21	Hartman Post Nency Jackson	2666	Jannetje b 5.26	
7.11	John Devoe Catharina Stockholm	2667	Cornelius b 6.16	
7.18	James Christie Annaatje Helm	2668	Cornelius b 6.16	

Bap	Parents	1802 Item	Child	Sponsors
7.25	Henry Compton Ellin Coyle	2669	Robert b 3.31	
8. 1	Cornelius Myer Martyntje Terhune	2670	Elizabeth b 6.16	Hendrick Banta Elizabeth Leeck
8. 1	Benjamin Force Annatje Haal	2671	David b 7.5	David Ackerman Metje Haal
8. 8	Cornelius V. Blerkom Maria Doremus	2672	Hendrick b 7.8	Catharina Terhune
8. 8	Arie Kierstede Jenneke V. Rypen	2673	Thomas b 7.15	Gerrit Post Marretje V. Rypen
8. 8	Rynier Kip Elizabeth V. Houten	2674	Fytje b 7.15	Fytje Pieterse
8.22	Cornelius Vreland Susanna Hellem	2675	Abraham b 7.18	
9. 2	Cornelius Van Rypen Maragrietje Post	2676	Maragrietje b 8.23	Hendrick F. Post Jannetje Van Houte
9.19	Hartman Degrauw Jannetje Vreland	2677	Hartman b 7.15	
10. 3	John R. Ludlow Elizabeth Vreland	2678	Antje b 8.1	
10. 3	John C. Van Houten Antje Post	2679	Cathalyntje b 9.9	
10.10	Casparus Van Vorst Grietje V. Boskerk	2680	Thomas b 9.11	
10.10	James Gilson Annaatje Messelaar	2681	Robert b 8.23	
10.31	Jacob J. Vreland Phebe Walls	2682	Jacob b 10.2	
10.31	Cornelius H. Doremus Marritje Vreland	2683	Hendrick b 9.30	
11. 7	Cornelius Van Campen Ludlow Catharina V. Eydestyn	2684	Elizabeth b 8.27	
11.11	Peter Westerveld Cathalyntje Westerveld	2685	Grietje b 10.20	
11.14	Abraham Snyder Marytje Kieslaar	2686	Sarah b 10.9	
11.21	Hendrick Printice Margrietje Kingsland	2687	William b 10.22	
11.21	Pieter Pier Selly Messeker	2688	Susanna b 10.10	
12. 5	Daniel Pickston Elizabeth Wood	2689	Hendrick b 11.6	Hendrick Pickston Marritje Post
12.10	Jacob Brinckerhoff Abigail Van Bussen	2690	Philip b 12.3	

Bap	Parents	1802-1803 Item	Child	Sponsors
12.12	Hendrick Laroe Antje Ackerman	2691	Catharina b 10.20	
1803 1.16	John J. Van Giesen Catharina Van Alen	2692	John b 12.5.1802	
1.23	Abraham Boss Claasje Hoghoort	2693	Rachel b 12.27.1802	Jacobus Demarest Catharina Hopper
1.23	Hendrick Labach Thyna Spier	2694	Sarah b 12.26.1802	Joseph Kogh Anna Spier
1.23	Gerrit Vreland Margrietje Van Rypen	2695	Jannetje b 12.15.1802	
1.30	Jurrie Van Rypen Rachel Meet	2696	Antje b 12.19.1802	
2.20	John Van Buren Antje Vreland	2697	John b 1.21	
2.27	Abraham Godwin Mary Mun(y)on	2698	Catharina b 2.14	
3. 6	Thomas Cadmus Margrietje Doremus	2699	Margrietje b 2.2	
3. 6	Hendrick Swin Rachel Brouwer	2700	Hendrick b 11.26.1802	Gideon Smith Catharina Smith
3.13	Johannis Spier Elizabeth Terhune	2701	Elizabeth b 2.10	
3.27	Helmich Van Houten Lena Van Blerkom	2702	Vrouwtje b 3.3	John Van Rype Vrouwtje Van Blerkom
5. 1	Adriaan J. Post Marretje Post	2703	Cathalyntje b 4.3	
5.30	Thomas Devorsne Susanna Folkonier	2704	Rachel b 4.19	
5.22	Enoch J. Vreland Maria Vreland	2705	Johannis b 4.24	
6.19	Johannis H. Post Elizabeth Ackerman	2706	Susanna b 5.6	
6.19	Peter Van Eydestyn Maria Tyse	2707	Henricus b 5.24	
7.17	Isaac Ackerman Syntje Post	2708	Rachel b 6.4	
8.21	Jacobus Demarest Catharina Hopper	2709	Samuel b 7.27	
8.28	John Toers Margrietje Kip	2710	Rynier b 8.3	Rynier Kip Elizabeth Van Houten
8.28	Johannes H. Post Geertje Degrauw	2711	Catharina b 7.30	
9.11	Peter Simmons Margrietje Westervelt	2712	Elizabeth b 8.20	

Bap	Parents	1803-1804 Item	Child	Sponsors
9.18	Hartman M. Vreland Thyna Post	2713	Lena b 8.31	
9.18	John Ennis Marytje Steger	2714	Neeltje b 6.4	
9.18	Hendrick Van Vorst Annaatje Peckston	2715	Isaac b 8.23	
10. 2	Cornelius Cadmus Jannetje Van Rypen	2716	Andries b 8.22	Andries Cadmus Pryntje Doremus
10. 2	Thomas Brass Maria Doremus	2717	Nellie b 8.17	
10. 2	father unknown Catharina Maria Folkonier	2718	Gerritje b 9.1	
10.27	Marcelus Wouterse Pryntje Post	2719	Gerrit b 10.16	
10.30	Fransiois Van Eydestyn Antje Tyse	2720	Jannetje b 10.6	George Van Eydestyn Jenneke Degrauw
10.30	Hendrick Pickston Marretje Post	2721	Johannes b 9.30	
10.30	Daniel Folkonier Johanna Boskerck	2722	Annaatje b 9.15	James Christie Annaatje Helm
11.13	Samuel Spier Maria Sigler	2723	Naomie b 10.8	
11.13	John Scidmoor Catharina Degrauw	2724	Jenneke b 9.14	
11.13	Cornelius C. Post Elizabeth Van Winkel	2725	Cornelius b 9.19	
11.27	Isaac Van Winkel Hester Van Giesen	2726	Eva b 10.28	
12. 4	Pieter Van Bussen Annaatje Paulusse	2727	Neeltje b 10.19	
12.11	Jacob Enog Vreland Marretje Vreland	2728	Joris b 11.4	Marritje Bertholf
12.11	Pieter Ackerman Annaatje Vreland	2729	Dirck b 11.3	
12.25	Benjamin Vreland Elizabeth Van Winkel	2730	Paulus b 11.22	Jacob Brinckerhof Abigail Van Bussen
1804 1.28	John H. Gerretse jr Polly Vreland	2731	Elizabeth b 12.22.1803	Elias J. Vreland Elizabeth Post
2. 5	Abram E. Vreland Lea Degrauw	2732	Hartman b 1.9	
2. 5	Jacob J. Van Winkel Annaatje Boss	2733	Stephan(ce) b 12.15.1803	
2. 5	Jurrie Van Rypen Rachel Meet	2734	Jenneke b 12.15.1803	

Bap	Parents	1804 Item	Child	Sponsors
2. 5	Isaac Schoonmaker Eva Vreland	2735	Henricus b 1.2	
2.19	Gerrit Van Houten Cornelia Van Ess	2736	Michael b 1.6	
2.19	Jacob J. Stagg Catharina Van Rypen	2737	Catharina b 1.15	John Vreland jr Geertje Rodebach
2.19	John Van Hoorn Maragrietje Van Bussen	2738	William b 1.23	Abraham Van Rypen Theodosia Westerveld
2.26	Jeremia Everse Neeltje Montanje	2739	Dirck b 2.1	Dirck Cadmus Jannetje Krom
3.11	Daniel Fielding Angonietje Huysman	2740	Cornelius b 2.23	
3.18	Joseph Gilliam Annaetje Cogh	2741	Christina b 2.9	Barent Spier Christina Cogh
3.18	John C. Jurrianse Elizabeth Van Hoorn	2742	Dirick b 2.19	Hessel Jurrianse Marytje Van Hoorn
3.18	Johannes A. Sip Hester Doremus	2743	Adrian b 1.17	
4. 1	George Van Eydestyn Jenneke Degrauw	2744	Jannetje b 12.10.1803	
4.15	Roelif Doremus Annaatje Doremus	2745	Marytje b 3.16	
4.15	Cornelius H. Doremus Marritje Vreland	2746	Cornelius b 3.15	Cornelius C. Vreland Catharina Doremus
5. 6	Henricus Vreland Lea Terhune	2747	Elizabeth b 3.31	
5.(6)	Jacob Van Rypen Jannetje Van Winkel	2748	Waling b 3.16	Waling Van Winkel Catharina Paulusse
5.10	Adriaan Van Houten Styntje Van Winkel	2749	Jenneke b 4.9	
5.10	Jacobus Brinkerhof Elizabeth Jurrianse	2750	Antje b 4.1	Magdalena Banta
5.20	Pieter Doremus Lena Berry	2751	Elizabeth b 4.14	
6.10	Isaac Van Rypen Maria Stagg	2752	Isaac b 4.28	
6.10	James Christie Annatje Helm	2753	Grietje b 5.4	Catharina Van Eydestyn
6.10	Casparus Degrauw Lena Jurrianse	2754	Johannis b 4.7	
6.24	Cornelius Holley Neeltje Vreland	2755	Gerrit b 5.21	Casparus Post Fytje Paulusse
7.22	Jacob Toers Marytje Post	2756	Joseph b 6.15	Marytje Cogg

Bap	Parents	Item	Child	Sponsors
8. 5	Cornelius A. Vreland Santje Helm	2757	Catharina b 7.1	James Christie Annatje Helm
8.26	Hendrick H. Post Jannetje Van Houten	2758	Lena b 8.2	
8.26	Daniel Schoonmaker Elizabeth Post	2759	Jacob b 8.1	
8.26	Cornelius Van Blerkom Marytje Doremus	2760	Jannetje b 7.24	
8.19	Gerrebrand Gerrebrandse Lea Ackerman	2761	Pieter b 7.18	Pieter Ackerman Annaatje Vreland
8.19	Casparus Van Rypen Antje Ackerman	2762	Laurence b 6.13	Selly Ackerman
9. 2	Jacob Brinckerhof Abigail Van Bussen	2763	Philippus b 8.6	
9.16	Adriaan Van Rypen Cathalyntje Spier	2764	Uriah b 8.20	
9.23	Hendrick J. Spier Metje Vreland	2765	Maria b 8.9	
9.30	William Van Leusden Hester Goetschius	2766	Sarah b 9.6	
10.14	Pieter Allen Marytje Drummond	2767	Jannetje b 8.12	
10.25	_____ Messeker	2768	Susanna, w of Abraham Ackerman b 11.2.1753	
10.28	Hartman Post Nancy Jackson	2769	Jacobus b 9.15	
11. 4	John C. Vreland Vrouwtje Van Blerkum	2770	Cornelius b 10.5	Cornelius Vreland Elizabeth Vreland
11.18	Abraham (R.) Van Houten Catharina Sip	2771	Molly b 10.6	Johannis Sip Geertje Van Winkel
12.25	John Vreland jr Geertje Rodebach	2772	John b 10.31	
12.25	Andrew Van Boskerck Theodosie Van Winkel	2773	Catharina b 11.19	Thomas V. Boskerk Maria V. Boskerk

1805

Bap	Parents	Item	Child	Sponsors
1. 1	Elias E. Vreland Antje Spier	2774	Jacob b 11.28.1804	
1. 4	John J: Goetschius Jannetje Ackerman	2775	John b 12.18.1804	John Goetschius Annatje Daty
1.16	David Smith Margrieta Marinus	2776	Thomas b 3.28.1804	Thomas Post Tryntje Vreland
1.20	John Van Buren Antje Vreland	2777	Blandina b 12.23.1804	
2.10	Daniel Pickston Elizabeth Wood	2778	Lena b 1.24	

Bap	Parents	1805 Item	Child	Sponsors
2.10	Isaac Ackerman Sytje Post	2779	Isaac b 12.31.1804	
2.17	Richard Outwater Catharina Kip	2780	Willemyntje b 12.16.1804	
3.18	Adriaan M. Post Lybetje Van Rypen	2781	Johannes b 2.9	
3.10	Isaac Aljee Antje Ryerse	2782	Catharina, twin b 1.24	John Burhans Catharina Burhans
3.10	Same as #2782	2783	David, twin b 1.24	
3.10	Hendrick J. Kip Claasje Sip	2784	Neeltje b 2.6	
3.24	Thomas Van Hoorn Elizabeth Retan	2785	Marretje b 2.11	
3.31	Daniel Folkonier Henckje Boskerck	2786	Abraham b 2.5	Catharina Folkonier
4. 7	Benjamin Weller Jean Dickey	2787	Jean b 2.28	
4.14	Cornelius C. Post Elizabeth Van Winkel	2788	Maria b 3.10	
5. 5	Rynier Kip Elizabeth Van Houten	2789	Isaac b 4.1	Isaac Kip Hendrikje Van Giesen
5.19	Hendrick Printice Margrietje Kingsland	2790	Maria b 4.12	
5.19	Pieter Westerveld Cathalyntje Westerveld	2791	Jannetje b 4.25	
5.19	Waling W. Van Winkel Catharina Van Voorhees	2792	Dirck b 3.28	
5.19	John G. Van Houten Elizabeth Gould	2793	Marian b 3.13	
6. 9	Abraham Godwin Mary Munson	2794	David Griffith b 5.25	Sarah Griffith
6. 9	John Parke Arriaanje Marcelusse	2795	John Kollock b 5.9	
6.16	Jacobus Stagg Lidea Schoonmaker	2796	Maria b 5.4	Isaac Van Rypen Maria Stagg
7. 7	John Losie Antje Van Rypen	2797	Isaac b 6.8	Isaac Van Rypen Maria Stagg
7. 7	Pieter Pier Selly Messeker	2798	Maria b 5.25	
7. 7	Peter Jackson Hester Brinckerhoff	2799	John b 6.8	
7.14	Hendrick Labach Thyna Spier	2800	Barent b 5.30	

Bap	Parents	Item	Child	Sponsors
		1805-1806		
7.28	Joris Banta Lisabeth Van Eydestyn	2801	John b 6.17	
7.28	Jurrie Jurrianse Catharina Van Hoorn	2802	Dirck b 7.11	Marritje Van Hoorn
7.28	Dirck Van Hoorn Maria Witlock	2803	Thomas b 6.26	
8.24	Thomas Cadmus Maragrietje Doremus	2804	Helmich b 8.14	
8.25	Harmen Van Rypen Rebecca Brouwer	2805	Jurrie b 8.5	Jacob Ackerman Susanna Doremus
8.25	Cornelius H. Doremus Marritje Vreland	2806	Cornelius b 7.24	
10. 6	Benjamin Forse Annaatje Haal	2807	John b 8.18	
10. 6	Cornelius V. C. Ludlow Catharina Van Eydestyn	2808	Lena b 8.3	
10.13	Isaac Van Rypen Maria Stagg	2809	Marian b 8.6	
10.23	Hendrick Van Vorst Annaatje Pickston	2810	Waling b 10.16	
11.10	Abraham Boss Claasje Haghort	2811	Elizabeth b 9.25	
11. 3	Isaac Schoonmaker Eva Vreland	2812	Lea b 10.14	Petrus Vreland Lea Winne
10.26	Cornelius Cadmus Jannetje Van Rypen	2813	Corneli(us), twin b 10.13	Cornelius Van Houten Lena Van Houten
10.26	Same as #2813	2814	Jacobus, twin b 10.14	
12. 1	Thomas Devorsne Susanna Folkonier	2815	Sietje b 9.25	
12.15	Albert Doremus Jannetje Vreland	2816	Gerritje b 11.7	
12.15	Casparus Boss Selly Blanchard	2817	Gerret b 11.19	
12.15	Gerret Gerritse Marritje Doremus	2818	Gerrebrant b 11.19	
12.18	Joseph Gillam Annaatje Cogh	2819	Arent b 11.20	Christina Kogh
12.22	John Van Houten Selly Van Bussen	2820	John b 11.6	
12.25	Gerret Van Rypen Maria Ecker	2821	Steve b 12.10	
1806 1. 5	Isaack Van Winkel Hester Van Giesen	2822	Jannetje b 12.7.1805	Jacobus Post Jinne Van Giesen

Bap	Parents	1806 Item	Child	Sponsors
1. 5	Hartman Vreland Thyna Post	2823	Jenneke b 12.8.1805	
1.19	Encreas Gould Agness Helme	2824	Benjamin Helme b 11.3.1805	
1.26	John H. (Spi)er Geertje Kiesler	2825	Hendrick b 11.17.1805	Matheus Spier Catharina V. Rypen
2.16	Jacob Vreland Marritje Vreland	2826	Marritje b 12.25.1805	Enoch Jor. Vreland Marritje Bertholf
2.16	Johannes Post Selly Goetschius	2827	Geertje b 1.16	
2.16	John C. Van Houten Antje Post	2828	Lena b 1.12	
2.16	Robert Glass Sarah Banta	2829	Joris b 1.13	
2.16	Hendrick Gerritse Thyna Doremus	2830	Annaatje b 12.1.1805	
2.16	Johannes Van Hoorn Marragritje Van Bussen	2831	Thomas b 1.9	
3. 2	Adriaan Van Houten Thyna Van Winkel	2832	Antje b 1.30	Waling Van Winkel Jannetje P(_____)
3. 2	John Van Winkel, deceased Elizabeth Brinckerhoff	2833	Johannes b 1.22	
3. 2	Abraham Snyder Marytje Kiesler	2834	Abraham b 1.28	
3. 9	Casparus Post Fytje Paulusse	2835	Cornelius b 2.1	
3. 9	Waling H. Van Winkel Margrietje Ackerman	2836	Helmich b 2.6	Helmich Van Winkel Marritje Post
4.13	Abraham Vreland, deceased Lea Degrauw	2837	Catharina b 3.13	George Van Eydestyn Jenneke Degrauw
4.20	Peter Simmons Marragrietje Westerveld	2838	Sarah b 3.28	
4.20	Abraham D. Ackerman Selly Hall	2839	Isaac b 3.20	Jacob Ackerman Susanna Doremus
4.27	Jacob Van Rypen Jannetje Van Winkel	2840	Gerrebrand b 3.23	
5. 4	Jacob J. Van Winkel Annaatje Boss	2841	Paulus b 3.31	
5.18	Andrias Cadmus (P)ryntje Doremus	2842	Pieter b 4.21	Peter Doremus Lena Berry
6.22	John Gerritse Polly Vreland	2843	Jenneke b 5.31	
6.22	Jeremia Boskerck Antje Gerritse	2844	Henricus b 5.14	Henry J. Gerritse Jamima Hopper

Bap	Parents	1806 Item	Child	Sponsors
7. 6	Adriaan J. Post jr Rachel Van Giesen	2845	Joris b 6.10	Isaac Van Winkel Hester Van Giesen
7. 6	Pieter Doremus Lena Berry	2846	William b 6.20	
7.27	Gerrebrand Gerrebrandse Sytje Evertse	2847	Jacob b 6.14	
7. 3	Daniel Fielding N(iet)je Huysman	2848	Jacobus b 5.9	
8.17	Jacob Brinkerhoff Abigail Van Bussen	2849	Lena b 8.3	
9. 7	Johannis Post Marritje Vreland	2850	Lea b 7.10	
9. 7	James Christie Antje Helme	2851	James b 8.15	
10. 1	John (J.) Van Giesen Catharina Van Aalen	2852	John Van Aalen b 8.31	
10. 1	Lucas Van Aalen Antje Van Der Hoef	2853	Cornelius b 7.31	
10.12	John Marinus Maragrietje Goetschius	2854	David b 9.13	
10.14	John S. V. Winkel Jenny Kip	2855	Cornelius b 9.3	Simon Jos. V. Winkel Claasse Gerritse
11.16	Dirck Stagg Selly Ackerman	2856	Annaetje b 9.20	
11.16	William Van Lausden Hester Goetschius	2857	Saartje b 10.1(6)	
10. 5	Samuel Spier Maria Sigler	2858	Sophia	
11. 2	Jeorge Van Eydestyn Jenneke Degrauw	2859	Geertje b 7.30	
11. 2	Hendrick Van Vorst Annatje Pickston	2860	Waling b 9.22	Gerret Van Vorst Elizabeth Bilju
11. 2	Cornelius Holly Neelje Vreland	2861	Cornelius	
11. 2	Elijah Hargrow Petty Ackerman	2862	Elizabeth b 9.29	
11.18	Gerret Van Houte Cornelia Van Ness	2863	Henricus b 10.29	
11.30	Casparus Degrauw Lena Jurrianse	2864	Henricus b 11.12	
11.30	Jacob J. Stagg Catharina Van Rypen	2865	John b 10.19	
12.21	John C. Jurrianse Elizabeth Van Hoorn	2866	Christophel b 11.9	

Bap	Parents	Item	Child	Sponsors
		1806-1807		
12.29	Hendrick Spier Metje Vreland	2867	Burnet Vreland b 10.17	
1807				
1. 1	Matheus Spier Cathalyntje Van Bussen	2868	Judick b 11.27.1806	
1.18	Hartman Post Nancy Jackson	2869	John b 12.19.1806	
2. 1	Henricus Vreland Lea Terhune	2870	Johannes b 12.3.1806	
2. 8	Cornelius Van Blerkum Maria Doremus	2871	Catharina b 12.3.1806	
2. 8	Matheus Spier Catharina Van Rypen	2872	Antje b 12.20.1806	
2.22	Hessel Doremus Jannetje Demrerest	2873	Catharina b 12.27.1806	
3.15	Jacob Ackerman Susanna Doremus	2874	David b 2.14	
3.22	David Cogh Metje Post	2875	Elizabeth b 1.23	Helmich Post Elizabeth Post
3.30	Henricus J. Gerritse Myntje Hopper	2876	Antje b 2.27	Gerrit Hopper Antje Hennion
4.19	Pieter Westerveld Cathalina Westerveld	2877	Grietje b 3.23	
4.22	Joseph Gillam Annetje Cogh	2878	Antje b 3.5	Hendrick Laroe Aanatje Ackerman
5. 7	Hendrick Printice Maragrietje Kingsland	2879	Elizabeth b 2.25	
5.10	Dirck Van Hoorn Maria Witlock	2880	Angonietje b 3.22	
5.18	Adrian Van Rypen Cathalyntje Spier	2881	Catharina b 4.8	
6.28	Daniel Folkonier Hannah Boskerck	2882	Rachel b 5.16	
7. 5	John (M.) Ryerse Claasje Van Winkel	2883	Marian b 6.6	
7.19	Cornelius Post jr Elizabeth Van Winkele	2884	Theodorus b 6.30	
7.19	Peter Jackson Hester Brinckerhoff	2885	Maria b 6.22	
7.26	Jacobus C. Stagg Lidea Schoonmaker	2886	Annaatje b 7.11	
8.16	Isaac Van Rypen Matia Stagg	2887	Cornelius b 6.21	
8.30	Johannes Spier Elisabeth Terhune	2888	Elizabeth b 7.27	

		1807		
Bap	Parents	Item	Child	Sponsors
9. 6	Hendrick Labach Cathalyntje Spier	2889	Barentje b 7.13	
9. 6	Andrew Breastead Van Bussen Jannetje Post	2890	Philippus b 8.7	
9.13	William Hunter Elenor Carter	2891	Jane b 4.16	
9.20	Adriaan (M.) Post Elizabeth Van Rypen	2892	Jannetje b 8.31	John Marselusse Jannetje Van Rypen
9.20	John Losie Antje Van Rypen	2893	John b 8.4	
9.20	John Van Eydestyn Catharina Van Winkel	2894	Teunis b 8.20	
9.20	Andrew Boskerck Theodosia Van Winkel	2895	Theodorus b 8.15	
9.27	Arie Banta Maria Debaen	2896	Lena b 8.7	
10.11	John E. Vreland Jenneke Van Winkel	2897	Helena b 9.15	
10.11	John Van Houten Selly Van Bussen	2898	Selly b 9.13	
10.11	Elias E. Vreland Anna Spier	2899	Sarah b 9.10	
10.11	Waling W. Van Winkel Catharina Van Voorhees	2900	Jannetje b 9.11	
10.11	Thomas Van Rypen Maria Van Houten	2901	Gerrit b 9.12	
10.11	Adrian (__) Post Altje Ackerman	2902	Sophia b 9.20	
10.18	John H. Spier Geertje (K)ieslaar	2903	Jinne b 8.31	
10.27	Isaac Van Winkel Hester Van Giesen	2904	Catharina b 10.1	
11. 1	Iddo Vreland Antje Vreland	2905	Enogh b 10.5	
12. 6	Jacob Folkonier Geertje Degrauw	2906	Daniel b 11.18	
12. 6	Egbert (Post) Cornelia Vreland	2907	Rachel b 11.30	
12.20	Peter Van Bussen Annaetje Paulusse	2908	Philipus b 12.6	
12.26	Gerrit Van Rypen Maria Ecker	2909	Cornelius b 11.11	
12.26	David Devoe Cornelia Ackerman	2910	John b 11.27	

Bap 1808	Parents	1808 Item	Child	Sponsors
1. 1	John G. Van Houten Elizabeth Gould	2911	Increase Gould b 11.18.1807	
1.17	Roelif Doremus Annaatje Doremus	2912	Johannes b 12.14.1807	
1.24	Michael Vreland Elizabeth Riddenar	2913	Michael b 12.28.1807	Lena Romyn
1.24	Thomas Devrosne Susanna Folkonier	2914	Thomas b 12.5.1807	
1.24	Gerrit Spier jr Cathalyntje Post	2915	John b 12.21.1807	
2.14	Albert Doremus Jannetje Vreland	2916	Catharina b 1.18	
2.28	Jacob En. Vreland Marritje Vreland	2917	Gerritje b 1.4	
3. 6	Jacobus Brinckerhoff Eizabeth Jurrianse	2918	Syntje b 1.27	
3.27	Adriaan Van Houten Thina Van Winkele	2919	Adrian b 2.20	Ed(_) P. Marcelusse Jannetje Van Winkel
3.27	John Van Hoorn Maragritje Van Bussen	2920	Abraham b 2.13	
3.27	John C. Jurrianse Elizabeth Van Hoorn	2921	Christofel b 2.27	
3.27	father deceased Metje Ackerman	2922	Elias b 2.15	
3.27	Samuel Spier Maria Sigler	2923	Cornelius b 2.2	
4.17	Isaac Schoonmaker Efje Vreland	2924	Maria Salome b 3.12	M. Salome Goetschius
4.17	Joris Haghoort Syntje Post	2925	Isaac b 3.11	
5. 1	Aaron A. Van Houten Annaatje Sip	2926	Marytje b 3.16	Cornelius Sip Marytje Van Rypen
5.15	Samuel Berry Jannetje Van Winkel	2927	Geertje b 4.1	
5.15	Johannes Sip Geertje Van Winkel, deceased	2928	Johannes b 4.17	Geertje Van Winkel
5.15	Cornelius Brinckerhoff Annaatje Jurrianse	2929	Lena b 4.16	
5.15	Hendrick Printice Maragritje Kingsland	2930	Elizabeth b 4.15	
5.22	John Ennis Maria Steger	2931	Peter b 3.28	
5.22	Thomas Cadmus Maragrietje Doremus	2932	Cathalyntje b 4.2(6)	

Bap	Parents	Item	Child	Sponsors
6. 5	Thomas Van Velsen Catharina Smith	2933	Rachel b 3.21	
6.19	Helmich A. Post Antje Berry	2934	Gabriel Ludlow b 1.23	
7. 3	Gerret Vreland Maragrietje Van Rypen	2935	Jenneke b 5.15	
7.10	Cornelius Vreland jr Lena Van Blerkum	2936	Cornelius b 6.12	
7.24	Thomas Van Hoorn Ellizabeth Retan	2937	Jannetje b 6.19	
7.24	Abraham Boss Claartje Haaghoort	2938	Annaatje b 6.26	
7.31	Jacob Zabriskie Annaatje Marinus	2939	Rachel b 7.12	
9. 4	Hartman Post Nancy Jackson	2940	Jannetje b 8.7	Hendrick Post Jannetje Van Houten
9. 4	Jurrie Jurrianse Catharina Van Hoorn	2941	Hendrick b 7.16	
10. 2	Hartman Vreland Thyna Post	2942	Marretje b 9.2	
10. 2	Abraham Snyder Maria Kieslaer	2943	Elizabeth b 8.28	
10. 2	Benjamin Forse Annaetje Haall	2944	Mous b 8.30	
11. 6	John Vreland Geertje Rodebach	2945	Elias b 8.27	
11.27	Jacob Brinkerhoff Abigail Van Bussum	2946	Elizabeth b 10.9	
11.27	John Devoe Elizabeth Post	2947	James b 10.8	
12.18	John Post Elizabeth Paulusse	2948	Catharina b 10.30	
12.26	James Christie Annaatje Helme	2949	Abraham b 10.31	
12.29	Henricus C. Van Houten Jenneke Van Winkel	2950	Lena b 12.20	
1809				
1. 1	Cornelius V. C. Ludlow Catharina V. Eydestyn	2951	Richard b 8.31.1808	
1.15	Peter Jackson Hester Brinkerhoff	2952	Maria b 12.4.1808	
1.22	Jacobus Demarest Catharina Hopper	2953	Gerret b 1.1	Anna Hopper
1.22	John C. Vreland Vrouwtje Van Blerkum	2954	Elizabeth b 12.20.1808	

		1809		
Bap	Parents	Item	Child	Sponsors
1.22	Cornelius Van Hoorn Sarah Wilson	2955	Sarah b 12.19.1808	
1.29	Johannes R. Van Horten Elizabeth Thomson	2956	James b 9.15.1808	
1.29	James McCowen Jane Jackson	2957	Thomas b 11.16.1808	
2.12	Hendrick F. Post Jannetje Ackerman	2958	Marytje b 1.19	
2.12	Hendrick Vreland Lea Terhune	2959	Nickasie b 12.1.1808	
2.12	Jacob J. Stagg Catharina Van Rypen	2960	Adriaan b 12.13.1808	
2.12	Jacob Van Hoorn Sally Vreland	2961	Maragrietje b 12.31.1808	Lena Vreland
4. 3	Benjamin Van Orden Regina Heymer	2962	Laurence b 2.1	
4. 9	Hendrick Van Vorst Annaatje Pickston	2963	Antje b 3.7	
4. 9	Cornelius Holly Neeltje Vreland	2964	Gerritje b 3.2	Elias Vreland Antje Spier
4. 9	Thomas Van Rypen Maria Van Houten	2965	Sophia b 2.22	
4.23	David Kogh Betty Post	2966	Antje b 3.9	John Laroe Peggy Laroe
4.23	Dirck Van Hoorn Maria Withlock	2967	Elizabeth b 3.19	
5. 2	Andrew Van Buskerck Theosia Van Winkel	2968	Annaetje b 4.16	Annatje Van Eydestyn
5.14	Jacob J. Van Winkel Annaetje Boss	2969	Rachel b 4.9	
6.11	Pieter Van Bussen Annaatje Paulusse	2970	Philippus b 4.28	
7. 2	Jacob Ackerman Susanna Doremus	2971	Neeltje b 6.2	
7. 9	Esechiel Webb Fanny Hall	2972	Emaline b 6.10	
7.23	Richard Outwater Catharina Kip	2973	Harriot b 6.22	
7.30	Hendrick Spier Metje Vreland	2974	Nelson b 6.25	
7.30	Henricus Gerritse Myntje Hopper	2975	John b 7.9	
8. 6	John Jeraalman Bu(r_)haus Sally Hopper	2976	John Hopper b 7.15	

Bap	Parents	Item	Child	Sponsors
8.13	Cornelius Doremus Marretje Vreland	2977	Catharina b 7.11	
8.13	Hessel Doremus Jannetje Demarest	2978	Lea b 6.27	
8.13	John Losie Antje Van Rypen	2979	Jannetje b 6.17	
8.20	Daniel Demarest Elizabeth Bensen	2980	John b 8.6	John Bensen Maria Lesier
9. 3	Iddo Vreland Antje Vreland	2981	Maragrietje b 8.4	
9. 3	Frederick Jurrianse Catharina Van Eydestyn	2982	John b 8.3	
9.16	William Cairns Maria Cogh	2983	Harriet b 9.15	Hendrickje Boss
9.20	Jacobus Stagg Lidia Schoonmaker	2984	Sarah b 9.2	
9.24	 Lena Christie	2985	Thomas Albert b 12.14.1808	
9.24	Isaac Aljee Antje Ryerse	2986	Dorotie b 8.27	
10. 1	Hendrick Labach Thyne Spier	2987	John b 8.22	
10.15	Harmen Van Rypen Rebecca Brouwer	2988	Hendrick b 9.26	
11. 5	Robert Glass Sarah Banta	2989	Susanna b 9.5	
11.11	Abraham Post Elizabeth Westervelt	2990	Arie, twin b 10.31	
11.11	Same as #2990	2991	Cornelius, twin b 10.31	
11.12	Joseph Gillam Annaatje Cogh	2992	Michael b 10.5	Dirck Cadmus Jannetje Krom
12.17	Gerrit Gerritse Marritje Doremus	2993	Simeon b 11.19	
12.17	Cornelius C. Post Elizabeth Van Winkel	2994	Maria b 11.14	
12.17	John C. Jurrianse Elizabeth Van Hoorn	2995	Annaatje b 11.15	
12.24	Hendrick C. Van Houten Jennetje Van Winkel	2996	Annaatje b 11.27	
1810 1. 7	Peter Simmons Maragrietje Westerveld	2997	Antje b 12.1.1809	
1. 7	Hendrick Wouterse Catharina Van Rypen	2998	Gerret b 12.7.1809	

Bap	Parents	1810 Item	Child	Sponsors
1. 7	Cornelius Van Blerkum Marytje Doremus	2999	Elizabeth b 11.15.1809	
1.14	Theunis Bruyn Sarah Outwater	3000	Sarah b 11.29.1809	
1.14	Nicholas Jeraalman Maria Louwis	3001	Rachel b 12.9.1809	
1.14	Isaac Van Winkel Hester Van Giesen	3002	Joris b 12.12.1809	
2.18	John Van Rypen Maria Bruyn	3003	Alette b 11.10.1809	
2.18	Robert Post Rachel Van Der Hoef	3004	Jacobus b 1.3	
3.11	Waling W. Van Winkel Catharina Van Voorhees	3005	Sophia b 2.6	
3.11	David Devoe Cornelia Ackerman	3006	Pieter b 2.4	
3.18	Theunis Van Bussen Catharina Goetschius	3007	Annaetje b 2.13	
3.22	(John) Ryerson Claasje Van Winkel	3008	Jane b 1.22	
4.22	Ariaan Van Houten Thina Van Winkel	3009	Maria b 3.28	
4.22	Abraham R. Van Houten Catharina Sip	3010	Annatje b 3.18	Manus Vreland Annatje Sip
4.22	Hessel Dorem(us) Catharina Berry	3011	John b 3.24	Hendrik Doremus Greetje Hennion
4.22	John J. Jurrianse Selley Van Noorstrand	3012	Jacob b 3.21	
4.22	Joel Snyder Maria Sandvoort	3013	Levi b 10.11.1809	
4.22	Gerrit (S.) Spier Catalyntje Post	3014	Antje b 3.20	
5. 3	John Ennis Maria Steger	3015	Maria b 3.30	
5. 6	Hendrick Pickston Marritje Post	3016	Richard b 3.20	
5. 6	John Van Hoorn Maragrietje Van Bussen	3017	John b 4.10	
5.20	Martinus Van Houten Catharina Van Houten	3018	Selly b 5.1	
5.27	Gerret Jurrianse Jannetje Post	3019	Antje b 4.22	Johannes Post Jannetje Degrauw
5.27	Daniel Folkonier Hanna Boskerck	3020	Daniel b 4.17	

Bap	Parents	Item	Child	Sponsors
		1810-1811		
5.31	John Van Blerkom Antje Jacobusse	3021	Catharina b 4.23	
6.10	Aaron Van Houten Annaatje Sip	3022	Elizabeth b 5.12	
6.10	Pieter Spier Margarita Gerrebrantse	3023	John b 4.8	
6.24	James Celsey Jenneke Degrauw	3024	Hartman b 4.4	
6.24	father deceased Jannetje Vreland	3025	Abraham b 5.28	Lea Degrauw
7.15	Thomas J. Van Rypen Maria Van Houten	3026	Cornelia b 6.5	
7.30	John Anderson Ann Cane	3027	Sarah b 6.24	
8.26	Adrian Van Rypen Cathalyntje Spier	3028	Adrian b 7.18	
10.28	John H. Gerritse jr Polly Vreland	3029	Catharina b 9.28	
10.28	John J. Post Elizabeth Paulusse	3030	Neeltje b 9.29	
11.17	Jacob Zabriskie Annaatje Marinus	3031	Thomas b 10.15	
11.17	Thomas Cadmus Maragrietje Doremus	3032	Helmich b 10.2	
12. 2	Casparus Degrauw Helena Jurrianse	3033	Elizabeth b 9.25	
12. 9	Pieter Paulusse Jannetje Van Houten	3034	Sophia, twin b 11.2	
12. 9	Same as #3034	3035	Maria, twin b 11.2	
12. 9	Michael Vreland Elizabeth Riddenar	3036	Hendrick b 10.5	
12. 9	Albert Doremus Jannetje Vreland	3037	Cornelius b 10.21	
12.25	Hendrick Printice Margerit Kingsland	3038	Rachel b (11).20	
1811				
1.13	Cornelius C. Vreland Lena Van Blerkom	3039	Jannetje b 12.4.1810	
1.20	Hartman Post Nan(cy) Jackson	3040	Ester b 12.18.1810	
1.20	Peter Jackson Hetty Bri-kerhoff	3041	Eliza b 12.12.1810	
2. 3	Jurrie Jurrianse Catharina Van Hoorn	3042	Syntje b 12.16.1810	

Bap	Parents	1811 Item	Child
2.24	Waling H. Van Winkel Maragrietje Ackerman	3043	Richard b 1.21
3. 3	Hendrick Van Vorst Annaatje Pickston	3044	Hendrick b 1.28
3. 3	John Hill Maria Camble	3045	David William b 2.6
3.17	Joris Haghoort Syntje Post	3046	Pieter b 1.31
3.24	Jacob Brinkerhoff Abigail Van Bussen	3047	Philippus b 2.8
3.31	Whorthy Clark Elizabeth Van Houten	3048	Richard b 2.12
4.21	Jacob Stagg Catharina Van Rypen	3049	Francis b 2.27
4.21	John Van Houten Antje Post	3050	Marretje b 3.11
4.21	Thomas Devorsne Susanna Folkonier	3051	Sophia b 2.10
5.12	James Christie Annaatje Helm	3052	Annaatje b 3.27
5.19	Cornelius Vreland Doretie Van Der Hoef	3053	Catharina b 3.19
5.19	John J. Sip Arriaantje Marselusse	3054	Edo b 4.7
6.16	Jacobus C. Stagg Lidia Schoonmaker	3055	Rachel b 5.29
6.16	Helmich A. Post Maria Snyder	3056	Adriaan b 5.2
7. 7	John C. Vreland Vrouwtje Van Blerkum	3057	John b 6.2
7. 7	Roelif Doremus Annatje Doremus	3058	Cornelius b 6.2
7.28	Edo Vreland Antje Vreland	3059	Elias b 7.2
7.28	John J. Vreland Lena Vreland	3060	Sarah b 7.1
7.28	Dirick Van Hoorn Maria Witlock	3061	Cathalyntje b 6.19
7.28	Hendrick Gerritse Thyna Doremus	3062	Hendrick b 6.18
8.18	Abraham Boss Claasje Haghoort	3063	Pieter b 7.10
8.18	Jacob Van Winkel Annatje Boss	3064	Selly b 7.20

Bap	Parents	1811-1812 Item	Child	Sponsors
8.18	Cornelius Holly Neeltje Vreland	3065	Abraham b 7.24	
9. 2	James McCowen Jane Jackson	3066	John b 7.1	
9. 8	Isaac Schoonmaker Eva Vreland	3067	Peter b 7.27	
9. 8	John Van Eydestyn Catharina Van Winkel	3068	Theodorus b 8.19	
9. 8	Benjamin Forse Annaatje Haal	3069	Catharina b 7.28	Martha Ackerman
9.22	Andrew Van Bussen Jannetje Post	3070	Ariaan b 8.22	
9.22	Richard Outwater Catharina Kip	3071	John b 8.21	
10.20	Isaac Van Winkel Hester Van Giesen	3072	Isaac b 9.18	
10.20	Benjamin Zabriskie Catharina Gerritse	3073	Joost b 9.4	
11. 3	Joris Banta Elizabeth Van Eydestyn	3074	Aaron b 10.10	
11.24	David Aljea Diana Boss	3075	Dirick b 10.11	
11.24	Henricus Vreland Lea Terhune	3076	Dirick b 9.13	
12.15	Frederick Jurrianse Catharina Van Eydestyn	3077	Casparus b 11.14	
12.15	John C. Jurrianse Elizabeth Van Hoorn	3078	Hessel b 11.18	
12.28	John D. Degrauw Marretje Gerritse	3079	Richard b 10.31	
12.29	Joseph Gillam Annatje Cogh	3080	Maria b 11.25	
1812				
1. 5	Henricus Gerritse Myntje Hopper	3081	Gerrit b 12.15.1811	
1.12	Hendrick Van Houten Jenneke Van Winkel	3082	Helena b 12.10.1811	
1.26	Hendrick Labach Thyna Spier	3083	Maragrita b 11.17.1811	
2.16	Adriaan Vreland Anna Herring	3084	Abraham Herving b 1.6	
2.16	Theodorus Terhune Maria Spier	3085	Elizabeth b 12.8.1811	
2.16	Claasje Post	3086	Helmich b 1.6	Adriaan Post Elizabeth Van Rypen

Bap	Parents	Item	Child	Sponsors
		1812		
3. 8	Jacobus Van Wagenen Grietje Cadmus	3087	John b 1.19	
3. 8	John Cadmus Cornelia Hopper	3088	Hendrick Hopper b 1.31	
3. 8	Daniel Demarest Elizabeth Bensen	3089	Maria b 2.5	
3.15	Cornelius H. Doremus Marritje Vreland	3090	Elizabeth b 12.28.1811	
3.29	Edo P. Marcelisse Heylie Kip	3091	Peter b 2.27	Peter Marcelisse Jannetje V. Winkel
4.22	_____ Holley	3092	Cornelius b 12.31.1779	
5. 3	Hartman C. Vreland Theodocy Snyder	3093	Cornelius b 3.15	
5.17	John Jurrianse Selly Van Noorstrand	3094	Syntje b 4.12	
6.28	John H. Gerritse Maragrita Post	3095	Susanna b 4.25	
6.28	Enoch Vreland Maria Vreland	3096	Enoch b 4.9	
7.10	Hendrick Wouterse Caty Van Rypen	3097	Catharina b 6.21	
7.26	Thomas Ryker Marritje Van Hoorn	3098	Peggy b 6.21	
7. 2	John Van Hoorn Maragritje Van Bussen	3099	Richard b 6.29	
5.31	Elias J. Vreland Marragritje Post	3100	Elizabeth b 4.9	
8. 3	Roeliph Vreland Marytje Ryker	3101	Dirick b 7.25	
8.23	Teunis Van Bussen Catharina Goetschius	3102	Hester b 7.31	
9. 6	Hendrick Post Jannetje Ackerman	3103	Marragrietje b 8.11	
10.18	Michael M. Vreland Elizabeth Riddener	3104	Elizabeth b 9.7	
10.25	Jacob B. Van Rypen Maria Van Rypen	3105	Jurian b 9.27	
10.25	Gerret Jurrianse Jannetje Post	3106	Annaatje b 9.27	
11.16	William Cairns Maria Kogh	3107	Elizabeth b 8.13	
12.13	Samuel Leuwis Marritje Van Rypen	3108	Anna Eliza b 11.8	

1812-1813

Bap	Parents	Item	Child	Sponsors
12.20	Waling Van Winkel Catharina Van Voorhees	3109	Nicasie b 11.17	

1813

Bap	Parents	Item	Child	Sponsors
1.11	Jerimia Buskerck Anna Gerritse	3110	Jane b 11.28.1812	
2.14	John G. Jurrianse Eva Vreland	3111	Alettie b 1.3	
2.14	Abraham J. Vreland Lena Romyn	3112	John b 1.10	
2.14	Jacob D. Ackerman Susana Doremus	3113	David b 1.26	
2.28	Jacobus Van Wagenen Grietje Cadmus	3114	Rachel b 1.27	
3. 7	John J. Post jr Elizabeth Paulusse	3115	Elizabeth b 1.20	
3. 7	John Losie Antje Van Rypen	3116	Cornelius b 1.30	
3. 7	Benjamin Zabriskie Catharina Gerritse	3117	Annaetje b 2.8	
3. 7	David Kogh Metje Post	3118	Annaetje b 1.27	
3.14	John M. Vreeland Elizabeth Van Eydestyn	3119	Michael b 12.30.1812	
3.21	Adrian Van Houten Thina Van Winkel	3120	Edo b 2.7	
3.21	John A. Van Rypen Elizabeth Post	3121	Aaron b 2.13	
4.11	Peter Jackson Hetty Brinckerhoff	3122	Julian b 3.7	
4.11	Jacob Brinkerhoff Abigail Van Bussen	3123	Joris, twin b 3.3	Hendrick Brinkerhoff Rachel Vreland
4.11	Same as #3123	3124	Hendrick, twin b 3.3	
4.11	Hendrick Van Vorst Annaatje Pickston	3125	Saartje b 2.12	
4.18	John Kip Jannetje Van Winkel	3126	Cornelius b 3.9	
5. 2	Cornelius C. Vreland Lena Van Blerkum	3127	Cornelius b 3.21	
5. 2	Andrew Van Bussum Jannetje Post	3128	Marritje b 4.13	
5.20	Peter Kip Claasje Marselusse	3129	Hendrick b 4.11	Hendrick Kip Catharina Gerrits
6. 6	John Sip Arrianje Marcelusse	3130	Geertje b 5.16	

Bap	Parents	1813 Item	Child	Sponsors
6. 6	John Vreland Lena Vreland	3131	Grietje b 4.27	
6.20	John A. Post Cornelia Demarest	3132	Angonietje b 5.22	Gerret Demarest Angonietje Durjee
6.25	John Ludlow Catalina Ditmis	3133	Ditmis b 4.7	
7. 4	James Christie Annaetje Helm	3134	John b 5.24	
7. 4	Daniel Folkonier Hanna Boskerck	3135	Leonard Pearsey b 6.6	
7. 4	Helmich Post Maria Snyder	3136	Martha b 5.8	
7.11	John Van Syce Elizabeth Ackerman	3137	Maria b 6.11	
7.25	Aaron Van Houten Annaetje Sip	3138	Claasje b 6.25	
7.27	Hartman Post Nancy Jackson	3139	John b 6.30	
7.27	Isaac Sip Maria Demarest	3140	Selly b 7.9	
8. 1	Jacob Zabriskie Annaatje (Ma)rinus	3141	Catharina b 7.4	
8.22	Waling H. Van Winkele Grietje Ackerman	3142	Marritje b 8.3	
9. 5	Elias A. Vreland Anna Spier	3143	Lea b 7.26	
9. 5	Hendrick Gerritse Thyna Doremus	3144	Catharina b 7.21	
9.26	Jacobus Stagg Lidia Schoonmaker	3145	Catharina b 8.30	
9.26	Thomas Cadmus Maragrietje Doremus	3146	Cornelius b 8.23	
10. 3	Abraham Collard Antje Vreland	3147	Jacob b 9.5	
10.17	Edo Vreland Antje Vreland	3148	Joris b 9.10	
10.17	Isaac Van Winkel Hester Van Giesen	3149	Salome b 9.4	
10.24	Jacob J. Stagg Catharina Van Rypen	3150	Mary Van Rypen b 8.22	
10.24	Henry Glass Hannah Post	3151	John Henry b 9.15	
12. 5	John Van Eydestyn Catarina Van Winkel	3152	Alettie b 10.11	

Bap 1814	Parents	1814 Item	Child	Sponsors
1. 1	Jurrie Jurrianse Catharina Van Hoorn	3153	Hendrick b 12.5.1813	
1. 2	Thomas Van Rypen Polly Van Houten	3154	Maria b 9.28.1813	
3. 6	John L. Kiersted Catharina Schoonmaker	3155	Daniel b 1.13	Daniel Schoonmaker Flizabeth Post
3.20	Henricus Vreland Lea Terhune	3156	Paulus b 2.5	
3.20	Waling Van Vorst Maria Kip	3157	Hendrik, twin b 1.21	
3.20	Same as #3157	3158	Gerrit, twin b 1.21	
3.20	Simeon Van Ripen Geertje Zabriskie	3159	Antje Vreland b 2.11	
3.20	John J. Outwater Cathalyntje Van Bussen	3160	Nicholas b 2.25	
3.27	Cornelius Jeraalman Neeltje Jurrianse	3161	Jirrard b 2.9	
3.27	Jacobus Post Jinny Van Giesen	3162	Elizabeth b 2.(2_)	
4.11	Waling J. Van Winkel Catharina Paulusse	3163	Geertje b 3.8	
4.11	William Van Leusden Hester Goetschius	3164	Marritje b 3.6	
5. 1	Adrian Vreland Anna Herring	3165	Elias b 3.30	
5. 1	Dirrick Van Hoorn Maria Witlock	3166	Maria Ten Eyck b 12.29.1813	
6.12	Helmich Post Annatje Vreland	3167	Elizabet b 4.25	
6.12	John Banta Rachel Post	3168	Pieter b 4.28	
6.12	John Devoe Elizabet Post	3169	Elizabeth b 5.10	
6.19	Frederick Jurianse Catarina Van Eydestyn	3170	Annatje b 5.27	
7.10	Adrian Van Rypen Cathalyntje Spier	3171	Jacob b 5.10	
7.10	John Hill Maria Camble	3172	Francis Frasher b 6.23	
7.10	Theodorus Terhune Maria Spier	3173	Jannetje b 6.21	
7.24	Abraham A. Bosch Claasje Haghoort	3174	Abraham b 6.22	

Bap	Parents	Item	Child	Sponsors
7.31	Jacob Van Winkele Annaatje Bosch	3175	Maria b 7.4	
8.21	David Aljee Dianna Boss	3176	Aanna Eliza b 7.18	
8.21	Richard Outwater Catharina Kip	3177	Pieter b 7.12	Hendrik Kip Catharina Gerritse
8.21	John Herring Anna Elsworth	3178	Anna Eliza b 6.23	
9. 4	Hendrick Leback Thyna Spier	3179	James b 7.12	
9. 4	Nicholas Van Rypen Maria Paulusse	3180	Antje b 8.12	
9.25	John C. Jurrianse Elizabeth Van Hoorn	3181	John b 8.15	
9.25	Hendrick C. Van Houten Jannetje Van Winkel	3182	Eizabeth b 8.10	
10. 2	Martin Van Der Haan Elizabeth Gerritse	3183	Cornelius b 8.30	
10.10	Johannes Ackerman Eva Sip	3184	Albert b 9.2	Albert Ackerman Antje V. Winkel
11. 6	Albert Doremus Jannetje Vreland	3185	Michael b 10.2	
11.27	Daniel Demarest Elizabeth Bensen	3186	Gerret, twin b 11.16	Gerret Demarest Angonietje Durjee
11.27	Same as #3186	3187	Rachel, twin b 11.16	
12.25	Cornelius G. Van Rypen Catalyntje New Kerk	3188	Jannetje b 12.5	

1815

2.12	Enoch Vreeland Maria Vreeland	3189	Gouda b 11.24.1814	
2.12	Hendrick Printice Peggy Kingsland	3190	Caty b 1.8	
3. 6	Hermanus Van Wagenen Jane Edsel	3191	Johannes b 1.13	
3.26	John Post Catharina Demarest	3192	Marritje b 3.3	
3.26	Thomas Ryker Marritje Van Hoorn	3193	Abraham b 2.16	
4.23	Cornelius Post Maragritje Gerritse	3194	Cornelius b 3.21	
4.23	Teunis Van Bussen Catharina Goetschius	3195	Hermanus b 3.18	
5.28	John J. Post jr Elizabeth Paulusse	3196	John b 5.4	

Bap	Parents	1815 Item	Child
5.28	John G. Jurrianse Eva Vreeland	3197	Gerrebrand b 4.23
5.28	Joris Banta Elizabeth Van Eydestyn	3198	Eliza b 4.20
5.28	Dirrick Post Neesje Van Rypen	3199	Adriaan b 5.1
5.28	Isaac Schoonmaker Eva Vreeland	3200	John b 4.22
6.11	Michael C. Vreland Dority Snyder	3201	Andrias b 5.21
6.11	Joseph Gillam Lena Van Houten	3202	Annaatje b 5.18
6.11	Pieter Doremus Lena Berry	3203	Cornelius b 5.19
6.11	Gabriel Devoe Hannah Brown	3204	William b 5.4
6.18	Gerrit Jurrianse Jannetje Post	3205	John b 5.23
7. 9	John Jurrianse Salley Van Noorstrand	3206	John b 6.14
7.10	James McGregor Juley Gray	3207	James Roberts b 12.15.1814
7.23	Peter Jackson Hetty Brinkerhoff	3208	Jane b 6.14
8.13	John J. Sip Arriantje Marselis	3209	Adrian b 7.15
9. 3	John A. Van Rypen Elizabeth Post	3210	Jane b 7.26
9. 3	Abraham Van Rypen Tryntje Van Winkele	3211	Joseph b 7.1
10. 1	Jacob Zabriskie Annaatje Marinus	3212	Joost b 9.6
10.22	Marselus Post Marriche Van Houten	3213	Halmagh b 9.17
11.12	Andrew Van Bussum Janneche Post	3214	Eliza Ann b 10.15
11.12	Samuel Speer Mary Sigler	3215	John b 9.15
11.12	Cornelius C. Vreeland Lena Van Blarcum	3216	Nicasie Van Blarcum b 8.13
11.12	Henry Van Vorst Annatie Peckstone	3217	Hannah b 9.30
11.12	John Van Sys Elizabeth Ackerman	3218	Eliza Ann b 10.6

Bap	Parents	Item	Child	Sponsors
11.19	Georg Van Riper Clarissa Vreeland	3219	Garrit b 10.16	
12. 3	Thomas Van Riper and wife	3220	Jacob b 8.18	
12. 3	James Christie and wife	3221	Henry b 9.9	
12.17	Hartman Post Nancy Jackson	3222	Abraham, twin b 11.6	Peter Jackson Hetty Brinkerhoff
12.17	Same as #3222	3223	Isaac, twin b 11.6	
12.24	Garret Cadmus Betsy Van Houten	3224	James G. b 11.22	
1816 1. 1	Garret J. Garritson Mary Romane (baptism year listed as "1815")	3225	Bregie b 12.5.1815	
2.26	Anthony A. Jacobus Hannah Van Blarcom	3226	Henry Van Blarcom b 12.2.1815	Henry Van Blarcom Jane Van Blarcom
2. 5	Isaac Harris Hannah	3227	Polly b 12.28.1815	
2.29	Wm. Miles Salledy Miles (baptism year listed as "1815")	3228	Cathrane b 1.2	
2.18	Teunis Van Idesteyn Sarah Freeland	3229	Michael b 1.25	
1. 3	Teunis J. Spear Sophia Van Houten	3230	Maria b 12.12.1815	
4. 2	Isaac Van Winkle Hester Van Gieson	3231	Daniel b 3.9	
4. 7	Jacob Bogert Eliza Westervelt	3232	Eliz Ann b 2.13	
4. 7	Chas. A. Vreeland Ann Speer	3233	Lydia b 12.26.1815	
4. 7	Henry Van Riper Myntje	3234	Eliza b 2.29	Uriah Van Riper and wife
4.14	Barnard Ryer Sarah Van Dean	3235	Susan b 2.27	
4.21	Charles Blewer Rachel Simmons	3236	Hannah b 12.8.1815	Hannah Youmans
4.21	Thomas Hancock Betsey Cartwright	3237	Maria b 11.26.1815	Rachel Simmons
6.16	Jeremiah Yurreance Caty Van Horn	3238	Jared b 4.4	
6.16	David Goetsh(iu)s Betsey Lose	3239	Henry b 3.6	

Bap	Parents	Item	Child
4.15		3240	Jeremiah Toers
	Catharine Mandeville		b 8.1.1815, illegitimate

Mother is the wife of Abraham Mandeville who's been absent for 5 years. The child's grandmother, Catharine Riker, adopted the child.

Bap	Parents	Item	Child
7.29	Richard P. Terhune Rachel	3241	Peter
6.29	Albert P. Terhune Elen Terhune	3242	Elen
8.18	James C. Stagg Lydia Schoonmaker	3243	Sally b 6.8
8.18	John Van Riper Gitty Doremus	3244	Simon b 7.10
8.18	George Houghwout Sintye Post	3245	Elizabeth b 5.25
8.18	John C. Jureance Elizabeth Van Horn	3246	Peter b 6.24
8.18	John Riker Jane Degraw	3247	John, twin b 4.29
8.18	Same as #3247	3248	Garret, twin b 4.30
10.27	Thomas Devosne Susana Falconer	3249	Rulif b 7.26
10.27	Theodores Terhune Maria Speer	3250	Maria b 8.29
10.27	Henry Vreeland Leah Terhune	3251	Rachel b 7.23
10. 1	John Kip Jane Van Winkel	3252	Clarrissa b 8.29
11. 3	Walling W. Van Winkel Caty Van Vorhese	3253	Richard b 10.16

END OF VOLUME III

KEY TO THE INDEXES

In indexing, an attempt was made to merge surnames only if the divergent spelling was clearly the same name when pronounced, or if sufficient evidence was present to indicate that two widely different spellings must be the same name because of the spouse. The surname will be found listed or cross-referenced under the regularized spelling or the spelling that occured most frequently in the record.

Baptism Index: pp 151-179 (parents) - blue paper
                 pp 181-203 (sponsors) - yellow paper

The numeral in these indexes refers to the sequential item number as presented in the chronological record. Wives will not be found in this index if their surname is the same as the husband's.

Marriage Index: pp 265-290 (principals) - blue paper
                pp 291-292 (others) - yellow paper

The numeral in these indexes refers to the sequential item number as presented in the chronological record.

General Index: pp 359-381 - blue paper

This index covers the names found on pages 293-358. The numeral refers to the page number where the item will be found. Figures in parenthesis following a number indicates the frequency with which that reference appears on the page.

(____)OSS
  Jacob, 2256

(____)uw - see DE GRAW

ABEEL
  Garret, 1256, 1446

ACKERMAN, Ackkerman
  Abraham, 221, 2839
  Albert, 1626, 2035, 2442
  Alida, 2902
  Anna, 168-172, 308, 1341, 1488, 1607,
    1816, 1878, 2111, 2266, 2306, 2391,
    2434, 2623, 2624, 2691, 2762
  Catherine, 2365
  Cornelia, 2910, 3006
  David, 286
  Elizabeth, 94-97, 205, 270, 300,
    2459, 2601, 2706, 3137, 3218
  Gulyn, 212, 2181
  Henrietta, 557, 1898, 2121
  Isaac, 2503, 2628, 2708, 2779
  Jacob, 354, 2874, 2971, 3113
  Janet, 1631, 2775, 2958, 3103
  John, 289, 1659, 1819, 2034, 3184
  Lawrence, 238
  Lea, 2761
  Margaret, 2836, 3043, 3142
  Marmaduke, 1184, 1513, 1584, 1682
  Matthew, 1329, 1423, 1523
  Metje, 2922
  Patty, 1722, 1886, 2143, 2343, 2862
  Peter, 1737, 1992, 2414, 2555, 2729
  Rachel, 1498, 2272, 2289
  Sally, 2856
  Sarah, 192, 258, 1665

ACKERT
  Maria, 1840, 2821, 2909

AELTSE
  Cornelius, 280, 359
  George, 284
  Lea, 237
  Rachel, 222, 297, 372

Aesben - see OSBORN

AGNEW
  William, 1632, 1741, 2002

Akkerman - see ACKERMAN

Alje, Aljea, Aljee, Aljie - see ALYEA

ALLEN
  Peter, 1934, 1941, 2064, 2211, 2375,
    2619, 2767
  Sarah, 1896, 2320

ALYEA
  Catherine, 1832
  David, 3075, 3176
  Isaac, 2652, 2782, 2783, 2986
  Maria, 1854
  Peter, 1755, 2133
  Rachel, 2394

AMERMAN
  John, 555

ANDERSON, Andriesse(n)
  Catlintje, 314
  Claasje, 358
  John, 3027
  Lena, 378
  Maria, 1853, 2103

Archabald, ARCHIBALD
  David, 1161, 1228
  Janet, 1240

ATTREDGE
  Catherine, 2500

BAKER
  Anna, 2281

Bant - see BOND

BANTA, Bantha
  Aaron, 2896
  Anna, 1990, 2230, 2550
  Janet, 580
  John, 1180, 3168
  Joris, 2047, 2262, 2487, 2801, 3074,
    3198
  Lena, 877
  Margaret, 109-115
  Maria, 2077
  Sarah, 1907, 2099, 2395, 2553, 2829,
    2989
  Sietje, 244
  Tytje, 139-144

BARCLAY
  James, 1148

BARENDSE
  Dirk, 78-82

Bartholf - see BERTHOLF

BASRET
  Maria, 762

BEEKHORN
  Anthony, 1867
  Thomas, 1707

BEL
  Maria, 1625

INDEX OF PARENTS

BENNET
Elizabeth, 583
Polly, 2172

BENSEN
Catherine, 1433
Daniel, 2327
Elizabeth, 2980, 3089, 3186, 3187

BERDAN
Albert, 228
Anna, 235, 339, 1966
Anthony, 2032, 2422, 2540, 2646
Jacob, 1043, 1219, 1363, 2203, 2364, 2546
John, 745, 814
Lea, 2403

Bergen, BERGER
Dirk, 1804, 1932

Berri, BERRY
Abraham, 853, 1740, 1869, 2048, 2212
Anna, 2934
Catherine, 3011
Catlintje, 2513
Dirk, 1294, 1410
John, 332, 1579, 1710, 1803, 2189
Lena, 2429, 2751, 2846, 3203
Margaret, 833
Maria, 1358
Martin, 216, 310, 374
Paul, 245, 401
Philip, 510, 1673, 1760, 1880, 2145, 2248, 2536
Samuel, 311, 2927

BERTHOLF
Sarah, 1993
Stephen, 2249

Beuis - see BOICE

Bighlie, BIGLEY
John, 1318, 1319

BILJU
Catherine, 2203, 2364, 2546
Elizabeth, 1701, 1843, 2298
Henrietta, 1742, 2180
John, 1625

BILLINGS
Joseph, 2485
Nathan, 2577

BILLINGTON
Edward, 1087

BLACKWELL, Blackwil
Sarah, 447, 567

BLAIR
David, 1555, 1658, 1818, 2029, 2659

BLANCHARD, Blancher, Blanshaer, Blanshar, Blansjaer
Anna, 2605
Janet, 93, 202, 288, 388
Maria, 213, 326
Reyner, 1066, 1137, 1254, 1371, 1716
Sally, 2501, 2817
Sarah, 1899, 2348

BLAUVELT
Daniel, 2102

Blekwil - see BLACKWELL

BLEWER
Charles, 3236

Board - see BORD

BOERUM
Maria, 1804, 1932

BOGERT
Abraham, 1614
Jacob, 3232

BOICE
Margaret, 138

BOMEN
Sarah, 1951

Bon, BOND
Catherine, 710
Emma, 659, 702, 772

BOOTH
Margaret, 1585

BORD
Catherine, 868, 993, 1072, 1127, 1458
Joris, 318, 376
Lena, 1180, 2042

Bordan - see BERDAN

BORRES
John, 1223, 1317, 1432

Bortens - see BERDAN

Bos, Bosch - see BOSS

Boskerck, BOSKERK
Andrew, 2773, 2895, 2968
Anna, 2722, 2786, 2882, 3020, 3135
Fytje - see Sophia
Jeremiah, 2633, 2844, 3110
Margaret, 2542, 2680
Maria, 2507
Sophia, 1055, 1177
Thomasina, 982

INDEX OF PARENTS

BOSS - see also ROSS
Aaron, 758, 820, 896, 1025, 1118, 1195, 1344
Abraham, 842, 933, 1026, 1334, 1527, 2693, 2811, 2938, 3063, 3174
Amy, 2303
Anna, 1670, 2076, 2083, 2282, 2318, 2421, 2482, 2606, 2733, 2841, 2969, 3064, 3175
Caspar, 1899, 2348, 2501, 2817
Catherine, 588, 1305
Conrad, 420, 427, 443
Diana, 3075, 3176
Dirk, 1768, 1995
Henry, 177, 318, 1892, 2148, 2323
Janet, 497, 559, 623
John, 2068
Joshua, 581, 835
Manus, 2059
Maria, 1380, 2151
Sarah, 513, 1770, 1849
Staats, 195, 260, 340
Thomas, 2168, 2295

BOUWDEN
Matthew, 2526

BRADFORD, Bradfort - see also PERVOO
Maria, 1641
Braedberry - see BROADBERRY

Brand, BRANT
Anna, 132, 264
Margaret, 1632, 1741, 2002

Bras, BRASS
Adolph, 1302, 1362, 1491
Catherine, 834, 953, 2567
Garret, 793
Herman, 2222, 2653
Lucas, 411, 418
Sarah, 657, 751, 801, 824, 879
Thomas, 2613, 2717

Breant - see BRANT

Brevoot - see PROVOOST

Brieant - see BRANT

BRIKKER
John, 187, 279, 373

Brinckerhoff, BRINKERHOFF
Cornelius, 2929
Elizabeth, 2163, 2407, 2570, 2833
Hester, 2799, 2885, 2952, 3041, 3122, 3208
Jacob, 2561, 2610, 2690, 2750, 2763, 2849, 2918, 2946, 3047, 3123, 3124
Joris, 877

BROADBERRY
Elizabeth, 565
Maria, 332
Susan, 392, 393

BROOKS
Thomas, 1533

Broun - see BROWN

Brouwer - see BROWER

Browen - see BROWN

BROWER
Abraham, 300, 701, 734, 2005, 2417, 2498
Anna, 892, 972, 1024, 1101, 1150, 1280, 1403, 1627
Catherine, 2066
David, 915, 1031
Garret, 1036, 1203
Isaac, 377
Jacob, 754
Janet, 2608
John, 447, 567, 826, 917, 1004, 1005, 1115, 1186, 1720, 1904, 2125
Lena, 2463
Metje, 522, 768, 823
Nelly, 303
Peter, 2350
Rachel, 2700
Rebecca, 2805, 2988
Susan, 2152
Ulrich, 1381

BROWN - see also BRUYN
Anna, 3204
Haly, 2217
John, 1576, 1651, 2202
Richard, 2445
Sally, 2233

Bruin, BRUYN - see also BROWN
Alida, 231, 381
Anthony, 1437, 1702, 1839, 2026, 2179, 3000
Barent, 339
Catherine, 1812, 2031
Elizabeth, 343
Gerrebrand, 2431
Henry, 2082
Hester, 1940, 2135
Hilda, 1897
Hillegond, 553, 784, 829, 908
Jacob, 1842
Janet, 368
John, 362, 479, 1303, 1526, 1691, 1798, 1965, 2176, 2383

BRUYN (con'd)
Lea, 389
Maria, 3003
Rachel, 1813, 2023
Sietje, 182, 234, 342, 355
Thomas, 1418, 1643

BUR(__)HAUS
John, 2976

Buskerck - see BOSKERK

BUTLER
Anna, 1548
Catherine, 1408, 1511, 1671, 1815,
1956, 2153, 2330

BYVANK
Maria, 1256, 1446

CADMUS
Abraham, 506, 1209
Andrew, 1588, 1684, 1928, 1933, 2169,
2359, 2522, 2662, 2842
Anna, 1874
Anthony, 1361
Cornelia, 1567, 1650, 1938, 2190,
2349, 2495
Cornelius, 1689, 1939, 2237, 2716,
2813, 2814
Dirk, 1015, 1271, 1810
Egje, 1188
Garret, 3224
Henry, 1383
John, 570, 658, 1821, 3038
Joris, 600, 1775
Lea, 1963
Margaret, 3087, 3114
Maria, 578, 619, 678, 737, 812, 1066,
1137, 1254, 1371, 1716
Peter, 988
Priscilla, 963, 1346
Pryntje, 1482
Rachel, 546, 804
Thomas, 789, 907, 1260, 2575, 2699,
2804, 2932, 3032, 3146

CAIRNS
David, 1977
John, 2078
William, 2983, 3107

Caljer - see COLLIER

Camble - see CAMPBELL

Camingoer, CAMMEGAREN
Veronica, 454, 726

CAMPBELL
Anna, 1613

CAMPBELL (con'd)
Ezechiel, 1149
Maria, 3045, 3172

Canada - see KENNEDY

Canceljie, Cancklin - see CONKLIN

CANE
Ann, 3027

Caneda - see KENNEDY

CANFIELD
Nathan, 1777

CARSON
Elizabeth, 1436, 1986

CARTER
Eleanor, 2186, 2283, 2891
Robert, 1192

CARTWRIGHT
Betsy, 3237

CASE
Elizabeth, 2168, 2295, 2430

CAVELIER
John, 314

Celsey - see KELSEY

CHAYS
Bryant, 2061

CHITTERLIN
Matthew, 1001, 1046, 1103

CHRISTIE, Christyn, Chrystien
Elizabeth, 282, 357
James, 1694, 1695, 1911, 2292, 2346,
2446, 2548, 2668, 2753, 2851, 2949,
3052, 3134, 3221
Lena, 2985
Maria, 73, 74, 291, 395

Claasse - see CLAWSON

CLARK
Worthy, 3048

CLAWSON
Frances, 1318, 1319
Gerrebrand, 225, 351

Coat - see NORTH COAT

Cockefeer, COCKEFER
Alexander, 145, 146
Anna, 1542
Charity, 1424
Elizabeth, 874
John, 940, 1088, 1425, 1522

DAY (con'd)
  Janet, 323
  Peter, 2042
  Richard, 201
  Thomas, 978

Deavenpoort - see DAVENPORT

DEBAEN
  Maria, 2896

DeBoog - see TIEBOUT

DeBooys - see DUBOIS

DEDRICK, Dedriks
  Gertrude, 626, 682
  John, 204, 285

Deeter - see TEATOR

Deeths, Deets - see TEATS

Deforeestes, DE FOREST
  Gerard, 1216, 1431

Defvenpoort - see DAVENPORT

DE GARMO
  John, 535
  Peter, 534, 651

DeGraau, DeGraauw, DeGraaw, DeGrauw,
  DE GRAW
  Anna, 2257
  Caspar, 1477, 1544, 1776, 1921, 2167,
    2309, 2450, 2595, 2754, 2864, 3033
  Catherine, 1247, 1251, 1484, 1580,
    1679, 1881, 2144, 2334, 2529, 2724
  Cornelius, 1060, 1281, 1325, 1493,
    1732
  Elizabeth, 754
  Francis, 1718, 2025, 2257
  Garret, 878, 967, 1082, 1152
  Gertrude, 1483, 1664, 1694, 1695,
    1911, 2292, 2604, 2711, 2906
  Hartman, 2269, 2433, 2557, 2677
  Henrietta, 265, 371
  Herman, 788, 904
  Janet, 1121, 1288, 1360, 2258, 2347,
    2464, 2596, 2744, 2859, 3024, 3247,
    3248
  John, 586, 1358, 3079
  Lea, 2556, 2657, 2732, 2837
  Lena, 510
  Walter, 1102, 1168, 1296, 1365, 1452

DeLamontanje - see MONTAINE

DeMaree, DEMAREST
  Catherine, 3192
  Cornelia, 3132

DEMAREST (con'd)
  Daniel, 2980, 3089, 3186, 3187
  David, 2024
  Jacob, 2703, 2953
  Janet, 2873, 2978
  Jemima, 289
  Maria, 3140
  Rachel, 377

DEMOTT, Demouth
  Maria, 200, 346, 391, 392

DEMSEY
  Elizabeth, 1507
  Margaret, 1553

Deremis - see DOREMUS

Devenpoort - see DAVENPORT

DEVOE
  David, 2910, 3006
  Gabriel, 3204
  John, 691, 2667, 2947, 3169
  Joseph, 1300

Devorsne, Devoseni, Devosne, DE VOSNEY,
  Devoursne
  John, 467, 495, 596, 1246, 2172
  Margaret, 1234, 1354, 1591
  Maria, 1308, 1460
  Thomas, 2471, 2580, 2704, 2815, 2914,
    3051, 3249

Dey - see DAY

DICKEY, Dicky
  Jane, 2787
  William, 2284, 2435

Dideriks, Didirks - see DEDRICK

DIERMAN
  Elizabeth, 1659, 1819, 2034

DIRKJE
  Maria, 214

DITMIS
  Catlintje, 3133

DODD
  Thomas, 1731

Doremes, Doremis, DOREMUS
  Abraham, 494, 635
  Albert, 2816, 2916, 3037, 3185
  Alida, 931, 1051, 1767
  Anna, 1326, 1381, 1494, 1663, 1863,
    2912
  Catherine, 811, 862, 930, 1033, 1126,
    1227, 1467, 1750
  Cornelius, 40-45, 538, 637, 761, 1711,

DOREMUS (con'd)
  Cornelius (con'd), 1969, 1991, 2594,
    2683, 2746, 2806, 2977, 3090
  Egbert, 1914
  Fytje, 1230
  Henry, 153-157, 208, 333, 989, 1074,
    1140, 1497, 1500, 1593, 1729, 2008,
    2425
  Hessel, 2873, 2978, 3011
  Hester, 2743
  Janet, 158-160, 448, 614, 669, 744,
    2648
  John, 94-97, 205, 1985
  Joris, 839, 983, 1037
  Kitty, 3244
  Lea, 805, 943, 944, 1295
  Lena, 1412, 1519, 1604, 1828, 1983
  Margaret, 1793, 1992, 2575, 2699,
    2804, 2932, 3032, 3146
  Maria, 520, 650, 1411, 1954, 2124,
    2228, 2352, 2512, 2547, 2636, 2672,
    2717, 2760, 2818, 2871, 2993, 2999
  Peter, 2429, 2751, 2846, 3203
  Polly, 2613
  Pryntje, 1588, 1684, 1928, 1933, 2169,
    2359, 2522, 2662, 2830, 2842, 3062,
    3144
  Rachel, 775, 2327
  Roelof, 2288, 2647, 2745, 3058
  Susan, 2874, 2971, 3113
  Syntje, 1715
  Thomas, 168-172, 308, 898, 942, 1067,
    1197, 1269, 1376, 1769
  Thyna, Tyna - see Pryntje

DOUCHEE
  Lea, 591

DOTY, Douty
  Anna, 2229
  Lily, 2366

DOW
  John, 1366, 1464
  Maria, 1894

DREEK
  Cornelius, 199, 312, 313

DRUMMOND, Drummund
  Hester, 1190
  John, 1851, 2054
  Maria, 1934, 1941, 2064, 2211, 2375,
    2492, 2619, 2767
  Robert, 717, 779, 827, 922, 1130

DUBOIS
  Anna, 472, 525, 603, 671, 760

DUNCAN
  Thomas, 1172

DUNN
  Letitia, 1999, 2316

DUPLACEY
  Henry, 1548

Durje, DURYEA
  Samuel, 2089

DUVAAL
  Anna, 2061
  Thomas, 999, 1191, 1310, 1393

D'Vasseni - see DE VOSNEY

Dye - see DAY

EARL
  Dorothy, 1073
  Elizabeth, 2189
  Theodosia, 747, 864

EASTERLY
  Catherine, 1844
  Gouda, 1146, 1243, 1421, 1562

Ecke - see OUKE

Ecker - see ACKERT

EDEN
  Polly, 2241

EDESON
  Cornelius, 1272, 1313

EDGERLY
  John, 2281

EDSEL
  Jane, 3191

Egberse, Egbertle, EGBERTS(e), Egbertze,
  Egtbertse - see also EVERTS
  Anna, 476
  Cornelius, 1154, 1248, 1419
  Egbert, 1078, 1349, 1725
  Elsie, 538, 637, 761
  Garret, 1619, 2252
  John, 520, 650, 2097, 2225, 2353, 2488
  Peter, 2036
  Rachel, 2075, 2259
  Waling, 622, 1540, 1823

EHLER
  Anna, 2222, 2653
  Catherine, 2388
  Peter, 2492

Ekbertse - see EGBERTS

Ellen - see ALLEN

Ellenthorn - see ELLERTON

Eller - see EHLER

ELLERTON
  Rachel, 429
  Zachariah, 218

ELLISON, Ellizon
  Hester, 2284, 2435

ELSWORTH
  Anna, 3178

Enderson, Endress - see ANDERSON

ENNIS
  Anna, 999, 1191, 1310, 1393, 1688,
    1831, 1865, 1973, 2193, 2268, 2400,
    2413
  George, 2152
  Jacob, 1466, 1590, 1676
  John, 2455, 2714, 2931, 3015
  Margaret, 1208, 1389, 1514, 1609,
    1739, 1931, 2166, 2342, 2486
  Maria, 1309, 2597
  Rebecca, 2315, 2461, 2607
  Richard, 2648
  William, 591

Erl - see EARL

EVENS
  George, 449

Everse, Everson, EVERTS(e) - see also
  EGBERTS
  Catlintje, 1372, 1728
  George, 532, 639, 977, 1668
  Geesje, 1113, 1176, 1321, 1459, 1656
  Janet, 1015, 1271
  Jeremiah, 1855, 2049, 2242, 2376,
    2493, 2615, 2739
  Judy, 2462, 2637
  Matthew, 1196, 1278, 1364, 1457, 1550,
    2063, 2219, 2494
  Sietje, 2516, 2635, 2847

FAIRCHILD
  Anna, 1906, 2175

FALCK
  Catherine, 218
  Frances, 352
  Margaret, 534, 651

Falconer, FALKNER
  Catherine, 2718
  Daniel, 1339, 1435, 1568, 1693, 1820,
    2051, 2207, 2379, 2722, 2786, 2882,
    3020, 3135
  Jacob, 2906

FALKNER (con'd)
  Peter, 2389, 2460
  Susan, 2471, 2580, 2704, 2815, 2914,
    3051, 3249

Fearchild - see FAIRCHILD

Ferdon - see VERDON

FIELDING
  Daniel, 2354, 2476, 2524, 2641, 2740,
    2848
  Eva, 1775

FIERE
  Margaret, 1447

FLEMING
  Samuel, 1284

Folkonier - see FALKNER

FORBES, Forbess
  Abigail, 542

Forester - se- FOSTER

Forguson - see FURGESON

Forrester - see FOSTER

FORSE
  Benjamin, 2531, 2671, 2807, 2944, 3069
  Obediah, 2104, 2308

FOSTER
  Susan, 1322, 1397

FRANSCISCO, Franscisko, Fransisco
  Barent, 242, 421
  Elizabeth, 1437
  Francis, 137, 197
  Henry, 829, 908
  Hilda, 1390
  John, 138, 426
  Margaret, 1785

FREDRICKSE
  Margaret, 1987
  Maria, 147-150
  Thomas, 116, 121, 251

Freeland - see VRELAND

Frerikse - see FREDRICKSE

FRIEBOS
  Dorcas, 1272

Fullwood, FULWOOD
  Charles, 1055, 1177

FURGESON, Furguson
  Bridget, 1474-1476, 1636
  John, 1633

INDEX OF PARENTS

INDEX OF PARENTS

JONES (con'd)
Thomas, 608

Jong(h) - see YOUNG

Joons - see JONES

JORDAN
John, 1785

Jureance, Juriance, Jurjaense, Jurreanse, JURRIANSE, Jurryanse
Anna, 2929
Christopher, 972, 1024, 1101, 1150, 1280, 1403, 1627
Elizabeth, 2322, 2610, 2750, 2918
Fred, 2982, 3077, 3170
Garret, 3019, 3106, 3205
George, 2110, 2361, 2499, 2627, 2802, 2941, 3042, 3153
Gerrebrand, 502, 549, 636, 1929, 1937, 2611
Helena, 3033
Herman, 147-152, 203, 267, 393, 394, 396
Janet, 2326, 2579
Jeremiah, 3238
John, 36-39, 971, 1020, 1151, 1282, 1465, 1583, 1779, 2525, 2649, 2742, 2866, 2921, 2995, 3012, 3078, 3094, 3111, 3181, 3197, 3206, 3246
Lena, 1477, 1544, 1776, 1921, 2167, 2309, 2450, 2595, 2754, 2864
Maria, 1198
Metje, 335
Nelly, 1199, 1323, 1541, 2280, 2416, 2518, 2629, 3161
Sarah, 1290, 2264
Thomas, 6-15

Kadmus - see CADMUS

Kaljer - see COLLIER

Kanclen - see CONKLIN

KARNEY
Peter, 2106

Keeler - see KIESLER

KEEN
Alida, 1810

Keersie - see CASE

Keeter - see CARTER

KELSEY
James, 3024

Kemble - see CAMPBELL

KEMPER
Daniel, 1599

KENNEDY
Maria, 1213, 1315, 1405, 1472

KENT
Cornelius, 2286

Kerck, KERK - see also NEWKERK
John, 2325
Lena, 1929, 1937, 2611
Maria, 693
Zachariah, 867, 945, 1035

KEYSER
Margaret, 1430

KIDNEY, Kidnie, Kidny
Jacob, 1947
John, 981, 1705, 1903

KIERSTEAD, Kierstede
Aaron, 2134, 2673
Anna, 1892, 2148, 2323
Catherine, 2405
Dina, 1970, 2165
Henry, 1791
John, 355, 1782, 3155
Lena, 1707, 1867
Margaret, 2194
Rachel, 1781
Sietje - see Lena

Kiese - see CASE

Kieslaar, KIESLER
Catherine, 2046
George, 1422, 1713, 1885
Gertrude, 2825, 2903
John, 2253, 2332, 2448, 2530
Maria, Polly, 2428, 2583, 2686, 2834, 2943

KIND
Anna, 145, 146
Elias, 407, 408, 429
Jacob, 409
Simon, 430

KING - see also KONING
Aaron, 1706, 1866, 1910, 2127, 2128, 2216
Abraham, 2058
Anna, 1149
John, 1813, 1825, 2023, 2071
Rachel, 2073
Stephen, 1802, 1994

KINGSLAND
Anna, 2089

KINGSLAND (con'd)
  Catherine, 1428, 1521
  Henry, 1211, 1307
  Hester, 232, 315
  Isaac, 184, 1390, 1835
  Margaret, 1156, 1225, 1438, 2572,
   2687, 2790, 2879, 2930, 3038, 3190
  Maria, 1262, 1400, 1789, 2013
  Rachel, 1079, 1216, 1431
  William, 1241, 1443, 1507, 1532, 1653,
   1788, 1975, 2204

KIP
  Anna, 766, 1000, 1119, 1387
  Blandina, 988
  Catherine, 220, 2780, 2973, 3071, 3177
  Catlintje, 571, 777
  Cornelia, 960
  Cornelius, 235
  Elizabeth, 660, 714
  Eva, 526, 597, 690, 750, 830, 918,
   1098
  Helen, 711
  Henry, 211, 580, 1953, 2094, 2639,
   2784
  Heylie, 3091
  Isaac, 72, 188, 306
  Janet, 529, 620, 670, 722, 756, 791,
   843, 919, 2039, 2855
  John, 1009, 3126, 3252
  Lena, 624, 798
  Margaret, 1761, 1989, 2710
  Maria, 3157, 3158
  Peter, 1014, 1442, 1566, 1674, 3129
  Rachel, 987, 1179
  Reyner, 2674, 2789

KIRRIS
  Aaron, 2033

Kirstien - see CHRISTIE

Klaesen, Klaesse - see CLAWSON

KLERCKEN
  Maria, 863

Knolin - see NOLAN

Kocjefer - see COCKEFER

Kock - see COOK

Kockefer - see COCKEFER

Koeck - see COOK

Koejeman - see COEYMAN

Koerte - see COERTE

Koerten - see COURTEN

Koeyeman - see COEYMAN

Kogh - see COGG

KOLVE
  Sarah, 286

KONING(h) - see also KING
  Aaron, 1404, 1811
  Anna, 1777
  David, 1259
  Francis, 1111, 1439
  Henry, 951, 1019
  John, 790, 901, 1185, 1229

Kook - see COOK

Kool - see COLE

Kraen - see KREIN

KRANCK
  Abraham, 2233
  Isaac, 1997

KREIN
  Anna, 184
  David, 1873

Kyrstede - see KIERSTEAD

LABACH
  Henry, 2590, 2694, 2800, 2889, 2987,
   3083, 3179

LAKE
  Elizabeth, 1838, 2205
  Gilbert, 2463

LAM
  John, 1038

LAMBART
  John, 957

LANSINGH
  Garret, 1621

LAROE
  Abigail, 1470, 2020
  Henry, 1878, 2111, 2306, 2434, 2691

Laurence - see LAWRENCE

LAURIER
  Susan, 1533

LAWRENCE
  Elizabeth, 1981
  Stephen, 2107

Leback - see LABACH

Lenkford - see LINFORD

LESLIE
  Edmund, 1262

INDEX OF PARENTS

Leuwis, LEWIS
Abigail, 978
John, 996
Maria, 3001
Samuel, 3108

LEZIER
Henrietta, 973

Liense - see LINSEY

Linckfoot, Linckford, Linkfoot, Linkford,
LINFORD
Abraham, 2410
Herman, 2338
Jacob, 1343
Rebecca, 1552, 1747, 2214, 2398, 2399
Thomas, 2197, 2423

LINSEY, Linsie
Janet, 1708
Maria, 1301

LISK
Anna, 1332, 1401, 2130

LIVINGSTON
Catherine, 1487

Locy, Loosie, Lose, LOSEE, Losie
Betsy, 3239
John, 2480, 2651, 2797, 2893, 2979,
3116

LOUW
Elizabeth, 1382
John, 71

Louwis - see LEWIS

Ludlam, Ludlouw, LUDLOW
Cornelius, 2684, 2808, 2951
John, 392, 393, 1717, 1887, 2164, 2365,
2384, 2541, 2678, 3133
Richard, 1637, 1952

Luthem, LUTHEN, Luthin
Elizabeth, 1049, 1112, 1159, 1258,
1331, 1413, 1520, 1634, 1861
Peter, 1212
Sarah, 1285

Mac (_____) - see MC (_____)

Maccarty, Mackerthy, Mackerty - see
MC CARTY

Macknes, Macknesh, Mackniss, Mackness -
see MC NIES

Mandeviel, MANDEVILLE, Mandevyl
Alida, 2338
Ariantje, 957

MANDEVILLE (con'd)
Catherine, 2092, 3240
Elizabeth, 2140
Giles, 389, 441, 920, 1011, 1153, 1415,
1766
Henry, 198, 275, 361
Hester, 1594, 1697, 1845, 2055, 2239
John, 1922, 2074, 2336
Lena, 1991
Margaret, 1974
Martina, 2024
Rachel, 2087
Sietje, 1824, 2072, 2312

Marcelisse, Marcelusse - see MARSELIS

Marines, MARINUS
Anna, 2939, 3031, 3141, 3212
David, 472, 525, 603, 671, 760, 1188
John, 1672, 2854
Margaret, 2776

MARIUS
Elizabeth, 1599

MARSELIS, Marselisse, Marselusse
Anna, 1649
Ariantje, 2795, 3054, 3130, 3209
Claasje, 3129
Cornelius, 2067
Edo, 3091
Helen, 366
Janet, 1348
John, 1883

MARTENSE
Geesje, 238

MARTESSE
Maria, 329

Massaker, Masseker - see MESSEKER

Masselaar - see METSELAER

Mauerse(n), Mauritsz(en), Mauritzs,
Maurusse - see MORRISON

MC CARTY
Abigail, 1505
John, 800, 1961, 2157, 2490

MC COWEN
James, 2957, 3066

MC CREA
Catherine, 1404, 1910, 2127

MC GREGOR
James, 3207

McKray - see MC CREA

MC LEAN
Nelly, 1633
William, 1738

MC NIES
Anna, 1856, 2053, 2226
Margaret, 2101, 2285, 2432
Samuel, 897, 948

MEAD, Meed, Meet
Christina, 320
Elizabeth, 869
Elsie, 341, 383
Giles, 368
Janet, 1293, 1394
John, 213, 326
Margaret, 1345, 1868
Peter, 550
Rachel, 2696, 2734

Mendevyl - see MANDEVILLE

Messecer, Messecor, MESSEKER
(_____), 2768
Abraham, 486, 487
Eva, 2216
Femmetje, 362
Helmich, 2021
Henry, 1976
John, 424, 478, 2037, 2250
Lea, 2126
Ludwich, 433, 489
Maria, 2256
Nelly, 176, 294, 347, 385
Sally, 2294, 2377, 2502, 2688, 2798

Messejaar, METSELAER
Abraham, 1392, 1613
Anna, 2681

MEYER(S)
Catherine, 802, 891, 995, 1076
Cornelius, 2011, 2254, 2470, 2585, 2670
John, 1840

MILES
William, 3228

MILLER
Elizabeth, 2041
Maria, 1699, 2065, 2263, 2392

MILLIDS
Jacob, 272

MILLS
William, 1865

Moeritszen - see MORRISON

MOLLEN
Bernard, 358

MONTAINE, Montanje
Isaac, 303, 1276
Nelly, 1668, 1855, 2049, 2242, 2376, 2493, 2615, 2739

MOOR(E)
Anna, 1369, 2018, 2621
John, 2046
Rachel, 2022, 2118

MORGEN
Ruth, 858, 968

MORRELL
Patience, 1582

MORRIS(ON), Mourusse
Abraham, 1594, 1697, 1845, 2055, 2239
Alida, 1283
David, 935, 985
Elizabeth, 1755, 2133
Frances, 1020, 1282, 1465, 1583, 1779
Fred, 415, 444
Henry, 1832
Isaac, 445
Lena, 937, 1068, 1196, 1278, 1364, 1457, 1550
Maria, 856, 991, 1086, 1356
Molly, 901
Morris, 1093, 1384, 2096
Peter, 419
Syntje - see Frances

MUNSON, Munyon
Mary, 2608, 2794

Myer - see MEYER

Neefius, Neefje(e), Neefjes, Nefius -
see NEVIS

Nes - see VAN NESS

NEVIS
Cornelius, 934
Fytje, 906, 1064, 1304, 1528, 1763, 1864
Garret, 2014
John, 223, 356
Jutje - see FYTJE
Maria, 1857

NEWKERK, etc - see also KERK
Catlintje, 3188
Janet, 1023, 1114, 1165
Jemima, 598, 664

Nexen - see NIXON

INDEX OF PARENTS

INDEX OF PARENTS

PHILIPS, Phillips
  Elsie, 771
  Jacob, 874
  Maria, 1730, 1871
  Matthew, 440
  Polly, 2436

PHOENIX
  Catherine, 1221

Pichstoon, Pickstoon, PICKSTON
  Anna, 2626, 2715, 2810, 2860, 2963,
    3044, 3125, 3217
  Anthony, 766, 1000, 1119, 1387
  Daniel, 2474, 2475, 2689, 2778
  Dirk, 1283
  Henry, 2574, 2721, 3016
  Joseph, 2390

PIER
  Abraham, 477
  Anthony, 438
  Catherine, 572, 832
  Cornelius, 1612
  Daniel, 1793
  Garret, 2608
  Henrietta, 618
  Isaac, 2045
  Jacob, 1372, 1728
  John, 665, 707, 765, 810, 882, 1091
  Matthew, 2621
  Peter, 2294, 2377, 2502, 2688, 2798
  Susan, 1677, 1872

Pieterse(n), Pieterssen - see PETERSON

Pingman - see PENGMAN

Poel - see PAULSON

POST
  Aaron, 947, 1417, 1597, 2003, 2582
  Abraham, 794, 872, 2335, 2990, 2991
  Adrian, 105-108, 254, 338, 543, 557,
    609, 653, 694, 708, 746, 757, 799,
    860, 923, 1052, 1124, 1224, 1352,
    1628, 1724, 1764, 1875, 2131, 2161,
    2328, 2467, 2663, 2703, 2781, 2845,
    2892, 2902
  Anna, 528, 698, 719, 880, 887, 1028,
    1587, 1669, 1850, 1851, 2054, 2465,
    2679, 2828, 3050, 3151
  Beletje, 2437, 2523
  Betty - see Metje
  Caspar, 2275, 2481, 2835
  Catherine, 509, 956, 1155, 1242,
    1617, 1672, 1709, 2302
  Catlintje, 2198, 2355, 2506, 2713,
    2823, 2915, 2942, 3014

POST (con'd)
  Claasje, 3086
  Clara, 162-167
  Cornelius, 737, 812, 1007, 1215, 2208,
    2661, 2725, 2788, 2884, 2994, 3194
  Dirk, 3199
  Egbert, 2907
  Elizabeth, 462, 523, 971, 975, 1069,
    1151, 1264, 1359, 1530, 1574, 1960,
    1962, 2069, 2142, 2224, 2243, 2380,
    2457, 2490, 2593, 2759, 2947, 3121,
    3169, 3210
  Francis, 492, 560, 627, 646, 729
  Fytje, 1279, 1808
  Garret, 16-23, 178, 253, 360, 471, 674,
    2360, 2456, 2600
  Geesje, 280, 359
  Gerritje, 1571
  Hartman, 2139, 2276, 2406, 2539, 2666,
    2769, 2869, 2940, 3040, 3139, 3222,
    3223
  Helen, 585, 705, 741
  Helmich, 524, 625, 730, 1032, 1071,
    1182, 1183, 1286, 1377, 1378, 1486,
    1554, 1759, 1912, 2934, 3056, 3136,
    3167
  Henry, 282, 357, 871, 1006, 1062,
    1142, 1351, 1473, 1575, 2044, 2114,
    2236, 2277, 2444, 2549, 2656, 2758,
    2958, 3103
  Jacob, 73, 74, 291, 395, 491, 561, 601,
    673, 2307, 2394, 2438, 2578, 3162
  Janet, 193, 573, 1223, 1317, 1432,
    2063, 2219, 2249, 2494, 2584, 2890,
    3019, 3070, 3106, 3128, 3205, 3214
  John, 24-29, 181, 261, 276, 277, 364,
    386, 620, 906, 1064, 1304, 1509, 1528,
    1567, 1641, 1650, 1763, 1857, 1859,
    1860, 1884, 1938, 1993, 2141, 2190,
    2247, 2349, 2459, 2495, 2601, 2604,
    2644, 2706, 2711, 2827, 2850, 2948,
    3030, 3115, 3132, 3192, 3196
  Lea, 1116, 1265
  Lena, 644, 786, 797, 936, 1097
  Marcellus, 490, 611, 2462, 2637, 3213
  Margaret, 1801, 1870, 2052, 2220, 2299,
    2676, 3095, 3100
  Maria, 1531, 1624, 1648, 1733, 1743,
    1944, 2016, 2045, 2067, 2221, 2397,
    2426, 2571, 2574, 2576, 2721, 2756,
    3016
  Metje, 2875, 2966, 3118
  Michael, 1631
  Peter, 505, 740
  Pryntje, 2719
  Rachel, 1946, 3168

ROME
  Henry, 1830
  Maria, 216, 310, 374
  William, 249

ROMEYN, Romyn
  Eva, 1762, 1917
  Lena, 1902, 2098, 2337, 2552, 3112
  Lydia, 2418
  Mary, 3225
  Myntje, 1652
  Sarah, 2004

Roome - see ROME

Roorbach - see ROHRBACH

Roos, ROSS - see also BOSS
  Maria, 1524, 1610, 1889

Rothan, Rutham, RUTHAN , Retan
  Barent, 1167   mos.
  Daniel, 273, (910, 950, 1030, 1106)   stegg
  David, 868, 993, 1072, 1127
  Elizabeth, 1949, 2469, 2573, 2785,
   2937
  Eva, 594, 655, 785
  Geesje, 2401
  John, 1275, 1838, 2205
  Paul, 274

Rycke - see RIKER

Ryer, Ryerse(n) - see REYERSEN

Ryke, Ryker - see RIKER

SANDERS(ON)
  Anna, 161, 239
  Catherine, 105-108, 254
  Harmtje, 137, 197
  Peter, 183, 295, 391

Sandfordt, Sandfort, Sandvoord, Sand-
 voort, Sandvordt, SANFORD, Santfort
  Anna, 511
  Janet, 715, 753, 803, 894, 970, 1034,
   1107
  John, 1220, 1434
  Maria, Polly, 1802, 1994, 3013
  Michael, 1770
  Rachel, 1095
  Sarah, 898, 1067, 1197, 1269, 1376

Scheerman - see SHERMAN

SCHERMERHORN, etc
  Fytje, 2006

Schidmoor - see SKIDMORE

Schoomaker, SCHOONMAKER
  Catherine, 3155

SCHOONMAKER (con'd)
  Daniel, 1962, 2142, 2243, 2380, 2457,
   2593, 2759
  Helena, 1988, 2372, 2443, 2589
  Henry, 1134, 1210, 1320
  Isaac, 2735, 2812, 2924, 3067, 3200
  Lydia, 2358, 2519, 2655, 2796, 2886,
   2984, 3055, 3145, 3243
  Maria, 2485, 2577
  Martin, 762

Schuiler, SCHUYLER
  Philip, 232, 315, 398

Scidmoor, Scidmore - see SKIDMORE

Scisco - see FRANCISCO

Secor(n) - see SEGER

SEELY
  Samuel, 1582

SEGER
  David, 1474-1476, 1636

Segg - see STEGG

SHAROW
  Benjamin, 1854

SHEPHERD
  Cornelius, 1661, 1784, 1996, 2201

SHERMAN
  Jacob, 347

Shipard, Shiphard - see SHEPHERD

SHIPPY
  William, 2388

Shitterlem, Shitterlen, Shitterlin -
 see CHITTERLIN

Sichels - see SICKELSE

Sichlers - see SICKLER

SICKELS
  Fytje, 87-91
  John, 741, 786
  Maria, 92

SICKLER, Siglar, Sigler
  Abigail, 1895, 2062, 2188
  Abraham, 2251, 2339
  Daniel, 2147, 2260
  Eunice, 1298, 1399
  Jacob, 725, 770, 890, 976, 1053, 1337,
   1338, 1454
  James, 816
  John, 1824, 2072, 2312
  Margaret, 1526, 1576, 1651

INDEX OF PARENTS

SPIER (con'd)
  Jacob (con'd), 1552, 1747, 1967, 1987,
    2073, 2214, 2398, 2399
  Janet, 126-131, 191, 977, 1174, 1226,
    1448, 1655, 1834, 2085, 2305, 2510,
    2527
  John, 599, 663, 764, 818, 854, 903,
    911, 974, 994, 1003, 1110, 1117,
    1170, 1200, 1207, 1316, 1573, 1683,1445
    1727, 1814, 1957, 2069, 2120, 2156,
    2224, 2231, 2291, 2402, 2559, 2701,
    2825, 2888, 2903
  Lea, 252, 1451, 1712, 1837, 1908,
    2091, 2182, 2255, 2296
  Lena, 1022, 1202, 1391, 2056, 2071
  Magdalena, 1825
  Margaret, 1154, 1248, 1419, 1726,
    1980
  Maria, 622, 790, 1166, 1222, 1330,
    1478, 1560, 1719, 1925, 2178, 3085,
    3173, 3250
  Matthew, 1888, 2159, 2374, 2517, 2868,
    2872
  Peter, 3023
  Rachel, 942, 981, 1104, 1512, 1619,
    1705, 1903
  Reyner, 1085, 1406, 1495, 1496, 1822
  Sally, 2661
  Samuel, 2452, 2532, 2634, 2723, 2858,
    2923, 3215
  Sarah, 867, 945, 1035, 1253, 1620,
    2411
  Thyna, 2590, 2694, 2800, 2987, 3083,
    3179

Ssmith - see SMITH

STAATS, Staets
  Catlintje, 133-136

Stager - see STEEGER

Stagg - see STEGG

STEEB
  Sally, 1057

STEEGER
  Abraham, 464, 1345, 1868
  Catlintje, 242
  Christopher, 1357, 1479, 1600, 1714,
    1901, 2150
  Dirk, 317
  Elizabeth, 296, 370
  Henry, 1083, 1268, 1380
  John, 2056
  Maria, 177, 319, 1080, 2455, 2597,
    2714, 2931, 3015
  Sarah, 921, 1012, 1540, 1823, 2059

Steg - see STEGG

Steger(s) - see STEEGER

STEGG, Stegh
  Anna, 1768, 1995, 2286, 2551
  Dirk, 2856
  Henrietta, 2078
  Jacob, 590, 667, 735, 1853, 2103, 2358,
    2519, 2655, 2737, 2796, 2865, 2886,
    2960, 2984, 3049, 3055, 3145, 3150
  James, 3243
  John, 229, 1166, 1222, 1330, 1478,
    1560, 1719, 1925, 2178, 2261, 2415,
    2605
  Joseph, 1382
  Margaret, 183, 295, 391, 910, 950,
    1030, 1106
  Maria, Matia, 2003, 2582, 2752, 2809,
    2887
  Nelly, 897, 948
  Thomas, 182, 234, 342

STEINMETS, Steynmets
  Anna, 185, 225, 334, 351, 674, 1441
  Ariantje, 915, 1031
  Benjamin, 268
  Christopher, 955, 1121
  Garret, 1198
  Henrietta, 1094, 1277
  Hester, 606, 668
  John, 509
  Joris, 551, 638
  Judith, 151, 152, 203, 267, 393, 394,
    396
  Sarah, 721, 831, 986, 1131, 1274

Stheg - see STEGG

STILLWELL, Stillwill
  Elizabeth, 540, 692

STIVES
  Samuel, 736

STOCKHOLM
  Catherine, 2667

STRAET
  Janet, 6-15
  Lea, 16-23

STREEH
  Lucretia, 535

STRYKER
  Elizabeth, 838, 902, 1008

Stymets, Stynmets, Stynmetz - see
  STEINMETS

INDEX OF PARENTS

INDEX OF PARENTS

INDEX OF PARENTS

VAN RIPER (con'd)
  Herman, 1367, 1451, 1712, 1908, 2015,
    2182, 2805, 2988
  Isaac, 545, 630, 724, 895, 2752, 2809,
    2887
  Jacob, 752, 837, 952, 1016, 1116,
    1169, 1236, 1265, 1385, 1470, 1685,
    1686, 1778, 2020, 2123, 2149, 2155,
    2270, 2287, 2404, 2409, 2427, 2520,
    2534, 2654, 2748, 2840, 3105
  Janet, 539, 547, 700, 703, 767, 1689,
    1883, 1939, 2134, 2237, 2673, 2716,
    2813, 2814
  John, 541, 606, 647, 668, 706, 763,
    819, 900, 956, 961, 1063, 1155, 1233,
    1242, 1273, 1335, 1449, 1543, 1639,
    1698, 1756, 1809, 1998, 2004, 2019,
    2240, 2367, 2521, 3003, 3121, 3210,
    3244
  Judith, 1368, 1468, 1758
  Lea, 518, 769, 1744, 1916, 2185, 2609
  Lena, 1559
  Margaret, 1771, 1964, 1985, 2244,
    2564, 2695, 2935
  Maria, 475, 530, 1027, 1120, 1204,
    1324, 1463, 1518, 1675, 1734, 2360,
    2410, 2456, 2600, 3108
  Marinus, 648, 685, 849, 1049, 1112,
    1159, 1258, 1331, 1413, 1520, 1634,
    1861
  Metje, 1032, 1071, 1182, 1183, 1286,
    1377, 1378, 1486, 1554
  Molly, 2010
  Neesje, 3199
  Nicholas, 3180
  Philip, 1754, 1852, 2267, 2504
  Pietertje, 1506, 1586, 1862, 2084
  Rachel, 1961, 2157
  Sietje, 1579, 1710, 1803
  Simon, 582, 796, 3159
  Styntje, 1711, 1969
  Thomas, 536, 615, 654, 699, 717, 847,
    884, 2901, 2965, 3026, 3154, 3220
  Ulrich, 1326, 1494, 1663, 1863

VAN SANT
  Hester, 1396
  Janet, 1070
  Maria, 925, 1002, 1125, 1266, 1420,
    1602, 1780

VAN SCHYVEN
  Elizabeth, 997, 1050, 1145, 1790

Van Seil - see VAN SEYL

Van Sendt, Van Sent - see VAN SANT

VAN SEYL
  Abraham, 367
  Dirk, 236
  Elizabeth, 66, 227, 348
  John, 224
  Rachel, 259, 382
  Stephen, 294, 385, 422

Van Sisco - see FRANSCISCO

VAN STEE
  Anna, 268

VAN SYCE, Van Sys
  John, 3137, 3218

Van Vechte, VAN VECHTEN, Van Vegte(n)
  Catherine, 2012
  Janet, 708, 746
  John, 466, 528, 719

VAN VELSEN
  Thomas, 2933

VAN VOORHEES(en), Van Vorhese
  Catherine, 2792, 2900, 3005, 3109,
    3253
  Elizabeth, 1009, 1977
  Rachel, 212

VAN VORST
  Caspar, 2542, 2680
  Catherine, 566
  Cornelius, 604, 679, 817
  Fytje, 549, 636
  Garret, 243, 349, 1701, 1797, 1843,
    2158, 2298, 2528
  Henry, 2626, 2715, 2810, 2860, 2963,
    3044, 3125, 3217
  Hillegond, 758, 820, 896, 1025, 1118,
    1195, 1344
  Janet, 579
  Maria, 569, 645, 776, 828, 909
  Waling, 605, 732, 813, 984, 1100, 3157,
    3158

VAN WAGENEN, Van Wagening(en)
  Catherine, 460, 461, 496
  Catlimtje, 1209
  Fytje, 840, 876, 1547
  Garret, 696, 1143, 1238, 1988, 2443,
    2589
  Helena, 1826, 2378
  Henry, 498, 562, 687, 1141
  Herman, 593, 3191
  Hessel, 710
  Jacob, 457, 533, 629, 684, 3087, 3114
  Janet, 2079, 2279
  John, 1630, 1879, 2138
  Lena, 1388, 1534, 1645

INDEX OF PARENTS

VRELAND (con'd)
Claasje, 676, 749, 815, 875, 1010, 1059
Clarissa, 3219
Charles, 3233
Cornelia, 2907
Cornelius, 584, 1175, 1299, 1504, 1569, 1817, 2246, 2344, 2441, 2472, 2566, 2618, 2675, 2757, 2936, 3039, 3053, 3127, 3216
Dirk, 109-115, 244, 840, 876, 1547
Echje, 57-61, 209
Edo, 2905, 2981, 3059, 3148
Elias, 237, 322, 556, 641, 713, 1530, 1648, 1801, 2299, 2774, 2899, 3100, 3143
Elizabeth, 198, 275, 361, 1340, 1508, 1596, 1717, 1773, 1887, 2164, 2384, 2541, 2678
Elsie, 841, 926, 1040
Enoch, 309, 960, 1041, 1044, 1096, 1133, 1163, 1201, 1312, 1348, 1407, 1503, 1616, 1765, 1950, 2304, 2705, 3096, 3189
Eva, 2735, 2812, 2924, 3067, 3111, 3197, 3200
Fytje, 1499
Garret, 661, 742, 889, 2022, 2118, 2244, 2564, 2695, 2935
Geesje, 1800
Gertrude, 609, 653, 694, 757, 799, 860, 923, 1052
Gouda, 2362, 2466
Hartman, 390, 499, 633, 2198, 2355, 2506, 2713, 2823, 2942, 3093
Helen, 250
Henrietta, 1998
Henry, 2640, 2747, 2870, 2959, 3076, 3156, 3251
Hessel, 540, 692
Hester, 495, 596
Isaac, 1652, 1841, 2060, 2273, 2453
Jacob, 698, 880, 1028, 1306, 1687, 1891, 2038, 2235, 2369, 2373, 2439, 2458, 2479, 2587, 2625, 2682, 2728, 2826, 2917
Janet, 328, 600, 717, 779, 827, 871, 922, 1006, 1062, 1130, 1142, 1351, 1361, 1635, 1748, 2128, 2269, 2433, 2557, 2677, 2816, 2916, 3025, 3037, 3185
John, 335, 459, 503, 573, 575, 616, 652, 656, 712, 748, 808, 855, 939, 980, 998, 1042, 1048, 1122, 1146, 1174, 1217, 1226, 1243, 1409, 1421, 1448, 1510, 1562, 1655, 1796, 1834

VRELAND (con'd)
John (con'd), 1896, 2079, 2085, 2162, 2279, 2320, 2510, 2770, 2772, 2897, 2945, 2954, 3057, 3060, 3119, 3131
Joris, 341, 383
Lea, 2082, 2555
Margaret, 301, 844, 938, 941, 1039
Maria, 595, 686, 743, 2155, 2594, 2683, 2746, 2806, 2850, 2977, 3090
Martje, 116-121, 251, 284
Metje, 330, 1618, 1723, 2000, 2206, 2477, 2614, 2765, 2867, 2974
Michael, 577, 610, 640, 773, 780, 859, 883, 949, 1013, 1058, 1135, 1239, 1640, 1902, 2098, 2337, 2552, 2913, 3036, 3104, 3201
Myntje, 1703, 1893, 2115, 2317, 2483, 2602
Nelly, 536, 1481, 2545, 2755, 2861, 2964, 3065
Nicholas, 997, 1050, 1145, 1790
Peter, 805, 943, 944, 1295, 1553
Rachel, 2581
Polly, 2632, 2731, 2843, 3029
Roelof, 931, 1051, 3101
Sally, 2961
Sarah, 1570, 1647, 3229
Sietje, 1490, 1556, 1644, 1772
Tiesje, 2537

WALDROM
Adolph, 1221
Joseph, 1882
Maria, 1250

Wallen - see WHALEN

Walls - see WELLS

WEAVER
Christina, 688, 728, 857

WEBB
Ezechiel, 2972

Weever - see WEAVER

WELLS
Phoebe, 2369, 2458, 2587, 2682

WELSTEAD
Susan, 1434

Weselse, WESSELS(E)
Anna, 1206, 1444, 1623
Evert, 52-56, 190, 266
Henry, 1288, 1360
Lucas, 552, 689, 1585
Maria, 514, 515, 564
Wessel, 628, 807, 929

Westerveld, WESTERVELT
  Anna, 217, 290
  Catlintje, 2791
  Cornelius, 132, 264, 2381, 2565
  Dorothy, 1936, 1943, 2218, 2497
  Eliza, 3232
  Elizabeth, 2990, 2991
  Geesje, 278
  John, 281, 1918, 2040, 2507
  Margaret, 983, 1037, 2599, 2712, 2838,
    2997
  Peter, 2535, 2685, 2877
  Rachel, 696

Wever - see WEAVER

WHALEN
  Rachel, 2108, 2109

WHEELER
  Benjamin, 2787
  Maria, 1595
  William, 771

WHITE
  John, 841, 926, 1040
  Margaret. 1720, 1904

WHITLOCK
  Maria (Polly), 2616, 2803, 2880, 2967,
    3061, 3166

Wieler, Willer - see WHEELER

Willes - see WILLIS

WILLIAMS
  Jemima, 1836, 2095

WILLIS
  Abraham, 1709, 2302
  John, 775
  Margaret, 1366, 1464
  Maria, 725, 770, 816, 890, 976, 1053,
    1337, 1338, 1454

WILSON
  Sarah, 2955

WINNE
  Catherine, 587
  Janet, 2057
  John, 1436, 1986
  Lea, 1233, 1335, 1449, 1543, 1639,
    1809, 2019, 2097, 2225, 2240, 2353,
    2367, 2488, 2521
  Peter, 1253
  Pietertje, 1303, 1798, 1965, 2176

WINTERS
  John, 1057

Wite - see WHITE

Withlock, Witlock - see WHITLOCK

WOOD
  Elizabeth, 2390, 2474, 2475, 2689,
    2778
  Joseph, 485
  Lea, 2199
  Lydia, 2638

WOORTENDYK
  Cornelia, 196

Woud - see WOOD

WOUTERS(E)
  Anthony, 905
  Emma, 1164
  Garret, 1571
  Henry, 2998, 3097
  Marcellus, 2719
  Margaret, 1383
  Styntje, 1811

WRIGHT - see also RIKER
  Albert, 1806, 1955
  Margaret, 2125
  Sarah, 1714

Wynand, WYNANT(S)
  Catherine, 527, 617, 697, 739, 809,
    886, 966
  Joris, 1290

Wyt - see WHITE

Xanders - see SANDERS

YORKS
  Elias, 1958, 2184, 2489, 2612

YOUNG
  Abigail, 2389, 2460
  Eleanor, 2106
  Jacob, 2092
  Jane, 2451
  Maria, 1461, 1564
  Peter, 302

Yurreance, Yurrianse - see JURRIANSE

Zaboiski, ZABRISKI(E)
  Albert, 1982
  Benjamin, 3073, 3117
  Caspar, 460, 461, 496, 2039
  Gertrude, 1123, 3159
  Jacob, 2403, 2940, 3031, 3141, 3212
  Polly, 2335

Zanderson - see SANDERS

INDEX OF SPONSORS

For note regarding the use of this index, see page 150

INDEX OF SPONSORS

Brouwer - see BROWER

Brouwn - see BROWN

BROWER
Abraham, 1904
Anna, 823, 1036, 1282, 1290, 1544, 2110, 2416, 2649
Ariantje, 218
Catherine, 754
David, 701
Elizabeth, 764, 768
Garret, 1101
Hessel, 514, 689, 807
Janet, 2125
John, 754
Maria, 300, 361, 721, 915
Metje, 447, 724
Ulrich, 300

BROWN - see also BRUYN
Anthony, 1390
Hester, 1576
John, 1464, 2219
Reyner, 1443

Bruin, BRUYN - see also BROWN
Alida, 161
Anna, 231
Anthony, 1526
Barent, 231, 381
Elizabeth, 1418
Femmetje, 489
Helena, 100, 153, 174
Henry, 389, 1253
Hilda, 1788
Hillegond, 873, 1721
Isaac, 770, 775, 1303
Jacob, 1437
Janet, 275, 1691, 2586
John, 339, 342, 489, 829, 1798
Lena, 131, 188, 232
Maria, 1526
Rachel, 1897
Rebecca, 478
Reyner, 908, 1383, 1813, 2217
Sarah, 362
Sietje, 391

Burd - see BORD

Burger - see BERGER

BURHANS
Catherine, 2782
John, 2782

BURK
Mary, 1172

Burtens - see BERDAN

BUTLER
John, 2201

BUTTERS
Mary, 968

Buys - see BOICE

Byard - see BAYARD

Cackefer - see COCKEFER

CADMUS
Abraham, 546, 578, 664, 1810
Andrew, 1567, 2716
Anna, 843, 1066
Catherine, 570
Cornelia, 1689
Cornelius, 1650, 1775, 1985, 2503, 2662
Dirk, 1026, 2739, 2992
Efje, 1939
Frances, 981
Fytje, 542
Gertrude, 546, 2190
Hartman, 506
Isaac, 452, 471, 660, 798
John, 542, 600, 804
Lea, 506, 2446
Maria, 740, 812, 814, 907, 919, 933, 1127, 1137, 1209, 1517, 1582, 1670
Peter, 1260
Rachel, 678
Thomas, 293, 681, 789

CAIRNS
John, 1977

Calyer - see COLLIER

CAMMENA
Engelbert, 1427

CAVELIER, etc
John, 358

Cha - see DOUCHEE

CHILDS
Lea, 2320

CHRISTIE, Christien, Christyn, Chrystien, Cirstien
Aenter, 454
Anna, 282
Elizabeth, 395, 729, 741, 871
James, 2144, 2309, 2722, 2757
Maria, 254, 357

CLARKSON
(_____), 1205

INDEX OF SPONSORS

INDEX OF SPONSORS

INDEX OF SPONSORS

INDEX OF SPONSORS

HARVEY
Elizabeth, 538

HASENFLOEG
Conrad, 1076

HELLING
Agnes, 139
Margaret, 143

HELM(E)
Anna, 2722, 2757
Arthur, 1249
Cornelius, 2446
Henry, 1610
Maria, 1610
Peter, 2151
Priscilla, 117, 147
Susan, 2378

HELMERICHSE, Helmerigse, Helmingse
Gerritje, 3
Peter, 58, 65, 78

HEN
Sarah, 1951

Hendirukse, HENDRIKSE
Anna, 380
Garret, 23, 316

HENNION
Abraham, 355
Anna, 1124, 1223, 1352, 1560, 1617, 2876
Anthony, 2066
David, 9
Janet, 1535
Margaret, 3011

HERMANS
Garret, 86
Geurtje, 8
Reykje, 7
Ryke, 36

Herris - see HARRIS

Hertje - see HARTE

HESSELS(E)
Anna, 97, 103, 158
Claasje, 257
Elizabeth, 102
Gertrude, 273
Peter, 257, 455
Rachel, 155
Vroutje, 81, 156, 206

Hoghoort - see HAGHERT

Holm, Hom - see HELM

HONEYSOET, Honeysoot
Maria, 1522
Naomi, 1471

Hooms - see HELM

Hoorn - see VAN HORN

Hoppe(n), HOPPER
Andrew, 96, 172
Anna, 2953
Catherine, 2693
Clara, 722, 756
Garret, 1230, 2876
Henry, 2273
Janet, 1101, 1627
Jemima, 2844
Maria, 702
Matthew, 1192

Horley - see HURLEY

HOSK
Nicholas, 416

Houten - see VAN HOUTEN

Houwerd, HOWARD
John, 276

Huin - see TERHUNE

Huisman(s) - see HUYSMAN

HURLEY
Catherine, 1661, 1688

HUSTON
Elsie, 1415
Paul, 889, 1316

HUYSMAN
Abraham, 220, 1482
Arientje, 178
Arthur, 1199
Isaac, 484
Jacob, 2641
Janet, 920
John, 620, 920
Maria, 620

IMMIT
Anna, 192

INTEREST
Christian, 1416

JACKSON
Peter, 3222

JACOBS, Jacobusse
(_____), 2200
Aaron, 2405
Adrian, 924, 1343, 1385

INDEX OF SPONSORS

KING(h) - see also KONING
Anna, 1653
John, 1866
Rachel, 1149

KINGSLAND
Aaron, 1216
Anna, 1532
Edmund, 184
Henry, 1532
Isaac, 1211
Isabel, 1507
Janet, 1216
John, 1225
Margaret, 1241, 1262, 1298
Maria, 1521, 2007
William, 1507

KIP
Anna, 624, 660, 714, 755, 760, 989
Blandina, 1260
Catlintje, 621, 677, 1000, 1050
Cornelia, 1014, 2493
Elizabeth, 211, 526
Elsie, 2287
Eva, 451, 626
Garret, 580
Helena, 670
Henry, 1674, 1891, 2632, 3129, 3177
Isaac, 2789
Jacob, 235, 306, 399
Janet, 594, 937, 1626, 1669, 1674, 1687
John, 750, 1055, 1114
Lena, 399, 466, 777
Nicasie, 526, 918
Peter, 1090, 1953
Rachel, 587
Reyner, 2710
Sarah, 798
Vroutje, 845

Kockefer - see COCKEFER

Koeck - see COOK

Koejeman - see COEYMAN

Koek - see COOK

Koerten - see COURTEN

Kogh - see COGG

KOLVE
Sarah, 270

KONING(H) - see also KING
Henry, 901
Janet, 1436
John, 1053, 1436
William, 818

Kook - see COOK

Kool - see COLE

KRANCK
Abraham, 1997

Krom, KRUM
Janet, 2739, 2992

Kuiper - see COOPER

Kyrstede - see KIERSTEAD

LACOMBA
Margaret, 389

LAKE
Elizabeth, 2670

Landt - see VAN EELSLANDT, VRELAND

LAROE
Henry, 2878
John, 2966
Maria, 1350
Peggy, 2966

Leeck - see LAKE

Lesier - see LEZIER

Lesley, LESLIE
James, 1241, 1262

LEZIER
Maria, 2980

Linckfoot, Linckford, Lineford,
LINFORD, Linkfoot, Linkford
Catherine, 2197
Herman, 1967
Maria, 1967, 2398, 2399
Rebecca, 1426, 1594
Thomas, 1747

Lodlo(o) - see LUDLOW

LOUW, Low
Abraham, 2041
Elizabeth, 1047

Ludlo, LUDLOW
John, 248, 501, 565, 922
Susan, 501

LUTHEN
Herman, 1258
Janet, 1159, 1285
Sarah, 1112

Macarty - see MC CARTY

Macfish - see MC FISH

Mackerty - see MC CARTY

Macknes, Mackniss - see MC NIES

Maclachlin - see MC LAUGHLIN

Madeviel, Mandeviel, MANDEVILLE, Mandevyl
Claasje, 1011
Henry, 2338
John, 1011, 2024
Rachel, 2005
William, 275

Marcelisse, Marcelusse - see MARSELIS

MARINUS
D., 511
David, 2237
John, 1188

MARSCHALK
Elizabeth, 1199

MARSELIS(se), Marselusse
Ed, 2919
Elizabeth, 20, 162
John, 2892
Peter, 1649, 3091

MARTENSE
Maria, 238

MARTESE
Geesje, 221

MATTEUSSE
Gerritje, 10

Maurits, Mauritsz, Mauritzs, Maurusse -
see MORRISON

MC CARTY
John, 1505, 1874

MC FISH
Abraham, 2303

McKnies - see MC NIES

McLaclin, MC LAUGHLIN
Lena, 2050, 2314

MC NIES, McNish
Anna, 1478
Jacob, 2101
John, 1995
Margaret, 1856

MEAD
Aaron, 1293
Giles, 213
Janet, 1268, 1353
John, 288, 550
Peter, 341, 383
Styntje, 368

MEASE
Sally, 2022

Meed, Meet - see MEAD

MERREL
Maria, 248, 393

Merselisse - see MARSELIS

Messecer, MESSEKER
Abraham, 422
Elizabeth, 1671, 1976
Femmetje, 294
Henry, 294, 362, 2037, 2294
Ludwich, 2126
Maria, 325, 422
Sarah, 2037
Susan, 1329

Messelaar, METSELAER
Elizabeth, 2213

MEYER(S)
Anna, 182
Catherine, 1955

MICHEL
John, 2007

MILLAGS
Anna, 480

MILLER
Charlotte, 392
Elizabeth, 438

MILLIDS
Anna, 272
John, 272

Moeritszen - see MORRISON

MONTAINE, Montanje
Isaac, 1084

Moor, MOORE
Cornelius, 2022
John, 2018

MORRISON, Mouristzen, Mourusse
Alida, 1196, 1457, 1465, 1550, 2574
Dirk, 990
Elizabeth, 425, 2201
Frances, 1024, 1198
Fred, 445
Henry, 425, 1196
Isaac, 415, 444
Jacob, 419
Janet, 444, 445
Josina, 415
Judith, 1278
Lena, 1228, 1283
Syntje, 419, 2579

Seeger, SEGER
  Christopher, 1345

SHEPHERD
  Samuel, 1784

Shiers - see SEARS

Shiphard - see SHEPHERD

Sichels(e), SICKELSE
  Catherine, 786
  Egje, 818
  Elizabeth, 1317
  Fytje, 61, 64, 302
  Henry, 88
  John, 570
  Maria, 90, 196, 266, 356, 364

SICKLER
  Abraham, 2100
  Hester, 2100
  Jacob, 1657
  Junis, 1368
  Maria, 1657
  Samuel, 1399
  Thomas, 874

Siers - see SEARS

Sigler - see SICKLER

Sikkelse - see SICKELSE

SIMMONS
  Elizabeth, 2565
  John, 1787
  Peter, 1900, 2086
  Polly, 2086, 2286, 2451
  Rachel, 3237
  Susan, 1787, 1900

SINDEL
  John, 1842
  Thomas, 2194

SIP
  Aaron, 3, 29
  Adrian, 881, 1135, 1453, 1675, 2504
  Anna, 52, 67, 83, 543, 589, 3010
  Arien, 89, 186
  Cornelius, 1578, 1852, 2639, 2926
  Dirk, 1377
  Edo, 5, 68
  Gerritje, 899, 1135, 1328
  Gertrude, 1675
  Helmich, 465, 642
  Hillegond, 1, 69, 85, 285
  Janet, 490, 700, 2185
  John, 1136, 1157, 1322, 1673, 2609,
    2771
  Margaret, 4, 80, 104

SIP (con'd)
  Metje, 881

Sisco - see FRANSCISCO

SKIDMORE
  Naomi, 1200, 1600, 1881
  Samuel, 1085

SKINNER
  William, 136

SLOT
  Margaret, 550

Smit, SMITH
  Abraham, 641, 826
  Alida, 713
  Ariantje, 1623, 1808, 1958
  Catherine, 2700
  Catlintje, 599
  Edward, 135
  Elias, 1115
  Elizabeth, 916, 1089, 2093
  Gideon, 2700
  Jacob, 764, 768
  Sarah, 1437
  Susan, 2519

SNYDER
  Anna, 2231
  Catherine, 1886
  George, 2208
  Maria, 1722, 1839
  Jonathan, 1665
  Zachariah, 2428

SPIER, Spyer, Spyr
  Abraham, 907, 988, 1113, 1419, 1444,
    1796, 2056
  Anna, 988, 1022, 1084, 1644, 1731,
    2661, 2694, 2964
  Anthony, 388, 459, 766, 772, 888, 941,
    969, 1166, 1936, 1943, 2005
  Barent, 1330, 1888, 2069, 2741
  Benjamin, 558
  Catherine, 1083
  Catlintje, 659, 785, 2224
  Cornelius, 707, 810, 942, 1545, 1685,
    2427, 2520
  Dirkje, 680, 1269, 1372, 1382
  Elias, 1003, 1380, 1619, 1984
  Francis, 1207, 1467
  Garret, 517, 632, 1075, 1170, 1445,
    1590
  Gerritje, 129, 1091
  Gertrude, 130, 187, 2069
  Henry, 191, 292, 423, 659, 779, 943,
    944, 977, 981, 1022, 1144, 1153, 1226,
    1270, 1338, 1451, 1676, 1683, 1727

INDEX OF SPONSORS

TERHUNE (con'd)
Cornelius, 1570
Dirk, 1589, 1729, 2603
Elizabeth, 2305, 2449
Gerrebreg, 220
Gertrude, 142
Jacob, 1645, 2050, 2314
Margaret, 1354, 1833, 2525
Maria, 586
Michael, 2476
Peter, 1757, 2593
Roelof, 1563
Stephen, 329
Tiesje, 2641

TERP
Wyntje, 1574

Thammis - see THOMASSE

Themouth - see DEMOTT

THOMASSE, Thomese, Tho's
Abraham, 50, 104, 336, 345, 378
Elias, 368
Elizabeth, 297
Garret, 121
George, 7, 264, 298, 331
Isaac, 246
Jacob, 203, 247, 328, 347
John, 51, 262, 338, 720
Maria, 51

Thymetz - see STEINMETS

Thyse - see TYSEN

TIEBOUT
John, 283
Maria, 286
Rachel, 990

TIEPEL
Catherine, 2151

TOEDER
Polly, 1150

TOERS(E)
Aaron, 130, 187, 192
Abraham, 473
Anna, 35, 645, 738, 896, 966, 1025,
  1103, 1118, 1271, 2146
Beletje, 473
Cornelius, 34
Elizabeth, 643
Frances, 30, 604
Garret, 1761
Jacob, 621, 677, 1000, 1050
John, 32, 312, 373, 751, 879
Lawrence, 31

TOERS (con'd)
Margaret, 1761
Maria, 32, 571, 872
Pietertje, 551
Samuel, 1271, 1949, 2571
Sarah, 767
Syntje, 1989

Tomasse - see THOMASSE

Toors - see TOERS

Torner - see TURNER

Tours - see TOERS

TRAPHAGE(N)
Catherine, 241
Henry, 722, 756
William, 241, 1879

TUCKER
John, 1605

TURK
Sarah, 216

TURNER
Janet, 693, 771, 1087, 1425

Tyse, TYSEN
Anna, 1558, 2090, 2258
Maria, 1719, 1930

ULDRICKSE
Ulrich, 1808

Valk - see FALCK

VAN ALE(N)
Henry, 448

VAN BLARCOM, Van Blercum, Van Blerkom,
 Van Blerkum
Anna, 1410
Anthony, 555
Brechje, 1949
Gilbert, 282, 454
Helena, 236
Henry, 652, 726, 808, 851, 3226
Janet, 2303, 3226
John, 259, 450, 845
Lea, 195
Molly, 433
Nicasie, 2469
Rachel, 307
Vroutje, 2702

Van Boskerck, Van Boskerk - see BOSKERK

Van Bossum - see VAN BUSSEN

VAN BUREN
Agnes, 1516

VAN BUREN (con'd)
  Beekman, 1516
  Elizabeth, 1427
  James, 2315
  Peter, 2229

Van Busen, Van Bussem, VAN BUSSEN,
 Van Busson
  Abigail, 2368, 2730
  Catherine, 1359
  David, 1534
  Elizabeth, 1505, 2137, 2501, 2605
  Herman, 800, 1147, 1238, 1574
  John, 1066
  Margaret, 1147, 2392
  Peter, 2368
  Philip, 1143, 1189
  Sally, 2291
  William, 1321, 2157

Van Cent - see VAN SANT

VAN CORTLAND, Van Courland
  Anna, 134
  Catherine, 1148
  Elizabeth, 136

Van Der Beeck, VAN DER BEEK
  Abraham, 1827
  Elsie, 289
  Isaac, 2329
  Janet, 838
  John, 1159, 1285
  Paul, 219, 245, 311, 375
  Sarah, 283, 310

Van Der Coek, VAN DER COOK - see also
 COOK
  Cornelia, 434
  Lena, 406
  Ma(_____), 434

Van Der Hoef, VAN DER HOOF, Van Der Hoev
  Abraham, 348
  Catherine, 1842
  Cornelius, 286
  Dinah, 1769
  Dorothy, 2555
  Elizabeth, 595
  Garret, 301
  Gilbert, 407, 408
  Henry, 728, 1502
  Isaac, 382
  Jacob, 319, 2234
  Matthew, 1430
  Michael, 1970

VAN DER POEL
  Maria, 71

VAN DEUSSE
  Maria, 293

VAN DE WATERS
  Cornelia, 1194

Van Dien - see VAN DUYN

VAN DRIESSEN
  John, 443

VAN DUYN
  Abraham, 327, 346
  Cornelius, 211
  Henrietta, 1219
  Jemima, 387

VAN DYCK
  Lena, 1645
  Magdalena, 1164
  Molly, 842
  Rachel, 2076

Van Dyn - see VAN DUYN

VAN EELSLANDT, Van Elsland
  Janet, 40, 94
  Maria, 154, 159, 341, 383

Van Enburgh - see VAN IMBURGH

Van Es, Vaness, Van Ess - see VAN NESS

Van Eydelstyn, Van Eyderstyn, VAN
 EYDESTEYN
  Anna, 697, 1461, 1668, 1681, 2968
  Anthony, 631, 672, 1082
  Caspar, 588, 1152, 1408, 1483, 1513,
   1797
  Catherine, 516, 636, 2753
  Christopher, 1184
  Clara, 1094
  Cornelia, 984
  Elizabeth, 878, 904, 1100, 1990, 2099,
   2606
  Francis, 1558, 2090, 2258
  George, 2720, 2837
  Herman, 623, 732, 788, 820, 967
  Janet, 809, 865, 1584
  Maria, 2065
  Michael, 2395
  Peter, 1930
  Pietertje, 521
  Rachel, 792, 1423, 1595, 1926
  Sietje, 1534
  Tade, 469, 649, 979, 1195, 1220, 1584,
   1745

VAN GELDER
  Jacob, 1488
  Sarah, 1030

INDEX OF SPONSORS

VRELAND (con'd)
  Anna (con'd), 1756, 2344, 2607, 2761
  Beletje, 633, 1142, 1299, 1340
  Benjamin, 2060
  Catherine, 1042, 1048, 1163, 1530,
    1570, 1580, 1634, 1652, 2025, 2087,
    2273, 2347, 2776
  Christina, 503
  Claasje, 109, 611, 717, 780, 827, 926,
    1085, 1369, 2048
  Cornelia, 2118
  Cornelius, 610, 748, 778, 2555, 2594,
    2746, 2770
  Dirk, 57, 117, 322, 467, 495, 595, 640,
    841, 844, 1348, 1579, 1693
  Egje, 119, 163, 199, 251, 261
  Elias, 59, 313, 503, 599, 1263, 1304,
    1417, 1529, 1597, 1654, 1834, 2016,
    2141, 2211, 2247, 2456, 2576, 2731,
    2964
  Elizabeth, 1470, 1529, 1648, 1803,
    1817, 2594, 2770
  Enoch, 113, 731, 1014, 1687, 2418,
    2826
  Fytje, 116, 590, 625, 704, 1174
  Garret, 633, 743
  Geesje, 1361
  Gertrude, 567, 906, 1624, 1631, 1801
  Hartman, 284, 361, 544, 572, 575, 616,
    703, 708, 883, 1006, 2161, 2246
  Helena, 60
  Henrietta, 1444, 1772
  Herman, 2264
  Hester, 577
  Isaac, 1042, 1163, 1691, 1902, 2375,
    2586
  Jacob, 35, 712, 742, 1007, 1052, 1264,
    1394, 1559, 1762, 1987
  Janet, 58, 121, 250, 541, 1010, 1029,
    1059, 1175, 1239, 1950
  John, 590, 596, 609, 625, 704, 749,
    815, 897, 971, 1028, 1057, 1130,
    1174, 1186, 1202, 1278, 1323, 1410,
    1441, 1636, 1644, 1756, 1772, 1925,
    2392, 2618, 2657, 2737
  Joris, 154, 320
  Lea, 2566
  Lena, 2046, 2961
  Manus, 3010
  Margaret, 301, 313, 373, 495, 640,
    897, 900, 943, 947, 977, 1028, 1179,
    2244, 2254, 2349, 2375, 2545, 2581
  Maria, 160, 320, 544, 653, 661, 688,
    757, 1064, 1320, 1638
  Marinus, 1029, 1361
  Martje, 110, 112, 118, 150, 222, 309

VRELAND (con'd)
  Metje, 1676, 1683
  Michael, 44, 584, 629, 653, 661, 688,
    757, 799, 825, 840, 859, 980, 1027,
    1062, 1065, 1073, 1504, 1555, 1596,
    2155, 2471
  Nelly, 573, 648
  Nicholas, 111, 118, 198, 303, 377,
    926, 2278
  Peter, 735, 796, 1051, 1140, 1369, 1510,
    1611, 1737, 2008, 2320, 2812
  Pryntje, 2657
  Rachel, 390, 2060, 2453, 3123
  Richard, 1875
  Roelof, 1411
  Sietje, 2082, 2471
  Thomas, 1647, 1841, 2354

Wahshaar - see WANSHAIR

WALINGS(zen)
  Anna, 2
  Hillegond, 404
  Jacob, 279
  John, 1, 285, 404

Wanshaar, WANSHAIR
  Christina, 405, 525
  John, 405, 525, 762, 1102, 1134, 2358,
    2372

WENDEL
  Catherine, 1249

Wenne - see WINNE

WESSELS(E)
  Anna, 929, 1139, 1288
  Helena, 689
  Henry, 1459
  Jacob, 929
  Janet, 416
  Lena, 514, 807
  Lucas, 466
  Wessel, 552

Westerveld, WESTERVELT
  Anna, 1918
  Cornelius, 281, 2451
  Fytje, 1231, 1630, 2138, 2589
  Garret, 1299
  Geesje, 759
  George, 132
  Janet, 290
  John, 1607, 1771
  Lena, 1180
  Margaret, 539, 696, 2381
  Martina, 1879
  Roelof, 290
  Theodosia, 2738

INDEX OF SPONSORS

1726-1727

*Date	Married	Item	Remarks
12.19.1725	Gerrit Post, wid	1	Akquegnonk
1. 4.1726	Fransyntje Peterse, j.d.		Akquegnonk
12.19.1725	Staes Bos, j.m.	2	Akquegnonk
1. 8.1726	Johanna Van Winkel, j.d.		Akquegnonk
12.26.1725	Frans Oudwaeter, wid	3	Akquegnonk
1.20.1726	Johanna Xandersen		widow Drury, Akquegnonk

1726

2.13	Isaac Van Der Hoef, j.m.	4	Akquegnonk
3.10	Elisabeth Van Seil, j.d.		Akquegnonk
3.21	Johan Van Blerkom	5	Sadel Rivier, Bergen Co.
3.25	Jannetje Lanker		Sadel Rivier, Bergen Co.
3. 6	Barend Fransisco, j.m.	6	Secund River
4.19	Catalyntje Stegers, j.d.		Secund River
4.19	Hendrik Van Nes, j.m.	7	Akquegnonk
5.20	Tryntje Roelofse, j.d.		Akquegnonk
5.21	Reynhard Erichson, j.m.	8	Hakkingsak preacher
5.22	Maria Provoost, j.d.		lives there
4.24	Johannes Brikker, j.m.	9	Akquegnonk
5.27	Fransyntje Toers, j.d.		Akquegnonk
6.12	Peter Mattheusse Nieuwkerk, j.m.	10	Bergen
7. 3	Tryntje Dirkse, j.d.		lives here
10.15	John Tenbroeck	11	Nieuw-Jork Stad
10.16	Mary King		Nieuw-Jork Stad
10.13	Johannes Mendevyl, j.m.	12	Akquegnonk
11. 9	Elisabeth Bruin, j.d.		Secund-River
10. 6	Sacharias Ellerton, j.m.	13	Akquegnonk
11.13	Catryntje Valk, j.d.		Akquegnonk
10.13	Jacob Vreeland, j.m.	14	Secund-River
12.21	Martje Jurjaense, j.d.		Akquegnonk
8.28	Stuven Van Seil, j.m.	15	Akquegnonk
12.26	Neeltje Messeker, j.d.		Akquegnonk
10. 6	Johannes Post, j.m.	16	Akquegnonk
12.26	Johanna Houwert, j.d.		Akquegnonk

1727

3.19	Peter Adolf, j.m.	17	Akquegnonk
5. 6	Martje Aeltse, j.d.		Akquegnonk
4. 1	Jacob Van Der Hoef, j.m.	18	Akquegnonk
5.11	Elisabeth Stegers, j.d.		Akquegnonk
4. 1	Jurjaen Aeltse, j.m.	19	Akquegnonk
5.13	Martje Vreeland, j.d.		Akquegnonk
5.20	Gerrit De Boog, j.m.	20	Akquegnonk
5.23	Maria Van Der Beek, j.d.		Akquegnonk
4. 9	Andries Van Gysen, j.m.	21	lives here
5.26	Martje Dirkse, j.d.		lives here

* - Date before groom's name - intention to marry (banns)
    Date before bride's name - marriage performed

*Date	Married	Item	Remarks
6. 4	Reinier Van Houte	22	j.m., Akquegnonk
7. 8	Gerritje Spyr		j.d., Akquegnonk
8. 9	John Kip	23	j.m., Secund-River
8.12	Sarah Spyr		j.d., Secund-River
9. 2	Jacob Spyr	24	j.m., lives here
10.18	Egje Van Houte		j.d., lives here
9.30	Antony Bruin	25	j.m., Secund-River
10.31	Aerjaentje Jraleman		j.d., Secund-River
10.14	Thomas Ager	26	j.m., Secund-River
11. 3	Geertje Bras		widow Spyr, Secund-River
10.21	Barend Van Hoorn	27	j.m., Akquegnonk
11.17	Rachel Aeltse		j.d., Akquegnonk
11.10	Hendrik Jraeleman	28	j.m., Secund-River
12. 6	Hester Vincent		j.d., Secund-River
11.10	Peter Wenne	29	j.m., Nieuw-Brittanje
12.13	Lea Spyr		j.d., Secund-River
12. 9.1727	Cornelis Aeltse	30	j.m., Akwuegnonk
1.19.1728	Geesje Post		j.d., Akquegnonk
1728			
4. 6	Lucas Bras	31	j.m., Akquegnonk
4.25	Lena Reyke		j.d., Akquegnonk
5. 4	Simeon Van Winkel	32	j.m., Nieuw-Brittanje
6. 5	Geertruy Kuuk		j.d., Akquegnonk
4.28	Abraham De Voor	33	j.m., Secund-River
6.11	Fransyntje Ganjon		j.d., Secund-River
5.21	Adam Wesenaer	34	j.m., Goosjen
7. 8	Lea Stheg		j.d., Rempug
7.19	Jacob Sjeerman	35	widower, Akquegnonk
8.15	Neeltje Messeker		Akquegnonk
9.22	Peter Bras	36	j.m., Secund-River
10.17	Marietje Thomasse		j.d., Secund-River
9.14	Casparus Tades	37	widower, Akquegnonk
10.19	Hendrikje D'Grauw		j.d., Hakkingsak
	David Van Gelder	38	j.m., Nieuw-Jork
10.21	Elisabeth Van Der Beek		j.d., Pomton
9. 7	Jacob Kool	39	j.m., Aesopus, lives here
10.31	Sara Deffenpoort		j.d., Aesopus, lives here
	Hendrik Blinkerhof	40	j.m., Hakkingsak
11. 1	Marietje Wester-Veld		j.d., Hakkingsak
10.12	Gerrit Van Hoorn	41	j.m., lives here
11.30	Elisabeth Thomasse		j.d., lives here
10.26	Petrus Van Blerkum	42	j.m., from here
12. 6	Rachel Van Seyl		j.d., from here
12.16	Jacob Thomasse	43	Akquegnonk
12.17	Maria Gerbrantse		Nieuw-Barbardos, Bergen Co.

* - see page 205

*Date	Married	Item	Remarks
11.18	Joris Vreeland	44	Akquegnonk
12.18	Elsje Meet		Pegquenek, Bergen Co.
11.15	Hendrik Post	45	j.m., Akquegnonk
12.25	Elisabeth Christyn		j.d., Hakkingsak
	Jan Bogard	46	j.m., Hakkingsak
12.31	Antje Westerveld		j.d., Hakkingsak
1729			
	Jacobus Bartholf	47	j.m., Hakkingsak
3. 1	Elisabeth Van Imburg		j.d., Hakkingsak
4.19	Isaac Van Nes	48	j.m., Akquegnonk
6.27	Neeltje Reike		j.d., Akquegnonk
4. 5	Peter Reike	49	j.m., Akquegnonk
6.30	Femmetje Reike		j.d., Akquegnonk
4.19	Hendrik Reike	50	j.m., Akquegnonk
6.30	Marta Gould		j.d., Akquegnonk
4.19	Jacob Milles	51	j.m., Akquegnonk
7. 4	Lena Deffenpoort		j.d., Akquegnonk
6. 7	Jurjaen Peterse	52	j.m., Akquegnonk
7. 5	Antje Gerritse		j.d., Akquegnonk
7. 5	Isaac Montanje	53	j.m., lives here
7.25	Nelletje Brouwer		j.d., lives here
7.25	Johannes Cavellier	54	widower, lives here
8.16	Catalynte Enderson		j.d., lives here
8.10	Abraham Thomasse	55	widower, Akquegnonk
9.13	Catryntje Andriesse		j.d., Akquegnonk
10.12	Boudewyn De Honeur	56	Rarethan River
10.14	Maria Thomas		Rarethan River
10.15	Barend Smak	57	j.m., Piskattoe Bouns
10.16	Marietje Beuis		j.d., Piskattoe Bouns
10.18	Adriaen Post	58	j.m., Akquegnonk
11.28	Rachel Hartte		j.d., Akquegnonk
11. 8	Dirk Steger	59	j.m., Akquegnonk
12.19	Jannetje Jacobusse		j.d., Akquegnonk
11. 8	Johannes Reike	60	j.m., lives here
12.24	Rachel Van Nes		j.d., lives here
11.26.1729	Adriaen Post	61	Essex Co. by Akquegnonk
1. 9.1730	Martje Thomas		Essex Co. by Akquegnonk
12. 6.1729	Joris Bord	62	j.m., Akquegnonk
1.10.1730	Antje Van Winkel		j.d., Akquegnonk
12.13.1729	Robbert Guuld	63	j.m., lives here
2.26.1730	Geertje Van Duin		j.d., lives here
1730			
1. 3	Nicolaes Joons	64	j.m., lives here
2. 4	Elisabeth Bruin		j.d., lives here
	Cornelis Janse Banta	65	j.m., Hakkingsak
4.25	Rachel Wyrtse Banta		j.d., Hakkingsak

*Date	Married	Item	Remarks
4.11	Jacobus Akkerman	66	j.m., Hakkingsak
5.19	Dirkje Van Gysen		j.d., Akquegnonk
8.12	Dirk Merlet	67	j.m., Rarethans River, mar at Milston
8.13	Jannetje Schamp		j.d., Rarethans River
6.27	Jan Cuurte	68	widower, lives here
8.28	Nelletje Steg		j.d., lives here
9. 6	Johannes Messeker	69	j.m., Akquegnonk
9.21	Hendrikje Messeker		j.d., Akquegnonk
7. 4	Stephen Basset	70	Essex Co., Nieuw-Jersey
10. 2	Ann Millidge		Essex Co-, Nieuw-Jersey
10.10	John Hall	71	Somerset Co.
10.14	Magdalena Governeurs		Somerset Co.
10.14	Willem Klaessen	72	j.m., Piskattie Bouns, mar at Milston
10.15	Sara Smak		j.d., Piskattie Bouns
9.26	Helmerich Van Houte	73	j.m., Akquegnonk
11. 6	Catharina Van Gysen		j.d., Akquegnonk
10.17	Jurje Jurjaense	74	j.m., Akquegnonk
11.13	Elisabeth Steinmets		j.d., Akquegnonk
	Johannes Bruin	75	j.m., Secund-River
12.21	Hillegond Van Gysen		j.d., Secund-River
11.21.1730	Bernardus Mollin	76	j.m., Akquegnonk
1. 2.1731	Klaesje Andriesse		j.d., Akquegnonk
1731			
1.16	Jillis Meet	77	j.m., Akquegnonk
2. 3	Jannetje Bruin		j.d., Akquegnonk
3.30	Benjamin Steinmets	78	widower, Riddenstoun, mar at Milston
4. 1	Sara Emans		j.d., Riddenstoun
4.10	Johannes Van Gysen	79	widower, Akquegnonk
4.29	Susanna Vincent		j.d., Secund-River
	Jan Lewis	80	j.m., Japog, with certificate from
4.30	Janneke Van Deursen		j.d., Japog /Hakkingsak
4.25	Elias Vreeland	81	j.m., Akquegnonk
5.22	Christina Thiese		j.d., Akquegnonk
5. 8	Johannes Bruin	82	j.m., Akquegnonk
5.24	Femmetje Messeker		j.d., Akquegnonk
5.15	Onphry Defvenpoart	83	j.m., Hanover Co.
7. 3	Elisabeth Heyle		j.d., Hanover Co.
9.14	John Ludlow	84	j.m., Essex Co. by Akquegnonk
9.23	Susannah Broed-Berry		j.d., Essex Co. by Akquegnonk
9.18	Hartman D: Vreeland	85	j.m., Akquegnonk
10.23	Lea Peterse		j.d., Akquegnonk
11.13	Frederik Muzelius	86	j.m., Tappan preacher
11.20	Mary Ludlow		j.d., Nieuw-Jork
11. 6	Willem Willemse	87	j.m., Akquegnonk
11.26	Johanna Xandersen		widow Oudwaeter, Akquegnonk

* - see page 205

*Date	Married	Item	Remarks
1732			
5. 6	Jan Thomasse	88	j.m., Akquegnonk
5.12	Martje Van Houte		j.d., Akquegnonk
5. 6	Gerrit Peterse	89	j.m., Japog
5.22	Egje Neefjes		j.d., Akquegnonk
5.23	Peter Nederman	90	j.m., Bergen Co.
6. 5	Judith Laeubets		widow, Bergen Co.
8.17	Jacob Bennet	91	j.m.
8.18	Mycay Wykhof		j.d.
9.__	(manuscript destroyed)	92	
9.__			
9.16	Dirk Thomasse	93	j.m., Akquegnonk
9.28	Petertje Post		j.d., Akquegnonk
10.14	Jan Vincent	94	j.m., Essex Co.
11.20	Elisabeth Doremes		j.d., Essex Co.
	Charles Bevand	95	Secund-River, Essex Co.
12.26	Tryntje Roset		Secund-River, Essex Co.
11. 2	Abraham Van Winkle	96	Akquegnonk & Secund-River,
	Marietje Van Dyk		Essex Co.
12.23.1732	Natanael Foort	97	j.m., Akquegnonk
1.11.1733	Maria Davids		j.d., Akquegnonk
1733			
3.21	Niclaes Romein	98	widower, Pompton, Bergen Co.
4.14	Rachel Dirkse Vreeland		j.d., Wesel, Essex Co.
4. 6	Johannes Snyer	99	j.m., Hanover Co.
5. 5	Catryntje Heyle		j.d., Hanover Co.
4.14	Abraham Spyr	100	j.m., Bergen
5.12	Annaetje Spyr		j.d., Akquegnonk
5.11	Thomas Thomasse	101	Secund River
5.19	Geertruid Wendal		lives here
__.__	(manuscript destroyed)		
5.18	Nicolaes Heyle	102	j.m., Hanover Co.
6.14	Rachel Defvenpoort		j.d., Hanover Co.
5.26	Jan Bogard	103	j.m., Hakkingsak
6.23	Rachel Van Nieuw-Kerk		Akquegnonk
6. 2	Peter Gerritse	104	widower, Akquegnonk
6.22	Antje Aeltse		j.d., Akquegnonk
7.__	Richard Broad Berry	105	j.m., Essex Co.
7.28	Elisabeth Van Dyk		j.d., Essex Co.
8.11	Hartman K: Vreeland	106	j.m., Akquegnonk
9.15	Jannetje Jacobusse		widow, Akquegnonk
8.18	Abraham Abr: Van Gysen	107,	j.m., lives here
9.25	Antje Dirkse		j.d., lives here
8.11	Frans Spyr	108	widower, both live within this
10. 4	Hester De Lameter		widow /congregation

* - see page 205

*Date	Married	1733-1734 Item	Remarks
9.22	Marselis Post	109	j.m., Akquegnonk, Essex Co.
10. 4	Annaetje Sip		j.d., Akquegnonk, Essex Co.
10. 5	Silvester Earle	110	j.m., Hakkingsak, Bergen Co.
10. 8	Martha Sobriesko		j.d., Hakkingsak, Bergen Co.
	Daniel Worms	111	widower, Hanover Co., mar at Secund-
10.19	Tryntje Van Winkel		j.d., Essex Co. /River
	Robbert Juiston	112	j.m., Essex Co., mar at Secund-
10.19	Alida Van Winkel		j.d., Essex Co. /River
10.12	Peter Peterse	113	j.m., Akquegnonk, Essex Co.
10.31	Catharina Van Winkel		j.d., Akquegnonk, Bergen Co.
1734			
1. 7	Peter Steinmets	114	j.m., Essex Co.
2. 2	Marietje Brouwer		j.d., Essex Co.
1.25	Abraham Rothan	115	j.m., Rempug
2.22	Sara Van Gelder		j.d., Rempug
2. 1	Simeon Van Winkle	116	widower, Akquegnonk
3. 3	Antje Peterse		widow, Akquegnonk
	Hermanus Burger	117	j.m.
3. 4	Annaetje Koeimans		j.d.
2.16	Isaac Van Duin	118	j.m., Hanover Co.
	Catharina Bruin		j.d., Puegguenek, Bergen Co.
2.19	William Steck	119	j.m., Pompton
3.21	Elisabeth Hervy		widow, Pompton
6. 1	Johannes Jacobusse	120	j.m., both live within this
7. 3	Saertje Bruin		j.d. /congregation
4. 4	Abraham Cadmus	121	j.m., Secund-River
4.__	Geertje Ager		widow, Secund-River
7. 5	Abraham Metseler	122	j.m., Akquegnonk
7.25	Rachel Van Blerkum		widow, Akquegnonk
6.22	Zacharias Sikkels	123	widower, Bergen
6.29	Rachel Van Winkle		j.d., Akquegnonk
8.10	Jacobus Jacobusse	124	j.m., lives here
9.20	Tytje Van Nes		j.d., lives here
8.17	Michiel Herty	125	j.m., Tappan
9.21	Hannetje Doremes		j.d., Akquegnonk
9.15	Benjamin Ooldis	126	j.m., lives here
10. 7	Nelly Valk		j.d., lives here
9.28	Helmerich Van Houte	127	j.m., Akquegnonk
10.25	Geertje Van Hoorn		j.d., Akquegnonk
10.26	Jan Willts	128	j.m., Akquegnonk
12.23	Anna Maria Van Gysen		j.d., Akquegnonk
11. 2	Robbert Dromment	129	j.m., lives here
12. 2	Sara Millits		j.d.
11.17	Adriaen Van Houte	130	j.m., Akquegnonk
12.19	Angenietje Boogaerd		j.d., Peremes

* see page 205

1734-1737

*Date	Married	Item	Remarks
11.23	Michiel Van Der Voort	131	Nieuw Nederland on Lang-Eyland
12.20	Jannetje Wesselse, j.d.		Nieuw Nederland on Lang-Eyland
11.12	Jacobus Van Winkle	132	widower, Akquegnonk
11.24	Catharina Bekling		j.d., Akquegnonk
11.30.1734	Cornelis Van Houte	133	j.m., Akquegnonk
1.11.1735	Rachel Post		j.d., Akquegnonk
1735	Arie Cadmus	134	j.m., Secund River, mar at Secund
1.22	Elisabeth _andevyl		widow, Secund River /River
2.28	Cornelis Spier	135	j.m., both live within this cong
	Susanna Vincent		widow of Johannes Van Giesen
7.26	Pieter Mauritzen	136	
	Mareytie Spier		
7.26	Willem Reyerszen	137	j.m.
	Elizabeth Reyerszen		
1736	Harmanus Van Bossen	138	j.m., b Neuw York, liv Hackinsak
__.__	Abigaal Forbes		j.d., b Hamstead, Lang Eyland
__.__	Jacob Van Winckel	139	j.m., b 2 River, liv here
	Margaretha Heyl		b Rempogh, liv Hanover Co.
__.__	Jacob Themout	140	wid, b Hooghwyzel, Darmstad, Germany
	Barbara Thewalt		wid. b Moxter, Germany
			both liv Tawachgouw
__.__	Hendrik Messeker	141	b Staaten Eyland, liv Gansegat
	Mareytie Van Zeyl(j)		b Aghquechnonck, liv here
1737	Gerrit Neefyes, j.m.	142	b Staten Eyland, liv Slooterdamm
__.__	Cathalyntje Westerveld		j.d., b Tapan, liv Weghgerouw
__.__	Abraham Broeks	143	j.m., b Neuw York, liv Perikenes
	Jannetje Doremus		j.d., b Aghquechnonk, liv there
__.__	Alexander Pietersze	144	j.m., b Neuworcks Bounds, liv there
	Maria Volks		j.d., b Aghquechnonk, liv here
__.__	Marten Reyerssen, j.m.	145	sn of Frans, b Neuw York
	Antje Van Rype, j.d.		dau of Jurriaan Thomasse, b Tapan
			both liv here
__.__	Johannes Francisko	146	wid of Margaretha Buys
	Claartje Coerte, j.d.		both b Aghquechnonck, liv Pomtan
__.__	Johannes Thymets	147	j.m., both b & liv Aghquechnonk
	Catharina Post		j.d.
__.__	Thades Van Winckel	148	j.m., b Aghquechnonk, liv here
	Catharina Bord		j.d., b Rarethans, liv here
__.__	Petrus Pieterszen	149	j.m., b Aghquechnonck, liv here
	Anna Kip		j.d., b Bergen, liv here
__.__	Joh's Gerritszen	150	j.m., both b Aghquechnonk, liv here
	Mareytje Gerritszen		j.d.

* - see page 205, however,
    dates for #136-137 are probably marriage dates

Date	Married	Item	Remarks
—.—	Abraham Van Giesen Jannetje Van Houten	151	j.m., b Aghquechnonk, liv here j.d., b & liv here
—.—	Dirck Thomusse Jannetje Van Houten	152	wid, b Aghquechnonk, liv here j.d., b Totua, liv there
—.—	Reynier Van Giesen Catharyntje Marselisze, j.d.,	153	sn of Bastyaan, liv Aghquechnonk dau of Marselis Pietersze, liv Bergen
—.—	Cornelis Hendrickzen Claassje Pietersse	154	j.m., sn of Hend: Gerritszen j.d., dau of Hessel Pieterszen both b & liv Aghquechnonk
—.—	Johannes Spier Johanna Van Ydersteyn	155	j.m., b Pem(_____) j.d., dau of Machiel Thadese, b & liv Aghquechnonk, she died as bride
1738 2. 4	Symon Kent Mareytje Spier	156	j.m., b Neuworks Bounds j.d., b Second River, liv Gan(segat)
—.—	Izaak Rycke, j.m. Lena Bruyn, j.d.	157	sn of P:, b Staaten Eyland, liv Gansegat dau of Joh's, b Gansegat, liv Peghquoneck
—.—	Simeon V. Winckel Elizabeth De Grauw	158	j.m., b & liv Aghquechnonk j.d., b & liv Hakkensak
—.—	Everth Wesselze Rachel Post	159	wid, b Neuw York, liv here wid, b Tappan, liv here
—.—	Cornelis Doremus Antje Jong	160	j.m., b Aghquechnk, liv here j.d., b Hanover, America, liv there
6. 9	Dirck Bourdan Antje Van Winckel	161	j.m., b & liv Hakkensak j.d., b & liv Aghquechnk
9.28	Nicolaas Jones Marretje Jong	162	wid, liv Pomtan j.d., liv Tawaggous
10.19	Simeon Van Winckel Annatje Bosch	163	j.m., b & liv Achquechnk j.d., b Tappan, liv here
10.19	Jurrie Jansze Van Rype Helena Van Houten	164	j.m., both b & liv Achquechnk j.d.
11. 9	Pieter Claassen Elizabeth Pietersze	165	j.m., both b & liv within this cong j.d.
11.11	Uldrik Brouwer Mareytje Van Der Vorst	166	j.m., b Bergen, liv Achq. j.d., b Neuw Y(___), liv there
11.11	Pieter Bras Rachel Philips	167	wid of Mareytie Cadmus, liv Aghquech j.d., b Ne(iu)-Ork, liv here /nonk
12.19	Abraham Rycke, j.m. Aaltje Smith, j.d.	168	b Staten-Eyland, liv Achquechnonk b Achquechnonk, liv there
12.20	Hendrik Rycke Lena Messeker	169	j.m., b Staaten-Eyland, liv Gansegat j.d., b Gansegat, liv there
1739 1.20	Hessel Brouwer, j.m. Lena Wesselsen, j.d.	170	sn of Uldrik, b Bergen, liv here dau of Everth, b Aghquechnonk, liv here
2. 1	Joh. Philips Antje Messeker	171	j.m., b Neuw York, liv Gansegat j.d., b Staaten Eyland, liv Gansegat

1737-1739

Date	Married	Item	Remarks
2. 5	Rycke Rycke Tryntje Franscisco	172	j.m., b Staaten-Eyland, liv Gansegat j.d., b Achquechnk, liv Gansegat
2.23	Adriyaan Post Jannetje Van Wageningen	173	j.m., b Neuw York, liv here j.d., b Aghquechnonk, liv here
4.12	Joh's Van Giesen Catharina Echtbersze	174	j.m., b here, liv this place j.d., b & liv this place
5. 9	Lauwrens Crawle Margriet Karries	175	j.m., b Yrland, both liv Pomtan j.d., not yet 13y old, b Hanover
5.10	Johannes Dideriks Hesther Vreeland	176	wid, b Bergen, liv there j.d., b Weesel, liv there
5.22	Hendrick Caller Elsebeth Jukhar	177	j.m., b Switszerland, liv this place j.d., b Switszerland, liv this place
5.24	Benjamin Coots Elisabeth Bos	178	j.m., b Boston, liv at the Neck j.d., b Neuw York
6. 2	Abraham Van Winckel Jacumyntje Van Neuwkerk	179	j.m., both b Achquechnonk, liv here j.d.
6.11	Johannes Van Houten Martyntie Bartholf	180	j.m., sn of Roelof, b Weesel j.d., dau of Carynus, b Hackinsak she liv Pannan; he liv Pomtan
7. 4	Hardman Cadmus Lea Van Hoorn	181	j.m., both b & liv Aghquechnonk j.d.
7. 5	Frans Hooghland Franseyntje Banta	182	j.m., from N. York j.d., from Hakkinsak
8.22	Hendrik Van Winckel Mareytje Gerritszen	183	j.m., sn of Joh., b & liv Second Riv. j.d., dau of Gerrit Thomasse, b /Neuw-ork Bounds, liv Aghquechnonck
8.23	Jacob Steck, j.m. Antje Vreeland, j.d.	184	sn of Jan, b N. Barbados Neck, liv there dau of Dirck, b Aghquechnk, liv Weesel
8.24	Joost Cogh, j.m. Mareytje Tours, j.d.	185	b Nassauw Dillenburgh, Germany, both liv b Sloterdam /Aghquechnonck
10.18	Jacob Smith, j.m. Elizabeth Brouwer, j.d.	186	sn of Elias, b Aghquechnonck, both liv dau of Uldrick, b Bergen /this place
10.19	Hessel Pieterzen Van Wageningen Cathryntje Bon, j.d.	187	j.m., b Sloterdam, both liv b Neuw York /Sloterdam
10.19	Jacobus Reyerszen Mareytje Van Blerkum	188	j.m., b Neuw York, liv Pomtan j.d., b & liv Per-Emmes
11.22	Joh's Steeger Anneke Rycke, j.d.	189	j.m., b Gansegat, liv there b Staaten-Eyland, liv Aghquechnonck
12.13	Gerbrant Gerbrantse Wyntje Van Winckel	190	j.m., both b Neuw-Barbados Neck, liv j.d. /Achquechnonk
12.22	Willem Cachelin Lea Spearling	191	j.m., b Second-River, both liv Ach j.d., b Lang-Eyland /quechnonck
1740 3. 6	Joris Stech Antje Van Yderstein	192	j.m., b N. Barbados Neck j.d., b Weeselen, liv Achquechnk

Date	Married	Item	Remarks
3. 6	Ludowyk Wycker	193	j.m., b Germany, liv Pomtan
	Elizabeth Van Der Poel		j.d., b Rarethans, liv Pomtan
11.14	Helmech Sip	194	j.m., b Achquechnonk, liv there
	Jannetje Van Houten		j.d., b Totua. liv there
11.15	Johannis Ouke	195	j.m., b & liv Lang-Eyland
	Janneke Spier		j.d., b & liv Akquechnk
11.21	Thomas Van Bremen	196	j.m., b Nieuw-Haarlem, liv Per-Emus
	Aaltje De Remis		j.d., b & liv Perikenes
11.22	Willem Hoppe, j.m.	197	sn of And's, b & liv Per Emmes
	Antje Weszels, j.d.		dau of Ev't, b & liv Aghquechnonk
12. 5	Helmech Post	198	j.m., both b Aghquechnonk, liv here
	Francyntje Tours		j.d.
1741			
1. 1	Thomas Van Rypen	199	j.m., b & liv Aghquechnonk
	Lena Van Wagenen		j.d., b Weesel, liv there
3.10	Abraham Mauritszen	200	j.m., b Hunterdon, liv there
	Jacumyntje De Mare		j.d., b Hackensak, liv Pechquonek
5.19	Joh's Brouwer	201	j.m., b Bergen. liv Aghquechnonk
	Sara Blakwell		j.d., b Albany, liv Aghquechnonk
5.24	John Van Houte	202	wid, from Bergen Co., both liv Agh
	Francis Vreland		j.d., from Essex Co. /quechnonk
6.23	Gerbrant V. Houten	203	j.m., b Hoboken, liv Totua
	Jannetje Sip		j.d., b Agquechnonk, liv there
6.24	Isaak Kingsland	204	gentleman, of Bergen Co.
	Johanna Schuyler		spinster, of Bergen Co.
7. 3	Elias Vreeland	205	j.m., b Agquechnonk, liv this place
	Cathalyntje Smith		j.d., b Gansegat, liv this place
9.29	Hendrik Van Houten	206	j.m., b & liv here
	Aaltje Jacobusze		j.d., b Aghquechnonk, liv Peghquoneck
10. 1	Arent Schuyler	207	j.m., b Pomtan, liv there
	Helena Van Wagenen		j.d., b Aghquechnonk, liv here
10. 2	Dirck Vreeland	208	j.m., b Achquechnonk, liv here
	Neefsje Neefsjes		j.d., b Aghquechnonk, liv Slooterdam
12.29	Harmanus Van Wageningen	209	j.m., b Aghquechnonk, liv there
	Geertruy Van Houten		j.d., b Totua, liv there
1742			
1. 6	Gerbrant Jurriyaansen	210	j.m., b Barb-Neck, liv there
	Feytje Van Vorscht		j.d., b B-Neck, liv there
1.13	Jacob Rycke, j.m.	211	b Staten Eyland, liv Aghquechnonk
	Tryntje Spier, j.d.		b Secon-River, liv there
1.15	Marynus Van Winckel	212	j.m., b Aghquechnk, liv here
	Mareytje Everszten		j.d., b Hakkingsak, liv here
2.11	Machiel Van Der Koek	213	j.m., b & liv Gansegat
	Cornelia Van Nes		j.d., b & liv Gansegat
2.20	John Coombe, wid	214	b Exeter, Old Engeland, both liv here
	Mary Ferril, wid of James Waacker, b London, Old Engeland		

Date	Married	Item	Remarks
3.12	Jacobus La Rou	215	j.m., b Rempoogh, liv there
	Rebekka Bartholf		j.d., b Hackingsack, liv Pomtan
4.23	Guljyaam Bartholph	216	j.m., b Hackingsack, liv Pomtan
	Helena La Rou		j.d., b Rempogh, liv there
5. 1	James Billinghton	217	schoolmaster
	Anna America		
5.27	Joh's Van Der Hoef	218	j.m., b Weezel, liv Hanover Co.
	Lena Franscisco		j.d., b Gansegat, liv there
6.11	Pieter Nevius, j.m.	219	b Freahold, Somerset Co., liv there
	Lea Nevius, j.d.		b Staten-Eyland, liv here
6.17	Pieter Doremus, j.m.	220	sn of Cornelis, b Aghquechnonk, both liv
	Elizab'th Hervie, j.d., dau of Thomas, b Nauwersing/this place
7. 3	George Stymatts	221	of Essex Co.
	Claertie Van Eydersteyn		of Bergen Co.
10.29	Helmech Van Houten	222	j.m., b Gemoenepan, liv Totua
	Antje Post		j.d., b Achquechnonk, liv here
11. 9	Abraham Jacobuszen	223	j.m., b & liv Hannover
	Evatje Kip		j.d., b & liv Prekenisse
11.13	Hessel Vreeland	224	j.m., b & liv here
	Elizabeth Stillewill		j.d., b Woodbrids, liv here
12. 1	Lodewyck Messeker	225	j.m., b Staten-Eyland, liv Gansegat
	Lena V. Zeyl		j.d., b Agquechnonk, liv Gansegat
12. 2	Frederick Van Rype	226	j.m., b & liv Aghquechnonk
	Annetje Van Vorst, j.d., b New-Barbados-Neck, liv Aghquechnonk
12. 9	Johannes V. Houten	227	j.m., both b Aghquechnonk, liv here
	Jannetje Doremes		j.d.
12. 9	Frederick Cadmus	228	j.m., b Sloterdam, liv there
	Saartje V. Winckel		j.d., b Weesel, liv there
12. 9	Abraham Rycke	229	j.m., b Staten-Eyland, liv Gansegat
	Mareytje Ricxz		j.d., b Gansegat, liv there
12.10	Cornelis Doremes	230	j.m., b Agquechnk, liv there
	Annatje V: Rype		j.d., b & liv Aghquechnonk
1743			
3. 4	Arend Klaaszen	231	j.m., b Agquechnk, liv here
	Sara Van Seyl		j.d., b Agquechnk, liv Gansegat
3. 5	Jurreyaan Evertszen	232	j.m., b Hackinsak, liv here
	Elizabeth Pettum		j.d., b N-York, liv here
3.12	Hendrick Bruyn	233	j.m., b Gansegat, liv Pechquoneck
	Mareytje Oudtwater		j.d., b Aghquechnonk, liv Periquones
4. 9	Johannes Messeker	234	wid, b Second River, liv Gansegat
	Catharina Rycke		j.d., b Totua, liv Gansegat
4.28	Abraham Smith	235	j.m., b Gansegat, liv Aghquechnonk
	Lena Jacobuszen		j.d., b Second-River, liv there
5.12	Hendrik Zabrisco	236	j.m., b & liv Per Emmes
	Neessye Van Hoorn		j.d., b & liv Slotterdam

Date	Married	Item	Remarks
6. 8	Waling Van Winckel Jannetje Van Houten	237	j.m., b Aghquechnk, liv there j.d., b & liv Totua
6.15	Joh's Doremes Franscyntje Mouritszen	238	j.m., b & liv Aghquechnonk Bounds j.d., b Hanover, liv there
12. 1	Samm'l Boss, j.m. Rebecka De Bonn, j.d.	239	b Staten-Eyland, liv Aghquechnk b Hackingsack, liv Per-Emmes
12.21	Cornelis Doremes Elsie Eghtbertsze	240	j.m., b Aghquechnk, liv this place j.d., b & liv this place
12.22	Johannes Vreeland Teytie Vreeland	241	j.m. j.d.
1744 1. 7	Theunis Slinggeland Hendrickje V. Ydersteyn	242	j.m., b Aghquechnk, liv Per-Emmes j.d., b Aghquechnk, liv here
1.26	Jacob Mauritszen Tryntie V. Houten	243	j.m., b Hanover, liv there j.d., b & liv Agquechnonk
4.28	Joh's Rycke Eva Ztierman	244	j.m., both b Achquechnonk, liv here j.d.
6. 9	Cornelis Van Wageninggen Helena Bon, j.d.	245	j.m., b Slotterdam, liv Staten-Ey b New York, liv Aghquechnonk /land
6.15	Helmech V. Houten Janneke V. Rype	246	j.m., both b & liv Achquechnonk j.d.
6.18	Pieter Jongh Mareytje Slot	247	j.m., b Hanover, liv there j.d., b Per Emmes, liv Pomtan
12. 6	Joh's Egberts Maria Doremus	248	j.m., both liv Ackwuechnk j.d.
12.12	Joh's Sip Annatie Van Winckel	249	j.m., both b & liv Ackquechnk j.d.
1745 1.10	Petrus Brouwer Catharina Van Der Oeff	250	j.m., of Hackensack, both liv Ack j.d., b N-Yorck /quechnonk
4.30	John Franssisco Aaltje Doremus	251	j.m., b Distorns-Neck, liv there j.d., b & liv this place
5. 9	Hendrik Ricks Elsie Pieterssen	252	j.m., b Ganse-Gat, liv there j.d., b Gansegat Bounds, liv there
5.29	John De Vauce, M. D. Hester Vreeland	253	both of Essex Co. spinster
6.11	Andries Ten Eyck Antje Reyjerszen	254	j.m., b New York j.d., b New York, liv Sommersett, Ra /rethans
6.14	Hessel Doremus Geessie Westerveld	255	j.m., b Ackquechnk, liv this place j.d., b & liv this place
6.27	Gerrit Van Houten Jannetie Kip	256	j.m., both liv Ackquechnonk j.d.
7. 3	Johannes Van Winkle jr Jannetje Van Ripen	257	yeoman, of Essex Co. spinster, of Essex Co.
8.15	Pieter Van Blerkum Susanna Calyer, j.d.	258	j.m., b & liv Per-Emmes b Newbardes-Neck, liv Sloterdam

Date	Married	Item	Remarks
9. 6	Jacob Van Houten Janneke Van Ripen	259	j.m., b Totua, liv this place j.d., b Tappan, liv this place
10.24	Nathanael Kingsland Rachel Van Zeyl	260	j.m., b Barbardos-Neck, liv there j.d., b Per-emmes, liv Zaal-Rivier
11. 4	Peter Theyssen Mareytie Tours	261	j.m., b Campga, liv there j.d., b Slooterdam, liv Pannen
11. 7	Gerrit Vreeland Marretje Stymetsz	262	j.m., b Ackquechnk, liv this place j.d., b & liv this place
11. 7	Ab: Claaszen Marretje Vreeland	263	j.m., b Ackquechnk, liv this place j.d., b & liv this place
11. 8	Joh's Van Houten Elizabeth V. Ripen	264	j.m., b Totua, liv there j.d., b Ackquechnonck, liv there
12. 6	Anthony V. Blerkum Marretje Reyerszen	265	j.m., b Hackingsack, liv there j.d., b Waggerouw, liv there
12.12	Johannes Rycke, wid of Rachel Van Ness Elizabeth Heess, j.d.,	266	b Staaten-Eyland b Elizabeth-Thown, both liv Ganssegat
12.26	Jan Yorckszen, j.m. Elizabeth Obenhouss, j.d.	267	b Polle-Valey, liv Schraalenburgh b Barbados-Neck, liv there
1746 4.16	Izaak Kingsland Elizabeth Don	268	j.m., both liv N-Barb: Neck wid of Alexander Gealt
4.24	Gerrit Van Wageninge Margarietje J. Van Winckel	269	j.m., b Pemrepoch, liv there j.d., b Ackquechnonk, liv there
4.25	Gerrit Post Elisabeth Tours	270	j.m., b Ackquechnk, liv this place j.d., b Per-Emmes, liv this place
5. 8	Samm'l Sidmon Angnitje V. Deusen	271	j.m., b Neworck, liv there j.d., b Rempogh, liv there
6.13	Theunis Hennion Annetje Doremus	272	j.m., b Perikenes, liv there j.d., b & liv Ackquechnonck
6.24	Jacob Vreeland Margaretha Gerritszen	273	j.m., both b Weezel, liv Achquech j.d. /nonck
6.29	Johannes Courte Pryna Post	274	wid of Anneke Stur wid of Sander Post
8.25	Joh's Du Garmoy, j.m. Lairesse Fruyt, j.d.	275	b Staaten-Eyland, liv Ackquechnonk b Philadelphia, liv Ackquechnonk
9.28	Isaac Cadmus, j.m. Sara Kip, j.d.	276	b Slooterdam, liv Achquechnonck b Bergen, liv Achquechnonck
__.__	Christoffel Van Ripen Mettie Brouwer, j.d.	277	j.m., b & liv Ackquechnonck b Hackensack, liv Ackquechnonck
__.__	Hendrick Spier Elisabeth Mandeviel	278	j.m., b Gansegat, liv there j.d., b Pomtan, liv there
12. 5	Joh's Van Winckel Janneke Reyjerszen	279	j.m., b Ackquechnonck, liv here j.d., b New York, liv here
12.15	Harmanus Stymets Annatje Immet	280	wid of Elsie Heeremans, both liv wid of Arje Toers /Ackquechnonck

1746, 1747, 1751, 1752

Date	Married	Item	Remarks
12.26	Johannes Ruthan	281	j.m., b Roozendaal, liv Bergen Co.
	Aaltje V. Hoorn		j.d., b Weezel, liv Wyckhoff
1747			
3. 2	_____ Livingston	282	j.m., b Albany, liv New York
	Susanna Franss		j.d.
4. 8	Harmanus De Grouw	283	j.m., b Hackensack, liv Per-Emmes
	Janneke V. Ydersteyn		j.d., b New-Barbados Neck, liv there
4.30	Casparus Ten Brisco	284	of Bergen Co.
	Catherine Wagener		of Essex Co.
5.10	Joris Wesselszen	285	j.m., b Ackquechnonk, liv here
	Lea Spier		j.d., b Ackquechnonk, liv Weezel
__.__	Edward Aarcher, j.m.	286	b Kinderhook, liv N-Barbados-Neck
	Catharina Asschton		wid of Thomas Asschton, liv New York
			mar at New York City Hall
11. 3	Edward Earl	287	of Berg. Co.
	Claassie Vreeland		of Essex Co.
12. 3	Hendrick Van Wageningen	288	j.m., b & liv Weesel
	Catha. Pauluszen		j.d., b & liv there
__.__	Corn'ls Vreelandt	289	of Essex Co.
	Margaretha V: Winckel		of Essex Co.
1751			
10.11	Hendrick Bruyn	290	j.m., b Second River, liv Achquechno
	Catrina Beem		j.d., b Peremies, liv Pomptan /nk
10.19	Pieter Pots	291	j.m., liv "de bogt"
	Maragrita Westervelt		j.d., liv Wegherew
12.__	Frans Post	292	j.m., b Achquechenonk
	Catlyntje Van Houte		b Totua
__.__	Hendrick Van Wageningen	293	j.m., Achquechenonk
	Annathje Van Winkele		j.d., Achquechenonk
1752			
3.24	Niclaes Ryke	294	j.m., Gansegat
	Marritje Bruyn		Gansegat
5. 9	Pieter Dirje	295	j.m., b Schralenburg
	Maria Post		j.d., b & liv Pompton
6.14	Johannis Hennion	296	j.m., b Perikenis
	Vrowtje Doremis		j.d., b Achquechenonk
7. 6	Simon Van Ess	297	j.m., Pompton
	Catlyna Deboog		j.d., Pompton
11.19	Lucas Wessels	298	j.m., Achquechenonk
	Annathje Van Driesen		j.d., Achquechenonk
11.23	Abraham Van Der Hoeff	299	j.m., b & liv Wesel
	Sarah Boss		j.d., b & liv Gansegat
12. 4	Simon Van Ess	300	j.m., both b & liv Pompton cong
	Elizabet Mandeviel		j.d.
12.21	Cornelus Van Vorst	301	j.m., both b & liv Achquechenonk
	Annetje Tours		j.d.

Date	Married	Item	Remarks
12.24	Tade Van Ydestien Elizabeth Nix	302	j.m., both b & liv Achquech. j.d.
1753 1. 5	Johannes Van Rype Cristiena Pieterse	303	j.m., both b & liv Achquechenonk j.d.
2.17	Abraham Van Winkele Rachel Van Rype	304	j.m., both b & liv in our cong j.d.
3.15	Pieter Jacobusse Lea Van Rype	305	, wid, both from our cong j.d.
4.29	Cornelus Westervelt Jenneke Van Hoorn	306	j.m., both b & liv in our cong j.d.
6. 5	Thomas Van Rype Neeltje Vreeland	307	j.m., both b & liv in our cong j.d.
6.11	Gerrit Van Wageninge Saartje Van Winkle	308	wid, both from our cong j.d.
6. 3	Helmich Van Houten Aegje Vreeland	309	j.m., both from Bergen j.d.
6. 2	Isaac Van Rype Catrina Van Rype	310	j.m., both from our cong j.d.
6.12	Jacob Toers Catlyntje Kip	311	j.m., both from our cong j.d.
8. 9	Rynhart Bartholf Jaccomyntje Berry	312	j.m., both from Pompton cong j.d.
9.24	Abraham Gerritse Annatje Roome	313	j.m., b Slotterdam, liv De Panne j.d., liv Pompton
10.15	Adriaen Post Annatje Post	314	wid, both from our cong j.d.
11.18	Pieter Meed Jenneke Van Winkele	315	j.m., both from our cong j.d.
1754 1. 1	Jacob Bovie Antje Kool	316	j.m., b Albany j.d., b Uylekill, liv there
1. 9	Hendrick Veltman Rachel Wesselse	317	wid, both from our cong wid
1.20	Johannis Eliasse Vreeland R. Jennicke Post	318	j.m., both from our cong j.d.
3.31	Abraham Beem Sarah Meed	319	j.m., Pompton j.d., Pompton
4. 6	Johannis Van Rype Hester Stynmets	320	j.m., both from our cong j.d.
5.27	Claes Vreland Catrina Van Duyn	321	j.m., both from Pompton cong j.d.
8.__	Christoffel Zindel Rebecca Bruyn	322	j.m., b Germany, liv Gansegat j.d., b Gansegat, liv there
9.15	Abraham Bertholf Maragrietje Mandeviel	323	j.m., b Schralenburg, liv Pompton j.d., b Hanover, liv Pompton

Date	Married	Item	Remarks
11. 9	Gysbert Peek Helena Van Winkele	324	j.m., b New York, liv Second River j.d., b Second River, liv there
11.17	Simeon Van Rype Maragrietje Pieterse	325	j.m., both b & liv Slotterdam j.d.
12. 2	Hendrick Mandeviel Rachel Spier	326	j.m., both b & liv Pompton j.d.
12. 8	Jacob J. Van Houte Helena Kip	327	j.m., b New Brunswyk, liv Achquechenk j.d., b Achquechenk, liv there
12.15	Hendrick Van Wageninge Neesje Van Wageninge	328	j.m., liv De Panne j.d., b & liv Slotterdam
1755 1.12	John Harris Elizabeth Kip	329	j.m., b Elizabethtown, both liv this j.d., b Achquechnonk /cong
1.19	Adrijaen A. Post Geertje Vreeland	330	j.m., Achquechenonk j.d., Achquechenonk
3.23	Arie Sisco Rachel Jacobusse	331	j.m., b Povershon, liv Hanover j.d., b & liv Pechquaneck
3.27	Anthony Bruyn Metje Van Giese	332	j.m., b & liv Second River j.d., b & liv our cong
5.19	Adam Tiemout Shalotte Hosk	333	j.m., b (B)wachaw, liv Rackerack j.d., b Uylekil, liv Steenaghte Val
6. 8	Christoffel Nix Sarah Hennion	334	j.m. j.d., b Esopus
6.15	Isaac Pouwelse Rachel Van Ess	335	j.m., b Povershon, liv "gebergte" j.d., b & liv Pomptansche Vlackte
7.27	Cornelius Ellis Magdalena Vanderbilt	336	wid, from Richmond Co., Staten Eyland j.d., from the same place
8.17	Barent Kool Catrina Post	337	j.m., b Hackensack, liv Pompton wid of Hendrick Kook, liv Pompton
8.24	James Collard Geertje Didirks	338	wid, both liv Niewbarbadoes Neck j.d.
8.30	Tomas Ellen Elizabeth Poulusse	339	both from Hackkensack cong
9.11	Jacob Rome Saartje Spier	340	j.m., both liv Pomptan cong j.d.
9.21	Frances Post Rachel Van Rype	341	wid, liv Wesel wid of Abraham Van Winkele, liv Wesel
9.21	Waling Van Vorst Catrina Van Eydestyn	342	j.m., both b & liv New Barbados Neck j.d.
10. 6	Johannis Maurisse Geertruy Steeger	343	j.m., b & liv Pechquaneck j.d., b Gansegat, liv Tawachaw
11.19	Samuell Rome Grietje Kool	344	j.m., b & liv Pompton j.d., b Hackensack, liv Weesel
11.30	Dirrick Van Rype Claasje Vreland	345	j.m., b & liv Achquechnonk j.d., b & liv Wesel

Date	Married	Item	Remarks
12. 1	Johannis Spier Lea Post	346	b Achquechenonk, liv "gebergte" j.d., liv Wesel
12.21	Thomas Van Rype Saertje Van Rype	347	j.m., both b & liv Ackquechenonk j.d.
12.21	Johannis Vreeland Antje Van Blerkom	348	j.m., b & liv Achquechenonck j.d., b & liv New Barbados N(eck)
12.28	Michiel E. Vreland Jannitje Van Winkele	349	j.m., both b & liv Achquechenonk j.d.
1756			
3.11	Cornelus Doremis Elizabeth Van Der Hoeff	350	wid of Rachel Demoree, liv Perckenis j.d., b & liv Achquechnonk cong
3.14	Jacob Meed Maria Derjee	351	j.m., b & liv Pompton wid, liv Pompton
3.30	Dirrick Deboe, j.m. Elizabeth Sanderse	352	b New Barbadoes Neck, liv Newark Mou j.d., b & liv Gansegat /ntains
5. 4	Samuell Johnson Maragrieta White	353	liv Second River liv Wesel
5.17	Nathaniel Ford Geesje Francisco	354	j.m. liv Gansegat
5.23	Johannis Winne Hannah Jeralleman	355	j.m., both b & liv Second River j.d.
9.25	Jacobus Slot Zophia Jeffers	356	j.m., liv Wenackkie "in de Nots" b Raritan, liv Stone House
12.20	Roelif Van Houte Annatje Kip	357	j.m., both liv Perckenis j.d.
12.26	France Post Marigrietje Van Wageninge	358	j.m., both b & liv Wesel j.d.
1757			
1.23	Johannis Cockkifer Jenny S(wi)ner	359	j.m., both b & liv this cong j.d.
3.13	Marthen Van Duyn Doritie Van Der Hoef	360	j.m., Pompton cong
2.14	Niccasie Kip Lea Mandeviel	361	j.m., b & liv Perckeniss j.d., b & liv Hanover
4.14	Jacobus Van Duyn Hester Jacobusse	362	j.m., b & liv Tawachaw j.d., b Pechquaneck, liv Gansegat
4.14	Syas Harvey Marritje Ryke	363	j.m., b Newersings, liv Pechquaneck j.d., b & liv Gansegat
4.14	Adolph Bras Sara Besset	364	j.m., b & liv Niew York j.d., b & liv Wesel
5. 8	Willem Mandeviel Elizabeth Nederman	365	j.m., b & liv on the Vlakte j.d., b & liv Slotterdam
6.29	Daniel Van Winkel Sarah Brass	366	j.m., liv Second River j.d., Achquechnonk
5.14	Marynis Van Rype Catrina Cogh	367	j.m., b & liv Saddle River b & liv Slotterdam

Date	Married	Item	Remarks
10.18	Johannis Toers Agnietje Va Winkel	368	j.m., both from our cong
__.__	Gerrit Van Rype Fytje Van Winkel	369	j.m., both b & liv Achquechnonk j.d.
11. 6	Barent Spier Jannitje Bond	370	j.m., b Pemmerepog j.d., b Niew York
12.10	Stephanus Bertholf Marytje Mandeviel	371	both liv Pompton
12.10	George Beaty Antje Snyder	372	j.m. j.d., liv Niewfoundland
12.11	Hendrick Mandeviel Sarah Bertholf (groom's given name "Pieter" crossed out)	373	j.m., both liv Pompton cong j.d.
12.13	Jacobus Hyler Antje Van Winkel	374	liv Uylekil j.d., liv Rackeway

1758

Date	Married	Item	Remarks
1. 8	Coenraet Lyn Claartje Van Houte	375	j.m., both liv Pompton cong j.d.
12. 2	Jacob E. Vreeland Antje Post	376	j.m., both b & liv Achquechnonk j.d.
12.14	Dirrick Jacobusse Sarah Steeger	377	j.m., both b & liv Gansegat "geberg j.d. /te"
12.27	Gerrit Gerritse Van Wagening Rachel Westervelt	378	j.m. j.d., liv Slotterdam

1759

Date	Married	Item	Remarks
4. 1	Robbert Drummond Jannitje Vreeland	379	j.m., both from our cong j.d.
10.20	Johannis G. Post Catrina Van Winkel	380	wid, both liv in our cong wid
12. 1	Gerrit Toers Maragrieta Van Winkel	381	j.m., Bergen Co., both from our cong j.d., Essex Co.

1760

Date	Married	Item	Remarks
12.13	Nicolaas Vreland Nancy Basset	382	wid j.d.
12.18	Cornelus Post Marritje Cadmus	383	j.m. j.d.
12.21	George Wynant Sarah Jurryanse Van Rype	384	

1761

Date	Married	Item	Remarks
12.19	Thomas Post Maria Vreelandt	385	

1763

Date	Married	Item	Remarks
4.13	Samuell Slingerland Marritje Cachlin	386	j.m., both liv Hanover j.d.
4.13	Dirk Francisco Maragrietje Cachlin	387	Hanover Hanover
4.14	Isaac Halenbeek Eva Slot	388	j.m., both from Hanover cong j.d.

1763, 1767, 1774, 1775

Date	Married	Item	Remarks
4.17	Pieter Vreland Leja Doremus	389	j.m., Achquechnonk j.d., Achquechnonk
9. 3	Johannis Brower Aaltje Smit	390	j.m., both from Achquechnonk cong j.d.
9. 4	Johannis Spier Catrina Doremis	391	j.m., both Stone Hoose Plains j.d.
9. 8	Hendrick Bruyn Hannah Clark	392	j.m., b & liv Gansegat j.d., b Raway, liv Gansegat
11.16	Abraham Van Rype Catrina Van Winkel	393	j.m., Achquechnonk j.d., Achquechnonk
11.20	Hendrick Van Blerkom Annatje Van Winkel	394	j.m., Achquechnonk j.d., Achquechnonk
11.26	Christopher Jurryanse Annatje Brower	395	(j.m.), both from our cong j.d.

1767

Date	Married	Item	Remarks
1. 4	Cornelus Post Anna Maria Cogh	396	wid j.d.
1.18	Adriaen Sip Gerritje Sip	397	j.m. j.d.
1.22	Dirk Van Rype Elizabeth Van Houte	398	j.m. j.d.
1.29	Jacob Jacobusse Sarah Jacobusse	399	j.m. j.d.
1.29	Josiah Stagg Elizabeth Low	400	j.m. j.d.

END OF VOLUME I

*Date	Married	Item	Remarks
8.14	Micha Gillam Christina Cogh	401	
8.14	Jacob Smith jr Fytje Post	402	
10.23 10.30	Robert McWilliams, wid Anna Nutter	403	b Ireland, both liv Achquechnonck b Nieuw York
11.26 12.25	Memmerduke Ackerman Lena Van Eydestyn	404	j.m., b Hackensack, liv at the Neck j.d., b & liv this cong
__.__	Roelof Boogert Hendrickje Ackerman	405	mar at Hackensack
12.25	Cornelius Vreeland Elizabeth Vreeland	406	

1775

Date	Married	Item	Remarks
1. 2	John Earl Catharina Hopper	407	
2.16	Cornelius Hall Catharina Van Imburgh	408	
2.11 3. 4	Johannis Stagg Marytje Spier	409	j.m., both b & liv Wesel j.d.

* - see page 205

*Date	Married	1775-1776 Item	Remarks
2.17 3. 5	Barent Retan Annaatje Van Rype	410	j.m., b Wykhoff, liv Wesel j.d., b & liv Wesel
4.29 6. 5	Casparus Stymets Maria Evertse	411	j.m., b Achquechnonck, both liv this j.d., b Pemberpock /cong
6.11	Petrus Christie Beletje Westervelt	412	mar at Schralenburgh
6.11	Jacob Haring Williamje Banta	413	mar at Schralenburgh
6.10 8. 3	Christophel Stager Sarah Ryker	414	j.m. j.d., liv in our cong
8.12	Abraham Huysman Marytje Terhune	415	
8.14	Marynus Vreland Geesje Vreland	416	
8.20	Thomas Van Horn Maragrieta Devorsne	417	
9. 9 9.30	Matheus Everse, wid Lena Mouritse, wid	418	b Hackensack, liv Achquechnonck b & liv Morris Co.
10.21 11. 5	Elias Vreeland jr Lea Van Vechten	419	j.m., b this cong, liv Chemoking j.d., b & liv our cong
10. 7 11.12	Johannis Evertse Sthntje Van Eydestyn	420	j.m., b & liv Bergen j.d., b & liv our cong
11.30	Dirck Boss Antje Stagg	421	
12. 7	John Bogert Lea Van Wagenen	422	
11.25 12.16	John Marinus Catharina Post	423	j.m., b Achquechnonck, liv Persippany j.d., b & liv Achquechnonck
12.24	Samuel Hudnut Heaty Drummond	424	
1776			
1.13 2.11	John Peek Annaatje Van Winkel	425	j.m., both b & liv Poverson j.d.
2.24	Dirck Stagg Annaatje Wesselse	426	
2.17 3.16	John Moor Sarah Boss	427	j.m., b Puremus, liv Slotterdam j.d., b Second River, liv Slotterda
4.13	Jacob Pier Cathalyntje Evertse	428	
5.26 6. 2	Jacobus Ennis Marytje Spier	429	j.m., both b & liv our cong j.d.
8.10 8.31	Gerret Spier Grietje Ennis	430	j.m., both b & liv our cong j.d.
8.11 9.22	John Van Rypen Lea Winne	431	j.m., both b & liv Second River j.d.

* - see page 205

*Date	Married	Item	Remarks
10.12	William Pharrow	432	j.m., b Egg Harbour, liv Wesel
11. 9	Salley Griffith, j.d.		b Second River, liv Nieuw Barbadoes Neck
11. 9	Arie Van Vorst	433	j.m., both b & liv Nieuw Barbadoes
1. 1.1777	Lena Berrie		j.d. /Neck

1777

	Dirck Stagg	434	wid
1.14	Peggy Stagg		wid
3.25	Johannes Durjee	435	j.m., b Lang Eyland, liv Hackensack
3.31	Maria Brinckerhoff		wid, b N. York, liv Hackensack
2.22	Dirck Pickstone	436	wid, b & liv Stonehouse
4.22	Aaltje Mouritze		j.d., b Pechkoneck, liv Stonehouse
5.15	Hendrick A: Zabriskie	437	j.m., both b & liv Schralenburgh
	Wyntje Leydecker		j.d.
	Jacob Ryker	438	
5.23	Sietje Vreland		
6.21	Joris Doremus	439	j.m., both b & liv Slotterdam
7. 7	Antje Berdan		j.d.
6.22	Frans Post	440	wid, both liv in the Boght
7.13	Maragrieta Van Rypen		wid
	Hendrick Ferdon	441	
7.24	Jenny Archibold		
	John Lawrence jr	442	
9.11	Elizabeth Wells		
9. 6	Frederick Stymets	443	j.m., both b New-York, liv Schralen
9.18	Ann Barrey		j.d. /burch
9.20	Thomas Van Rypen	444	wid, both b & liv Achquechnonck
9.21	Sarah Post		wid of Wesel Wesselse
	Gerret Van Rypen jr	445	
9.25	Lea Simmons		
	Francois Van Winkel	446	
10. 3	Susannah Forister		
9.20	Ewout Van Gelder	447	j.m., b Nieuw-York, liv Pomptan
10.13	Geesje Van Wagenen		j.d., b & liv Achquechnonck
11. 8	Hendrick Spier	448	j.m., both b & liv our cong
12. 6	Jannetje Van Giesen		j.d.
	John Hoogelandt	449	
12.27	Susanna Piearson		
12.31	Hermanus Brass	450	wid, liv Hackensack
1.4.1778	Cornelia Smith, j.d.		b Peremus, liv Nieuw Barbadoes Neck

1778

1.23	Hendrick Harris	451	j.m., b Perikenis, liv Slotterdam
2.14	Neesje Van Hoorn		j.d., b & liv Slotterdam
	Jacobus Spier	452	
3.21	Rachel King		
	James Boggs	453	
4.14	Lane Lisk		

* see page 205

*Date	Married	Item	Remarks
4.21	Doctor Nicholas Roach Antje Gerritse	454	
5. 9 5.10	John Westerveldt Grietje Ackerman	455	j.m., b & liv Schralenburgh j.d., b Peremus, liv Hackensack
5.10	Enoch Vreeland, wid Janneke Marcelis, wid	456	b Bergen, liv Nieuw Barbadoes Neck b Perikenis, liv there
5.19	Arie King Caty McCrea	457	
5.31	Marinus Gerritse Annaatje Lisk	458	
6.28	Hendrick Van Derlinde Verbryck Antje Johnson	459	
6. 6 7. 2	Cornelius Van Vorst Annaatje Outwater	460	wid, both b & liv Nieuw Barbadoes wid of Ab'm Berrie /Neck
6.20 7. 5	Adolph Brass Maragrieta Van Der Hoef	461	j.m., b & liv Achquechnonck j.d., b Gansegat, liv our cong
6.20 7. 7	David Doremus Sarah Drummond	462	wid, b & liv Perikenis j.d., b Perikenis, liv our cong
7.22 7.26	Albert Van Voorhees Rachel Hopper	463	j.m., b & liv Hackensack j.d., b & liv Perremus
7.11 9. 8	Johannis Van Der Hoef Maria Linsie, j.d.	464	j.m., b Menonkong, liv N. Barbadoes b & liv N. Barbadoes Neck /Neck
11. 8	Richard Berry Antje Vreland	465	
10.23 11.15	Hendrick Wesselse Jannetje Degraauw	466	j.m., b & liv Achquechnonck j.d., b Peremus, liv our cong
11.28 12.20	Egbert Doremus Geesje Jacobusse	467	j.m., both b & liv Peckmans River j.d.
12.12 1.14.1779	Joost Kogh Hendrickje Boss	468	j.m., both b & liv Slotterdam j.d.

Date	Married	Item	Remarks
1.17	Joseph Devoe Aaltje Outwater	469	
1.10 1.31	John Bruyn Pietertje Winne	470	j.m., both b & liv Second River j.d.
1.28	William Baker Geertje Brass	471	j.m., b Engeland, liv Hackensack j.d., liv Hackensack
3. 4 3. 7	John Goetschius Catharina Butler	472	wid, b Philadelphia, both liv Poll j.d., b N. Barbadoes Neck /evly
3. 8	Albert Westerveldt Marytje Van Saan	473	
3.27 4.11	Jacobus Van Seyl Catharina Goetschius	474	j.m., b & liv Paremus j.d., b Schralenburgh, liv Paremus
5. 2	Richard Van Houten Rachel Van Eydestyn	475	

* see page 205

*Date	Married	Item	Remarks
		1779-1780	

*Date	Married	Item	Remarks
5.30	Johannis Corby Elizabeth Sinderbox	476	wid wid
6. 4	Abraham Treve(s) Hannah Van Oostrandt	477	
6. 6	Petrus Paulusse Jenneke Van Winkele	478	wid wid
6.12 6.27	Johannis Bigley Franscyntje Van Giesen	479	wid, both liv our cong wid
8. 7	John Van Beuren Catharina Vreeland	480	
8.15	Gerret Van Alen Lea Vreeland	481	wid wid
8.15	Abraham Van Der Beeck Margarita Godwin	482	
9. 5	Jacobus Chappel Sarah Bebout	483	
9.12	Jacobus Jacobusse Catharina Gerrebrantse	484	
9.17 9.26	Arent Cogh Annaatje Ackerman	485	j.m., b & liv Slotterdam j.d., b Peremus, liv Hackensack
11.15 11.30	Cornelius Van Rypen Elizabeth Vreeland	486	wid, both b & liv Wesel j.d.
12.26	John Terhune Sarah Vreeland	487	
	1780		
1.24	Josua Townley Charlotte Eyons	488	
1.22 2. 6	William Gustavus Kingsland Elizabeth Demsey	489	j.m., both b & liv N. Barbadoes j.d. /Neck
2. 6	Coll. Samuel Hay Elizabeth Neil	490	wid
5.11 5.15	Jacobus Beem Rachel Van Voorhees	491	j.m., b & liv Wenagge j.d., b & liv Wyckhoff
5.12	Gerrit Degrauw Sarah Devoor	492	j.m., b Nieuw Bronswyck, liv Hanover j.d., b Nieuw York, liv Hanover
6.11 6.11	Cornelius Hopper Catharina Terhune	493	j.m., b & liv Pollovlay j.d., b N. York, liv Pollovlay
6. 1 6.11	Jacob Van Winkelen sr Jenneke Van Winkelen	494	j.m., b & liv our cong j.d., b & liv Weggereuw
8.27	Hermanus Van Rypen Maria Van Rypen	495	
7. 8 10.29	Lukas Van Winkelen Lena Van Wagenen	496	j.m., both b & liv our cong j.d.
8.19	Abraham Spier Metje Van Giesen	497	j.m., both b & liv Stonehouse j.d.

* see page 205

*Date	Married	Item	Remarks
11.17	Jacob Huston	498	j.m., b Second River, both liv our
12.24	Jannetje Stymets		j.d., b Achquechenonck /cong
1781			
	Michiel E. Vrelandt	499	wid
1. 7	Martha Bruyn		wid
1. 3	John Earl	500	wid, both b & liv Hackensack
1.14	Elizabeth Ackerman		j.d.
	John J. Roosevelt	501	
1.23	Mary Schuyler		
12.30.1780	Cornelius Tho's Joh's Doremus	502	j.m., b Wachauw, liv
1.28.1781	Marytje Billington, wid, b & liv Stonehouse		/Gansegat
	Pieter Aal	503	
2.13	Cathalyntje Syndel		
	Abraham Van Rypen	504	wid
3. 4	Neesje Gerritse		wid of Geurt Gerrebrantse
	Jacobus Bruyn	505	wid
3.10	Selly Smith		wid of Mr: Immory
5.26	Joris Wissel	506	j.m., b Germany, liv Wesel
6. 4	Anna Vreeland		j.d., b & liv Wesel
6. 7	Johannis Gerrebrantse	507	j.m., both b & liv our cong
8.16	Marytje Gerrebrantse		j.d.
6.23	Daniel Toers	508	j.m., b & liv Povershom
	Marytje Jacobusse		j.d., b & liv Peckmans River
7.15	Isaac Kingsland jr	509	j.m., liv Povershon
7.22	Hillitje Franscisco		j.d., b & liv Second River
	Pieter Gerritse	510	wid
8. 5	Jannetje Van Veghten		wid of Ad. Post
	William Kingsland	511	
10.21	Maragrita Jeraalman		
	Jacob Smalley	512	
11. 3	Tabitha Moore		
11.15	Thomas McDonald	513	j.m., b N. York, liv Gemoenepah
	Annaatje Van Schyven		j.d., b Peremus, liv Pemmerpoch
	Anthony Brown	514	
11.24	Elizabeth Francisco		
12.29	Pieter Post	515	wid, b & liv Slotterdam
2.10.1782	Elizabeth Bosch, wid of Henry Glass, b & liv N. Barbadoes		/Neck
1782			
	Resolve Waldrom	516	
1.30	Betty Godwin		
	James Ennis	517	wid
5.26	Jannetje Brouwer		wid
5. 8	Marcelus Post jr	518	b Achquechnonck, liv Wesel
6.11	Jenneke Ouke		j.d., b Lange Eylandt, liv Wesel
	Isaac Kip	519	wid
6.27	Jannetje Van Winkele		

* see page 205

*Date	Married	Item	Remarks
9. 1	David Demarest Maria King	520	wid wid
9.15	John Devoursne Anna Vreeland	521	wid wid
10. 6 10.26	Johannis C. Post Cornelia Cadmus	522	j.m., both b & liv Slotterdam j.d.
10.22 11.10	Hendrick F. Post Jannetje Van Houten	523	j.m., b Wesel, liv Bergen j.d., b & liv Wesel
12.13 12.29	Theodorus Van Winkelen Annaatje Van Eydestyn	524	j.m., both b & liv our cong j.d.
12.28 1.9.1783	Elias J. Vreeland Elizabeth Post	525	j.m., both b & liv our cong j.d.

(mar date gives groom's middle initial of "E.")

| 12.31
1.19.1783 | Dirck Van Der Hoef
Nency Thomas | 526 | j.m., b Gansegat, liv our cong
j.d., b Perikenis, liv our cong |
| 12.31
1.26.1783 | Johannis Pier
Lena Vreeland | 527 | j.m., both b & liv our cong
j.d. |

1783

1. 9 1.19	Thade J. Van Eydestyn Theodosie Erl	528	wid, both liv our cong wid of Thade Van Winkelen
1.12 1.19	Pieter Sandvoort Neeltje Van Ess	529	j.m., both liv Gansegat wid of Stephen Berry
1.25	John C. Westervelt Anna Van Rypen	530	
2. 1 3. 4	Gerret Egbertse Rachel Spier	531	j.m., both b & liv Stone House j.d.
2. 7 2.23	Waling Van Winkele Pietertje Van Rypen	532	j.m., both b & liv our cong j.d.
2.26	James Butler Anna Kingsland	533	
3. 1	Casparus Degraw Lena Jurrianse	534	
2. 8 3. 2	Jacob Van Noorstrand Geertje Degrauw	535	j.m., liv our cong j.d., b Peremus, liv our cong
3.23	David Blair Belitje Vreeland	536	
3.29 4.20	Hendrick Kool Abigail McCartie	537	j.m., b Pomptan, liv in the Boght j.d., b & liv Slotterdam
5. 1	John Gerritse Antje Toers	538	
6. 7 8. 3	George Van Eydestyn Lena Van Rypen	539	j.m., both b & liv our cong j.d.
6.21 7.12	John Skidmore, j.m. Catharina Degrauw, j.d.	540	b Second River, liv Nieuw Barbadoes b Nieuw Barbadoes Neck, liv there /Neck
9.21	Gulielmus Delmot Sophia Vreelandt	541	

* - see page 205

*Date	Married	Item	Remarks
9.26	Anthony Steenbeck	542	wid, b N. Bronswyck, both liv Peck
	Aaltje Smith		wid of Joh's Brouwer /mans River
12.17	Lothen Heddey	543	j.m., b New-Ark Mountains, both liv
2.8.1784	Mary Marygold		j.d., b Lange Pand /Achquechnonck
	Johannis Emmans	544	
12.20	Selley Schoonmaker		
12.24	Casparus Van Eydestyn	545	j.m., both b & liv New Barbadoes
2.1.1784	Sarah Van Vorst		j.d. /Neck

1784

*Date	Married	Item	Remarks
	John Spier	546	
1. 3	Jannitje Van Imburgh		
	Henry Edeson	547	
1. 3	Elizabeth Furlow		
1. 3	Helmich Van Winkelen	548	j.m., both b & liv our cong
1.24	Marrytje Post		j.d.
	Henry Duplacey	549	
1.22	Anna Buttler		
2. 5	Michael G. Vreeland	550	j.m., both b & liv our cong
3.13	Marrytje Van Rypen		j.d.
	Simeon Van Imburgh	551	wid
2. 1	Marragrietje Finly		(wid)
	Cornelius Sip	552	
2. 8	Marytje Van Rypen		
3.13	Pieter Terhune	553	j.m., b Pollevly, liv Saddle River
4.11	Jenneke Van Winkele		j.d., b & liv our cong
	Arie Bos	554	
5.15	Elizabeth Cadmus		
	Roeliph Van Wagenen	555	
6.17	Saartje Jurrianse		
6.17	John Parrot	556	j.m., b Nieuw York
7. 8	Rachel Koejeman		j.d., b & liv Stoonhouse
7. 3	Angus McLean, j.m.	557	b Schotland, liv Nieuw-Barbadoes Neck
	Catharina Kingsland, wid of William Garven, b & liv Nieuw-Barbad		/oes Neck
7.10	David Van Bussen	558	j.m., both b & liv our cong
8. 8	Sietje Van Eydestyn		j.d.
	Hendrick Van Blerkum	559	wid
7.15	Elizabeth Zabriskie		wid
7.24	Adoniram Pritten	560	j.m., b Morris Town, both liv Ach
8.19	Abigail Holstead		j.d., b Keckiat /quechnonck
7.31	Albert Ackerman	561	j.m., b & liv Peremus
8.21	Antje Van Winkelen		j.d., b & liv Achquechnonck
	Adriaan Van Rypen	562	
8. 1	Sarah Kelliham		
8. 7	Cornelius Van Giesen	563	j.m., both b & liv Stoonhouse
11.17	Sophia Sigler		j.d.

* - see page 205

1784-1785

*Date	Married	Item	Remarks
	Jacob Vreeland	564	wid
8.18	Catharina Van Rypen		wid
8.24	John Berry	565	j.m., b & liv Nieuw-Barbadoes Neck
9.12	Sietje Van Rypen		j.d., b & liv Wezel
9.11	Casparus Van Eydestyn	566	j.m., b & liv Nieuw-Barbadoes Neck
	Annaatje Post		j.d., b & liv Slotterdam
9.18	Abraham Brouwer	567	j.m., b & liv Peckmans River
10.14	Lena Sindel		j.d., b & liv Gansegat
10.30	Andrias Cadmus	568	j.m., b & liv Slotterdam
11.20	Pryntje Doremus		j.d., b Wachchauw, liv Slotterdam
	Hermanus Spier	569	
11.27	Mary Dow		
11.27	William Morris, j.m.	570	b Ireland, liv in the Bocht
12.30	Elizabeth Styles, wid of Joh's Hennion, b Remmerspoch, liv in		/the Bocht

<u>1785</u>

	Lucas Wesselse	571	wid
2. 4	Peggy Booth		
	Fransois Van Winkelen	572	wid
2. 5	Elizabeth Dowe		wid
2.12	Abraham Ryker jr	573	b Gansegat
3.10	Hannah Ennis		j.d., liv Achquechnonck
3. 5	Fransois Van Eydestyne	574	j.m., b & liv N. Barbadoes Neck
3.20	Antje Tyse		j.d., liv our cong
	Capt. Henry Jeraalam	575	wid
3.28	Maria Spier		wid
4. 3	Benjamin Demill, j.m.	576	b Philips Burgh, liv Nieuw Barbadoe
4.24	Maria Hurly, j.d.		b & liv Nieuw Barbadoes Neck /Neck
	Abraham King	577	
4.16	Elizabeth Spier		
	John Spier jr	578	
4.23	Margarieta Jeraleman		
5.15	Gerret J. Zabriskie	579	j.m., b & liv Peremus
6.12	Martha Mills		j.d., b Waggerauw, liv Wesel
5.21	John Holm	580	j.m., b Second River, both liv Ach
6.25	Marytje Roos		b Keckeyet /quechnonck
4.23	John Fergeson	581	j.m., both liv Nieuw-Barbadoes Neck
5.26	Elenor McLean		j.d.
6.11	John Gendor	582	j.m., b Hesse Cassel, liv Pollevly
6.25	Maria Bruyn		wid of Michael Vreeland, liv Pollevly
	Jacob Spier	583	wid
6.12	Saartje Wynants		wid
6.17	Hendrick J. Spier	584	j.m., b & liv Achquechnonck
7.10	Metje Vreeland		j.d., b Totua, liv Stoonhouse
	John Maghee	585	
7.14	Sarah Dow		

* see page 205

*Date	Married	Item	Remarks
6.25	Jacob Toers	586	j.m., both b & liv Slotterdam
7.17	Marytje Post		j.d.
7.16	Cornelius Pier	587	j.m., b & liv our cong
8.14	Antje Vreelandt		wid of Richard Berrie, b & liv our cong
	James Adams	588	wid
8.22	Catharina Van Inmburgh		wid
7.18	Jacob Morris	589	j.m., b & liv N. York
8.28	Marrytje Van Rypen		j.d., b & liv Wezel
7.21	Isaac Van Houten	590	j.m., b Wesel, liv Slotterdam
10.16	Annaatje Boss		j.d., b & liv Saddle River
8.19	James Hodge	591	j.m., b New Wimsor, liv Hackensack
8.29	Salley McCreere		j.d., liv Hackensack
	John Eaton	592	
10. 2	Mary Brouwer		
9.24	Isaac Vreeland	593	j.m., b & liv Pollvly
10. 2	Jinne Bruyn, wid of Paulus Van Winkele, b Wanagje, liv Pollevly		
	David Demarest	594	wid
12.27	Elizabeth Deeder		wid
1786			
3. 4	Isaac Pier	595	j.m., b & liv Gansegat
	Marytje Post		j.d., b & liv Peckmans River
	John Gomez	596	
4. 1	Cornelia Berdan		
3.11	Abraham Brouwer	597	wid, both b & liv Peckmans River
4. 5	Fytje Jacobusse		j.d.
3.26	Roeliph Post	598	j.m., b & liv Peckmans River
	Marretje Post		j.d., b & liv Wesel
3.11	John Evet	599	both liv Second River
4. 6	Elizabeth Davie		wid
4.22	Michael Post	600	j.m., b & liv Slotterdam
5.11	Jannetje Ackerman		j.d., b & liv Polle Vley
4.22	Adriaan M. Post	601	j.m., both b & liv Achquechnonck
5.14	Lybetje Van Rypen		j.d.
4.29	Paulus Ratan jr	602	j.m., b & liv in the Boght
5.14	Metje Spier		j.d., b & liv Stoonhouse
4.29	Pieter Van Giesen	603	j.m., both b & liv Stoonhouse Plains
5.14	Sarah Spier		j.d.
5. 4	Johannes A. Post	604	j.m., b & liv Slotterdam
	Maria Prefoort		j.d., b & liv Per Emmis
	Roeliph Post	605	
5.14	Marretje Post		
	Dinnis McPick	606	wid
5.18	Jinne Kingsland		
	David Lynsem	607	
7. 4	Susanna Romyn		

* see page 205

*Date	Married	Item	Remarks

1786-1787

6.18 Gilbert Van Emburgh   608 j.m., b & liv Nieuw Barbadoes Neck
7. 4 Maria Kerck, j.d., b Nieuw Arck Mountains, liv N. Barbadoes Neck

John Van Wagenen   609
7.23 Rachel Traphagen

6.21 Gerret Van Vorst   610 j.m., both b & liv Nieuw Barbadoes
8. 5 Maria Van Eydestyn   j.d.   /Neck

7.13 David Ackerman   611 wid, b Hackensack
8.31 Peggy Jeraalman, wid of Aaron Kingsland, b & liv Nieuw Barbadoes
                                                                /Neck

7.14 Gerret Van Vorst jr   612 b & liv Nieuw Barbadoes Neck
8.19 Elizabeth Bilju   j.d., b Staten Eyland, liv Remmerpoch

9. 9 Christophel Vreeland   613 j.m., b & liv Morris Co.
9.30 Catharina Wesselse   j.d., b Essex Co., liv Morris Co.

11. 4 Abraham Vreeland   614 j.m., both b & liv Pollevly
11.30 Rachel Ackerman   j.d.

11.18 Philip Barry   615 j.m., b & liv Nieuw Barbadoesneck
12.16 Eva Van Winkelen   j.d., b & liv Achquechnonck

11.18 Albert Ryker   616 j.m., b Gansegat
12. 7 Catharina Hurley   j.d., b & liv Nieuw Barbadoes Neck
1787

Abraham Koejeman   617
1.11 Jacomyntje Vreelandt

Adrian J. Post   618 wid
1.23 Marretje Post

Adrian Sip   619
1.23 Lea Van Rypen

Daniel L. Schoonmaker 620
2.22 Elizabeth Jeraalman

2.17 Elias J. Vreeland   621 j.m., b & liv Wezel
3. 8 Maragrietje Post   j.d., b & liv Slotterdam

2.24 Dirck Paulusse   622 j.m., b & liv Povershon
4.19 Annaatje Gerrebrantse   j.d., b & liv our cong

3. 5 Johannis Van Winkelen jr 623 j.m., both b & liv our cong
4.15 Sarah Van Winkelen   j.d.

4. 7 John Sulivan   624 j.m., b Sussex, liv Bergen Co.
5. 7 Anna Willer   j.d., b Essex, liv Bergen Co.

4. 7 Cornelius Shepard   625 j.m., both liv Bergen Co.
5. 7 Marritje Ryker   j.d.

4.28 George Van Eydestyn   626 wid, both b & liv our cong
5.28 Geesje Vreeland   wid

6. 6 Cornelius Doremus   627 j.m., b Wachchaw, liv Slotterdam
6.10 Styntje Van Rypen   j.d., b & liv Slotterdam

5.28 Henry Kingsland   628 wid, both liv Essex Co.
7. 1 Jannetje Brown   j.d.

5.31 Jacobus Van Rypen   629 j.m., b & liv Achquechnonck
6.30 Aaltje Vreeland   j.d., b & liv Poverson

* see page 205

*Date	Married	Item	Remarks
6.20	Johannes Van Rypen	630	wid, both b & liv Achquechnonck
8. 5	Jannetje Van Noorstrand		j.d.
7. 8	Theunis Bruyn	631	j.m., both b & liv in Second River
7.15	Sarah Ontwater		j.d. /cong
8. 3	Cornelius Cadmus	632	j.m., b & liv Slotterdam
8.19	Jannetje Van Rypen		j.d., b Wezel, liv Slotterdam
8. 3	Jacob E. Vreeland	633	j.m., both b & liv our cong
9. 2	Marretje Vreeland		j.d.
8. 3	John Van Blerkum	634	j.m., b & liv in the Boght
9. 2	Antje Jacobusse		j.d., b Wachauw, liv Achquechnonck
8.20	Anthony Steenbeck	635	wid, b Nieuw Bronswyck, liv the Notch
9.16	Dirckje Spier		wid of Jan Pier, b & liv the Notch
	Dirck Van Rypen	636	wid
10.14	Fytje Van Wagenen		wid of Dirck Vreland
10.26	Johannes H. Gerritse	637	j.m., b & liv in the Bogt
11.11	Maragrietje Van Rypen		j.d., b & liv Slotterdam
	John R. Ludlow	638	
11.25	Elizabeth Vreeland		
10.31	Gerrit Jacobusse	639	j.m., b & liv our cong
1.12.1788	Marytje Coerte		j.d., b Knobroek, liv Achquecknonck
11. 2	John Drummond jr	640	j.m., b Perikenis, liv our cong
12. 1	Grietje Boss		j.d., b Gansegat, liv Stoonhous
11.17	Jacob Van Der Beeck	641	j.m., b & liv Per Emus
1.6.1788	Maria Van Bussen		j.d., b & liv Slotterdam
12.23	Rynier Spier	642	j.m., liv Stoonhouse
3.9.1788	Marya Jacobusse		j.d., b & liv Peckmans Rivier
12.24	Francois Degrauw	643	j.m., b & both liv Nieuw Barbadoes
3.2.1788	Antje Degrauw		j.d., b Horsesymus /Neck
1788			
	William Davie	644	
1. 2	Nancy Furlong		
1.11	Jonathan Snyder	645	j.m., b Ulster Co., both liv Ach
2. 2	Martha Ackerman		j.d., in Pensylvania /quechnonck
2. 8	Hermanus P. Van Bussen	646	j.m., b Tappan, liv Slotterdam
3.16	Fytje Gerritse		j.d., b & liv Wezel
4.26	Johannes Brouwer	647	j.m., b & liv Peckmans River
6. 1	Grietje Wite, j.d.		b Achquechnonck, liv Peckmans River
	John Jorsan	648	
6.14	Margarita Sisco		
	William McLean	649	
6.24	Hester Jeraalman		
	Casper Kronick	650	
7. 6	Suca Vane		
	Stephen Kingsland	651	
7.31	Elenor Stymets		

* - see page 205

1788-1789

*Date	Married	Item	Remarks
6.28	Pieter Ackerman	652	j.m., b & liv Pollevly
8.28	Annaatje Vreland		b & liv Wezel
9.27	Joris Brinckerhoff	653	j.m., b & liv Hackensack
10.10	Rachel Terhune		j.d., b & liv Nieuw Barbadoes Neck
	John Van Rypen	654	
11.23	Henrietta Vreland		
	Gerrit Neefjes	655	
12. 6	Cathalyntje Post		
10.17	John B. Spier	656	j.m., b Nieuw-York, liv Slotterdam
12.14	Elizabeth Post		j.d., b & liv Wezel
12.24	Pieter Vreland jr	657	j.m., b Achquechnonck, liv Peckmans
1.22.1789	Maria Kerr		j.d., b & liv Pomptan /River
1789			
1.17	Jacob Ryker	658	j.m., b & liv Peckmans River
2. 8	Catharina Van Rypen		j.d., b & liv our cong
	Henry Kerck	659	
2.15	Jane Van Imburgh		
1.30	Helmich Van Giesen	660	j.m., b & liv Totua
2.22	Selly Van Noorstrand		j.d., b & liv Achquechnonck
2.14	Hermanus Degrauw	661	j.m., b Sterling, liv our cong
3. 7	Antje Montanje		j.d., b Peremus, liv our cong
2.21	Casparus Van Rypen	662	j.m., b & liv our cong
	Antje Ackerman		j.d., b & liv Pollevly
2.22	John H. King	663	j.m., both b & liv Second River
3.10	Rachel Bruyn		j.d.
	Philip Van Rypen	664	
3.29	Jannetje Sip		
	Joh. W. King	665	
4. 1	Lena Spier		
3.28	Isaac Kranck	666	j.m., liv Wezel
4. 5	Jannetje Van Houren		j.d., b Totua, liv Slotterdam
	Nicholaas Jeraalman	667	
4.18	Hester Bruyn		
	Arent King	668	
4.18	Christina Woutersse		
	Johannes Doremus	669	wid
5.31	Maragrietje Van Rypen		
5.10	Thomas Sigler	670	j.m., both b & liv Stone Hous-
6.21	Lea Spier		
6.18	William Mills	671	j.m., both liv Nieuw Barbadoes Neck
7.19	Anna Ennis		j.d.
	Gabriel Sprong	672	
7.30	Maria Byert		
7.11	Abraham A. Van Rypen	673	j.m., b & liv Wezel
8. 8	Theodosia Westerveldt		j.d., b Weggeraw, liv in the Bogt

* see page 205

*Date	Married	Item	Remarks
	Reynier Blanchard	674	
8.29	Elizabeth Van Bussen		
	John Porter	675	
8.30	Maria Snyder		
8. 6	John Sigler	676	j.m., both b & liv Stoone House
9.20	Sietje Mandeviel		j.d.
	William Ryerse jr	677	
9.20	Elienor Cook		
8.13	Pieter Gerrebrantse	678	j.m., b Stone House, liv our cong
10.31	Catharina Gerritse		j.d., b Slotterdam, liv our cong
8.15	Johannes Hemmion	679	j.m., b Keckiat, liv Rempoch
10.29	Syntje Vors		j.d., b & liv Rempoch
9. 5	Isaac Hervy	680	j.m., liv Peckmans River
9.27	Aaltje Van Houten		j.d., b Tam Point, liv Peckmans River
9.11	Hendrick Steger	681	wid, b Horse Neck, liv Povershon
10.25	Marytje Van Rypen		j.d., b & liv our cong
9.19	John M. Earl	682	j.m., b & liv Hackensack
10.25	Rachel Ackerman		j.d., b & liv Per-Eemus
	Abraham Vreland	683	
10. 5	Catharina Easterley		
10.22	Thomas Jones	684	j.m., b Keckiat, liv Rempoch
	Maria Thys		j.d., b & liv Rempoch
	Daniel Schoonmake-	685	
11.28	Elizabeth Post		
11.20	Pieter Van Eydestyn	686	j.m., b & liv our cong
12.24	Maria Furgeson		b Weschester, liv Achquechnonck
11.20	Robert Glass	687	j.m., b New-York
12.27	Sarah Banta		j.d., liv our cong
11.21	George Gerrebrantse	688	j.m., b Stone House, liv Warsession
12.17	Hannah Poulusson		j.d., b & liv Povershon
11.21	Jacob Van Rypen	689	j.m., b & liv Perikenis
12.19	Marritje Vreland		j.d., b Totua, liv Wezel
12. 5	Thomas Doremus	690	wid, liv Gansegat
	Maragrietje Ryker		wid of Siemon Van Ess, liv Gansegat
	Jonathan Holsted	691	
12.10	Isabella Neil		
12. 5	Matheus Spier	692	j.m., b Nieuw York, liv Slotterdam
1.9.1790	Cathalyntje Van Bussen		j.d., b Slotterdam, liv Wezel
1790	Isaac E. Vreland	693	
2.10	Grietje Vreland		
1. 9	Johannes Marcelusse	694	j.m., b & liv Perikenis
2.13	Jannetje Van Rypen		j.d., b & liv Achquechnonck
1. 9	Cornelius Van Der Haan	695	j.m., b & liv Achquechnonck
2.21	Maragrietje Post		j.d., b Pomptan, liv Achquechnonck

* - see page 205

1790-1791

*Date	Married	Item	Remarks
1.30	Isaac Alje	696	j.m., b Kindagkomeck, liv Wezel
2.28	Antje Ryerse		j.d., b & liv Weggerauw
	Isaac Storms	697	
3. 4	Elizabeth Parlman		
5. 1	Hendrick Laroe	698	j.m., b Remmerpock, liv Slotterdam
5.22	Annaatje Ackerman		wid of Arendt Cogh, liv Slotterdam
	John J. Berry	699	
6.13	Claasje Vreeland		
6.13	Jacob J. Vreland	700	j.m., b & liv Pollevly
6.27	Aaltje Carmer		j.d., b Tappan, liv Pollevly
	John H. Hopper	701	wid
6.27	Catharina Van Bussen		wid
7.10	Elias Yorks	702	j.m., b Nieuw York, both liv Peckmans
8.15	Rachel Ryker		j.d. /River
5.22	Casparus Boss	703	j.m., both b & liv our cong
8. 1	Selly Blanchard		
	Michael B. Terhune	704	
8. 8	Marytje Huysman		wid
8.15	Roeliph Ryker	705	j.m., both b Horseneck, liv Morris
9.23	Aaltje Jacobusse		j.d. /Co.
	Hendrick Jeraalman jr	706	
9.22	Hillegont Brown		
	Theodorus Brouwer	707	
10. 2	Maria Berry		
9. 2	Gerrebrand J. Jurrianse	708	j.m., b & liv Nieuw Barbadoes Neck
10.11	Helena Kerck, j.d.		b Stone House, liv in the Boght
	Cornelius Sip	709	
10.1(2)	Hester Haghoort		
	David Griffies	710	
10.16	Sarah Conger		
	John Van Emburgh	711	
10.24	Mary Jeraalman		
10.29	Peter Porter	712	j.m., liv Bergen Co.
11.21	Sarah Griffits		j.d., b Bergen Co., liv Essex
	Hendrick Kip jr	713	
12.11	Catharina Gerritse		
11.19	John Mac Carty	714	j.m., b Nieuw York, liv Slotterdam
12.19	Rachel Van Rypen		j.d., b & liv Wezel
	John Harrison	715	
12.24	Maragrita Ennis		
1791			
1. 5	Gerrit G. Van Wagenen	716	j.m., b & liv Slotterdam
	Helena Schoonmaker		j.d., b Esopus, liv Wesel
	Gerrebrand Van Houten	717	
1.30	Jannetje Gerritse		

* - see page 205

*Date	Married	1791 Item	Remarks
1. 8	Harme Van Rypen	718	j.m., b & liv Peckmans River
2. 6	Grietje Jacobusse		j.d., b & liv Horse Neck
2.10	Jurrie Jurrianse	719	j.m., b & liv Nieuw-Barbadoes Neck
3.12	Elizabeth Van Blercum,		j.d., b in the Gaffel, lin in the Boght
	Peter Ellen	720	
4.10	Marytje Drummond		
	Gerrit G. Gerritse	721	
4.17	Marritje Doremus		
	Hendrick B. Bruyn jr	722	
5.28	Lea Vreland		
5.22	Gerret Vreland	723	j.m., b Achquechnonck, both liv Peck
5.29	Rachel Moore		j.d., b Schoth Plaines /mans River
6.11	Jacob Van Winkelen jr	724	j.m., b Poveshom, liv Slotterdam
9.17	Annaatje Boss		j.d., b Slotterdam, liv there
	Thomas Van Hoorn	725	wid
7.24	Antje Mac Manners		wid
9. 6	Joris Banta	726	j.m., b Totua cong, liv Slotterdam
	Elizabeth Van Eydestyn		j.d., b & liv our cong
	Cornelius Helm	727	
9.18	Lea Cadmus		
	Henricus H. Schoonmaker	728	mar at Rochester
10.14	Maria Schoonmaker		
9.1(0)	Michael Van Eydestyn	729	j.m., b & liv our cong
10.23	Antje Banta		j.d., b Totua, liv Slotterdam
	Cornelius Smith	730	
10.23	Sarah Boss		
10.29	Philip Row	731	j.m., both b & liv Panne
11.12	Maria Van Syl		j.d.
	David Berdan	732	
10.30	Susannah Simmons		
	Cornelius Van Rypen	733	wid
10.30	Vrouwtje Gerritse		
	Jacob Miller	734	
11. 6	Catharina Hofman		
	Aaron Mire	735	
11. 6	Santje Storm		
	Frans Spier	736	
11.17	Lybetje Miller		
	John J. Berdan	737	
12. 3	Helena Bruyn		
10.29	Pieter Jacobusse	738	j.m., b & liv Peckmans River
12.10	Rachel Egbertse		j.d., b & liv our cong
	Joris Banta	739	
12.11	Elizabeth Van Eydestyn		

* - see page 205

*Date	Married	Item	Remarks
	Anthony Franscisco	740	
12.17	Maria Van Winkele		
	John Shipard	741	
12.17	Maragrieta Van Winkele		
11. 6	Helmich Van Wagenen	742	j.m., both b & liv Pomtan cong
1.15.1792	Tietje Van Duyn		j.d.
12. 9	Teunis Spier	743	j.m., b & liv our cong
1.26.1792	Rachel Mandeviel		j.d., b Pompton, liv Povershon
12.10	Nicholaus Hemmion	744	j.m., b Germany, liv Rempoch
1.26.1792	Lea Quackenbosch		j.d., b Schralenburgh, liv Wyckhoff
12.24	Gerrit Brouwer	745	j.m., b & liv Peckmans River
1.26.1792	Lena Spier		j.d., b & liv Wezel
12.31	Joris Doremus	746	wid, b & liv Perikenis
1.8.1792	Antje Rethan		j.d., b & liv in the Bogt

1792

	Cornelius Bogert	747	
1. 8	Annaatje Vreland		
	Thomas Person	748	
1.19	Elizabeth Cusaart		
	David Bensen	749	
1.21	Elizabeth Van Houten		
1.10	Roelif Doremus	750	j.m., b & liv Perikenis
2. 5	Annaatje Doremus		j.d., b & liv Wezel
1.14	Helmich Gerritse	751	j.m., b & liv Panne
2.25	Maria Van Aalen		j.d., b & liv Japoch
	Henry Brown	752	
1.28	Sietje Van Winkele		
	Thomas Vreland	753	
2. 5	Maragrietje Fielding		
2.10	Arie Kirris	754	j.m., b Pechkoneck, liv Wachauw
3. 4	Anneke Vreland		j.d., b & liv Peckmans River
	Johannis Ja. Vreland	755	
2.23	Jannetje Van Wagenen		
2.18	John G. Van Rypen	756	j.m., b Achquechnonck, liv Pechkoneck
3.18	Lea Kip		j.d., b & liv Perikenis
3. 3	Matheus Evertse	757	j.m., b Remmerpoch, liv our cong
4. 7	Janneke Post		j.d., liv our cong
	John Terhune	758	
4. 8	Elizabeth Zabriskie		
	Johannes Hennion	759	
4.10	Margrieta Wannemaker		
	Bryant Sheehys	760	
4.21	Anna Duvall		
	John Wilmott	761	
4.21	Selly Simmons		

* - see page 205

*Date	Married	1792 Item	Remarks
3.16	Hartman Post	762	j.m., b & liv Wezel
4.28	Nency Jackson		j.d., b Nieuw Winsor, liv Perikenis
	John Steger	763	
5.19	Lena Spier		
5. 5	Jacobus Van Houten	764	j.m., b & liv Panne
6. 9	Maria Banta		j.d., b Hackensack, liv Panne
	Arie Boss	765	
6. 9	Sytje Maurusse		
	Hendrick Coerte	766	
6. 9	Antje Bensen		
	Gerrit Halenbeeck	767	
6.10	Maria Kip		
5.19	John H. Ryerse	768	j.m., b & liv Weggeraw
6.16	Anna Van Aalen		j.d., b Japoch, liv Weggeraw
5.26	Thomas Boss	769	j.m., b & liv Slotterdam
7.15	Elizabeth Keerse		j.d., b Lange Eyland, liv Wezel
	John J. Berdan	770	
6.23	Maria Degrauw		
	Isaac S. Van Saan	771	
6.23	Cathalyntje Marselusse		
6.23	Adrian Van Rypen	772	j.m., b Wawejander, liv Wesel
8. 4	Cathalyntje Spier		j.d., b & liv Wesel
	Gerrebrand Gerrebranse	773	
8. 5	Elizabeth Messelaer		
7. 7	Even Barkow	774	j.m., b North Corolina, liv Weggerauw
8.11	Mary Dougherty		wid, b Pensylvania, liv Weggerauw
	Hendrick Post	775	wid
8.11	Hester Dey		wid
7.13	Michael Boss	776	j.m., b Nieuw York, liv our cong
8.26	Anna Smith		j.d., b Bergen, liv our cong
8.19	Daniel Blauveld	777	j.m., b Tappan, liv Wyckhoff
9.15	Maragrietje Preevo		j.d., b Per Emus, liv Panne
	John Lamb	778	
9. 1	Hilletje Brown		
	Joost Dierman	779	
9. 9	Catharina Van Winkelen		
	Elias Wheeler	780	
9.22	Temperence Wheyley		
9.16	Hendrick Van Nes	781	j.m., b & liv Pompton cong
9.30	Marytje Doremus		j.d., b & liv Peckmans River
	Jacob J. Van Nes	782	
10.10	Christianah Mead		
	Pieter Van Eydestyn	783	
10.14	Maria Tyse		

* - see page 205

*Date	Married	Item	Remarks
		1792-1793	
9.28	Christian Carlogh	784	j.m., both b & liv Remmerpoch
10.27	Maragrieta Ackerman		j.d.
	John G. Hoppen	785	
10.28	Rachel Hoppen		
9.30	Jacobus Van Duyn	786	j.m., both b & liv Tawaggauw
12. 1	Catharyntje Van Nes		j.d.
10.21	Johannes Egbertse	787	j.m., b & liv Stone House
11.11	Lea Winne		j.d., b & liv Second River
	Jacob G. Van Rypen	788	
11. 8	Jannetje Van Winkelen		
	Obadiah Forse	789	
11.10	Elizabeth Van Houten		
11.17	Hartman Degrauw	790	j.m., both b & liv our cong
12.23	Jannetje Vreland		j.d.
11.25	Nicholaas Winne	791	j.m., both b & liv Second River
12.15	Salley Franscisco		j.d.
12. 8	David Ker	792	j.m., b Pomptan, liv Perikenis
12.23	Antje Westerveld		j.d., b & liv Slotterdam
12.15	George Ryerse	793	j.m., b & liv Pechkoneck
12.30	Catharina Hoppen		j.d., b Slotterdam, liv Pechkoneck
	Nathan Coon	794	
12.21	Elizabeth Gray		
	Abraham Lyn	795	
12.22	Catharina Slot		
12.29	William G. Kingsland	796	wid, liv Nieuw Barbadoes Neck
1.6.1793	Catharina Wood		wid, liv Second River
12.30	Barent Franscisco	797	j.m., b & liv Rockoway
1.31.1793	Rachel Mandeviel		j.d., b & liv Stoonhouse
12.31	Abraham Van Blerkum	798	j.m., both b & liv Totua cong
1.19.1793	Vrouwtje Van Blerkum		j.d.
1793			
	Arie Kierstead jr	799	
1.17	Jenneke Van Rypen		
1.19	Gerret Storm	800	j.m., b & liv Rempoch
4. 1	Maragrieta Hennion		j.d., b Rempoch, liv Panne
2. 9	John Poelis	801	j.m., liv Rempogh
(3).16	Sarah Ham		j.d., liv Panne
2.22	William Van Ess	802	j.m., b & liv Gansegat
3.23	Elizabeth Van Blerkum		j.d., b Per Emus, liv Pechkoneck
	David Bertholf	803	
3. 4	Catharina Storm		
	Aaron King jr	804	
3.31	Eva Messeker		
	Gilbert Kuyper	805	
4. 1	Sarah Van Houten		

* - see page 205

*Date	Married	1793 Item	Remarks
3.31	Jacob Eckerson	806	j.m., b Keckiat, liv Patterson Town
4.21	Selly Kool		j.d., b & liv Totua cong
	Pieter Stur	807	wid
4. 1	Sarah Van Winbel		wid of Jan Romyn
4. 1	John T. Spier	808	j.m., b & liv Perikenis
5.18	Abigail Van Bussen		j.d., b & liv our cong
4.13	Roelif C. Van Houten	809	both b & liv Totua
5. 2	Antje Van Giesen		j.d.
	Martin Clark	810	
4.28	Femmetje Griffith		
	Robbert Van Houten	811	
5.18	Lena Van Giesen		
5.23	Laurence Van Orden	812	j.m., b Per Emus, liv Weggeraw
6.16	Henckje Bilju		j.d., b Brabant, liv Slotterdam
	Abraham Allen	813	
5.19	Christie Van Hoorn		
	David Pier	814	
5.19	Sally Berry		
	John Ja. Van Winkelen	815	
6. 2	Elizabeth Brinckerhoff		
7.20	Abraham Van Syl	816	j.m., b & liv Panne
8.31	Rachel Degrauw		j.d., b Keckiet, liv Panne
7.20	Coenraad Row	817	j.m., both b & liv Panne
9.15	Catharina Ryker		j.d.
	John G. Ryerse	818	
7.21	Lea Westerveldt		
	Walter Nep	819	
8. 1	Sarah Chapman		
8.17	Gerret C. Post	820	j.m., both b & liv our cong
10.18	Maragrietje Vreland		j.d.
	Stephen Bogert	821	
9. 7	Tyntje Stor		
	Simeon Van Blarcom	822	
9.18	Bregje Van Blercom		
	Pieter Banta	823	
9.21	Dolly Van Orden		
	John Ludlow	824	
9.22	Catharina Ackerman		
10. 4	Jacob Stur	825	j.m., b & liv Panne
11.16	Geesje Van Rypen		j.d., b Achquechnonk, liv Panne
	(1st reference gives bride's name as "Caziah")		
10.19	Roelif Romyn	826	j.m., b Schralenburgh cong
12.14	Elizabeth Stur		j.d., b South River, liv Panne
11.16	Jacob Mourusse	827	j.m., b Essex Co., liv Morris Co.
	Marritje Van Ess		j.d., b & liv Morris Co.

* - see page 205

*Date	Married	Item	Remarks
11.17	Hermanus Van Orden Fytje Westerveld	828	
11.18 12.15	Hartman M. Vreland Tyna Post	829	j.m., both b & liv our cong j.d.
11.19 12.26	Daniel Worden Christina Ero	830	j.m., b & liv Bergen Co. j.d., b Essex Co., liv Bergen Co.
1794			
1. 2	Philip Dial Pryntje Van Houten	831	
1.19	Albert Van Saan Jannetje Van Houten	832	
1.18 2.15	Pieter Van Blarkum Majeke Jacobusse	833	j.m., b Per Emus, liv Pechkoneck j.d., b Peckmans River, liv Gansegat
2. 2	Johannes Bruyn Sarah Koejeman	834	
3. 1	Helmich Van Houten Lena Van Blercum	835	
3.15	John Humble Margeret Martin	836	wid of John Crawford
3.15	John Parke Arriaantje Marselusse	837	
3.20	Pieter Pier Selly Messeker	838	
3.23	Morgan Morgan Dorcas Shepherd	839	
3.30	Jessey Ockly Elizabeth Outwater	840	
5.11	Jacob Outwater Elizabeth Brinckerhoff	841	
5.17	Benjamin Force Annaatje Hall	842	
6.11	Marthe Berry Rachel Van Rypen	843	
6.28	Theunis T. Hennion Rachel Ackerman	844	
7. 5	George Van Eydestyn Jenneke Degrauw	845	
7.12	Gerrit Gerritse Maragrietje Van Rypen	846	
8. 7	Abraham Van Giesen Fytje Nefius	847	wid wid
8. 9	Pieter Halm Maria Kingsland	848	
6.21 8.14	Cornelius Banta Catharina Brush	849	j.m., b Hackensack, liv Panne j.d., b Rempoch, liv Panne

* - see page 205

*Date	Married	Item	Remarks
8.14	John Kiesler Maria Snyder	850	
6.28 8.16	Gerret Vreland Maragrietje Van Rypen	851	j.m., both b & liv Achquechnonck /cong
7.19 8.23	Pieter P. Poelis Elizabeth Pecker	852	j.m., both b & liv Panne cong wid of Joh's Poelis
8.24	John Jo. Doremus Geertje Ryer	853	
8.26	Asa Perry Achsa Perry	854	
9. 4	Jacobus (J.) Post Jannetje Van Giesen	855	
9. 7	John Westerveld Annaatje Stymets	856	wid wid of Christophel Van Noorstrand
9. 7	Joseph Cooper Annaatje Kranck	857	
9.10	Abraham Brouwer Marytje Gerrebrantse	858	wid
9.21	Christophel Brouwer Lena Van Houten	859	
9.21	Johannis Kierstede Fytje Clark	860	wid wid of Abraham Ryker
10. 5	John Tyse jr Caty Stagg	861	
8. 9 10. 9	Joseph Scisco Selly Jacobusse	862	j.m., b & liv Gansegat j.d., b & liv Peckmans River
11. 1	Casparus Post Fytje Paulusse	863	
11. 3	Johannis Kerck Hester Jeraalman	864	wid
11.23	Cornelius Kent Antje Stagg	865	
11.29	Jan Mandeviel Antje Beyerse	866	
12.11	Thomas Dodd Phebe Allen	867	wid wid
12.20	William Van Houten Rebecca Brouwer	868	
12.25	John Bailey Jacomyntje Maurusson	869	
	1795		
1.11	Nicasie Van Blerkum Jannetje Rethan	870	wid wid
1.17	Michael Moore Elizabeth Willis	871	

1794-1795

* - see page 205

*Date	Married	1795 Item	**Remarks
1.11	Gerr-brand Bruyn	872	j.m., b Second River, liv our cong
2.14	Catharina Van Der Hoef		j.d., b Gansegat, liv our cong
	James Thredwell	873	
2.25	Polly Van Winkele		
	Hendrick Van Aalen	874	wid
3.15	Abigail Ecker		
2.21	Cornelius Doremus	875	j.m., b & liv Peckmans River
3.22	Jannetje Van Orden		j.d., b Per Emus, liv Totua
2.21	Simeon Van Ess	876	j.m., b Pompton, liv Wachchauw
3.22	Elizabeth Doremus		j.d., b & liv Peckmans River
	Jacobus Laroe	877	A
4. 4	Lena Messeker		
	Lodewyck Messeker	878	A
4.18	Sarah Spier		
	Albert Wright	879	A
5.16	Hanna Myer		
	Aaron Baffard	880	A
5.31	Polly Maclain		
	Jacob Zabriskie	881	B
8. 2	Lea Berdan		
	Gerrit A. Post	882	A
9. 5	Helena Manning		
	Abraham Toers	883	A
9.17	Catharina Ennis		
	Kemena Van Buren	884	A
9.27	Rebecca Ennis		
	Silas Munson	885	A
10. 1	Elizabeth Yorks		
	John N. Romein	886	A
10.10	Catharina Terhune		wid
	John H. Banta	887	A
10.11	Jannetje Van Saan		
	Jacobus Mandeviel	888	A
11.22	Susanna Van Houten		
	Cornelius Jeraalman	889	A
11.22	Jannetje Jurrianse		
	Daniel Bensen	890	E
11.29	Rachel Doremus		
	Nicholaes Outwater	891	E
12. 6	Rachel Brinckerhoff		
11.20	Hendrick H. Doremus	892	E, j.m., b & liv Perikenis
12.12	Marretje Jacobusse		j.d., b & liv Totua
10.31	Cornelius P. Vreland	893	E, j.m., both b & liv Wezel
1.23.1796	Dorothe Van Der Hoef		j.d.

** - Marriages numbered 877 - 1311 have letter designations the meaning of which is not disclosed by the recorder. Perhaps they refer to the location of the marriage. If so, the letters may represent:
A - Acquackenonck
B - Bergen
E - Essex

* - see page 205

*Date 1796	Married	1796 Item	**Remarks
1. 1	John Van Syle Arriaantje Post	894 E	
1. 3	Daniel Fielding Nietje Huysman	895 E	
1.17	Hessel Jurrianse Marytje Van Hoorn	896 E	
1.23	Petrus Paulusse Jannetje Van Houten	897 E	
1.23 2.14	Jacob John Vreland Phebe Wells	898 E, j.m., both b & liv our cong j.d.	
1.23 2.14	John Deeths Gouda Vreland	899 E, j.m., b Nieuw-York, liv Achquechno j.d., b Achquechnonck, liv there /nck	
2. 6 3. 3	Hermanus Linkfoot Aaltje Mandeviel	900 E, j.m., b & liv Achquechnonck j.d., b Pompton, liv Second River cong	

(groom's surname in 2nd entry given as "Linkford")

3.13	Hendrick Messeker Jamyme Ryker	901 E	
3.22	James Pinkerton Syntje Ackerman	902 E	
3.27	James D. Christie Annaatje Helm	903 B	
3.27 3.31	Rem Onderdonk Geesje Rethan	904 E, wid, b Nieuw Hemstead, liv Patter b Wezel /son	
4. 3	Hendrick Van Blerkom Dirckje Ackerman	905 E	
4.10	Gerrit J. Post Marritje Van Rypen	906 E	
5.15	Joseph Coekro Sarah Fredericks	907 E	
5.15	John J. Van Rypen Hendrica Van Ess	908 E	
5.21	John Earl Annaatje Bilju	909 E	
5.22	Jacob Willer Catharina Van Der Hoef	910 E	
6. 4	Stephen Dod Mahetible Gould	911 E	
8. 8	Enoch Greenleaf Mary Ryckman	912 E	
8.21	Isaac Van Winkelen Helena Schoonmaker	913 E	
9. 4	Johannes Luthen Geertruy Spier	914 E	
9.25	Peter Van Wagenen Sarah Plum	915 E	

* - see page 205   ** - see page 245

1796-1797

*Date	Married	Item	**Remarks
10.22	Hendrick H. Berry Lea Lamberts	916 E	
11.13	Cornelius Westervelt Maria Simmons	917 E	
11.13	Pieter Doremus Susanna Jacobusse	918 E	wid of Nicholaas Jones
11.20	Teunis Gerrebrantse Jannetje Spier	919 E	
11.26	Pieter Doremus Lena Berry	920 B	
12. 2	Abraham Snyder Maria Kiesler	921 E	
12.18	John Van Houten Selly Van Bussen	922 E	

1797

*Date	Married	Item	**Remarks
1. 5	James Elsworth Caty Brower	923 E	
1. 6	Lucas Van Aalen Anna Van Der Hoef	924 E	
1.22	Johannes C. Van Houten Antje Post	925 B	
1.29	Marcelus Van Giesen Jannetje Doremus	926 E	
4. 2	Simeon Van Houten Marytje Van Blerkum	927 E	
4.16	David Demarest jr Annaatje Van Saan	928 E	
5. 7	John Stagg Antje Blanchard	929 E	
5. 7	Hermanus Van Bussen jr Beletje Post	930 B	
6.19	Pieter Van Rypen Lydia Ryker	931 E	
5.13 6.22	Paulus Paulusse Elizabeth Cadmus	932 E,	wid, b & liv Povershon j.d., b Nieuw Town, liv Povershon
8.26	Hendrick Van Duyn Rachel Vreland	933 E	
8.26	William Van Duyn Elizabeth Doremus	934 F	
9. 9	John R. Gould Nancey Sandford	935 E	
9.20	Pieter Simmons Maragrietje Westerveldt	936 E	
10.22	Abraham Bloodgood Hannah Ennis	937 E	

* - see page 205, from this page on, date indicates marriage
** - see page 245

Date	Married	1797-1798 Item	*Remarks
10.29	Waling J. Van Winkel Selly Gerrebrantse	938 E	
11.18	Cornelius A. Vreland Santje Helm	939 E	
11.23	Hermanus Vreland Annaatje Sip	940 E	
12.10	Jacobus Doremus Maria Goetschius	941 B	
12.11	Samuel Spier Maria Sigler	942 E	
12.14	John Mac Carty Elizabeth Post	943 B, wid wid	
12.17	Hendrick H. Post Jannetje Van Houten	944 E	
1798 1.18	Thomas Van Hoorn Lybetje Rethan	945 E, wid wid	
3.10	Nathanael Tharp Sarah Doremus	946 E	
3.11	Johannis Van Rypen Geertje Doremus	947 E	
3.22	I(s)aac Ryker Lena Smith	948 E	
3.25	John P. Ennis Mary Steger	949 E	
5. 5	Hermanus Coerte Jannetje Spier	950 E	
5.24	Jacob Egbertse Jenneke Yorks	951 E	
5.26	Marcelus Post Judick Evertse	952 E	
5.27	Johannes Jacobusse Elizabeth Cokerooch	953 E	
5.27	Casparus Van Dien Maria Cogg	954 E	
5.29	John J. Berry Maria Dey	955 E	
7. 8	John F. Post Jannetje Degrauw	956 E, wid wid	
8. 2	James McCarday Jane Ryerse	957 B wid of Richard Stanton	
9. 2	John Doremus Maria Sich	958 E, wid	
9. 8	Isaac D. Ackerman Syntje Post	959 E	

* - see page 245

1798-1799

Date	Married	Item	*Remarks
9.20	Thomas Devorsne Susanna Folkonier	960	
9.29	Jacob E. Smith Cathalyntje Berry	961	E
10. 4	Encrease Gould Esqr. Agness Helme	962	E
10.21	Peter Terhune Elizabeth Witlock	963	E, wid
10.28	Richard Ennis Jenny Doremus	964	E
11.17	Hermanus Van Blerkum Elizabeth Van Aalen	965	B
12. 2	John King Jane Wells	966	E
12. 6	George Bolsbey Phebe Stiles	967	B
12.23	Henricus Vreland Lea Terhune	968	F
12.25	Pieter Terhune Hester Camble	969	E
1799 2.24	John Van Buren Antje Vreland	970	E
3. 3	Jurrie Jurrianse Catharina Van Hoorn	971	E
4.21	Gerrebrand Gerrebrantse Syntje Evertse	972	E
4.28	Paulus Terhune Sarah Paulusse	973	E
4.28	Guliam Hopper Anna Stegg	974	E
5.11	Henricus Goetschius Selly Van Bussen	975	B
5.11	Benjamin Vreland Elizabeth Van Winkel	976	E
5.13	Cornelius Van Blerkom Catharina Van Blerkom	977	E
5.14	Abraham Rethan Maragrita Ennis	978	E
5.25	Petrus Brouwer Jannetje Vreeland	979	E
5.25	Jacobus Brinckerhoff Elizabeth Jurrianse	980	E
6. 8	Abel Mac Pherson Elizabeth Goetschius	981	wid wid

* - see page 245

Date	Married	1799-1800 Item	*Remarks
6. 9	Casparus Van Vorst Grietje Boskerck	982	E wid
7.14	Cornelius Corsen Geertje Van Voorheese	983	E
7.21	Cornelius Van Blerkum Marytje Doremus	984	E
8. 3	Jacob Brinckerhoff Abigail Van Bussen	985	B
9. 7	Johannes Van Hoorn Maragrietje Van Bussen	986	E
9.28	Abraham E. Vreeland Lea Degraauw	987	E
10.12	Jacob Evertse Lea Vreeland	988	E
10.13	Robert Blair (H)ighly Messeler	989	E
10.20	John C. Yurrianse Elizabeth Van Hoorn	990	E
10.26	Hendrick Kneght Margaret Kingsland	991	E
11. 5	Petrus Van Ess Marytje Cadmus	992	E, wid wid
11.10	Jurrie Van Rypen Rachel Meedt	993	B, wid
11.17	Thomas Cadmus Grietje Doremus	994	E
12. 1	Johannis A. Post Elizabeth Van Winkel	995	E
12.22	Pieter Van Bussen Annaatje Paulusse	996	E
12.25	Jacobus Van Winkel Jannetje Van Winkel	997	E
12.29	Cornelius Austin Antje Van Houten	998	E
1800 1. 4	Jacobus Spier Lea Spier	999	E
2.23	Waling C. Van Winkele Jannetje Post	1000	E
3. 6	Jarvis Pearsaal Rachel Killy	1001	E
3. 9	Hendrick Labach Thyna Spier	1002	E
4. 5	Abraham Peek Catharina Brass	1003	E

* - see page 245

1800-1801

Date	Married	Item	*Remarks
4.14	Gerrebrand C. Van Houten Rachel Meet	1004	E
4.14	Elias Baldwin Naomie Scidmore	1005	E
4.27	John J. Ryerse Maria Bogert	1006	E
5. 3	Gerrit Marselusse Lena Degrauw	1007	B
6.15	Samuel Prime Jinny Dixon	1008	E
6.19	John Gerritse Polly Vreland	1009	E
8. 9	Hendrick Pickstone Marritje Post	1010	E
8.24	Cornelius Doremus Marritje Vreland	1011	E
9.14	Gerret Pier Jenneke Brouwer	1012	E
10. 4	Jacob Ryker Catharina Leeth	1013	E
10. 4	Helmich Post Nancy Berry	1014	E
10.19	Barent Spier Sarah Jacobusse	1015	E
10.25	Johannis H. Post Geertje Degrauw	1016	F
11.30	Dirck T. Van Hoorn Polly Witlock	1017	E
12. 7	Thomas Brass Maria Doremus	1018	E
12. 7	Hendrick Van Vorst Annaatje Pickston	1019	E
12.21	Peter Hennion Maria Van Blerkom	1020	E
12.27	Henry Simmons Marretje Van Rypen	1021	E
1801			
2.14	Simeon J. Van Ess Elizabeth Van Giesen	1022	E
2.22	Abraham Stagg Polly Ackerman	1023	E wid
2.28	Barent Spier Christina Cogh	1024	B, wid wid
2.28	Dirck Cadmus Jannetje Krom	1025	B

* - see page 245

Date	Married	Item	*Remarks
		1801-1802	
3.23	Matheus Pier Anna Moore	1026	E
5. 3	Adriaan Van Houten Thyna Van Winkele	1027	E
5.10	Hendrick J. Kip Claasje Sip	1028	E
5.17	Rynier Kip Elizabeth Van Houten	1029	E
5.26	Hendrick Mandeviel Fytje Bruyn	1030	E
6.13	Egbert Bruyn Rachel Goetschius	1031	B
6.28	Helmich D. Van Houten Metje Van Giesen	1032	E
10.20	Ely Frost Sarah Brown	1033	E wid of William Coffie
11.15	Jacob Berdan jr Antje Van Houten	1034	B
11-22	Henry Gerritse Annaatje Lisk	1035	E, wid wid
12. 5	Anthony Van Blerkom Annaatje Van Blerkom	1036	
12.26	Cornelius A. Post Selly Spier	1037	E
12.26	Johannis A. Post Margrietje Vreland	1038	
12.27	Cornelius Van Rypen Margarietje Post	1039	E
1802			
2.14	Gerrit Demott Marytje Westervelt	1040	B, wid wid
5. 9	Cornelius Van Campen Ludlow Catharina Van Eydestyn	1041	E
6. 7	Jacob J. Stagg Catharina Van Rypen	1042	E
7. 3	Jacobus Demarest Catharina Hopper	1043	E
7.10	Samuel Taylor Sarah Doremus	1044	E
9.11	John Marinus jr Maragrietje Goetschius	1045	B
9.12	Albert Terhune Marretje Post	1046	E
9.26	Nicasie Kip Jenneke Paulusse	1047	

* - see page 245

Date	Married	1802-1804 Item	*Remarks
10.17	Enoch J. Vreeland Maria Vreeland	1048	(E)
10.19	Peter Jackson Hester Brinckerhoff	1049	E
11.18	Cornelius Norrid Elizabeth White	1050	E
11.20	Cornelius C. Post Elizabeth Van Winkele	1051	E
11.27	John C. Van Rypen Vrouwtje Van Blerkom	1052	E
12.18	Frans Bruyn Lea Cadmus	1053	E wid of Cor. Helm
1803 1. 2	Isaac Schoonmaker Efje Vreland	1054	B
1.16	John J. Van Giesen Catharina Van Alen	1055	B
1.29	Abraham Van Houten Geertje Mouritse	1056	E
2. 6	Jacob Gerritse Lea Wesselse	1057	B
4. 3	John H. Gerritse Maragrietje Post	1058	E, wid wid
4.17	Joseph Gillam Annaatje Cogh	1059	B
7. 3	Joseph Sherburne Rachel Fine	1060	E wid
7.10	Adrian J. Post Rachel Van Giesen	1061	B
7.17	Andreas Boskerck Theodocie Van Winkele	1062	E
9.10	Gerrit H. Post Elizabeth Doremus	1063	E
9.11	Isaac Van Rypen Maria Stagg	1064	E
9.19	Charles Kip Jane Crawford	1065	E
12.11	William Doremus Geertje Jacobusse	1066	E
12.22	Abraham D. Van Houten Catharina Sip	1067	E
12.25	John C. Vreland Vrouwtje Van Blerkum	1068	E
1804 1. 1	Elias A. Vrelandt Annaatje Spier	1069	E

* - see page 245

Date	Married		Item	*Remarks
			1804-1805	
1.28	John Vreland jr Geertje Rodebach		1070 E	
2. 3	Nicholas Van Blerkum Maria Kip		1071 E	
3.17	John Van Bussen Jannetje Goetschius		1072 B	
3.28	Benjamin Youmans Catharina Cranck		1073 E	
4. 1	Edward Earl Maria Van Blerkum		1074 E	
4. 1	John Ennis Susanna Doremus		1075 E	
5.10	Dirck Berdan Antje Berdan		1076 B	
5.13	Jurrie Van Rypen Marretje Blair		1077 E	
5.26	Benjamin Weller Jane Dickey		1078 E	
6.10	Abraham Outwater Maria Bogert		1079 E	
7.29	Richard Outwater Catharina Kip		1080 B	
8.11	Cornelius G. Doremus Geertje Demarest		1081 E	
8.19	Helmich J. Van Winkel Antje Van Houten		1082 E	
10.27	Maris Ackerman Cornelia Smith		1083 E	
11.29	William Rosekrants Gitty L. Lee		1084 E	
12. 2	Albert Doremus Jannetje Vreland		1085 E	
12. 8	Rynier Van Giesen Catharina Van Eydestyn		1086 E	
12.23	Pieter P. Van Aalen Jannetje Doremus		1087 E	
12.25	John En. Vreland Jenneke Van Winkel		1088 E	
12.26	John A. Post Sally Goetschius		1089 B	
12.27	Hendrick M. Gerritse Catharina Doremus		1090 E	
1805				
1. 3	Harmen Van Rypen Rebecca Brouwer		1091 E	wid of Will. Van Houten

* - see page 245

1805-1806

Date	Married	Item	*Remarks
1.12	John H. Spier Geertje Kieslaer	1092	E
3.24	John S. Van Winkel Jannetje Kip	1093	B
4.15	Jacob Ackerman Susanna Doremus	1094	E
4.21	Daniel F. Lockwood Lena Jeraalman	1095	E
5.26	Edo Van Winkel Jannetje Van Der Hoef	1096	E
6. 8	Benjamin Van Wert Maria Wilson	1097	E
6.16	Hendrick T. Spier Rachel Van Dyck	1098	E, wid wid
8.31	Abraham Post Elizabeth Westervelt	1099	E
9. 6	Waling H. Van Winkel Maragrietje Ackerman	1100	B
9. 8	Robert Blair Mary Booth	1101	E wid	(bride's surname "Van Blerkum" crossed out)
9.21	Peter Tyse Annaatje Van Blerkum	1102	E
9.21	Peter A. Westervelt Catharina Burhans	1103	B
10. 5	Dirck Stagg Selly Ackerman	1104	E
10.13	Richard Voorhis Maria Berdan	1105	E
10.20	Peter Van Winkel Phebe Godwin	1106	E
11.24	Jurrie Brouwer Catharina Kool	1107	E
12.25	Robert Slator Elizabeth Moore	1108	E
12.29	Matheus Spier Catharina Van Rypen	1109	E

1806

Date	Married	Item	*Remarks
1. 1	David Cogh Metje Post	1110	E
1. 5	Robert Parck Elizabeth Van Aalen	1111	E wid
1. 7	Rev'd Jacob Schoonmaker Catharina Ludlow	1112	E
3. 2	John M. Ryerse Claasje Van Winkele	1113	E

* - see page 245

Date	Married	Item	*Remarks
3. 2	Jacob J. Van Winkel Elizabeth Van Der Hoef	1114	E
3.30	Helmich Sip jr Maragrietje Linkford	1115	E
4.10	Jacob H. Spier Maria Gerritse	1116	E
4.12	Peter Van Duyn Antje Ryker	1117	E
6. 8	Henry G. Doremus Elizabeth Van Giesen	1118	E
6.21	Hendrick J. Gerritse Jamyma Hopper	1119	E
6.29	Cornelius C. Vreland Lena Van Blerkom	1120	E
7.12	Charles Frerick(e) Caty Gould	1121	E
7.13	John T. Van Eydestyn Catharina Van Winkel	1122	E
8. 9	Hessel Doremus Jannetje Demarest	1123	E
9.18	Adriaan M. Post Aaltje Ackerman	1124	E
9.28	Christophel Brouwer Elizabeth Gerritse	1125	E
10.11	Thomas Van Rypen Maria Van Houten	1126	E
11. 8	Andries Ackerman Susanna Ryers	1127	E
11.30	Michael M. Vreland Elizbeth Reddanor	1128	E

1807

Date	Married	Item	*Remarks
1.29	Edo Vreland Antje Vreland	1129	E
2. 8	Andrew Breasted Van Bussen Jannetje Post	1130	E
2. 8	John W. Davis Susanna Godwin	1131	E
4.11	Lodewyck Smith Catharina Dolhaven	1132	E
4.12	Hendrick T. Spier Elizabeth Van Houten	1133	E, wid wid
4.16	Adrian A. Van Houten Annaetje Sip	1134	E
5.10	Johannes J. Sip jr Geertje Van Winkel	1135	E

1806-1807

* - see page 245

Date	Married	Item	*Remarks
5.17	Barney Pier Jannetje Rethan	1136 E	
5.18	David Van Blerkum Sarah Vreland	1137 E	
6. 3	John Flood Isabella King	1138 E	
8.30	John R. Berdan Maria Van Houten	1139 B	
9.13	Hendrick Van Blerkum Jannetje Post	1140 E	
9.20	Egbert Post Cornelia Vreeland	1141 E	(groom's name "Adri(an)" crossed out)
10. 3	Hendrick T. Van Blerkum Tryntje Van Der Haan	1142 E	
10.11	David Marinus Lena Gerritse	1143 E	
10.11	Samuel Berry Jannetje Van Winkele	1144 E	
11. 7	Jacob Zabriskie Annaatje Marinus	1145 E	
11.15	Hendrick Van Houten Jannetje Van Winkele	1146 E	
12. 6	George Livingston Charlotte Coleman	1147 E	
12.12	Joseph Baldwin Rebecca Degrauw	1148 E	
12.19	Jacob Van Hoorn Selly Vreeland	1149 E	
12.25	John Devoe Elizabeth Post	1150 E	
12.25	Cornelius C. Van Houten Salome Schoonmaker	1151 E	
12.26	John Insley Catharina Willis	1152 E	
12.28	Gilbert Mc Ilwrick Fytje Kranck	1153 E	

1808

Date	Married	Item	*Remarks
1.23	John J. Post Elizabeth Paulusse	1154 E	
1.30	Worthy Clark Elizabeth Van Houten	1155 E	
2.20	Marten Van Houten Catharina Van Houten	1156 E	
4.17	Hendrick F. Post Jannetje Ackerman	1157 E	

* - see page 245

Date	Married	Item	*Remarks
4.17	Peter J. Post Lea Doremus	1158	E
6.19	David Alje Dina Boss	1159	E
7.10	Frederick Jurrianse Catharina Van Eydestyn	1160	E
9.24	Stephen Baker Jannetje Van Winkele	1161	E
10. 2	Casparus Wesselse Neefje Van Houten	1162	B
10.22	Richard Berdan Lena Ryerse	1163	E
12.10	Antony Jacobusse Maragrietje Boss	1164	E
12.10	William Cairns Maria Kogh	1165	B
12.11	John J. Jurrianse Selly Van Noorstrand	1166	E
12.24	Hendrick Wouterse Catharina Van Rypen	1167	E
12.27	Peter Rednaer Catharina Spier	1168	E
12.31	Isaac Cubberley Susanna Van Noorstrand	1169	E
1809			
1.16	Jacob Van Rypen Rachel Boss	1170	E
1.29	Jacob Mourusse Marritje Van Giesen	1171	E
2. 4	Jacob Van Der Hoef Lea Vreland	1172	E
2.11	Oliver Cannon Maria Low	1173	E
3. 4	Abraham Mandeviel Catharina Degrauw	1174	E
4. 2	Gerret Jurrianse Jannetje Post	1175	E
4.15	James Leary Anna Doremus	1176	E
4.15	James Boon Elizabeth Weeks	1177	E
9. 9	Jacob Spier Fytje Riddenaer	1178	E
9.30	Samuel Post Maragrietje Aljee	1179	E

* - see page 245

Date	Married	Item	*Remarks
12.20	Stephen Boss Sally Osborn	1180	E
1810			
1.15	John Koejeman Jacomyntje Van Winkele	1181	E
1.20	Peter Willis Harriot Hennion	1182	E
1.28	Jacob N. Vreland Maria Cochlin	1183	E
2.17	Robert King Jane Griffith	1184	E
2.24	Isaac Van Rypen Rachel Boss	1185	E
2.26	John J. Vreland Helena Vreland	1186	E
4. 7	Bortis Winters Esther Dickey	1187	E
4.22	Theodorus (F.) Terhune Marytje Spier	1188	E
4.24	John Hancock Peggy Lions	1189	E
5.31	John Hatharington Phebe Conger	1190	E
6.10	Adrian Van Giesen Elizabeth Kip	1191	E
6.12	John Spier Anna Yeomans	1192	E
7. 8	John Sip Arriaantje Marselusse	1193	E, wid
8. 5	John R. Degrauw Maria Gerritse	1194	E
10.20	John N. Jeraalman Magdalena Spier	1195	E
11.17	Simion Van Rypen Geertje Zabrikie	1196	E
12. 8	Jacob Van Rypen Maria Van Rypen	1197	E
12. 9	Benjamin Zabriskie Catharina Gerritse	1198	E
12. 9	Adrian Vreland Antje Herring	1199	E
12.29	Edward Mitchel Dorothe Westervelt	1200	E, wid wid
1811			
2. 9	John S. Van Ess Elizabeth Kooper	1201	E

* - see page 245

Date	Married	1811 Item	*Remarks
2.12	Helmich Post Maria Snyder	1202 E	
3.31	Thomas Van Rypen Rachel Van Winkele	1203 E	
3.31	John G. Gerritse Elizabeth Van Giesen	1204 E	
4.14	Cornelius Van Rypen Maragrietje Maurusse	1205 E	
4.21	Isaac Sip Marytje Demarest	1206 E	(bride's surname "Wester-velt" crossed out)
5.23	Edo P. Marcelusse Heylia Kip	1207 B	
6. 9	John Doremus Eleanor Morris	1208 E	
6.15	Gerret Cadmus Elizabeth Van Houten	1209 E	
7.27	John Cadmus Cornelia Hopper	1210 E	
8. 4	Cornelius H. Bogert Rachel Kip	1211 E	
8. 8	Pieter H. Kip Claasje Marcelusse	1212 E	
8.11	Abraham Brower Nancy Van Aarsdelen	1213 E	
9. 1	Samuel Leuwis Marritje Van Rypen	1214 E, wid wid	
9. 7	John Jurrianse Eva Vreland	1215 E	
9.21	Jacobus Van Wagenen Grietje Cadmus	1216 E	
9.22	John J. Goetschius Hannah Goetschius	1217 B	
11.24	John W. Bensen Ruth Backman	1218 E	
12. 1	Edo Van Winkele Jannetje Van Houten	1219 E, wid wid	
12.22	John Kip Jannetje Van Winkele	1220 B	
12.22	John M. Vreland Elizabeth Van Eydestyn	1221 E	
12.25	John Crank Salley Selif	1222 E	
12.25	John Hancock Hannah Youman	1223 E	

* - see page 245

Date	Married	1811--1813 Item	*Remarks
12.29	John Pelt Margerit Cairns	1224 E	
1812			
1.12	John J. Spier Annaatje Van Winkele	1225 E	
1.25	Jacob Smith Nancy Reybert	1226 E	
2. 8	John Van Syce Elizabeth Ackerman	1227 E	
2. 9	Henry G. Gerritse Margerit Blair	1228 E	
3. 8	William Nickol Hannah Van Horn	1229 E	
3.29	Abraham Van Rypen Tryntje Van Winkele	1230 E	
3.31	Joseph Kingsland jr Martha Ackerman	1231 B	
5.17	Helmich Van Houten Maria Godwin	1232 E	
6.18	John A. Ackerman Eva Sip	1233 E	(marriage month "May" crossed out)
6.20	John L. Kierstede Catharina Schoonmaker	1234 E	
6.28	Nicholas Ackerman Annaatje Van Winkele	1235 E	
7. 4	David Ackerman Egje Doremus	1236 E	
8. 9	John A. Van Rypen Elizabeth Post	1237 E	
9.13	Job F. Baker Jane Flowers	1238 E	
9.27	John Seagar Mary Rue	1239 E	
10.15	John A. Post Cornelia Demarest	1240 E	
11.22	John Crane Mariann Weekes	1241 E	
12.17	Hermanus Van Wagenen Jinny Etsel	1242 E	
12.20	John Berry Maria Aljea	1243 E	
12.26	Paulus Post Catharina Doremus	1244 E	
1813			
1. 9	Philip T. Van Bussen Annaatje Van Blerkum	1245 F	

* - see page 245

Date	Married	1813 Item	*Remarks
2. 1	John J. Outwater Catharina Van Bussen	1246 E	
2.14	Samuel Van Saan Lena Banta	1247 E	
2.14	Nicholas McDugal Margerit Ackerman	1248 E	
3.17	Jacob Van Winkele jr Ann Kingsland	1249 E	
3.21	John J. Gerritse jr Mary Brouwer	1250 E	
5.15	George Van Voorhees Sally Van (B)uren	1251 B	
6. 5	William Amon Hannah Spier	1252 E	
6. 6	David Demarest Gerritje Van Houten	1253 B	
6. 6	Helmich Post Annaatje Vreland	1254 E	
6. 9	Hendrick Glass Annaetje Post	1255 E	
7.18	Teunus Spier Fytje Van Houten	1256 E	
8.17	Cornelius Post jr Maragrietje Gerritse	1257 E	
8.23	Greenleaf S. We(bb) Hannah Querean	1258 E	
9.11	Albert Van Houten Gerritje Vreland	1259 E	
9.19	George J. Ryerson Hillegont Van Houten	1260 B	
10. 2	John Deeths Claasje Gerritse	1261 E	
10.14	Matheus Spier Jannetje Vreland	1262 E, wid wid	
10.16	Mitchel Saunier Elisa Vreland	1263 E	
11. 6	Martinus Van Der Haen Elizabeth Gerritse	1264 E	
11.13	John Peck Sophia Spier	1265 E	
12. 5	Hendrick Van Rypen Myntje Van Rypen	1266 E	
12.11	Hendrick Jurrianse Gerritje Van Blerkum	1267 E	

* - see page 245

Date	Married	1813-1814 Item	*Remarks
12.31	James McGrigor Julia Gray	1268 E	
12.31	Archibald Stayley Sally Clark	1269 E	
1814 1.16	John Earl Laticie Terhune	1270 E	
2. 6	Joseph Gillam Lena Van Houten	1271 E	
4. 9	George Brinckerhoff Caty Doremus	1272 E	
4.10	Joseph Blauvelt Maria Van Saan	1273 E	
4.11	Gabriel Devoe Hanah Brown	1274 E	
5.15	John Schoonmaker Jamima Berry	1275 E	
5.28	Samuel Taggert Mary Dickeay	1276 E	
5.30	Philip H. Earle Charlott Nickelness Earle	1277 E	
6. 4	George Mandevill Caty Ryerse	1278 E	
6.11	James Bruen Rachel Koeyeman	1279 E	
7. 2	Gerrebrant G. Van Rypen Hannah Van Blerkom	1280 E	
7. 3	John Stager Magdalena Paulusse	1281 E	
7. 4	Elijah Strickland Eliza Quereau	1282 E	
7.30	Cornelius J. Bogert Jannetje Post	1283 E, wid wid	
8. 6	Adam Banta Cathalyntje Vreland	1284 E	
9.17	Albert P. Terhune Elenor Van Winkele	1285 E	
10.13	Thomas Cammel Sophia Crank	1286 E	
10.30	Mercelus Post Marietje Van Houten	1287 B	
11. 4	William Griffen Ward Margeret Henry Walworth	1288 E	
11.15	Jacob Durjee Regana Heymer	1289 E wid	

* - see page 245

Date	Groom	Item	Bride	*Remarks
12. 4	Dirick Post	1290	Neesje Van Ry(pen)	E
12.10	Cornelius Hopper	1291	Lena Van Houten	B
1815				
1. 8	Jacob Van Winkel jr	1292	Antje Koejeman	E
1.15	Mathew Alexander	1293	Anney Colwell	E
2. 4	Anthony Jacobusse	1294	Hanna Van Blerkum	E
2. 7	Laurance Ackerman	1295	Lena Vreland	E
2.26	Flavel R. Herrison	1296	Unice Lingford	E
3.26	Hendrick Cadmus	1297	Annaatje Vreland	E
5.20	William Miles	1298	Sally Van Blerkum	E
6. 3	Pieter J. Bogert	1299	Eva Vreland	E
__.__	David Goetschius	1300	Elizabeth Losie	E
7. 8	Jacob Hopper	1301	Geertje Vreland	E
7.16	Jacob Morris	1302	Antje Van Eydestyn	E
7.22	Cornelius Blerkum, wid (groom's surname "Vreland" crossed out)	1303	Antje Ackerman, wid	E
8. 5	Andre(w) C. Post	1304	Syntje Ryers	B
8.27	Albert Hopper	1305	Jaannetje Ryerse	B
8.31	Pieter Van Houten	1306	Lena Van Wagenen	B
9.10	Teunus Van Eydestyn	1307	Selly Vreeland	E
9.16	Teunus Spier	1308	Hannah Anthony	E
10. 1	Thomas Rogers	1309	Maria Small	E
10.23	Derick Terhune	1310	Lauke Van Winkle	B. C
11.18	George Ouwater	1311	Marea Terhune	B. Co.
1816				
3.20	Anthony Batrem	1312	Elizabeth Brinckerhoof wid of John J. Van Winckle	
3.23	James Post	1313	Sophia Vreeland	
1. 4	Peter Steger	1314	Margaret Vrieland	
10.12	Daniel Christie	1315	Margaret Yereance	

* - see page 245

MARRIAGE INDEX

For note regarding the use of this index, see page 150

BANTA (con'd)
Maria, 764
Peter, 823
Rachel, 65
Sarah, 687
Wilhelmina, 413

BARKOW
Evan, 774

Barrey, Barry - see BERRY

Bartholf, Bartholph - see BERTHOLF

BASSET
Nancy, 382
Sarah, 364
Stephen, 70

BATREM
Anthony, 1312

BEATY
George, 372

BEBOUT
Sarah, 483

BEEM
Abraham, 319
Catherine, 290
Jacob, 491

Bekling - see BIGLEY

BENNET
Jacob, 91

BENSEN
Anna, 760
Daniel, 890
David, 749
John, 1218

BERDAN
Anna, 439, 1076
Cornelia, 596
David, 732
Dirk, 161, 1076
Jacob, 1034
John, 737, 770, 1139
Lea, 881
Maria, 1105
Richard, 1163

BERGER
Herman, 117

Berrie, BERRY
Ann, 443
Catlintje, 961
Henry, 916
Janet, 1157

BERRY (con'd)
Jemima, 312, 1275
John, 565, 699, 955, 1243
Lena, 433, 920
Maria, 707
Martin, 843
Morris, 1083
Nancy, 1014
Philip, 615
Richard, 465
Sally, 814
Samuel, 1144

BERTHOLF
Abraham, 323
David, 803
Guiliam, 216
Jacob, 47
Martina, 180
Rebecca, 215
Reinhard, 312
Sarah, 373
Stephen, 371

Besset - see BASSET

Beuis - see BOICE

BEVAND
Charles, 95

BEYERSE
Anna, 866
Maria, 672

BIGLEY
Catherine, 132
John, 479

BILJU
Anna, 909
Elizabeth, 612
Henrietta, 812

BILLINGHTON
James, 217
Maria, 502

BLACKWELL
Sarah, 201

BLAIR
David, 536
Margaret, 1228
Maria, 1077
Robert, 989, 1101

Blakwell - see BLACKWELL

BLANCHARD
Anna, 929
Ryner, 674

MARRIAGE INDEX

Blauveld, BLAUVELT
  Daniel, 777
  Joseph, 1273

Blerkum - see VAN BLARCOM

Blinkerhof - see BRINKERHOFF

BLOODGOOD
  Abraham, 937

Bogard, BOGERT
  Agnes, 130
  Cornelius, 747, 1211, 1283
  John, 46, 103, 422
  Maria, 1006, 1079
  Peter, 1299
  Roelof, 405
  Stephen, 821

BOGGS
  James, 453

BOICE
  Maria, 57

BOLSBEY
  George, 967

Bon, BOND
  Catherine, 187
  Helena, 245
  Janet, 370

Boogaerd, Boogert - see BOGERT

BOON
  James, 1177

BOOTH
  Mary, 1101
  Peggy, 571

BORD
  Catherine, 148
  Frances, 182
  Joris, 62

Bos, Bosch - see BOSS

Boskerck, BOSKERK
  Andrew, 1062
  Margaret, 982

BOSS
  Aaron, 590, 724
  Anna, 163, 590, 724
  Caspar, 703
  Dinah, 1159
  Dirk, 421
  Elizabeth, 178, 515
  Henrietta, 468
  Margaret, 640, 1164
  Michael, 776

BOSS (con'd)
  Rachel, 1170, 1185
  Samuel, 239
  Sarah, 299, 427, 730
  Staats, 2
  Stephen, 1180

Bourdan - see BERDAN

BOVIE
  Jacob, 316

Bras, BRASS
  Adolph, 364, 461
  Catharine, 1003
  Gertrude, 26, 471
  Herman, 450
  Lucas, 31
  Peter, 36, 167
  Sarah, 366
  Thomas, 1018

BRIKKER
  John, 9

Brinckerhoff, BRINKERHOFF
  Elizabeth, 815, 841, 1312
  George, 1272
  Henry, 40
  Hester, 1049
  Jacob, 980, 985
  Joris, 653
  Maria, 435
  Rachel, 891

BROADBERRY, Broedberry
  Richard, 105
  Susan, 84

Broeks, BROOKS
  Abraham, 143

Brouwer, BROWER
  Abraham, 567, 597, 858, 1213
  Anna, 395
  Catherine, 923
  Christopher, 859, 1125
  Elizabeth, 186
  Garret, 745
  George, 1107
  Hessel, 170
  Janet, 517, 1012
  John, 201, 390, 647
  Maria, 114, 592, 1250
  Metje, 277
  Nelly, 53
  Peter, 250, 979
  Rebecca, 868, 1091
  Theodore, 707
  Ulrich, 166

MARRIAGE INDEX

BROWN - see also BRUYN
  Anna, 1274
  Anthony, 514
  Henry, 752
  Hilda, 778
  Hillegond, 706
  Janet, 628
  Sarah, 1033

Bruen, Bruin - see BRUYN

BRUSH
  Catherine, 849

BRUYN - see also BROWN
  Anthony, 25, 332, 631
  Catherine, 118
  Egbert, 1031
  Elizabeth, 12, 64
  Francis, 1053
  Fytje, 1030
  Gerrebrand, 872
  Helena, 737
  Henry, 233, 290, 392, 722
  Hester, 667
  Jacob, 505
  James, 1279
  Janet, 77, 593
  John, 75, 82, 470, 834
  Lena, 157
  Maria, 294, 582
  Martha, 499
  Rachel, 663
  Rebecca, 322
  Sarah, 120

Burger - see BERGER

BURHANS
  Catherine, 1103

BUTLER, Buttler
  Anna, 549
  Catherine, 472
  James, 533

Byert - see BEYERSE

Cachelin, Cachlin - see CONKLIN

CADMUS
  Aaron, 134
  Abraham, 121
  Andrew, 568
  Cornelia, 522
  Cornelius, 632
  Dirk, 1025
  Elizabeth, 554, 932
  Fred, 228
  Garret, 1209
  Hartman, 181

CADMUS (con'd)
  Henry, 1297
  Isaac, 276
  John, 1210
  Lea, 727, 1053
  Margaret, 1210
  Maria, 383, 992
  Thomas, 994

CAIRNS
  Margaret, 1224
  William, 1165

CALLAGHAN
  Sarah, 562

Caller, Calyer - see COLLIER

Camble, Cammel, CAMPBELL
  Hester, 969
  Thomas, 1286

CANNON
  Oliver, 1173

CARLOGB
  Christian, 784

CARMER
  Alida, 700

CARSON
  Cornelius, 983

CASE
  Elizabeth, 769

CAVELLIER
  John, 54

CHAPMAN
  Sarah, 819

CHAPPEL
  Jacob, 483

CHRISTIE, Christyn
  Daniel, 1315
  Elizabeth, 45
  James, 903
  Peter, 412

Claasjen, Claassen - see CLAWSON

CLARK
  Anna, 392
  Fytje, 860
  Martin, 810
  Sally, 1269
  Worthy, 1155

CLAWSON
  Aaron, 231
  Abraham, 263

CLAWSON (con'd)
  Peter, 165
  William, 72

Cochlin - see CONKLIN

COCKEFER, Cockkifer
  John, 359

COEKRO
  Joseph, 907

COERTE
  Clara, 146
  Henry, 766
  Herman, 950
  John, 68, 274
  Maria, 639

COEYMAN
  Abraham, 617
  Anna, 117, 1292
  John, 1181
  Rachel, 556, 1279
  Sarah, 834

COGG, Cogh - see also COOK
  Aaron, 485
  Anna, 396, 1059
  Catherine, 367
  Christina, 401, 1024
  David, 1110
  Joseph, 185, 468
  Maria, 954, 1165

COKEROOCH
  Elizabeth, 953

COLE - see also GOULD
  Anna, 316
  Barent, 337
  Catherine, 1107
  Henry, 537
  Jacob, 39
  Margaret, 344
  Sally, 806

COLEMAN
  Charlotte, 1147

COLLARD
  James, 338

COLLIER
  Henry, 177
  Susan, 258

COLWELL
  Anna, 1293

CONGER
  Phoebe, 1190
  Sarah, 710

CONKLIN
  Margaret, 387
  Maria, 386, 1183
  William, 191

COOK - see also COGG
  Eleanor, 677
  Gertrude, 32

COOMBE
  John, 214

COON
  Nathan, 794

COOPER
  Elizabeth, 1201
  Gilbert, 805
  Joseph, 857

COOTS
  Benjamin, 178

CORBY
  John, 476

Corsen - see CARSON

Courte - see COERTE

Cranck - see KRANCK

Crane - see KREIN

Crank - see KRANCK

CRAWFORD
  Jane, 1065

CRAWLE
  Lawrence, 175

CUBBERLEY
  Isaac, 1169

CUSSART
  Elizabeth, 748

DAVENPORT
  Humphrey, 83
  Lena, 51
  Rachel, 102
  Sarah, 39

Davie, Davids, DAVIS
  Elizabeth, 599
  John, 1131
  Maria, 97
  William, 644

DAY
  Hester, 775
  Maria, 955

Deboe - see TIEBOUT

DE BONN
  Rebecca, 239

De Boog - see TIEBOUT

DEDRICK
  Gertrude, 338
  John, 176

Deeder - see TEATOR

Deeths - see TEATS

Deffenpoort, Defvenpoort - see
 DAVENPORT

DE GARMO
  John, 275

DeGraauw, DeGrauw, DE GRAW, DeGrouw
  Anna, 643
  Caspar, 534
  Catherine, 540, 1174
  Elizabeth, 158
  Francis, 643
  Garret, 492
  Gertrude, 535, 1016
  Hartman, 790
  Henrietta, 37
  Herman, 283, 661
  Janet, 466, 845, 956
  John, 1194
  Lea, 987
  Lena, 1007
  Maria, 770
  Rachel, 816
  Rebecca, 1148

DE HONEUR
  Boudewyn, 56

DE LAMETER
  Hester, 108

DELMOT
  Gulielmus, 541

DeMare, DEMAREST
  Cornelia, 1240
  David, 520, 594, 928, 1253
  Gertrude, 1081
  Jacob, 1043
  Janet, 1123
  Jemima, 200
  Maria, 1206

DEMILL
  Benjamin, 576

DEMOTT
  Adam, 333
  Garret, 1040
  Jacob, 140

DEMSEY
  Elizabeth, 489

DE REMIS
  Alida, 196

Derjee - see DURYEA

De Vauce - see DE VOSNEY

DEVOE
  Gabriel, 1274
  John, 1150
  Joseph, 469

DE VOOR,etc
  Abraham, 33
  Sarah, 492

Devorsne, DE VOSNEY, Devoursne
  John, 253, 521
  Margaret, 417
  Thomas, 960

Dey - see DAY

D'Grauw - see DE GRAW

DIAL
  Philip, 831

Dickeay, DICKEY
  Esther, 1187
  Jane, 1078
  Mary, 1276

Dideriks, Didirks - see DEDRICK

DIERMAN
  Joseph, 779

DIRKJE, Dirkse, Dirje
  Anna, 107
  Catherine, 10
  Maria, 21
  Peter, 295

DIXON
  Janet, 1008

Dod, DODD
  Stephen, 911
  Thomas, 867

DOLHAVEN
  Catherine, 1132

DON
  Elizabeth, 268

Doremes, Doremis, DOREMUS
  Albert, 1085
  Alida, 251
  Anna, 125, 272, 750, 1176
  Catherine, 391, 1090, 1244, 1272

DOREMUS (con'd)
  Cornelius, 160, 230, 240, 350, 502,
    627, 875, 1011, 1081
  David, 462
  Egbert, 467
  Egje, 1236
  Elizabeth, 94, 874, 934, 1063
  Gertrude, 947
  Henry, 892, 1118
  Hessel, 255, 1123
  Jacob, 941
  Janet, 143, 227, 926, 964, 1087
  John, 238, 669, 853, 958, 1208
  Joris, 439, 746
  Lea, 389, 1158
  Margaret, 994
  Maria, 248, 721, 781, 984, 1018
  Peter, 220, 918, 920
  Pryntje, 568
  Rachel, 890
  Roelof, 750
  Sarah, 946, 1044
  Susan, 1075, 1094
  Thomas, 690
  Vroutje, 296
  William, 1066

DOUGHERTY
  Mary, 774

DOW, Dowe
  Elizabeth, 572
  Mary, 569
  Sarah, 585

Dromment, DRUMMOND
  Heaty, 424
  John, 640
  Maria, 720
  Robert, 129, 379
  Sarah, 462

DuGarmoy - see DE GARMO

DUPLACEY
  Henry, 549

Durjee, DURYEA, etc
  Jacob, 1289
  John, 435
  Maria, 351

DUVALL
  Anna, 760

EARL, Earle
  Charlotte, 1277
  Edward, 287, 1074
  John, 407, 500, 682, 909, 1270
  Philip, 1277

EARL (con'd)
  Sylvester, 110
  Theodosia, 528

EASTERLEY
  Catherine, 683

EATON
  John, 592

Echtbersze - see EGBERTS

Ecker - see ACKERT

ECKERSON
  Jacob, 806

EDESON
  Henry, 547

EDSEL
  Jane, 1242

EGBERTS(e), Eghbertsze - see also EVERTS
  Catherine, 174
  Elsie, 240
  Garret, 531
  Jacob, 951
  John, 248, 787
  Rachel, 738

Ellen - see ALLEN

ELLERTON
  Zachariah, 13

ELLIS
  Cornelius, 336

ELSWORTH
  James, 923

EMANS, Emmans
  John, 544
  Sarah, 78

Enderson - see ANDERSON

ENNIS
  Anna, 573, 671, 937
  Catherine, 883
  Jacob, 429
  James, 517
  John, 949, 1075
  Margaret, 430, 715, 978
  Rebecca, 884
  Richard, 964

ERICHSON
  Reinhard, 8

Erl - see EARL

ERO
  Christina, 830

MARRIAGE INDEX

GARRISON (con'd)
Peter, 104, 510
Vroutje, 733

GENDOR
John, 582

Gerbrantse, Gerrebrandse, GERREBRANT(se)
Anna, 622
Anthony, 919
Catherine, 484
George, 688
Gerrebrand, 190, 773, 972
John, 507
Maria, 43, 507, 858
Peter, 678
Sally, 938

Gerritse, Gerritszen - see GARRISON

GILLAM
Joseph, 1059, 1271
Micah, 401

GLASS
Henry, 1255
Robert, 687

GODWIN
Betty, 516
Margaret, 482
Maria, 1232
Phoebe, 1106
Susan, 1131

GOETSCHIUS
Anna, 1217
Catherine, 474
David, 1300
Elizabeth, 981
Henry, 975
Janet, 1072
John, 472, 1217
Margaret, 1045
Maria, 941
Rachel, 1031
Sally, 1089

GOMEZ
John, 596

GOULD - see also COLE
Catherine, 1121
Increase, 962
John, 935
Mahetible, 911
Martha, 50
Robert, 63

GOVERNEURS
Magdalena, 71

GRAY
Elizabeth, 794
Julia, 1268

GREENLEAF
Enoch, 912

Griffies, GRIFFITH, Griffits
David, 710
Femmetje, 810
Jane, 1184
Sally, 432
Sarah, 712

Guuld - see GOULD

HAERING
Anna, 1199
Jacob, 413

HAGHERT, Haghoort
Hester, 709

Halenbeeck, Halenbeek - see HALLENBECK

HALL
Anna, 842
Cornelius, 408
John, 71

HALLENBECK
Garret, 767
Isaac, 388

Holm - see HELM

HAM
Sarah, 801

HANCOCK
John, 1189, 1223

Haring - see HAERING

HARRIS(on)
Flavel, 1296
Henry, 451
John, 329, 715

HART, Hartte
Michael, 125
Rachel, 58

HARVEY
Elizabeth, 119, 220
Isaac, 680
Syas, 363

Hatharington - see HETHERINGTON

HAY
Samuel, Col., 490

HEDDEY
Lothen, 543

HEESS
  Elizabeth, 266

HELM(e)
  Agnes, 962
  Anna, 903
  Cornelius, 727
  John, 580
  Peter, 848
  Susan, 939

Hemmion - see HENNION

HENDRICKZEN
  Cornelius, 154

HENNION
  Anthony, 272, 844
  Harriet, 1182
  John, 296, 679, 759
  Margaret, 800
  Nicholas, 744
  Peter, 1020
  Sarah, 334

Herring - see HAERING

Herrison - see HARRIS

Herty - see HART

Hervie, Hervy - see HARVEY

HETHERINGTON
  John, 1190

HEYL(E)
  Catherine, 99
  Elizabeth, 83
  Margaret, 139
  Nicholas, 102

HEYMER
  Regina, 1289

HODGE
  James, 591

HOFMAN
  Catherine, 734

Holm - see HELM

HOLSTEAD, Holsted
  Abigail, 560
  Jonathan, 691

Hoogelandt - see HOUGHLAND

Hoppe, Hoppen, HOPPER
  Albert, 1305
  Catherine, 407, 793, 1043
  Cornelia, 1210
  Cornelius, 493, 1291
  Guliam, 974

HOPPER (con'd)
  Jacob, 1301
  Jemima, 1119
  John, 701, 785
  Rachel, 463, 785
  William, 197

HOSK
  Charlotte, 333

HOUGHLAND
  Francis, 182
  John, 449

Houwert, HOWARD
  Anna, 16

HUDNUT
  Samuel, 424

HUMBLE
  John, 836

HURLEY, Hurly
  Catherine, 616
  Maria, 576

HUSTON
  Jacob, 498

HUYSMAN
  Abraham, 415
  Maria, 704
  Nietje, 895

HYLER
  Jacob, 374

IMMET
  Anna, 280

INSLEY
  John, 1152

JACKSON
  Nancy, 762
  Peter, 1049

JACOBS, Jacobusse, Jacobusze(n)
  Abraham, 223
  Alida, 206, 705
  Anna, 634
  Anthony, 1164, 1294
  Dirk, 377
  Fytje, 597
  Garret, 639
  Geesje, 467
  Gertrude, 1066
  Hester, 362
  Jacob, 124, 399, 484
  Janet, 59, 106
  John, 120, 953
  Lena, 235

JACOBS (con'd)
  Margaret, 718
  Maria, 508, 642, 892
  Mayke, 833
  Peter, 305, 738
  Rachel, 331
  Sally, 862
  Sarah, 399, 1015
  Susan, 918

JEFFERS
  Sophia, 356

Jeraalam, Jeraalman, JERALEMAN,
 Jeralleman
  Anna, 355
  Ariantje, 25
  Cornelius, 889
  Elizabeth, 620
  Henry, 28, 575, 706
  Hester, 649, 864
  John, 1195
  Lena, 1095
  Margaret, 511, 578, 611
  Mary, 711
  Nicholas, 667

JOHNSON
  Anna, 459
  Samuel, 353

JONES
  Nicholas, 64, 162
  Thomas, 684

Jong(h) - see YOUNG

Joons - see JONES

JORDAN
  John, 648

Jraleman, Jraeleman - see JERALEMAN

JUISTON
  Robert, 112

JUKHAR
  Elizabeth, 177

Jurjaense, JURRIANSE, Jurriyaansen,
 Jurryanse
  Christopher, 395
  Elizabeth, 980
  Fred, 1160
  Garret, 1175
  George, 74, 719, 971
  Gerrebrand, 210, 708
  Henry, 1267
  Hessel, 896
  Janet, 889
  John, 990, 1166, 1215

JURRIANSE (con'd)
  Lena, 534
  Margaret, 1315
  Maria, 14
  Sarah, 555

KARRIES
  Margaret, 175

Keerse - see CASE

Kelliham - see CALLAGHAN

KELLY
  Rachel, 1001

KENT
  Cornelius, 865
  Simon, 156

Ker - see KERR

Kerck, KERK - see also NEWKERK
  Helena, 708
  Henry, 659
  John, 864
  Maria, 608

KERR
  David, 792
  Maria, 657

KIERSTEAD, Kierstede
  Aaron, 799
  John, 860, 1234

Kieslaer, KIESLER
  Gertrude, 1092
  John, 850
  Maria, 921

Killy - see KELLY

KING
  Aaron, 457, 668, 804
  Abraham, 577
  Isabella, 1138
  John, 663, 665, 966
  Maria, 11, 520
  Rachel, 452
  Robert, 1184

KINGSLAND
  Anna, 533, 1249
  Catherine, 557
  Henry, 628
  Isaac, 204, 268, 509
  Janet, 606
  Joseph, 1231
  Margaret, 991
  Maria, 848
  Nathan, 260
  Stephen, 651

MARRIAGE INDEX

KINGSLAND (con'd)
  William, 489, 511, 796

KIP
  Anna, 149, 357
  Catherine, 1080
  Catlintje, 311
  Charles, 1065
  Elizabeth, 329, 1191
  Eva, 223
  Helena, 327
  Henry, 713, 1028
  Heylia, 1207
  Isaac, 519
  Janet, 256, 1093
  John, 23, 1220
  Lea, 756
  Maria, 767, 1071
  Nicasie, 361, 1047
  Peter, 1212
  Rachel, 1211
  Ryner, 1029
  Sarah, 276

KIRRIS
  Aaron, 754

Klaaszen, Klaessen - see CLAWSON

KNEGHT
  Henry, 991

Koeiman - see COEYMAN

Kogh - see COGG

Koijeman - see COEYMAN

Kool - see COLE

Kooper - see COOPER

KRANCK
  Anna, 857
  Catherine, 1073
  Fytje, 1153
  Isaac, 666
  John, 1222
  Sophia, 1286

KREIN
  John, 1241

KROM
  Janet, 1025

KRONICK
  Caspar, 650

Kuuk - see COOK

Kuyper - see COOPER

LABACH
  Henry, 1002

Laeubets - see LAMBERTS

LAMB
  John, 778

LAMBERTS
  Judith, 90
  Lea, 916

LANKER
  Janet, 5

LAROE, LaRou
  Helena, 216
  Henry, 698
  Jacob, 215, 877

LAWRENCE
  John, 442

LEARY
  James, 1176

LEE
  Kitty, 1084

LEETH
  Catherine, 1013

Leuwis, LEWIS
  John, 80
  Samuel, 1214

LEYDECKER
  Wyntje, 437

LINFORD, Lingford, Linkfoot, Linkford
  Eunice, 1296
  Herman, 900
  Margaret, 1115

LINSEY, Linsie
  Maria, 464

LIONS
  Peggy, 1189

LISK
  Anna, 458, 1035
  Jane, 453

LIVINGSTON
  (_____), 282
  George, 1147

LOCKWOOD
  Daniel, 1095

LOSEE, Losie
  Elizabeth, 1300

LOW
  Elizabeth, 400

MARRIAGE INDEX

LOW (con'd)
  Maria, 1173

LUDLOW
  Catherine, 1112
  Cornelius, 1041
  John, 84, 638, 824
  Mary, 86

LUTHEN
  John, 914

LYN
  Abraham, 795
  Conrad, 375

LYNSEM
  David, 607

Mac (_____) - see MC (_____)

Maghee - see MC GHEE

Mandeviel, MANDEVILL(E), Mandevyl
  Abraham, 1174
  Alida, 900
  Elizabeth, 278, 300
  George, 1278
  Henry, 326, 373, 1030
  Jacob, 888
  John, 12, 866
  Lea, 361
  Margaret, 323
  Maria, 371
  Peter, 373
  Rachel, 743, 797
  Sietje, 676
  William, 365

MANNING
  Helena, 882

Marcelis, Marcelusse - see MARSELIS

MARINUS
  Anna, 1145
  David, 1143
  John, 423, 1045

MARSELIS, Marselisze, Marselusse
  Ariantje, 837, 1193
  Catherine, 153
  Catlintje, 771
  Claasje, 1212
  Edo, 1207
  Fred, 86
  Garret, 1007
  Janet, 456
  John, 694

MARTIN
  Margaret, 836

MARYGOLD
  Mary, 543

Maurisse, Mauritszen, Mauritzen,
  Maurusse, Maurusson - see MORRIS

McCarday, McCartie, MC CARTY
  Abigail, 537
  James, 957
  John, 714, 943

MC CREA
  Catherine, 457

MC CREERE
  Sally, 591

MC DONALD
  Thomas, 513

MC DUGAL
  Nicholas, 1248

MC GHEE
  John, 585

MC GRIGOR
  James, 1268

MC ILWRICK
  Gilbert, 1153

McLain, MC LEAN
  Angus, 557
  Eleanor, 581
  Polly, 880
  William, 649

MC MANNERS
  Anna, 725

MC PHERSON
  Abel, 981

MC PICK
  Dennis, 606

MC WILLIAMS
  Robert, 403

MEAD, Meed, Meedt, Meet
  Christina, 782
  Elsie, 44
  Giles, 77
  Jacob, 351
  Peter, 315
  Rachel, 993, 1004
  Sarah, 319

Mendevyl - see MANDEVILLE

MERLET
  Dirk, 67

MARRIAGE INDEX

MESSEKER
  Anna, 171
  Eva, 804
  Femmetje, 82
  Henrietta, 69
  Henry, 141, 901
  John, 69, 234
  Lena, 169, 877
  Ludwich, 225, 878
  Nelly, 15, 35
  Sally, 838

Messelaer, Messeler, METSELER
  Abraham, 122
  Elizabeth, 773
  Highly, 989

MEYER
  Aaron, 735
  Anna, 879

MILES
  William, 1298

MILLER
  Elizabeth, 736
  Jacob, 734

Milles - see MILLIDS

MILLIDGE
  Anna, 70

MILLIDS, Millits
  Jacob, 51
  Sarah, 129

MILLS
  Martha, 579
  William, 671

Mire - see MEYER

MITCHEL
  Edward, 1200

MOLLIN
  Bernard, 76

MONTAINE, Montanje
  Anna, 661
  Isaac, 53

MOOR(E)
  Anna, 1026
  Elizabeth, 1108
  John, 427
  Michael, 871
  Rachel, 723
  Tabitha, 512

MORGAN
  Morgan, 839

MORRIS, Mouritse, Mouritszen, Mouritze, Mourusse
  Abraham, 200
  Alida, 436
  Eleanor, 1208
  Frances, 238
  Gertrude, 1056
  Jacob, 243, 589, 827, 1171, 1302
  Jemima, 869
  John, 343
  Lena, 418
  Margaret, 1205
  Peter, 136
  Sietje, 765
  William, 570

MUNSON
  Silas, 885

Muzelius - see MARSELIS

Myer - see MEYER

NEDERMAN
  Elizabeth, 365
  Peter, 90

Neefjes, Neefyes, Nefius - see NEVIS

NEIL
  Elizabeth, 490
  Isabella, 691

NEP
  Walter, 819

NEVIS, Nevius
  Egje, 89
  Fytje, 847
  Garret, 142, 655
  Lea, 219
  Neffsje, 208
  Peter, 219

NEWKERK - see also KERK
  Jemima, 179
  Peter, 10
  Rachel, 103

NICKOL
  William, 1229

Nieuwkerk - see NEWKERK

NIX
  Christopher, 334
  Elizabeth, 302

NORRID
  Cornelius, 1050

NUTTER
  Anna, 403

OBENHOUSS
Elizabeth, 267

OCKLY
Jesse, 840

ONDERDONK
Rem, 904

OOLDIS
Benjamin, 126

OSBORN
Sally, 1180

Oudtwater, Oudwaeter - see OUTWATER

OUKE
Janet, 518
John, 195

OUTWATER, Ouwater
Abraham, 1079
Alida, 469
Anna, 87, 460
Elizabeth, 840
Francis, 3
George, 1311
Jacob, 841
John, 1246
Maria, 233
Nicholas, 891
Richard, 1080
Sarah, 631

Parck, Parke, PARKER
John, 837
Robert, 1111

PARLMAN
Elizabeth, 697

PARROT
John, 556

PAULSON, Paulusse, Pauluszen
Anna, 688, 996
Catherine, 288
Dirk, 622
Elizabeth, 339, 1154
Fytje, 863
Isaac, 335
Janet, 1047
John, 801
Magdalena, 1281
Paul, 932
Peter, 478, 852, 897
Sarah, 973

PEARSAAL
Jarvis, 1001

PEARSON
Susan, 449
Thomas, 748

Peck - see PEEK

PECKER
Elizabeth, 852

PEEK
Abraham, 1003
Gilbert, 324
John, 425, 1265

PELT
John, 1224

PERRY
Achsa, 854
Asa, 854

Person - see PEARSON

PETERSE
Alexander, 144
Anna, 116
Christina, 303
Claasje, 154
Elizabeth, 165
Elsie, 252
Frances, 1
Garret, 89
George, 52
Lea, 85
Margaret, 325
Peter, 113, 149

Pettum - see POTTUM

PHARROW
William, 432

PHILIPS
John, 171
Rachel, 167

PICKSTON(E)
Anna, 1019
Dirk, 436
Henry, 1010

Piearson - see PEARSON

PIER
Barney, 1136
Cornelius, 587
David, 814
Garret, 1012
Isaac, 595
Jacob, 428
John, 527
Matthew, 1026
Peter, 838

MARRIAGE INDEX

Pieterse, Pieterssen, Pietersze(n) -
see PETERSE

PINKERTON
James, 902

PLUM
Sarah, 915

Poelis - see PAULSON

PORTER
John, 675
Peter, 712

POST
Abraham, 1099
Adrian, 58, 61, 173, 314, 330, 601,
618, 1061, 1124
Andrew, 1304
Anna, 222, 314, 376, 566, 925, 1255
Ariantje, 894
Beletje, 930
Caspar, 863
Catherine, 147, 337, 423
Catlintje, 655
Cornelius, 383, 396, 1037, 1051, 1257
Dirk, 1290
Egbert, 1141
Elizabeth, 525, 656, 685, 943, 1150,
1237
Francis, 292, 341, 358, 440
Fytje, 402
Garret, 1, 270, 820, 882, 906, 1063
Geesje, 30
Hartman, 762
Helmich, 198, 1014, 1202, 1254
Henry, 45, 523, 775, 944, 1157
Jacob, 855
James, 1313
Janet, 757, 1000, 1130, 1140, 1175,
1283
John, 16, 380, 522, 604, 956, 995,
1016, 1038, 1089, 1154, 1240
Lea, 346
Margaret, 621, 695, 1039, 1058
Maria, 295, 548, 586, 595, 598, 605,
618, 1010, 1046
Marselus, 109, 518, 952, 1287
Metje, 1110
Michael, 600
Paul, 1244
Peter, 515, 1158
Pietertje, 93
Pryna, 274
R. Janet, 318
Rachel, 133, 159
Roelof, 598, 605
Samuel, 1179

POST (con'd)
Sarah, 444
Syntje, 959
Thomas, 385
Tyna, 829

Pots, POTTS
Peter, 291

POTTUM
Elizabeth, 232

Poulusse, Poulusson, Pouwelse - see
PAULSON

Preevo, Prefoort - see PROVOOST

PRIME
Samuel, 1008

PRITTEN
Adoniram, 560

PROVOOST
Margaret, 777
Maria, 8, 604

QUACKENBOSCH
Lea, 744

QUEREAN, Quereau
Anna, 1258
Eliza, 1282

Ratan - see RUTHAN

Reddanor, Rednaer - see RIDDENAR

Reike - see RIKER

Retan, Rethan - see RUTHAN

REYBERT
Nancy, 1226

REYERS, Reyerssen, Reyerszen, Reyjerszen
Anna, 254, 696
Catherine, 1278
Elizabeth, 137
George, 793, 1260
Gertrude, 853
Jacob, 188
Janet, 279, 957, 1305
John, 818, 1006, 1113
Lena, 1163
Maria, 265
Martin, 145
Susan, 1127
Syntje, 1304
William, 137, 677

Reyke - see RIKER

RICKS, Ricxz
Henry, 252

RICKS (con'd)
  Maria, 229

Riddenaer, RIDDENAR
  Elizabeth, 1128
  Fytje, 1178
  Peter, 1168

RIKER - see also WRIGHT
  Abraham, 168, 229, 573
  Albert, 616
  Anna, 189, 1117
  Catherine, 234, 817
  Henry, 50, 169
  Isaac, 157, 948
  Jacob, 211, 438, 658, 1013
  Jemima, 901
  John, 60, 244, 266, 768
  Lena, 31
  Lydia, 931
  Margaret, 690
  Maria, 363, 625
  Nelly, 48
  Nicholas, 294
  Peter, 49
  Rachel, 702
  Roelof, 705
  Rycke, 172
  Sarah, 414

ROACH
  Nicholas, 454

Rodebach - see ROHRBACH

ROELOFSE
  Catherine, 7

ROGERS
  Thomas, 1309

ROHRBACH
  Gertrude, 1070

ROME
  Anna, 313
  Jacob, 340
  Samuel, 344

Romein, ROMEYN, Romyn
  John, 886
  Nicholas, 98
  Roelof, 826
  Susan, 607

Roome - see ROME

Roos - see ROSS

ROOSEVELT
  John, 501

ROSEKRANTS
  William, 1084

ROSET
  Catherine, 95

ROSS
  Maria, 580

Rothan - see RUTHAN

ROW, Rue
  Conrad, 817
  Mary, 1239
  Philip, 731

RUTHAN
  Abraham, 115, 978
  Anna, 746
  Barent, 410
  Elizabeth, 945
  Geesje, 904
  Janet, 870, 1136
  Johannes John, 281
  Paul, 602

Rycke - see RIKER

RYCKMAN
  Mary, 912

Ryer, Ryers, Ryerse, Ryerson - see REYERS

Rycke(r) - see RIKER

Sanderse, SANDERSON
  Anna, 3, 87
  Elizabeth, 352

Sandford, Sandvoort, SANFORD
  Nancy, 935
  Peter, 529

SAUNIER
  Mitchel, 1263

SCHAMP
  Janet, 67

SCHOONMAKER
  Catherine, 1234
  Daniel, 620, 685
  Helena, 716, 913
  Henry, 728
  Isaac, 1054
  Jacob, 1112
  John, 1275
  Maria, 728
  Sally, 544
  Salome, 1151

SCHUYLER
  Aaron, 207

MARRIAGE INDEX

SNYER
  John, 99

Sobriesko - see ZABRISKIE

SPEARLING
  Lea, 191

SPIER
  Abraham, 100, 497
  Anna, 100, 1069, 1252
  Anthony, 743, 1256, 1308
  Barent, 370, 1015, 1024
  Catherine, 211, 1168
  Catlintje, 772
  Cornelius, 135
  Dirkje, 635
  Elizabeth, 577
  Francis, 108, 736
  Garret, 430
  Gerritje, 22
  Gertrude, 914
  Henrietta, 448
  Henry, 278, 584, 1098, 1133
  Herman, 569
  Jacob, 24, 452, 583, 999, 1116, 1178
  Janet, 195, 919, 950
  John, 155, 346, 391, 546, 578, 656,
    808, 1092, 1192, 1225
  Lea, 29, 285, 670, 999
  Lena, 665, 745, 763
  Magdalena, 1195
  Maria, 136, 156, 409, 429, 575, 1188
  Matthew, 692, 1109, 1262
  Metje, 602
  Rachel, 326, 531
  Ryner, 642
  Sally, 1037
  Samuel, 942
  Sarah, 23, 340, 603, 878
  Sophia, 1265
  Thyna, 1002

SPRONG
  Gabriel, 672

Spyr - see SPIER

Stager - see STEEGER

Stagg - see STEGG

STAYLEY
  Archibald, 1269

Stech, Steck - see STEGG

STEEGER
  Catlintje, 6
  Christopher, 414
  Dirk, 59

STEEGER (con'd)
  Elizabeth, 18
  Gertrude, 343
  Henry, 681
  John, 189. 763, 1281
  Mary, 949
  Peter, 1314
  Sarah, 377

STEENBECK, Steenbeek
  Anthony, 542, 635

Steg - see STEGG

Steger(s) - see STEEGER

STEGG
  Abraham, 1023
  Anna, 421, 865, 974
  Catherine, 861
  Dirk, 426, 434, 1104
  Jacob, 184, 1042
  John, 409, 929
  Joris, 192
  Josiah, 400
  Lea, 34
  Maria, 1064
  Nelly, 68
  Peggy, 434
  William, 119

STEINMETS
  Anna, 856
  Benjamin, 78
  Caspar, 411
  Eleanor, 651
  Elizabeth, 74
  Fred, 443
  George, 221
  Herman, 280
  Hester, 320
  Janet, 498
  John, 147
  Maria, 262
  Peter, 114

Stheg - see STEGG

STILES
  Elizabeth, 570
  Phoebe, 967

STILLEWILL
  Elizabeth, 224

Stor - see STORR

STORM(S)
  Catherine, 803
  Garret, 800
  Isaac, 697

MARRIAGE INDEX

STORM (con'd)
  Santje, 735

STORR
  Elizabeth, 826
  Jacob, 825
  Peter, 807
  Tyntje, 821

STRICKLAND
  Elijah, 1282

Styles - see STILES

Stur - see STORR

Stymatts, Stymets, Stymetsz, Stynmets -
  see STEINMETS

SULIVAN
  John, 624

SWINER
  Janet, 359

Syndel - see SINDEL

TADES
  Caspar, 37

TAGGERT
  Samuel, 1276

TAYLOR
  Samuel, 1044

TEATOR
  Elizabeth, 594

TEATS
  John, 899, 1261

Ten Brisco - see ZABRISKIE

TEN BROECK
  John, 11

TEN EYCK
  Andrew, 254

TERHUNE
  Albert, 1046, 1285
  Catherine, 493, 886
  Dirk, 1310
  John, 487, 758
  Lea, 968
  Letitia, 1270
  Maria, 415, 1311
  Michael, 704
  Paul, 973
  Peter, 553, 963, 969
  Rachel, 653
  Theodore, 1188

THARP
  Nathan, 946

Themout - see DEMOTT

THEWALT
  Barbara, 140

Theyssen, Thiese - see TYSEN

Thomas, THOMASSE, Thomusse
  Abraham, 55
  Dirk, 93, 152
  Elizabeth, 41
  Jacob, 43
  John, 88
  Maria, 36, 56, 61
  Nancy, 526
  Thomas, 101

Thredwell - see TREADWELL

Thymets - see STEINMETS

Thys - see TYSEN

TIEBOUT
  Catlintje, 297
  Dirk, 352
  Garret, 20

Tiemout - see DEMOTT

TOERS, Tours
  Abraham, 883
  Anna, 301, 538
  Daniel, 508
  Elizabeth, 270
  Frances, 9, 198
  Garret, 381
  Jacob, 311, 586
  John, 368
  Maria, 185, 261

TOWNLEY
  Joshua, 488

TRAPHAGEN
  Rachel, 609

TREADWELL
  James, 873

TREVES
  Abraham, 477

Tyse, TYSON
  Anna, 574
  Christina, 81
  John, 861
  Maria, 684, 783
  Peter, 261, 1102

Valk - see FALCK

Van Aalen - see VAN ALEN

Van Aarsdelen - see VAN ARSDALE

VAN ALEN
Anna, 768
Catherine, 1055
Elizabeth, 965, 1111
Garret, 481
Henry, 874
Lucas, 924
Maria, 751
Peter, 1087

VAN ARSDALE
Nancy, 1213

Van Beuren - see VAN BUREN

VAN BLARCOM, Van Blarkum, Van Blercom,
 Van Blercum, Van Blerkom, Van Blerkum
Abraham, 798
Anna, 348, 1036, 1102, 1245, 1280,
 1294
Anthony, 265, 1036
Brechje, 822
Catherine, 977
Cornelius, 977, 984, 1303
David, 1137
Elizabeth, 719, 802
Gerritje, 1267
Henry, 394, 559, 905, 1140, 1142
Herman, 965
John, 5, 634
Lena, 835, 1120
Maria, 188, 927, 1020, 1074, 1101
Nicasie, 870
Nicholas, 1071
Peter, 42, 258, 833
Rachel, 122
Sally, 1298
Simon, 822
Vroutje, 798, 1052, 1068

Van Bossen - see VAN BUSSEN

VAN BREMEN
Thomas, 196

VAN BUREN
John, 480, 970
Kemena, 884
Sally, 1251

VAN BUSSEN
Abigail, 808, 985
Andrew, 1130
Catherine, 701, 1246
Catlintje, 692
David, 558
Elizabeth, 674

VAN BUSSEN (con'd)
Herman, 138, 646, 930
John, 1072
Margaret, 986
Maria, 641
Peter, 996
Philip, 1245
Sally, 922, 975

Van Der Beeck, VAN DER BEEK
Abraham, 482
Elizabeth, 38
Jacob, 641
Maria, 20

VANDERBILT
Magdalena, 336

VAN DER HAAN, Van Der Haen
Catherine, 1142
Cornelius, 695
Martin, 1264

Van Der Hoef(f), VAN DER HOFF
Abraham, 299
Anna, 924
Catherine, 250, 872, 910
Dirk, 526
Dorothy, 360, 893
Elizabeth, 350, 1114
Isaac, 4
Jacob, 18, 1172
Janet, 1096
John, 218, 464
Margaret, 461

VAN DER KOEK
Michael, 213

Van Der Oeff - see VAN DER HOFF

VAN DER POEL
Elizabeth, 193

Van Der Voort, Van Der Vorst - see
 VAN VORST

Van Deursen, VAN DEUSEN
Agnes, 271
Janet, 80

Van Dien - see VAN DUYN

VAN DRIESEN
Anna, 298

Van Duin, VAN DUYN
Caspar, 954
Catherine, 321
Gertrude, 63
Henry, 933
Isaac, 118

MARRIAGE INDEX

VAN HOUTEN (con'd)
  John, 180, 202, 227, 264, 922, 925
  Lena, 859, 1271, 1291
  Maria, 1126, 1139, 1287
  Martin, 1156
  Martje, 88
  Neefje, 1162
  Peter, 1306
  Pryntje, 831
  Ryner, 22
  Richard, 475
  Robert, 811
  Roelof, 357, 809
  Sarah, 805
  Simon, 927
  Susan, 888
  William, 868

VAN IMBURG(H), Van Inmburgh
  Catherine, 408, 588
  Elizabeth, 47
  Gilbert, 608
  Janet, 546, 659
  John, 711
  Simon, 551

Van Nes, VAN NESS
  Catherine, 786
  Cornelia, 213
  Henrietta, 908
  Henry, 7, 781
  Isaac, 48
  Jacob, 782
  John, 1201
  Maria, 827
  Nelly, 529
  Peter, 992
  Rachel, 60, 335
  Simon, 297, 300, 876, 1022
  William, 802

Van Neuwkerk, Van Nieuw-Kerk - see
NEWKERK

Van Noorstrand, VAN NOSTRAND,
Van Oostrandt
  Anna, 477
  Jacob, 535
  Janet, 630
  Sally, 660, 1166
  Susan, 1169

VAN ORDEN
  Dolly, 823
  Herman, 828
  Janet, 875
  Lawrence, 812

Van Ripen, VAN RIPER, Van Rype(n)
  Abraham, 393, 504, 673, 1230
  Adrian, 562, 772
  Anna, 145, 230, 410, 530
  Caspar, 662
  Catherine, 310, 564, 658, 1042, 1109,
    1167
  Christopher, 277
  Cornelius, 486, 733, 1039, 1205
  Dirk, 345, 398, 636
  Elizabeth, 264, 601
  Fred, 226
  Garret, 369, 445
  George, 164, 993, 1077
  Gerrebrand, 1280
  Henry, 1266
  Herman, 495, 718, 1091
  Isaac, 310, 1064, 1185
  Jacob, 629, 689, 788, 1170, 1197
  Janet, 246, 257, 259, 632, 694, 799
  John, 303, 320, 431, 630, 654, 756,
    908, 947, 1052, 1237
  Lea, 305, 619
  Lena, 539
  Margaret, 440, 637, 669, 851
  Maria, 495, 550, 552, 589, 681, 906,
    1021, 1197, 1214
  Marinus, 367
  Myntje, 1266
  Neesje, 1290
  Peter, 931
  Philip, 664
  Pietertje, 532
  Rachel, 304, 341, 714, 843
  Sarah, 347, 384
  Sietje, 565
  Simon, 325, 1196
  Styntje, 627
  Thomas, 199, 307, 347, 444, 1126, 1203

Van Saan, VAN SANT
  Albert, 832
  Anna, 928
  Isaac, 771
  Janet, 887
  Maria, 473, 1273
  Samuel, 1247

VAN SCHYVEN
  Anna, 513

Van Seil, VAN SEYL
  Abraham, 816
  Elizabeth, 4
  Jacob, 474
  John, 894
  Lena, 225

MARRIAGE INDEX

VERBRYCK
  Henry, 459

VERDON
  Henry, 441

VINCENT
  Hester, 28
  John, 94
  Susan, 79, 135

VOLKS
  Maria, 144

Voorhis - see VAN VOORHEES

VORS
  Syntje, 679

Vreeland(t), VRELAND, Vrelant, Vrieland
  Abraham, 614, 683, 987
  Adrian, 1199
  Aegje, 309
  Alida, 629
  Anna, 184, 465, 506, 521, 587, 652,
    747, 754, 970, 1129, 1254, 1297
  Beletje, 536
  Benjamin, 976
  Catherine, 480
  Catlintje, 1284
  Christopher, 613
  Claasje, 287, 345, 699
  Cornelia, 1141
  Cornelius, 289, 406, 893, 939, 1120,
    1303
  Dirk, 208
  Edo, 1129
  Elias, 81, 205, 419, 525, 621, 1069
  Eliza, 1263
  Elizabeth, 406, 486, 638
  Enoch, 456, 1048
  Eva, 1054, 1215, 1299
  Frances, 202
  Garret, 262, 723, 851
  Geesje, 416, 626
  Gerritje, 1259
  Gertrude, 330, 1301
  Gouda, 899
  Hartman, 85, 106, 829
  Helena, 1186
  Henrietta, 654
  Henry, 968
  Herman, 940
  Hessel, 224
  Hester, 176, 253
  Isaac, 593, 693
  Jacob, 14, 273, 376, 564, 633, 700,
    898, 1183
  Janet, 379, 790, 979, 1085, 1262

VRELAND (con'd)
  Jemima, 617
  John, 241, 318, 348, 755, 1068, 1070,
    1088, 1186, 1221
  Joris, 44
  Lea, 481, 722, 988, 1172
  Lena, 527, 1295
  Margaret, 693, 820, 1038, 1314
  Maria, 19, 263, 385, 633, 689, 1011,
    1048
  Marinus, 416
  Metje, 584
  Michael, 349, 499, 550, 1128
  Nelly, 307
  Nicholas, 321, 382
  Peter, 389, 657
  Polly, 1109
  Rachel, 98, 933
  Sally, 1149, 1307
  Sarah, 487, 1137
  Sietje, 438
  Sophia, 541, 1313
  Thomas, 753
  Tytje, 241

Wagener - see VAN WAGENEN

WALDROM
  Resolve, 516

WALWORTH
  Margaret, 1288

WANNEMAKER
  Margaret, 759

WARD
  William, 1288

WEBB
  Greenleaf, 1258

Weekes, WEEKS
  Elizabeth, 1177
  Mariann, 1241

Weller - see WHEELER

WELLS
  Elizabeth, 442
  Jane, 966
  Phoebe, 898

WENDAL
  Gertrude, 101

Wenne - see WINNE

WESENAER
  Adam, 34

MARRIAGE INDEX

MISCELLANEOUS INDEX, MARRIAGES

ASSCHTON
Thomas, 286

Bartholf - see BERTHOLF

Berrie, BERRY
Abraham, 460
Richard, 587
Stephen, 529

BERTHOLF
Carynus, 180

BOICE
Margaret, 146

Brouwer, BROWER
John, 542
Ulrich, 170, 186

BRUYN
John, 157

Buys - see BOICE

CADMUS
Maria, 167

COFFIE
William, 1033

COGG, Cogh - see also COOK
Aaron, 698

COOK - see also COGG
Henry, 337

CRAWFORD
John, 836

DEMAREST, Demoree
Rachel, 350

DOREMUS
Cornelius, 220

DRURY
(_____), 3

GARRISON
Henry, 154

GARVEN
William, 557

GEALT
Alexander, 268

GERREBRANT(se)
Geurt, 504

Gerritszen - see GARRISON

GLASS
Henry, 515

HARVEY
Thomas, 220

Heeremans - see HERMANS

HELM
Cornelius, 1053

HENNION
John, 570

HERMANS
Elsie, 280

Hervie - see HARVEY

HOPPE(R)
Andrew, 197

IMMORY
Mr., 505

JONES
Nicholas, 918

KINGSLAND
Aaron, 611

Kook - see COOK

Oudwaeter, OUTWATER
(_____), 87

PAULSON
John, 852

PETERS
Hessel, 154
Marcelus, 153

PIER
John, 635

Pietersze - see PETERS

Poelis - see PAULSON

POST
Ad., 510
Alexander, 274

RIKER
Abraham, 860
P., 157

ROMEYN, Romyn
John, 807

Rycke, Ryker - see RIKER

SMITH
Elias, 186

SPIER, Spyr
(_____), 26

MISCELLANEOUS INDEX, MARRIAGES

CHURCH MEMBERSHIP

Register of Members tabulated as a result of house visits by Rev. Henricus Coens, preacher at Akquegnonk, Secund-River, and the Noord, during:

MEN	WOMEN
1726	
3.__ Stratemaker, Jan	Michielse, Catarina
Post, Frans	Fransen, Marietje
Van Gysen, Bastiaen	Sip, Annaetje
Petersen, Hessel	Stratemaeker, Jannetje
Egberts, Alexander	Van Winkel, Annetje
Jurjaense, Thomas	Van Gysen, Magdalena
Gerritse, Hermannus	Petersen, Elsje
Post, Arien	Messeelisse, Elisabeth
Vreeland, Klaes Hartmans	Bruin, Lena
Van Winkel, Simon	Meet, Margrita
Steinmets, Christopher	Van Blinkerhof, Aeltje
Pauwelse, Peter	Klaesen, Petertje
Thomasse, Cornelis	Van Winkel, Margrietje
Thomasse, Johannes	Andriessen, Fietje
Schuyler, Arend	Steinmets, Annetje
Jraleman, Jacob	Gerbrands, Neeltje
Vreeland, Abraham	Marselisse, Hilligonda
Wouterse, Gerrit	Van Winkel, Saertje
Van Gysen, Abraham	Van Winkel, Tryntje
Jurjaense, Jan	Santvoort, Dimmi
Vreeland, Isaac	Bruin, Aeltje
Tades, Casparus	Post, Jannetje
Van Winkel, Michiel Walinchs	Steinmets, Annetje
Van Winkel, Jacob Walinchs	Sip, Hillegonda
Van Winkel, Johannes Walinchs	Brikkers, Geertrui
Van Houte, Reinier Cornelisse	Van Winkel, Catarina Jacobse
Jurjaense, Harmen	Beuis, Geertrui
Wesselse, Evert	Steinmeths, Judith
Vreeland, Dirk Johannisse	Reyersen, Annaetje
Roman, Willem	Glars, Saertje
Van Wageningen, Gerrit Hermanusse	Van Nest, Sara
Oudewaeter, Frans	Banta, Sytsje
Doremes, Thomas	Van Houte, Gerritje
Valk, Klaes	Turk, Sara
Smit, Elias	Marselisse, Elisabeth
Van Winkel, Marinus	Sip, Annaetje
Van Gysen, Hendrik Bastiaens	Akkerman, Anneke
Van Gysen, Reinier Bastiaens	Peterse, Rachel
Van Gysen, Joris Bastiaens	Westerveld, Aeltje
Van Winkel, Jacob Jacobse	Joosten, Sara
Van Winkel, Johannes Jakobse	D'lameter, Hester
Pauwelse, Dirk	Hendrikse, Geesje
Van Gysen, Reinier Abrahamse	Merrel, Maria
Spyr, Johannes	Pauwelse, Echje
Vincent, Levinus	Banta, Sytje Hendrikse
Thomasse, Thomas	Vreeland, Fietje Hartm:
St(o)uten(berg), (Jan)	Kind, Johanna
Van Winkel, Gideon	Jurjaense, Martje
Koeiman, Johannes	Wouters, Sara
Van Dyk, Frans	Van Winkel, Tryntje Walings
Van Deusse, Mattheus	De Vuu, Hester

CHURCH MEMBERSHIP

3.__ House visits (con'd)

MEN	WOMEN
Roset, David	Van Deusse, Marietje
Stoutenburg, Peter	Van Deusse, Sara
Pyr, Teunis Jansen	Deuker, Henrica
Douwe, Johannes	Koeimans, Jannetje
Gerritse, Peter	Van Winkel, Rachel
Reyersen, Johannes	Borger, Fietje
Van Houte, Dirk	Bras, Geertje
Van Houte, Jacob	Van Imburg, Rachel
Van Houte, Roelof	Koeimans, Marietje
Doremes, Johannes	Slingerland, Engeltje
Doremes, Joris	Slingerland, Sara
Reyersen, Joris	Spyr, Tryntje
Dey, Dirk	De Voreest, Sara
Hennion, Johannes	Varik, Margrietje
Rothan, Daniel	Peterse, Tryntje
Gerritse, Johannes	Thomasse, Catarina
Gerritse, Gerrit	Bortens, Annetje
Thomasse, Jurjaen	Hesselse, Froutje
Frerikse, Thomas	Gerbrands, Metje
Frerikse, Andries	Sichels, Marietje
Van Houte, Cornelis	Sichels, Fietje
Van Houte, Peter	Akkerman, Elisabeth
Tuurs, Arent	Bordan, Marietje
Van Winkel, Arien	Schouten, Antje
Post, Johannes	Martens, Catalintje
Post, Adriaen	Roman, Maria
Van Houte, Johannes Cornelisse	Spyr, Harmtje
Van Winkel, Simeon	Tuurs, Marietje
Van Houte, Roelof Cornelisse	Sip, Margrietje
Vreeland, Dirk Hartmanse	Gerbrants, Martie
Doremes, Hendrik	Gerritse, Elisabeth
Van Winkel, Jacob Simense	Van Winkel, Aeltje
Post, Gerrit	Vreeland, Marietje Hartmanse
Gerritse, Hendrik	Vreeland, Aegje Johannisse
	Post, Klaertje
	Thomasse, Fransyntje
	Akkerman, Sara Abrahams
	Spyr, Geertrui
	De Groot, Wilmtje
	Dito, Antje
	Tades, Jannetje
	Van Winkel, Lea
	Van Houte, Elisabeth
	Hesselse, Elisabeth
	Alexanderse, Tryntje
	Peterse, Fryntje
	Van Gyse, Prientje Abrahamse
	Spyr, Jannetje
	Van Schy(ven), Helena
	Banta, Margrietje
	Hesselse, Annetje
	Van Nieukerken, Jakomyntje
	Cornelisse, Sara

1726	MEN	WOMEN

1726

3.___ House visits (con'd)

Van Nieuw-Kerken, Gerritje
Herte, Tryntje Jacobs
Jansen, Doretie
Van Elsland, Marietje
Tuurs, Antje
Vreeland, Rachel Eliasse
Stratemaeker, Margrietje
Vroom, Judith
Herrits, Elisabeth

1726

3.31 <u>By letter</u>:
Re(i)ken, Peter   Messeker, Maria
Westerveld, Cornelis   Oliver, Wyntje
                         Oliver, Susanna

<u>Confession</u>:
Reyersen, Frans   Dey, Janneke
Dideriks, Johannes   Van Winkel, Geertrui Jacobse
Neefjes, Johannes   Gerritse, Antje
Doremes, Cornelis   Hesselse, Rachel
Gerritse, Abraham   Van Noortstrand, Anna
Kip, Isaac   Christyn, Marietje
Post, Jacobus   Kyrstede, Maria
Hendrikse, Gerrit   Van Houte, Jannetje
Thomasse, Abraham   Kyrstede, Annaetje
Barense, Dirk   Petersen, Fransyntje
Roman, Peter   Hesselse, Geertje
Dr(ee)k, Cornelis   Van Hoorn, Marietje
Sip, Arien   Aelse, Antje
Hennion, Daniel   Post, Catarina
Hennion, Abraham   Berri, Johanna
Thomassen, Jacob   Andriessen, Lena
                         Breant, Antje

6.23 <u>By letter</u>:
Van Tilburg, Peter   Klaesen, Geertje
                         Leidekker, Cornelia

9.28 <u>By letter</u>:

                         Akkerman, Sara
                         Smith, Elisabeth

<u>Confession</u>:
Van Der Beek, Paulus   Van Der Beek, Saraetje
Berri, Marten   Berri, Debora
Berri, Samuel   Van Der Beek, Marietje
Van Duin, Marten   Van Duin, Jakomyntje
                         Van Der Beek, Elisabeth - dism
                         /to Jorck

1727

2.12 <u>Confession</u>:

                         Walters, Maria

2.24 <u>By letter</u>:
Westerveld, Jan   Provoost, Belia
                         Suidam, Antje

6. 1 <u>By letter</u>:
Byvank, Evert - dism to
/Nieuw-Jork

CHURCH MEMBERSHIP

MEN	WOMEN

1727
10.14 By letter:

                                      Petersen, Adryaentje
                                        Haering, Fietje

Confession:
Meet, Peter   Meet, Christyntje
Meet, Gilles   Meet, Elsje
12.31 By letter:

                                        De Foreest, Femmetje - dism to
                                          /Hakkingsak 11.26.1731

Confession:
De Boog, Gerrit   Vreeland, Martje
Van Hoorn, Barend   Aeltse, Raechel
Berri, Paulus   Aeltse, Martje
Aeltse, Cornelis

1728
12.31 By letter:

                                        De Grauw, Hendrikje

Confession:

                                        Thiese, Christina
                                        Doremes, Jannetje

1729
12. 4 Confession:
Peterse, Johannes   Huismans, Aerjaentje
1730
6. 5 Confession:
Gerbrandse, Klaes   Vreeland, Metje
Lodloo, Jan   Gerbrandse, Mariedje
Van Gysen, Andries   Dirkse, Martje
Akkerman, Jacobus   Thomasse, Martje
Post, Adriaen   Van Gysen, Dirkje
Sjeerman, Jacob   Messeker, Neeltje

9. 5 By letter:
Marinus, Jan   Salomons, Maeike
                                        Pauwelse, Christina

Confession:

                                        Post, Geesje
                                        Harte, Rachel
                                        Van Gysen, Maria
                                        Van Gysen, Catrina

12. 4 Confession:
Klaese, Gerbrand   Steinmets, Johanna
Thomasse, Jan   Spyr, Gerritje
Van Gysen, Johannes   Paelding, Margrieta
Van Gysen, Dirk   Post, Petertje
Post, Adrian
Van Gysen, Cornelis
1731
3. 3 Confession:
Spyr, Jacob   Van Houte, Egje
Bruin, Baerend
Guuld, Robert

By letter:

                                        Christyn, Elisabeth

5.26 By letter:

                                        Ennis, Sara, wid of Barend Hibon

CHURCH MEMBERSHIP

MEN	WOMEN

1731
5.26 Confession:
Vreeland, Hartman D:

Van Duyn, Geertje
Vreeland, Rachel
Vreeland, Margrietje

9. 2 By letter:
Van Duyn, Abraham

Reyerse, Geertje
Blainchard, Maria

Confession:
Van Houte, Helmerich Roelofse

Vincent, Susanna

12. 2 Confession:
Vreeland, Enoch Hartmanse
Van Der Hoef, Isaac

Van Blerkum, Jannetje
Van Seyl, Elisabeth
Andriesse, Catarina
Reyerse, Elisabeth

1732
3. 1 Confession:
Adolph, Peter

Spyr, Rachel

6. 4 By letter:

Marcelis, Helena

8.31 Confession:
Vreeland, Michiel Eliasse

1733
6. 9 By letter:
Koul, Christiaen

Spang, Christina

Confession:
Van Der Hoef, Jacob

Steger, Elisabeth

1734
9. 6 Confession:
Spyr, Cornelis

Bekling, Anna Catharina

1735
10.__ & 11.__ Confession:
Bredberry, Richard
Post, Pieter

Smith, Aaltje

1736
3.13 Confession:
Cogh, Johan Caspar
Pieterszen, Paulus

Cogh, Catharina
Smith, Cornelia
*Thomasse, Marretje
*Voord, Maria
Van Houten, Rachel

1737
__.__ Confession:
Sanderszen, Eghbert
Thomasse, Gerrit
Vreeland, Elias
Willis, John

Vreeland, Jannetje, w of
/G. Thomasse
Aaltszen, Lea, w of E. Vreeland
Blanschar, Jannetje, w of D. Dy
Bos, Elizabeth

12.11 By letter:

Oothoud, Margaretha, w of
/Dom. J. V. Driessen

Confession:
Romeyn, Claas

Everthze, Barbar, w of J. Everthze
Huysman, Antje, w of J. G. Post
Romeyn, Rachel, w of Claas Romeyn

* - original has a line between "Marretje" and "Maria". Reason
     is unknown

CHURCH MEMBERSHIP

MEN	WOMEN

1738

__.__ Confession:

(T)earbos, William	(T)earbos, Maria
Boghaart, Jan	Pieterszen, Lea
Pieterszen, Petrus	V. Winckelen, Catharina
Van Houten, Cornelis	Kip, Anna
Van De Voort, Machiel	Pieterszen, Claasje
Van Houten, Robberth	Wessels, Jannetje
Barry, John	Post, Elisabeth
Dreak, Cornelis	Dreak, Mareytje

12.23 Confession:

Thomasse, Isaak	Pieterszen, Antje
Pieterszen, Jurrie	Van Houten, Geertje
V. Houten, Helmech Pietersze	

1739

4.20 Confession:

Vincent, Jan	Schuyler, Maria
Van Giesen, Johannes	Vincent, Elizabeth
Van Blerkum, Jan	Van Giesen, Catharina
Post, Adriyaan	Van Blerkum, Vrouwtje
	Neuwkerk, Antje
	Van Winckel, Sara
	Neuwkerk, Jacumyntie
	Spier, Janneke
	Post, (Ja)nettje

8.11 Confession:

	Van Winckele, Wyntje
	Doremes, Aaltje

12.22 By letter from Rev. G: D: Bois:

	Marzelissen, Catharina, w of
	/Reynier Van Giese

1740

4. 5

Van Winckel, Abraham	Sip, Annatje, w of Marselis Post
Post, Marzelis	Van Dyck, Hanna
Post, Hendrick	Van Wageningen, Lena
	Van Wageningen, Catharina
	Post, Antje
	Van Houten, Jannetje
	(T)earboss, Catharina

1741

3.28 By letter from Rev. G. DuBois:

Wanshaar, Johannes	Nys, Susanna, wid
	Egbers, Christina, w of J. Wanshaar

6.27

	Tours, Annatje
	Van Ydesteyn, Claartje
	Vreeland, Hesther

9.20 By letter from Rev. G: DuBois:

	Van Winkel, Annatje

12.26

Kings Land, Isaak	Schuyler, Johanna, w of I. Kingsland

1742

4.18

Neefjes, Gerrit	Westerveld, Cathalyntje, w of
	/Gerrit Neefjes

6.26

Rycke, Ryk	Rycke, Willempie
	Van Seyl, Lea

CHURCH MEMBERSHIP

1743 MEN	WOMEN
4. 9 Coek, Frans	
1744 V. Houten, Helmech	
10.13 Sippe, Helmich	Sippe, Jannetje
	Van Winckel, Rachel
	Van Winckel, Margrietje
1746	
___._ Vreeland, Elias	Vreeland, Cathr.
1747	
___._ Stymetsz, Joris	

1753
3.17 By letter:
Stynmets, Hermanus   Sandvoort, Hannah, w of
/Hendrick Veltman

Confession:
Van Winkele, Marinus   Dubois, Anna, w of Rev. David
Van Giese, Abraham   /Marinus

11.17 Confession:
Van Winkele, Abraham   Van Giese, Maria
Van Rype, Thomas

1754
3.16 Confession:
Van Winkele, Waling

By letter:
Post, Johannis   Kool, Femmetje
Post, Anna

6.15 Van Houte, Johannis, & w------Van Houte, Lybetje
Post, Frans, & w--------------Post, Catlyntje
Van Wageninge, Hermanus, & w---Van Wageninge, Geertruy
Vreeland, Johannis
Vreeland, Elias J.
Sip, Johannis

1755
9. 6 Van Vorst, Cornelius, & w-----Toers, Antje

Received By Confession   Received By Letter

1774
10.29 Van Winckel, Johannis, &
Van Vorst, Jenneke, his wife
Wanshair, Johannis
Van Blerkum, Antje, w of
/Joh's E. Vreeland

1775
3. 1 Van Rypen, Dirck, &   from S. Van Voorhees:
Vreland, Claasje, his wife   Goetschius, Salome, w of
Vreland, Dirck, &   /Hen. Schoonmaker
Van Wagenen, Fytje, his wife
Vreland, Johannes Enoch
Davis, Jinne, wid of Charles
/Leuwis

1776
5.25 Berdan, Jan D., &
Van Hoorn, Catharina, his wife
Vreland, Pieter

8.12   from H. Meyer:
Gerritse, Henry, Esq.

CHURCH MEMBERSHIP

1781	Received By Confession	Received By Letter
5. 3	Paulusse, Paulus, &	
1783	Jurrianse, Neeltje, his wife	
12. 6	Van Giesen, Abraham	
1784		
9.16	Vreeland, Enoch J.	
	Vreeland, Enoch C., &	
	Van Winkelen, Lea, his wife	
9.19		from W. Kuypers:
		Outwater, Annaatje, w of
		/Cornelius Van Vorst
1785		
6.30	Post, Thomas, &	
	Vreeland, Tryntje, his wife	
	Stymets, Annaatje, w of	
	/Christophel V. Orstrand	
	Van Wagenen, Maragrita, w of	
	/Arie Van Winkelen	
7.10	Van Noorstrand, Christophel	
	Post, Adriaan J.	
1786		
4.13	Sip, Johannes jr, &	
	Van Winkele, Geertje, his wife	
	Van Houten, Fytje, w of	
	/Hessel Pieterse	
	Van Houten, Cornelius J., &	
	Van Houten, Helena, his wife	
11. 2	Van Winkelen, Catharina, w of	
1787	/Jacob Vreeland	
6. 7	Wesselse, Lucas	
	Pieterse, Hessel	
	Vreeland, Elias J., &	
	Post, Elizabeth, his wife	
	Seely, Samuel	
11.25		from W. Kuypers:
		Kip, Hendrick, &
		Banta, Jannetje, his wife
12. 9		from B. Van Der Linde:
		Stegg, Cornelius, &
		Banta, Maragrietje, his wife
12.13	Van Bussen, Hermanus	
	Van Bussen, Philippus, &	
1788	Post, Elizabeth, his wife	
5. 8	Kip, Pieter, &	
	Van Winkelen, Jacomyntje, his wife	
	Berdan, Jacob, &	
	Bilju, Catharina, his wife	
12.10	Van Wagenen, Gerret P.	
1789		
4. 9	Van Rypen, Cornelius, &	
	Vreland, Elizabeth, his wife	

1791	Received By Confession	Received By Letter
4. 4		from H. Meyer:
		Van Winkelen, Jacob, &
		Kip, Elsje, his wife
4.21	Doremus, Hendrick C.	
	Spier, Barent	
	Spier, John B.	
	Wesselse, Helena, wid of	
	/Hessel Brouwer	
9.29	Van Winkelen, Maragrieta, w	
	/of Hendrick Doremus	
10. 2	Vreland, Jacob H.	

1792		
10.25		from Totua:
		Westervelt, Fytje, w of
		/Gerret P. Van Wagenen

1793		
5.16	Gerrebrantse, Geertje, w of	
	/Gerrit Van Rypen	
5.19		from Pomptan Church:
		Bertholf, Marretje, w of
		/Enoch Jo. Vreland
6.27	At Totua:	
	Westerveld, Jurrie	from N. York & Lange Eyland:
		Van Houten, Cornelius
		Brouwer, Abraham, &
		/Maria, his wife
6.30		from Per Emus Church:
		Ackerman, Albert, &
		Van Winkele, Rachel, his wife
9.26	At Achquechnonck:	
	Winne, Lea, w of John Van Rypen	

1794		
9.21		from Totua Church:
		Cadmus, Abraham
10. 2	Mourusse, Abraham	
	Van Wagenen, Cathalyntje, w	
	/of Abr. Cadmus	
10. 9	At Totua:	
	Van Houten, Abraham, &	from Hackensack Church:
	Wesselse, Annaatje, his wife	Demarest, David, &
	Kool, Barent	Brouwer, Hester, his wife
	Van Winkele, Simeon Joh., &	
	Gerretse, Claasje, his wife	
	Ryerse, Lena, wid	

1795		
4.30	Van Wagenen, Johannes G.	
5. 7	At Totua:	from N. Lansing:
	Van Houten, Adriaan, &	Onderdonk, Rem, &
	Cadmus, Marytje, his wife	Blauveld, Helena, his wife
	Van Houten, Johannes J., &	
	Earl, Catharina, his wife	
	Van Houten, Dirck, &	
	Van Rypen, Maria, his wife	

CHURCH MEMBERSHIP

Received By Confession	Received By Letter

1795

5. 7 con'd
Marcelusse, Edo jr, &
Van Houten, Lena, his wife
Bensen, Lena

11. 5 Traphagen, Rachel, w of
   /Joh's G. Van Wagenen

11.19 At Totua:
Coerte, Hendrick, &
Bensen, Antje, his wife
Demarest, Pieter, &
Bensen, Cathalyntje, his wife
Marcelusse, Cornelius, &
Post, Marytje, his wife
Van Houten, Pieter H., &
Van Rypen, Lea, his wife
Doremus, Roelif, &
Doremus, Annaatje, his wife
Reyerse, Geertje, w of
   /John J. Doremus

1796

5.12 At Totua:
Van Saan, Isaac, &
Marcelusse, Cathalyntje, his wife
Hennion, Theunis, &
Kip, Catharina, his wife
Westerveld, Jacobus, &
Demarest, Elizabeth, his wife
Van Houten, Elizabeth
Mandeviel, Hester, w of
   /Abraham Maurusse
Yeomans, Elizabeth, w of
   /David Spier

5.15 At Totua:

from Nicolas Lansing:
Witting, Joseph, &
Miller, Cathalyntje, his wife

10.20 At Totua:
Van Saan, Albert, &
Van Houten, Jannetje, his wife

1797

5.11 At Achquechnonck:
Pieterse, Maragrietje, wid of
   /Simeon Van Rypen
Yong, Marritje, w of John Tyse
Post, Marritje, w of
   /Adrian J. Post

9.21 At Achquechnonck:
Van Winkelen, Jacob A.
Everse, Jerimia
Van Wagenen, Gerrit G., &
Schoonmaker, Lena, his wife
Terhune, Jacobus, &
Meclachlin, Lena, his wife

Received By Confession	Received By Letter

1797
9.21 con'd
Van Winkelen, Jenneke, w of
  /Pieter Terhune
Van Winkelene, Lena

1798
4.30 At Totua:

from Panne Church:
Van Aalen, Pieter

5. 3 At Achquechnonck:
Van Rypen, Gerret
Paulusse, Pieter
Post, Hartman
Spier, Gerritje, w of
  /Joh's En. Vreland
Vreland, Catharina, wid of
  /Cor. Degrauw
Montanje, Nellie, w of
  /Jeremia Evertse

from Gansegat Church:
Ryker, Abraham,
and wife

5. 6 Vreland, Michael
Schoonmaker, Jacob

5.24 At Totua:
Van Winkele, Cornelius, &
Van Rypen, Annaetje, his wife
Gerritse, Gerrit, &
Ryerse, Marytje, his wife
Ryerse, Lena
Gerritse, Hessel, &
Leuwis, Selly, his wife

10.25 At Achquechnonck:
Vreland, Cornelius H. Esq'r, &
Vreland, Elizabeth, his wife
Kip, Hendrick, &
Gerritse, Catharina, his wife

1799
5. 5 Jurrianse, Gerrebrand

5.10 At Totua:
Goetschius, Johannis
Van Houten, Cornelius (R.), &
Van Houten, Fytje, his wife
Bensen, Daniel, &
Doremus, Rachel, his wife

1800
5.29 At Achquechnonck:
Jackson, Nancy, w of
  /Hartman Post
Kerck, Lena, w of
  /Gerrebrand Jurrianse
Van Houten, Jannetje, w of
  /Peter Paulusse - d 11.4.1858

from Gerrardus A. Kuypers: Nieuw
                            /York:
Ackerman, Dirck, &
Demarest, Maragrietje, his wife -
  living in 1826 (which one or
  both?)

9.14 At Achquechnonck:
Meyers, Cornelius, &
Terhune, Martyntje, his wife
Van Rypen, Jacobus H.

CHURCH MEMBERSHIP

Received By Confession	Received By Letter

1801

5.28 At Achquechnonck:
Bradford, Richard

9.24 At Achquechnonck:
Fielding, Daniel, &
Huysman, Angonietje, his wife
Van Winkele, Waling J.

1802

6.10 At Achquechnonck:
Ackerman, Albert - living in 1826
Van Rypen, Jacob
Paulusse, Catharina, w of
  /Waling Van Winkel
Bilju, Elizabeth, w of
  /Gerrit Van Vorst

6.17 At Totua:
Degauw, John
Moffat, John
Hopper, Marytje, w of
  /Petrus Van A(len)

7.26 At Achquechnonck: from Wilhelmus Elting. Per Emus:
                                  Van Winkel, Antje, w of
                                    /Albert Ackerman - living in 1826

10.14 At Totua:
Doremus, Hendrick
Etsel, Elizabeth, wid of
  /Antally Earl
Tam, slave of Pieter Van Aalen

11.11 At Achquechnonck:
Spier, John, &
Terhune, Elizabeth, his wife
Winne, Lideja, w of
  /Pieter Vreland

1803

4.21 At Totua:
Remsen, Jacobus, &
Stagg, Antje, his wife

4.24 Demarest, David D., &   from Hackensack Church:
Van Saan, Annaatje, his wife   Smith, Elizabeth, w of
                                    /Johannes Post

4.28 At Achquechnonck:
Van Winkele, Helmich
Van Winkele, Jacobus, &
Van Winkele, Jannetje, his wife
Boss, Gerrit - living 1826
Van Winkele, Jacob J.

5. 1 At Achquechnonck:
Cadmus, Dirck, &
Crom, Jannetje, his wife

10.13 At Totua:
Bilju, Hendrika, w of   from Sal. Fraligh:
  /Laurence Van Orden   Bensen, Cathalina, wid of
                                    /Jacobus Brinckerhoff

CHURCH MEMBERSHIP

1804	Received By Confession	Received By Letter

10.18 At Totua:
Van Houten, Gerrebrand, Esq'r
Brown, John, &
Jones, Elizabeth, his wife
Hennion, Antje, wid of
/Cornelius Van Houten

10.25 At Achquechnonck:
Ackerman, Abraham, &
Messeker, Susanna, his wife
Van Houten, Gerret, & - d 8.23.1826
Van Ess, Cornelia, his wife
Doremus, Pieter, &
Berry, Lena, his wife
Van Rypen, Gerret, &
Winne, Jannetje, his wife
Van Wagenen, Lea, w of
/John Bogert
Vreland, Marretje, w of
/Jacob Vreland

1805
6. 7 At Totua:
Jeraalman, Grietje, wid of
/Samuel Burhans
Post, Rachel, w of
/Dirck Van Houten
Burhans, Catharina

9. 5 At Achquechnonck:
Vreeland, Jacob En.
Van Houten, Elizabeth, wid
/of Dirck Van Rypen

11.14 At Totua:
Van Houten, Dirck
Ryerse, Pieter

11.17 At Totua: from Keckeatt Church:
                                      Oldes, John, &
                                      Johnson, Elizabeth, his wife

1806
5.25 At Totua:
Van Sant, Margeret, w of
/Asa Wright

6. 5 Van Blerkum, Martin, &
Van Vleck, Antje, his wife
Van Houten, Roelif C., &
Van Giesen, Antje, his wife
Marcelusse, Pieter, &
Van Winkel, Jannetje, his wife
Van Houten, Robert, &
Van Giesen, Lena, his wife
Van Houten, Gerrebrant C., &
Meet, Rachel, his wife

6.(_) At Achquechnonck: from Hackensack Church:
                                      Debaan, Karel, &
                                      Bogert, Maria, his wife

CHURCH MEMBERSHIP

Received By Confession	Received By Letter
<u>1806</u> 6.15 Cadmus, Thomas, & Doramus, Maragrietje, his wife	<u>from Totua Church:</u> Doremus, Roelif, & Doremus, Annaatje, his wife

<u>1807</u>
1. 8 <u>At Achquechnonck:</u>
Printice, Hendrick - living in 1826
Vreland, Elias (A.)
Brouwer, Petrus - living in 1826
Evertse, Jacob

7. 9 <u>At Totua:</u>   <u>from Keckiath Church:</u>
Bensen, David, &   Onderdonck, Andries, &
Van Houten, Elizabeth, his wife Van Houten, Maria, his wife

10.21 <u>At Totua:</u>
Jacobusse, Marritje, w of
 /Hendrick Doremus

<u>1808</u>
10.27 <u>At Totua:</u>
Doremus, John

<u>1809</u>
5. 4 <u>At Totua:</u>
King, John, &
Hunter, Isabella, his wife

10. 8 Ryerse, Nancy, w of
 /John Doremus

<u>1810</u>
5.17 <u>At Totua:</u>
Van Houten, Abraham D.

10.18 <u>At Totua:</u>   <u>from N. Lansing:</u>
         Blauvelt, Johannes Joseph, &
         Van Orden, Rachel, his wife

<u>1811</u>
5.17 <u>At Achquechnon(ck):</u>
Van Rypen, John A. - living in 1826
Vreeland, Elias Ja. - living in 1826

5.19 <u>At Achquechnonc(k):</u> <u>from Jacobus V. C. Romeyn:</u>
         Demarest, Gerret, & - living 1826
         Durjee, Angonietje, his w - liv 1826

10.24 <u>At Totua:</u>
Van Houten, Metje, w of
 /Corneli(us) Van Houten
Van Houten, Jannetje

<u>1812</u>
4.22 <u>At Achquechnonck:</u>
Holley, Cornelius

<u>1813</u>
5.20 <u>At Achquechnonck:</u>
Post, Marretje, w of
 /Helmic(h) Van Winkele

11. 4 <u>At Achquechnonck:</u>
Bogert, Roelif

<u>1814</u>
5.26 Post, Casparus, & - living in 1826
Paulusse, Fytje, his wife
Paulusse, Annaatje, wid of
 /P. Van Buss(on)

CHURCH MEMBERSHIP

1814	Received By Confession	Received By Letter

10.13 <u>At Achquechnon(ck)</u>:
Sip, John J.

1815
5.25 <u>At Achquechnonk</u>:
Van Winkele, Waling, & - living in 1826
Van Rypen, Pietertje, his wife - living in 1826

6. 1 <u>At Totua</u>:   <u>from Jacobus Demarest</u>:
Van Houten, Maria   Pulis, William
Sip, Catharina, w of
/Ab'r Van Houten

6.14 <u>At Achquechnonck</u>:   <u>from Gerardus A. Kuypers</u>:
Van Zyl, Eva, w of
/Cor. Van Hoorn

10. 5 <u>At Totua</u>:   <u>from John Demarest</u>:
Van Houten, Antje   Stor, Abraham, &
Rothan, Anna, his wife

CHURCH CONSISTORY

Register of Elders and Deacons at Akquegnonk as extracted from an old church book at Hakkingsak while Rev. William Bartholf was minister there, together with the dates of their election.

	ELDER	DEACON
1694 3.18	Vreeland, Elias	Van Gysen, Basteaen Peterse, Hessel
1695 4.16		Post, Frans
1696 5.__	Van Winkel, Waling Jacobse	Steynmets, Christoffer
1697 5. 2		Van Gysen, Basteaen
1698 5.22	Vreeland, Elias	Gerritse, Hermannus
1699 5. 4	Post, Frans	Peterse, Hessel
1700 5. 9	Van Gysen, Basteaen	Jurjaense, Thomas
1701 5.20	Van Winkel, Waling Jacobse	Van Gysen, Abraham
1702 5.__	Peterse, Hessel	Gerritse, Hermannus
1703 5.__	Vreeland, Elyas	Jurjaense, Aelt
1704 5.25	Toers, Lourens	Walings, Jacob
1705 5.__	Post, Frans	Jurjaense, Thomas
1706 5. 2	Van Gysen, Basteaen	Post, Adriaen
1707 5.__	Peterse, Hessel	Hartmans, Klaes
1708 5.__	Gerritse, Hermannus	Gerritse, Hendrik
1709 5.__	Van Winkel, Simon	Jraeleman, Jacob
1710 5.__	Jurjaense, Thomas	Van Houte, Peter Helmerichse
1711 5. 9	Post, Frans	Walings, Jacob
1712 5.__	Van Gysen, Basteaen	Jurjaense, Jan
1713 5.14	Steynmets, Christopher	Hartmans, Klaes
1714 5.__	Peterse, Hessel	Jraleman, Jacob

CHURCH CONSISTORY

	ELDER	DEACON
1715 5.__	Gerritse, Hermanus	Jurjaense, Harmen
1716 5.__	Post, Frans	Van Gysen, Abraham Reyersen, Joris
1717 5.30	Post, Adriaen	Van Houte, Peter Helmerichse
1718 5.22	Jurjaense, Jan	Post, Gerrit Van Nes, Simon
1719 5.__	Van Gysen, Basteaen	Hennion, David
1720 5.26	Van Houte, Peter Helmerichse	Vreeland, Dirk Hartmans Van Houte, Roelof Helmerichse
1721 5.__	Van Gysen, Basteaen	Hennion, David
1722 5.__	Jraleman, Jacob	Toers, Arent Lourense
1723 5.__	Peterse, Hessel	Walings, Johannes

Early 1724 in the presence of Rev. Gualtherus DuBois, Nieuw Jork minister, and before a new call was issued for the Noorden and the Noorder part of the (parish), the following were elected:

Jurjaense, Thomas	Gerritse, Johannes
Vreeland, Dirk Hartmanse	Thomasse, Jurjaen

	New Member	In Place Of
1726 e5.19 16.12	Elder: Gerritse, Hendrik Van Houte, Peter Helmerichse Deacon: Gerritse, Peter Vreeland, Dirk Johannesse	 Jraeleman, Jacob Vreeland, Dirk Hartmanse Gerritse, Johannes Toers, Aerend Lourense
1727 11.29	Elder: Vreeland, Klaes Hartmanse Post, Gerrit Gerritse, Johannes Deacons: Jurjaense, Harmen Hermanusse, Gerrit Neefjes, Johannes Gerritse, Gerrit	These Elders and Deacons were elected to increase the number of members on the consistory
e5.11 16. 4	Elder: Gerritse, Hermannus Jurjaense, Jan Vreeland, Dirk Hartmanse Toers, Arend Lourense Deacon: Sip, Arien Post, Johannes Barendse, Dirk Frerikse, Thomas	 Peterse, Hessel Jurjaense, Thomas Van Houte, Peter Helmerichse for a vacant position Walings, Johannes Vreeland, Dirk Johannesse Thomasse, Jurjaen Gerritse, Peter

CHURCH CONSISTORY

	New Member	In Place Of
1728		
e5.30 i6.16	**Elder:**	
	Peterse, Hessel	Gerritse, Hendrik
	Post, Adriaen	Vreeland, Klaes Hartmanse
	Van Houte, Peter Helmerichse	Post, Gerrit
	Gerritse, Peter	Gerritse, Johannes
	Deacon:	
	Vreeland, Dirk, Johannesse	Jurjaense, Harmen
	Thomasse, Jacob	Hermanusse, Gerrit
	Frerikse, Andries	Neefjes, Johannes
	Westerveld, Jan	Gerritse, Gerrit
1728 6.24	**Achquechnonck Churchmasters:**	
	Gerritse, Hendrik	Van Gysen, Bastiaen
	Van Winckel, Jacob Simonse	Gerritse, Hermanus
	Remaining:	
	Peterse, Hessel	
	Jurjaense, Thomas	
1730 5. 7	Van Winkel, Simeon	Van Winkel, Jacob Simonse
	Hermanusse, Gerrit	Gerritse, Hendrik
1731 —.—	Sip, Arie	Van Rypen, Abraham
	Thomasse, Jurjaen	Vreeland, Klaes Hartmanse
1732 5.18	Van Houte, Jacob	
	Tades, Casparus	
1733 5. 3	Hennion, Johannes	Thomasse, Jurjaen
	Thomasse, Abraham	Sip, Arie

1729
6. 9 Consistory members elected in 1727 are retired from office without being replaced. Those elected in 1728 remain as Consistory.

	New Member	In Place Of
1730 e5. 7 i5.31	**Elder:**	
	Van Gysen, Basteaen	Post, Adriaen
	Van Houte, Roelof Helmerichse	Gerritse, Peter
	Deacon:	
	Doremes, Cornelis	Vreeland, Dirk Joh:
	Van Houte, Cornelis Helmerichse	Westerveld, Jan
1731 e5.27 i6.13	**Elder:**	
	Jurjaense, Harmen	Peterse, Hessel
	Gerritse, Gerrit	Van Houte, Peter Helmerichse
	Deacon:	
	Post, Johannes	Frerikse, Andries
	Post, Adriaen jr	Thomasse, Jacob
1732 e5.18 i6.11	**Elder:**	
	Gerritse, Hermanus	Van Gysen, Basteaen
	Frerikse, Thomas	Van Houte, Roelof Helmerichse
	Deacon:	
	Walings, Johannes	Doremes, Cornelis
	Van Der Beek, Paulus	Van Houte, Cornelis Helmerichse

CHURCH CONSISTORY

	New Member	In Place Of
1733		
e5. 3	**Elder:**	
16. 3	Post, Arie	Jurjaense, Harmen
	Gerritse, Johannes	Gerritse, Gerrit
	Deacon:	
	Smit, Elias	Post, Johannes
	Hendrikse, Gerrit	Post, Adriaen
1734		
e5.23	**Elder:**	
16. 9	Post, Johannes	Gerritse, Hermanus
	Thomasse, Jacob	Frerikse, Thomas
	Deacon:	
	Van Houte, Dirk	Walings, Johannes
	Thomasse, Jan	Van Der Beek, Paulus

1735-1738

recorded 5.11.1738:

		Elder
	Pietersze, Hessel	Post, Arie
	Van Winckel, Joh's W.	Gerritszen, Joh's
	------------	------------
	Van Houten, Roelof	Post, Joh's
	Jurrijaanse, Harmen	Thomusse, Jacob
	------------	------------
	Frerickszen, Thomas	Pietersze, Hessel
	Harmanusse, Gerrit	Van Winckel, Joh's W.

		Deacon
	Van Winckel, Simeon	Smith, Elias
	Doremes, Thomas	Hendrickse, Gerrit
	------------	------------
	Vreeland, Dirck Jansze	V. Houten, Dirck
	Post, Adriaan Fransze	Thomasse, Jan
	------------	------------
	V. Winckel, Marynus	Doremes, Thomas
	Thomasse, Abraham	V. Winckel, Simeon

1739		
e5.31	**Elder:**	
16.11	Gerritszen, H.	Jurriaansse, H.
	V. Houten, J.	V. Houten, R.
	Remaining: Frerickszen, Th.	
	Harmanusse, G.	
	Deacon:	
	Thades, Casp.	Vreeland, Dirck
	Aaltszen, Cor.	Post, Adriaan
	Remaining: V. Winckel, Mar.	
	Thomasse, Abr.	

1740 no elections or installations

1741		
e5.24	**Elder:**	
15.24	Vreland, Dirck	Frerickszen, Thomas
	Doremus, Cornelis	Harmanusse, Gerrit
	Remaining: Gerritszen, Hend.	
	V. Houten, Jacob	
	Deacon:	
	Thomasse, Isaak	V. Winckel, Marynus
	Post, Jacobus	Thomasse, Ab.

CHURCH CONSISTORY

New Member   In Place Of

1740 (con'd)
Remaining: Thades, Casp.
           Aaltszen, Cor.

Churchwardens and Churchmasters

New Member	In Place Of	Remaining
1736		
Post, Adriyaan	Henniyon, Joh's	V. Giesen, Reynier
Aalstzen, Cornelis	Thomasze, Abraham	V. Winckel, Marynus
1737		
V. Giesen, Hendrick	V. Giesen, Reynier	Post, Adriyaan
Ludlouw, John	V. Winckel, Marynus	Aalstzen, Cornelis
1738		
Broadberry, Richard	Post, Adriyaan	V. Giesen, Hendrik
Pietersze, Johannes	Aalstzen, Cornelis	Ludlouw, John
1739		
Thomasse, Gerrit	Van Giesen, H.	Broadberry, Richart
Vreeland, Elias Mach.	Ludlouw, John	Pietersze, Joh's
1740 no elections		
1741		
V. Giesen, Dirck	Brodberry, Rich'd	Thomasze, Gerrit
Vreland, Hardman	Pieterszen, Joh's	Vreland, Elias Mach.
1742		
Van Winckel, Simeon	Thomuszen, Gerrit	Vreeland, Hardman
Thomauszen, Jan	Vreeland, Elias Mach.	V. Giesen, Dirk
1743		
Gerritszen, Gerrit	V. Giesen, Dirck	V. Winckel, Simeon
NB: niet gedient	Vreeland, Hardman	Thomuszen, Jan
1744		
Walingszen, Jacob	V. Winckel, Simeon	Gerritszen, Gerrit
Post, Ad. Arendze	Thomassen, Jan	
Kingsland, Isaak		
1745		
V. Houten, Reynier	Post, Ad.	Walingzen, Jacob
Pieterszen, Petrus	Gerritszen, Gerrit	Kingsland, Izaak
1746		
Hesselzen, Pieter	Van Giesen, Reynier	Walingszen, Jacob
Van Winckel, Waling	Pieterszen, Petrus	Kingsland, Isaak

New Member	In Place Of
1742 16.13 Elder:	
Jurreyaansze, Harmen	Gerritzen, Hendrik
Post, Joh's	V. Houten, Jacob
Remaining: Vreeland, Dirck	
Doremus, Cornelis	
Deacon:	
Pieterszen, Jurry	Thades, Casparus
V. Houten, Helmech R.	Aaltszen, Cornelis
Remaining: Thomusse, Izaak	
Post, Jacobus	
1743 15.23 Elder:	
V. Houten, Cornelis Hel.	Vreeland, Dirck
Walingzen, Johans	Doremes, Corn's
Remaining: Jurreyaansze, Harmen	
Post, Joh's	

CHURCH CONSISTORY

New Member	In Place Of

1743 (con'd)

Deacon:
Post, Marcelis   V. Rype, Isaak
V. Houten, Hel. Piet.   Post, Jacobs
Remaining: Pieterszen, Jurry
         V. Houten, Hel. R.

1744

Elder:
V. Winckel, Marynus   Jurreyaanszen, Har.
Thomaszen, Jurry   Post, Johannes
Remaining: V. Houten, Cornelis Hel.
         Walingszen, Joh's

Deacon:
Vreeland, Enoch   Pietersen, Jurry
V. Houten, Robb't   V. Houten, Helm. R.
Remaining: V. Houten, Helm. Piet.
         Post, Marselis

1745

Elder:
Post, Joh's   V. Houten, Corn'l H.
V. Wageningen, Gerrit   Walingszen, Joh's
Remaining: Thomussen, Jurry
         V. Winckel, Marynus

Deacon:
Reyierszen, Joh's   Post, Marselis
Vincent, John   V. Houten, Helm.
Remaining: Vreeland, Enoch
         V. Houten, Robb't

1746

Elder:
Thadeszen, Casp.   V. Rypen, Jurrie Tho.
Aalstzen, Corn's   V. Winckel, Marynus
Remaining: Post, Joh's
         V. Wageningen, Gerrit

Deacon:
Paulussen, Joh's   Vreeland, Enoch
Zip, Helm.   V. Houten, Robb't
Remaining: Reyerszen, Joh's
         Vincent, John

1753
5.31

Elder:
Vreeland, Dirrik   Post, Johannis
Van Houte, Dirrick   Van Wageninge, Gerrit

Deacon:
Post, Hendrick   Ryerse, Johannis
Van Houte, Gerrebrand   Van Cent, John

Churchmaster:
Van Wageninge, Hermanus   Pouwelse, Patries
Sip, Johannis   Van Houte, Rinier

Elder Assistant:

     Gerritse, Cornelus
     Spier, Cornelus
     Cadmus, Hartman
     Jurryanse, Gerrebrand

CHURCH CONSISTORY

	New Member	In Place Of
1754		
5.23	**Elder:**	
	Walingse, Johannis	Van Eydestyn, Casparus
	Pieterse, Jurrie	Aalse, Cornelus
	Deacon:	
	Wanshair, Johannis	Sip, Helmich
	Vreeland, Elias	Powelse, Johannis
	Churchmaster:	
	Vreeland, Elias J.	Van Winkele, Waling
1755	Van Winkele, Johannis	Pieterse, Pieter
6.22	**Elder:**	
	Post, Jacobus	Vreeland, Dirrick
	Vreeland, Enoch	Van Houte, Dirrick
	Deacon:	
	Vreeland, Hartman	Post, Hendrick
	Van Houte, Johannis	Van Houte, Gerrebrand
	Churchmaster:	
	Vreeland, Johanis	Van Wageninge, Hermanus
	Vreeland, Johannis (E.)	Sip, Johanis
1756		
5.27	**Elder:**	
	Van Wageninge, Gerrit	Post, Jacobus
	Sip, Helmich	Walingse, Johannis
	Post, Johannis	Pieterse, Jurrie
	Deacon:	
	Van Blerkom, Jan	Van Houte, Johannis
	Van Wageninge, Hermanus	Wanshair, Johannis
	Jurryanse, Gerrebrand	Vreeland, Elias
	Churchmaster:	
	Gerritse, Hendrik	Vreeland, Elyas J.
	Van Winkele, Marinis A.	Van Winkele, Johannis
1757		
5.19	**Elder:**	
	Aalse, Cornelus	Van Wageninge, Gerrit
	Vreeland, Elias	Vreeland, Enoch
	Deacon:	
	Pieterse, Petrus	Van Blerkom, Jan
	Sip, Johannis	
	Churchmaster:	
	Van Eydestyn, Tade	Vreeland, Johannis
	Cadmus, Johannis	Vreeland, Johannis E.
1758		
5.__	**Elder:**	
	Vreeland, Elyas	Sip, Helmich
	Post, Johannis	Post, Johannis
	Deacon:	
	Vreland, Hartman	Van Wagening, Hermanus
	Van Winkele, Marinis	Jurryanse, Gerrebrand
	Churchmaster:	
	Vreland, Johanis	Gerritse, Hendrik
	Vreeland, Michiel	Van Winkel, Marinus
1759		
__.__	**Elder:**	
	Wanshair, Johannis	Vreeland, Elyas
	Post, Hendrick	Walingse, Johannis
	Deacon:	
	Van Winkel, Abraham	Sip, Johannis
	Vreeland, Johannis	Powlusse, Petrus

CHURCH CONSISTORY

New Member	In Place Of

Churchmaster:
Vreeland, Johannis E. — Cadmus, Johannis
Van Vorst, Cornelus — Jurryanse, Gerrebrand

1760
6.__ (Elder:)
Poulusse, Petrus — Van Wageninge, Gerret
Pieterse, Jurrie — Aalse, Cornelus
(Deacon:)
Vreland, Hartman — Van Winkel, Waling
Van Winkel, Marinis — Vreland, Elyas
(Churchmaster:)
Van Rype, Gerret — Vreland, Johannis
Pieterse, Hessel — Vreland, Michiel

1761
__.__ Elder:
Vreeland, Dirk — Wanshair, Johannis
Van Rype, Cornelus — Post, Hendrick
Deacon:
Berdan, Dirk — Van Winkel, Abraham
Doremis, Cornelus — Vreeland, Johannis
Churchmaster:
Van Rypen, Dirk — Vreland, Johannis E.
Van Hoorn, Johannis — Van Vorst, Cornelus

1762
__.__ Elder:
Van Wageninge, Gerret — Powlusse, Petrus
Vreeland, Johanis — Pieterse, Jurrie
Deacon:
Post, Gerret — Vreland, Hartman
Van Vorst, Cornelus — Van Winkel, Marinis
Churchmaster:
Drummond, Robbert — Van Rype, Gerret
Post, Adryaen A. — Pieterse, Hessel

At Achquechnonck

1775
e5.25 Elder:
16. 5 Jurrianse, Gerrebrand — Poulusse, Petrus
Post, Adriaan A. — Van Winckel, Waling
Deacon:
Van Winckel, Johannis A. — Vreland, Jacob
Vreland, Dirck — Drummond, Rob't
Churchmaster:
Van Eydestyn, Thade — Van Winckel, Johannis
Pieterse, Hessel — Van Rypen, Dirck

1776
e5.16 Elder:
16. 2 Vreland, Hartman M. — Van Wagenen, Hermanus
Sip, Helmich — Doremus, Cornelius H.
Deacon:
Van Rypen, Dirck — Van Vechten, Jan
Vreeland, Johannis F. — Van Vorst, Cornelius
Churchmaster:
Van Rypen, Abr. — Van Wagenen, Jacob
Vreeland, Michiel H. — Van Rypen, Gerret

1777
e5. 8 Elder:
15.19 Gerrittse, Henry — Jurrianse, Gerrebrand
Vreeland, Johannis El. — Post, Adriaan A.

CHURCH CONSISTORY - At Achquechnonck

New Member	In Place Of
Deacon:	
Berdan, Jan	Van Winkel, Johannis A.
Vreeland, Pieter	Vreeland, Dirck
Churchmaster:	
Van Houten, Cornelius J.	Van Eydesteyn, Thade
Van Winkel, Jacob	Pieterse, Hessel

1778
e6. 7
16.21

Elder:	
Van Winkele, Marynus	Vreland, Hartman M.
Sip, Johannis	Sip, Helmich
Deacon:	
Van Vorst, Cornelius	Van Rypen, Dirck
Vreland, Dirck	Vreland, Joh's E.
Churchmaster:	
Van Wagenen, Hermanus	Vreland, Michiel H.
Post, Thomas	Van Rypen, Ab'm

1779
e5.16
15.24

Elder:	
Van Winckelen, Abraham	Gerritse, Henry
Post, Adriaan A.	Vreland, Joh's El.
Deacon:	
Sickelse, Joh's	Berdan, Jan
Vreland, Jacob	Vreland, Pieter
Churchmaster:	
Van Eydestyne, Thade Joh's	Van Houten, Cornelius J.
Post, Hendrick jr	Van Winkele, Jacob

1780
e5. 4
15.15

Elder:	
Van Wagenen, Hermanus	Van Winkelen, Marynus
Jurrianse, Gerrebrand	Sip, Johannes
Deacon:	
Van Rypen, Dirck	Van Vorst, Cornelius
Berdan, Jan	Vreeland, Dirck
Churchmaster:	
Paulusse, Paulus	Van Wagenen, Hermanus
Van Bussen, Philip	Post, Thomas

1781
e5.24
16. 4

Elder:	
Vreeland, Johannis El.	V. Winkelen, Abraham
Van Vorst, Cornelius	Post, Adrian
Deacon:	
Vreeland, Dirck	Sickelse, Johannis
Paulusse, Paulus	Vreeland, Jacob
Churchmaster:	
Van Giesen, Cornelius	Van Eydestyn, Thade J.
Van Rypen, John A.	Post, Hendrick

1782
e5. 9
15.20

Elder:	
Gerritse, Henry	Van Wagenen, Hermanus
Post, Adriaan	Jurianse, G.
Deacon:	
Vreeland, Joh's E.	Van Rypen, Dirck
Wanshair, Johannis	Berdan, Jan
Churchmaster:	
Wesselse, Lucas	Paulusse, Paulus
Post, Adrian J.	Van Buussen, Philip

CHURCH CONSISTORY - <u>At Achquechnonck</u>

	<u>New Member</u>	<u>In Place Of</u>

<u>1783</u>
e6. 9 <u>Elder</u>:
16.22 Van Wagenen, Hermanus — Vreeland, Joh's El.
Van Winkelen, Marynus — Van Vorst, Cornelius
<u>Deacon</u>:
Berdan, Jan — Vreeland, Dirck
Vreeland, Pieter — Paulusse, Paulus
<u>Churchmaster</u>:
Post, Thomas — Van Giesen, Cornelius
Gerritse, Hendrick jr — Van Rypen, John A.

<u>1784</u>
e5.23 <u>Elder</u>:
16.13 Jurrianse, Gerrebrand — Gerritse, Henry
Vreeland, Johannis El. — Post Adriaan
<u>Deacon</u>:
Van Giesen, Abraham jr — Vreland, Joh's E.
Paulusse, Paulus — Wanshair, Joh's
<u>Churchmaster</u>:
Van Winkelen, Jacob — Wesselse, Lucas
Van Winkelen, Waling — Post, Adriaan J.

<u>1785</u>
e5. 5 <u>Elder</u>:
15.29 Post, Adriaan — Van Wagenen, Hermanus
Van Rypen, Dirck — Van Winkelen, Marynus
<u>Deacon</u>:
Vreeland, Enoch J. — Berdan, Jan
Vreeland, Enoch C. — Vreelandt, Pieter
<u>Churchmaster</u>:
Pieterse, Hessel — Post, Thomas
Post, Hendrick jr — Gerritse, Hendrick jr

<u>1786</u>
e5.25 <u>Elder</u>:
16.11 Van Vorst, Cornelius — Jurrianse, Gerrebrand
Berdan, Jan D. — Vreeland, Johannes E.
<u>Deacon</u>:
Post, Thomas — Van Giesen, Abraham
Sip, Johannes jr — Paulusse, Paulus
<u>Churchmaster</u>:
Vreeland, Elias J. — Van Winkelen, Jacob
Van Wagenen, Roeliph — Van Winkelen, Waling

<u>1787</u>
e5.17 <u>Elder</u>:
15.28 Sip, Johannes — Post, Adriaan A.
Vreland, Johannis E. — Van Rypen, Dirck
<u>Deacon</u>:
Van Noorstrand, Christophel — Vreland, Enoch J.
Post, Adriaan J. — Vreland, Enoch C.
<u>Churchmaster</u>:
Pieterse, Hessel
Post, Hendrick

<u>1788</u>
e5. 1 <u>Elder</u>:
15.12 Gerritse, Henry — Van Vorst, Cornelius
Kip, Hendrick — Berdan, Jan
<u>Deacon</u>:
Pieterse, Hessel — Post, Thomas
Van Houten, Cornelius — Sip, Johannes jr

CHURCH CONSISTORY - At Achquechnonck

New Member	In Place Of

Churchmaster:
Van Winkelen, Johannis   Vreland, Elias J.
Wouterse, Gerret   Van Wagenen, Roelef

1789
e5.21 **Elder:**
i6. 1 Wesselse, Lukas   Sip, Johannes
Post, Thomas   Vreland, Johannes E.
Deacon:
Van Bussen, Philip   Van Noorstrand, Christophel
Vreland, Elias   Post, Adriaan A.
Churchmaster:
Gerritse, Henry
Van Wagenen, Hermanus

1790
e5.13 **Elder:**
i5.24 Jurrianse, Gerrebrand   Kip, Hendrick
Sip, Johannes jr   Gerritse, Henry
Deacon:
Van Wagenen, Gerrit P.   Pieterse, Hessel
Van Rypen, Cornelius   Van Houten, Cornelius
Churchmaster:
Van Winkelen, Johannes
Wouterse, Gerrit

1791
e6. 2 **Elder:**
i6.13 Post, Adriaan A.   Wesselse, Lucas
Van Rypen, Dirck   Post, Thomas
Deacon:
Kip, Pieter   Van Bussen, Philip
Doremus, Hendrick   Vreland, Elias J.
Churchmaster:
Gerritse, Henry
Van Rypen, Gerret
Pieterse, Hessel

1792
e5.17 **Elder:**
i5.28 Vreland, Enoch Jo.   Jurrianse, Gerrebrand
Van Houten, Cornelius   Sip, Johannes jr
Deacon:
Spier, Barent   Van Wagenen, Gerret P.
Berdan, Jacob   Van Rypen, Cornelius
Churchmaster:
Vreland, Johannes El.   Gerritse, Henry
Post, Thomas   Wouterse, Gerret

1793
e5.16 **Elder:**
i6. 2 Post, Thomas   Post, Adrian A.
Pieterse, Hessel   Van Rypen, Dirck
Deacon:
Post, Adrian J.   Doremus, Hendrick
Van Winkelen, Jacob W.   Kip, Pieter
Churchmaster:
Jurrianse, Christofel   Van Rypen, Gerrit
Vreland, Cornelius H.   Pieterse, Hessel

CHURCH CONSISTORY - At Totua

1793
e5. 9 Elder:
i6. 9 Doremus, Hessel
Westervelt, Cornelius
Deacon:
Van Winkelen, Johannes
Doremus, Hendrick
Churchmaster:
Van Winkelen, Simeon J.
Marselusse, Pieter

1794
e6.28 Elder:
i7.20 Ackerman, Albert   Post, Johannes
Kip, Nicasie   Van Saan, Samuel
Deacon:
Westerveld, Jurrie   Van Winkelen, Simeon jr
Brouwer, Abraham   Benson, John jr

At Achquechnonck

1794
e6. 1 Elder:
Paulusse, Paulus   Vreland, Enoch Jo.
Van Bussen, Philip   Van Houten, Cornelius
Deacon:
Vreland, Elias J.   Spier, Barent
Spier, John B.   Berdan, Jacob
Churchmaster:
Post, Adrian M.   Vreland, Johannis El.
Ludlow, John   Post, Thomas

1795
e5.14 Elder:
i5.25 Kip, Hendrick   Pieterse, Hessel
Sip, Johannes jr   Post, Thomas
Deacon:
Berdan, Jacob   Van Winkelen, Jacob W.
Van Wagenen, Johannes G.   Post, Adriaan J.

At Totua

1795
e5.24 Elder:
i6. 7 Bensen, Johannis Esq'r   Doremus, Hessel
Spier, Hendrick Esq'r   Westerveld, Cornelius
Deacon:
Van Houten, Abraham   Van Winkelen, Johannes
Van Winkelen, Simeon   Doremus, Hendrick
Churchmaster:
Bensen, Johannes jr   Marselusse, Edo jr
Doremus, Hendrick   Van Houten, Adrian

1796
e5.12 Elder:
i5.29 Van Winkelen, Simeon jr   Ackerman, Albert
Demarest, David   Kip, Nicasie
Deacon:
Marcelusse, Edo jr   Westerveldt, Jurrie
Van Houten, Adriaan   Brouwer, Abraham
Churchmaster:
Van Winkele, Cornelius
Gerritse, Johannis

CHURCH CONSISTORY - <u>At Achquechnonck</u>

	New Member	In Place Of
<u>1796</u> 5. 8	<u>Elder:</u> Cadmus, Abraham Vreland, Johannes El.	Paulusse, Paulus Van Bussen, Philip
	<u>Deacon:</u> Post, Adriaan J. Van Winkelen, Jacob W.	Vreland, Elias J. Spier, John B.
<u>1797</u> e5.28 16.18	<u>Elder:</u> Van Rypen, Dirck Spier, Barent	Kip, Hendrick, deceased Sip, Johannis jr
	<u>Deacon:</u> Kip, Pieter Vreland, Elias J.	Berdan, Jacob Van Wagenen, Johannis G.

<u>At Totua</u>

<u>1797</u> e5.25 16. 5	<u>Elder:</u> Post, Johannis Van Saan, Samuel	Benson, Johannis Spier, Hendrick
	<u>Deacon:</u> Van Houten, Dirck Marcelusse, Cornelius	Van Houten, Abraham Van Winkelen, Simeon
	<u>Churchmaster:</u> Westerveld, John C. Van Saan, Albert	Benson, Johannis jr Doremus, Hendrick
<u>1798</u> e5.24 16.10	<u>Elder:</u> Van Winkele, Johannes Doremus, Hendrick	Van Winkele, Simeon Demarest, David
	<u>Deacon:</u> Van Houten, Johannes J. Van Saan, Isaac	Marcelusse, Edo Van Houten, Adriaan
	<u>Churchmaster:</u> Van Houten, Adriaan Van Winkele, Simeon J.	Van Winkele, Cor. Gerritse, Johannis

<u>At Achquechnonck</u>

<u>1798</u> e5.17 16.17	<u>Elder:</u> Van Wagenen, Gerrit P. Vreland, Enoch Jo.	Cadmus, Abraham Vreland, Joh's El.
	<u>Deacon:</u> Van Winkelen, Jacob A. Evertse, Jeremiah	Post, Adriaan J. Van Winkel, Jacob W.
<u>1799</u> e5. 2 15.23	<u>Elder:</u> Doremus, Hendrick Paulusse, Paulus	Van Rypen, Dirck Spier, Barent
	<u>Deacon:</u> Vreeland, Cornelius H. Esq'r Terhune, Jacobus	Kip, Pieter Vreeland, Elias J.

<u>At Totua</u>

<u>1799</u> e5.10 16.16	<u>Elder:</u> Spier, Hendrick Van Houten, Abraham	
	<u>Deacon:</u> Van Winkele, Cornelius Gerritse, Hessel	

CHURCH CONSISTORY - <u>At Totua</u>

New Member	In Place Of

<u>Churchmaster</u>:
Bensen, Johannis J.
Coerte, Hendrick

<u>1800</u>
e5. 8 <u>Elder</u>:
15.25 Bensen, Johannis Esq'r   Post, Joh's
Van Winkele, Simeon Jo.   Doremus, Hendrick
<u>Deacon</u>:
Van Houten, Cornelius R.   Van Houten, Johannis J.
Demarest, Petrus   Van Saan, Isaac
<u>Churchmaster</u>:
Van Houten, Roelif R.
Bensen, David
Van Aalen, Petrus

<u>At Achquechnonck</u>

<u>1800</u>
e5.22 <u>Elder</u>:
16. 2 Van Houten, Cornelius   Van Wagenen, Gerret P.
Post, Adriaan J.   Vreland, Enoch Jor.
<u>Deacon</u>:
Post, Hartman   Van Winkel, Jacob A.
Kip, Hendrick   Evertse, Jeremiah

<u>1801</u>
e5.14 <u>Elder</u>:
15.25 Vreland, Johannes Enoch   Doremus, Hendrick
Sip, Johannes   Paulusse, Paulus
<u>Deacon</u>:
Jurrianse, Gerrebrand   Vreland, Cornelius H.
Van Wagenen, Gerrit   Terhune, Jacobus

<u>At Totua</u>

<u>1801</u>
e5.24 <u>Elder</u>:
16. 7 Westerveld, Cornelius   Spier, Hendrick
Marcelusse, Cornelius   Van Houten, Abraham
<u>Deacon</u>:
Van Aalen, Petrus   Van Winkel, Cornelius
Bensen, Daniel   Gerritse, Hessel
<u>Churchmaster</u>:
Van Houten, Roeliph J.   Coerte, Hendrick
Van Winkel, Simeon jr   Van Aalen, Petrus

<u>1802</u>
e6. 6 <u>Elder</u>:
16.17 Post, Johannes   Bensen, Joh's Esq'r
Doremus, Hendrick   Van Winkel, Simeon Jo.
<u>Deacon</u>:
Van Saan, Albert   Van Houten, Cor. R.
Doremus, Roeliph   Demarest, Petrus
<u>Churchmaster</u>:
Ryerse, Joris
Van Houten, Adriaan

<u>At Achquechnonck</u>

<u>1802</u>
e5.27 <u>Elder</u>:
16. 7 Vreland, Cornelius H. Esq'r   Van Houten, Cornelius
Vreland, Elias J.   Post, Adrian J.
<u>Deacon</u>:
Ackerman, Dirck   Post, Hartman
Paulusse, Pieter   Kip, Hendrick

CHURCH CONSISTORY - At Achquechnonck

	New Member	In Place Of

1803
6. 9 Elder:
Van Wagenen, Gerrit P.   Vreland, Joh's En.
Kip, Pieter   Sip, Joh's
Deacon:
Spier, Johannis   Jurrianse, Gerrebrand
Ackerman, Albert   Van Wagenen, Gerrit

At Totua

1803
e4.21
15.29 Elder:
Van Winkele, Cornelius   Westervelt, Cornelius
Van Houten, Abraham   Marcelusse, Cornelius
Deacon:
Degrauw, John   Van Aalen, Petrus
Van Houten, John   Bensen, Daniel
Churchmaster:
Godwin, Abraham   Van Houten, Roeliph J.
Van Houten, Robert   Van Winkele, Simeon jr
Van Houten, Jacob   Ryerse, Joris

1804
e5.13
15.27 Elder:
Demarest, David   Post, Johannes
Van Winkel, Simeon Joh.   Doremus, Hendrick
Deacon:
Goetschius, John   Van Saan, Albert
Demarest, David D.   Doremus, Roeliph
Churchmaster:
Benson, David
Van Houten, Gerrebrand   At Achquechnonck

1804
e5.10
15.21 Elder:
Vreland, Enoch Jor.   Vreland, Cornelius
Van Winkel, Jacob   Vreland, Elias J.
Deacon:
Winkel, Helmich   Ackerman, Dirck
Kip, Hendrick   Paulusse, Pieter

1805
e5.23
16. 3 Elder:
Spier, Barent   Van Wagenen, Gerrit P.
Sip, Johannes   Kip, Pieter
Deacon:
Van Rypen, Gerrit   Spier, Johannes
Ackerman, Abraham   Ackerman, Albert

At Totua

1805
e5.26
16. 9 Elder:
Marcelusse, Edo   Van Winkele, Cornelius
Van Houten, Adriaan   Van Houten, Abraham
Deacon:
Brown, John   Degrauw, John
Van Houten, Gerrebrand   Van Houten, John
Churchmaster:
Doremus, John   Godwin, Abraham
Van Winkel, Frans   Van Houten, Robert

1806
e5.25
16. 5 Elder:
Van Winkel, Cornelius   Demarest, David
Doremus, Hendrick   Van Winkel, Simeon Joh's

CHURCH CONSISTORY - At Totua

New Member	In Place Of
Deacon:	
Bensen, Daniel	Goetschius, John
Onderdonck, Rem	Demarest, David D.
Churchmaster:	
Marselusse, Pieter	
Van Houten, Robert	At Achquechnonck

1806
e5.15 Elder:
15.26

Vreland, Elias J.	Vreland, Enoch Jor.
Berdan, Jacob	Van Winkel, Jacob W.
Deacon:	
Van Houten, Gerret Esq'r	Van Winkel, Helmich
Doremus, Pieter	Kip, Hendrick

1807
e5. 7 Elder:
15.18

Van Houten, Cornelius	Spier, Barent
Post, Adriaan J.	Sip, Johannes, deceased
Deacon:	
Debaan, Karel	Ackerman, Abraham
Doremus, Roeliph	Van Rypen, Gerrit
	At Totua

1807
e5.17 Elder:
16.21

Degrauw, John	Marcelusse, Edo
Van Houten, Cornelius R.	Van Houten, Adriaan
Deacon:	
Van Houten, Robert	Brown, John
Marcelusse, Pieter	Van Houten, Gerrebrand
Doremus, Hendrick H.	Onderdonck, Rem
Churchmaster:	
Doremus, John	
Van Winkele, Frans	

1808
e5.26 Elder:
16. 6

Spier, Hendrick	Van Winkel, Cornelius
Van Houten, Abraham	Doremus, Hendrick
Deacon:	
Van Houten, Gerrebrand C.	Bensen, Daniel
Bensen, David	Doremus, Hendrick H.
Churchmaster:	
Van Saan, Albert	
Van Houten, Gerrebrand	At Achquechnonck

1808
e5.29 Elder:
17. 3

Vreland, Cornelius	Berdan, Jacob
Van Winkel, Helmich	Vreland, Elias
Deacon:	
Evertse, Jacob	Van Houten, Gerret Esq'r
Boss, Gerret	Doremus, Pieter

1809
e5.11 Elder:
15.22

Van Rypen, Gerret	Van Houten, Cornelius
Vreland, Enoch Jor.	Post, Adriaan J.
Deacon:	
Doremus, Roeliph	
Jurrianse, Gerrebrand	
Vreland, Jacob En.	

CHURCH   CONSISTORY - At Totua

	New Member	In Place Of

1809
e5.21 Elder:
16.25 Van Houten, Dirck   Degrauw, John
Van Saan, Albert   Van Houten, Cornelius R.
Deacon:
Doremus, John   Van Houten, Robert
Demarest, Pieter   Marselusse, Pieter
Churchmaster:
Van Winkel, Simeon J.
Marselusse, Edo

1810
e6. 3 Elder:
17. 8 Doremus, Hendrick   Spier, Hendrick
Marcelusse, Edo   Van Houten, Abraham
Deacon:
Van Houten, Gerrebrand Esq'r   Van Houten, Gerrebrand C.
Demarest, David D.   Benson, David
Benson, Daniel   Demarest, Pieter
Churchmaster:
Van Houten, Abraham
Van Aalen, Pieter

At Achquechnonck

1810
e5.31 Elder:
16.11 Van Houten, Gerret Esq'r   Vreland, Cornelius
Kip, Hendrick   Van Winkele, Helmich
Deacon:
Doremus, Pieter   Doremus, Roeliph
Van Winkele, Jacobus   Boss, Gerret

1811
e5.26 Elder:
16.16 Ackerman, Dirrick   Vreland, Enoch Jor.
Post, Hartman   Van Rypen, Gerrit
Deacon:
Vreland, Elias Ja.   Jurrianse, Gerrebrand
Van Winkele, Waling J.   Vreland, Jacob E.

At Totua

1811
e5.23 Elder:
16. 3 Degrauw, John   Van Saan, Albert
Marcelusse, Peter   Van Houten, Dirick, deceased
Deacon:
Van Aalen, Peter   Doremus, John
Blauvelt, John Joseph   Bensen, Daniel
Churchmaster:
Doremus, John
Bensen, David

1812
e5.10 Elder:
16.14 Van Winkele, Cornelius   Doremus, Hendrick
Van Houten, Abraham   Marcelusse, Edo
Deacon:
Bensen, David   Van Houten, Gerrebrand Esq'r
Van Houten, Abraham R.   Demarest, David
Churchmaster:
Doremus, John
Bensen, David

CHURCH CONSISTORY - <u>At Achquechnonck</u>

	New Member	In Place Of

<u>1812</u>
e5. 7 <u>Elder</u>:
i5.31 Ackerman, Abraham   Van Houten, Gerret Esq'r
       Van Winkele, Jacob W.   Kip, Hendrick
       <u>Deacon</u>:
       Van Rypen, John   Doremus, Peter
       Cadmus, Thomas   Van Winkele, Jacobus

<u>1813</u>
e5.30 <u>Elder</u>:
i6.13 Vreland, Elias
       Doremus, Roelif
       <u>Deacon</u>:
       Paulusse, Pieter
       Printice, Hendrick   <u>At Totua</u>

<u>1813</u>
e5.27 <u>Elder</u>:
i6. 7 Spier, Hendrick
       Goetschius, John
       <u>Deacon</u>:
       Doremus, John
       Van Houten, Gerrebrand C.
       <u>Churchmaster</u>:
       Bensen, Daniel
       Van Houten, Abraham R.

<u>1814</u>
e5.22 <u>Elder</u>:
i6. 5 Blauvelt, Johannes Joseph
       Van Houten, Gerrebrand Esq'r
       <u>Deacon</u>:
       Van Houten, Robert
       Van Houten, John J.
       Van Aalen, Peter
       <u>Churchmaster</u>:
       Van Houten, Abraham
       Van Saan, Albert   <u>At Achquechnonck</u>

<u>1814</u>
e5.19 <u>Elder</u>:
i5.30 Van Houten, Gerrit Esq'r   Van Winkele, Jacob W.
       Van Winkele, Helmich   Ackerman, Abraham
       <u>Deacon</u>:
       Bosch, Gerrit   Van Rypen, John
       Bogert, Roelif   Cadmus, Thomas

<u>1815</u>
e5. 7 <u>Elder</u>:
i5.21 Demarest, Gerrit
       Vreland, Elias Ja.
       <u>Deacon</u>:
       Post, Casparus
       Sip, John   <u>At Totua</u>

	Elder	Deacon	Churchmaster

<u>1815</u>
e5. 4 Degrauw, John   Bensen, Daniel   Bensen, David
       Marselusse, Edo   Doremus, Jobn   Marcelusse, Pieter
       (the above entry entirely crossed out)

<u>1815</u>
e8. 6 Van Winkele, Cornelius Doremus, John   Marcelusse, Pieter
i8.27 Van Houten, Abraham   Van Aalen, Pieter   Bensen, David

At Aquacknonck

1795
3. 2 <u>Trustees elected</u>:
Schoonmaker, Rev. Henry - declined
Gerrise, Henry
Peterse, Hessel
Post, Thomas - declined
Powleson, Paul
V: Bossen, Phillip
V: Rypen, Richard
3. 7 <u>Trustees elected</u> in place of those that declined:
Kip, Henry
Van Winkle, Jacob

PEW RENTALS: 10.14.1803

Pew #	Person	# Of Seats
1	Van Ryper, Isaac	2
	Stagg, James	2
2	Van Houten, Garret Esq'r	2
	Berry, Philip	2
3	Van Wincle, Francis	2
	/sold to Helmegh Sip (__0.18.1812	
	Van Wincle, Isaac	2
4	Vreeland, Jacob E.	2
	Vreeland, John C.	2
5	Van Ryper, Jacob	4
6	Feeland, Danel	4
7	Duremus, Henry	4
8	Buskark, Jeremiah	2
	Van Ryper, Adrian	2
	/sold to Edo Vreeland	
	Garretse, Doc'r John	3
9	Post, Henry	5
10	Van Wincle, Jacob jr	3
	/trans to Isaac J. Van Winkel	
	Cudmus, Thomes	2
11	Van Houten, Cornelius J.	3
	Cudmis, Cornelius	2
12	Post, Adrian M.	5
13	Vreeland, Harmones	2
	Jureancy, Garrebrant	2
	Sip, John	1
14	Wauters, Garret	1
	Wauters, Hanry	1
	Wauters, Marcetius	2
	Vreeland, Rulph	1
15	Vreeland, Elies J.	4
16	Kip, Pieter	4
17	Van Wincle, Jacob W.	4
18	Van Waggener, Rulph	4
19	Van Wincle, Helmegh	4
20	Powlisson, Peter	4
21	Van Waggener, Garrit	4
22	Van Ryper, John A.	4
23	Van Wincle, Walling	4
24	Jacson, Peter	4

PEW RENTALS 10.14.1803

Pew #	Person	# Of Seats
25	Ludlow, Cornelius R.	4
	/trans to Abraham Ackerman 10.25.1810 from Cornelius N. C. Ludlow	
26	Kip, Henry P.	4
27	Ackerman, Abraham	4
28	Vreeland, Cornelius Esq'r	4
29	Van Winkle, Jacob A.	2
	Speer, Garret J.	1
30	Garritse, John H. jr	4
31	Sip, Cornelius	4
32	Mersalus, John	2
	/sold to Henry Kip 10.17.1816	
	Kip, Henry	2
33	Van Houten, Adrian	4
	/sold to John Merseles	
34	Sip, Adrian	4
35	Zebrisce, Christian A.	4
36	Van Iderstine, George	2
	Van Norstrant, Jacob	1
	Degraw, Catherine	1
37	Van Riper, Garrit	3
	/sold to Fradereck Yereance 3.28.1826	
	Van Riper, Elisabeth	1
38	Vreeland, Elias J.	4
39	Ludlow, John R.	3
	Van Norstrant, Winche	1
40	Post Adrian A.	4
41	Van Winkle, Walling C.	2
	/to Edo Vreeland 12.28.1807, Waling then deceased	
	Post, James	2
42	Sip, John	4
43	Post, Henry F.	4
	Ryerson, John M.	1
44	Post Adrian J.	2½
	Post, John A.	1½
	Post, Thomas	2½ (crossed out)
	Zabriskie, Jacob	1
	(seems as though "John A." and "Jacob" were entered at a late date in place of "Thomas")	
45	Ackerman, Richard	5
46	Brinckerhof, Henry G.	4
	Vreeland, Benjemin	1
47	Ackerman, Albert	3
	/to John A. Ackerman 7.27.1820	
	Bogert, John	2
	/sold to Frederick Yereance 5.13.1824	
48	Bantaw, Richard	5
49	Van Winkle, Theodorus	2
	Van Iderstine, Tuniss	3
	Van Winkle, James	2
50	Post Cornelius	4
51	Vreeland, Isaac E.	2
	Vreeland, Peter	2
52	Demarest, James	2
	/to Ralph Doremus	
	Vandebake, Abraham A.	2
	/to Abraham A. Bush	

PEW RENTALS 10.14.1803

Pew #	Person	# Of Seats	
53	Cadmus, Andrew	2	
	Van Bussen, Peter	2	
54	Bush, Aron	2	
	Van Iderstine, Peter	2	
55	Simmons, Peter	2	
	Speer, John J.	2	
56	Van Horn, John, Richard, & /Thomas	4	
57	Garitse, Henry jr /sold to David Alyea 10.17.1814	2	
	Vreeland, Jacob	2	
58	Vreeland, Enoch G.	3	
	Ludlow, Henmore	1	
	/these now, 1820, belong to Albert Ackerman & Isaac Ackerman		
59	Yereance, Hessel	2	
	Yereance, Christopher	2	
60	Speer, Samuel /to James Maloney 1.5.1820	2	
	Speer, John	2	
3	Van Burin, John	2	on the galliree
	Van Blarcom, Cornelius	2	ditto
6	Christie, James	2	ditto
	Van Iderstine, Francis	2	ditto
7	Westervelt, Peter	4	ditto

Inscriptions

from tombstones in graveyard of the

PROTESTANT REFORMED DUTCH CHURCH

at Acquackanonck

made by

WILLIAM W. SCOTT

in 1920

Includes all graves with stones. First
buriel was about 1698

This copy made in 1942 from pencil list in the Julius Forst-
mann Library of Passaic, N.J. and rechecked with it by

Herbert S. Ackerman
and
Arthur J. Goff

Note: The number at left is page number of field book used when
copying was done and tends to identify family groups.

Compiler's Note: The above is a copy of the Title page of the inscriptions which follow. The cemetery stones were not rechecked by the
compiler but were copied and rearranged from the typescript on file
at the Holland Society of New York's library. The History and Tradi-
tions Committee of The Society recommended that these inscriptions
be included with the church record since there is no known plan to
publish these death records elsewhere.

CEMETERY RECORD

The reader should be aware that:

1. There are some obvious errors.
2. No relationships, such as wife of, son of, etc., are given.
3. Death dates range from 1738 to 1896

*#		Death	Age
	ACKERMAN		
84	Albert	4.20.1837	79- 1-11
90	Albert I.	3. 8.1877	58- 6-28
83	Ann VAN WINKEL	2. 9.1847	81- 0- 3
38	Anny	9. 4.1849	29- 6- 0
87	Auletty	8.21.1834	43y
19	David I.	10.22.1873	74- 2-14
30	Elizabeth	7. 6.1832	69y
39	Eve SIP	2. 1.1845	53- 1-11
38	Gertrude	9.14.1849	0- 6- 3
39	Herman	10.12.1843	16- 2-27
90	Isaac	2.23.1850	51- 7-20
90	Isaac	1. 9.1852	0- 1- 4
51	Jacob W.	2. 3.1879	15- 4- 2
83	Jane	7.26.1865	58- 4-25
38	John A.	6.21.1850	58- 0- 7
51	John H.	2. 6.1865	34- 1- 0
90	Kitty PAULSON	5.27.1847	50- 8- 9
87	Margaret	12.16.1852	87- 0-19
51	Margaret E.	10.17.1884	49- 9- 0
16	Maria VAN HOUTEN	3.22.1869	66- 6- 9
16	Mary L.	4.27.1851	27- 9- 6
30	Morris	5.24.1821	56y
19	Rachel	12.27.1862	59- 7-22
86	Richard	8.22.1830	67-11-__
17	William P.	2.11.1877	85- 0-12
	ANDERSON		
75	Anna	7. 4.1858	67- 6-12
76	Clara	9. 5.1872	42y
75	David I.	4. 8.1873	81y
16	Holger P. P.	9.15.1871	0- 2- 7
76	John	7. 4.1874	15y
77	Katie		
76	Sarah E.	11.22.1889	37- 5-21
76	William S.	3.16.1887	59- 8-27
	ANDRUSS		
5	A.		
6	Ann ZABRISKIE	3.14.1896	80-11-17
7	Annie L.	8.13.1866	0- 1-10
7	Hattie C.	4.13.1891	18- 2-23
6	Maria L.	3.22.1862	24- 2-__
6	Sarah	8.21.1864	76- 2-18
7	William L. jr	7.14.1876	33- 3-12
	ARANTS		
79	Daniel	12.30.1738	0
	ARCULARIUS		
10	Caroline	8.29.1843	35y

* - see page 328

CEMETERY RECORD

*#		Death	Age
	BADELL		
60	Mary J.	8. 7.1886	18- 2-16
	BAFY		
59	_____		
	BAKER		
36	Melissa MONTROSE	8.11.1881	19- 0- 0
	BALMER		
27	Margaret	2. 1.1843	2-11- 0
27	Sarah	12.13.1881	77- 0- 0
27	Walter	7.10.1845	54- 6- 0
	BANTA		
32 & 51	Aaron	1.15.1810	33-11-28
2	Eleanor	5.10.1844	51- 9-11
91	Elizabeth	10.15.1847	76-10- 3
56	Frankie		
91	George	5.30.1831	63- 1- 0
56	Henry E. M.	9.26.1861	2m
93	John G.	3.13.1868	62- 8-24
94	John R.	3.27.1857	36- 2- 0
56	Mary E.	6.19.1860	7- 6-21
94	Rachel Ann VAN RIPER	1.14.1851	24- 9-28
94	Richard I.	2.18.1834	53-11-__
94	Sarah	10.14.1863	78- 7-26
56	Willie	7.30.1866	1- 6-11
	BARKLEY		
45	John F.	5.21.1880	29- 7-10
	BASSETT		
91	Eleanor	2.24.1742	14-10- 5
78	Stephen	1. 4.1763	56- 0- 4
	BECK		
39	Frans J.	8.24.1878	22-10-16
	BERRY		
44	John B.	10.28.1807	63- 9-17
17	John I.	2.13.1872	59- 6-25
98	Maria ALYEA	11.28.1863	68- 2- 5
85	Maria E.	11.11.1858	2- 8- 3
17	Sarah LINFORD	3.15.1889	80- 7-16
75	Willie H.	8.23.1868	9- 8- 7
	BERTHOLF		
82	Mary	4. 8.1820	82y
	BIEGEL		
40	Elizabeth	11.17.1888	57-10- 5
40	Lena	11. 4.1877	20- 6- 0
	BLAIR		
42	Millaca	8. 2.1800	30- 0- 0
42	Robert	11.29.1829	85- 0- 0
43	Robert	7.30.1800	0- 0- 3
	BLAKISTON		
45	Agnes JURRIANSE	8. 3.1880	31- 4-15

* - see page 328

CEMETERY   RECORD

*#		Death	Age
	BLANCHARD		
10	Hiram	2.20.1848	59- 2-18
	BOGARDUS		
63	Charlotte WILTSIE	2. 3.1861	72- 1- 5
64	Mary	8. 1.1869	43- 8-11
63	Stephen	2.22.1853	34-11-22
63	Wm. R., Rev.	2.12.1862	72-11-19
	BOGERT		
120	Abraham	11.14.1892	68- 8-__
81	Agnes W. JERALEMAN	2. 6.1884	41- 4-27
71	Andrew B.	5.23.1873	0- 4-16
81	Blanche A.	5.28.1891	20- 2-14
81	Cornelius J.	5.15.1886	23- 0-10
108	Ella	4.17.1868	5- 6- 8
74	Etta	9. 7.1878	1- 8-10
120	James E.	10.10.1889	33- 7- 1
71	Solomon	6.27.1881	67-10-14
108	Willie	8. 3.1867	2- 7- 0
	BOYLE		
47	Byron G.	2.18.1881	22- 7-17
	BREVOORT		
38	Clara J.	7.14.1879	44- 0-26
39	Edward S.	4. 9.1884	0-10-21
38	Elvira E.	5.15.1886	28- 9- 0
37	Jacob Z., N.J. 13th Reg't Vol.	4.22.1888	53- 0- 0
	BRINKERHOFF		
40	Abigail VAN BUSSEN		
43	Anny	5.19.1803	4-10-15
58	Cornelius	6.19.1860	79- 8-28
58	Cornelius	12. 4.1849	5-10- 7
58	Hannah	3.28.1869	87- 3-16
90	J. Romaine	4.18.1890	57- 4-22
41	John		
58	Mary	10.14.1860	1- 8- 5
41	Philip	9.16.1802	0- 0-13
41	Philip	7.15.1805	0-11-15
	BROWER		
98	Clayborne	5. 7.1856	6- 1- 5
73	James H.	10. 1.1888	40y
98	Louis N.	5.24.1856	2- 8- 7
9	Mary	11.28.1871	88- 0- 0
	BROWN		
111	Anna	8. 6.1865	0- 3-11
108	Ellen ENNIS	4. 7.1876	74- 3- 6
108	Jacob P.	12. 9.1874	71- 5- 0
111	Jane Ann CADMUS	5. 9.1865	27- 7-15
112	Mable	6.28.1887	1- 1- 6
40	Margaret	11.19.1883	62- 9-10
111	Willie	6.22.1865	0- 1-26

* - see page 328

CEMETERY RECORD

	Death	Age
BUSH		
15 Aaron	9. 1.1815	79-11- 5
90 Ann Eliza	9. 3.1843	27- 9- 6
90 Clarissa HOWARD	5. 2.1845	65- 4-22
15 Hyly	7.28.1821	82- 1-23
97 Peter A.	3.21.1858	46- 8-11
BUYS		
44 Peter J.	4.13.1883	44- 4-25
CADMUS		
111 Andrew C.	3.14.1884	80- 6-21
64 Cornelius G.	6.21.1891	78- 6-11
64 David	8. 5.1869	74- 7-21
63 Elizabeth VAN HOUTEN	9. 5.1849	60- 0- 0
111 Ellen	9.25.1877	71- 8-13
63 Garret	11. 9.1879	79- 0- 0
64 Garret D.	7.28.1847	0- 5-14
104 Gertrude SIP	6.12.1887	49- 4-15
109 Henrietta	8.30.1863	0- 8-19
70 Henry	9.19.1857	6-10- 9
62 James	3.16.1878	72- 5- 2
63 James G.	3.30.1893	78- 0- 3
16 Jane	5.29.1831	2- 3-13
63 Lydia V. S. BANTA	3.22.1887	65- 6- 7
64 Maggie	1.14.1870	0- 1-24
64 Margaret VREELAND	1.14.1890	80- 5-10
70 Margaret Anna	5.21.1855	1- 4- 3
62 Mary DEMOTT	12.31.1891	89- 8- 8
70 Peter Helmus	9.12.1857	1- 5-16
111 Rittie	12. 9.1881	25- 3-__
64 Sarah A.	9. 1.1852	2- 8- 0
70 Thomas	5. 9.1862	85-13- 0
CAMPBELL		
13 Jane VREELAND	12.19.1874	67y
CARPENTER		
105 Jesse P.	2.17.1850	25- 1- 5
105 Mary L.	12. 4.1854	71- 3-10
105 Noah S.	7.19.1864	82- 6- 5
CASTLE		
43 Agnes ROSE	1838-1895	57y
102 Catherine	10.19.1891	80- 5- 4
102 Philip	4. 1.1893	92- 3- 1
CHAMBERLAIN		
12 John Joseph	2. 3.1858	28- 9- 6
CHASE		
65 Lydia	1.29.1863	2- 6- 0
CHRISTIE		
71 Eva	7.10.1865	5- 4- 4
71 Gussie	7.20.1873	0- 0-19
71 John	6. 4.1875	20- 4- 9
71 Mary E. BOGERT	8.10.1873	39- 7-28

* - see page 328

*#		CEMETERY RECORD Death	Age
	CLAUDIUS		
31	John	1.27.1874	4- 1- 0
	CLEMONS		
74	Charles A.	7. 9.1875	10y
74	John W.	1. 1.1895	65- 2-28
	CLEVELAND		
23	Benjamin N.	10.31.1870	75y
24	Catherine P.	7. 1.1862	35- 9-10
23	Eliza HENDRICKSON	2. 2.1871	58- 0- 0
23	Eunice LINFORD	4.25.1867	73-10-21
23	Jane E.		
23	Martha FORCE	2. 1.1835	42- 6-15
23	Peter		
24	Phoebe	6.30.1887	56- 3-14
	COEYMAN		
102	Abram	9.20.1888	70- 9- 1
	COLLINS		
30	Barnabus V., Rev.	7.23.1877	63- 0- 0
30	Sarah	1.26.1880	33- 6- 0
	COHOON		
68	Josiah	2.28.1851	62- 0- 0
	CAMPTON		
49	Fanny	3. 3.1849	53- 9- 9
	CONKLIN		
86	Susan SCUDDER	1. 1.1877	77y
	COON		
46	Jane	2. 5.1891	81y
46	Samuel	2.27.1864	58y
	COURTER		
35	Ellen	2. 8.1841	24- 9-17
	COWENHOVEN		
71	David W.	1837-1840	3y
71	John H.	1834-1894	60y
71	Nellie POST	1810-1888	78y
71	Samuel G. W.	1810-1880	73y
	CRAIG		
29	T. H., Corp, Co. D, 9th NY Inf		
29	J.D.C.; A.C.C.; E.H.C., and S.E.G.		
	CROSBY		
11	Elizabeth	2. 3.1862	83- 3- 0
	CRAWFORD		
19	Charlotte	3.22.1855	2- 6- 0
35	Henry C.	11. 2.1890	78- 8- 5
35	Jessie	3.20.1880	7- 9- 6
	DAVIDSON		
113	Agnes	4.16.1877	84y
113	Alexander	10.20.1853	65y

* - see page 328

	CEMETERY RECORD	
*#	Death	Age

DAVIDSON (con'd)

114	Elizabeth DONALD	1.30.1882	46y
113	John	2.11.1854	54y

DAY

46	Mary	9.23.1866	40y

DE BIRD

50	Johanna HELLER	3.26.1891	70y
50	Tice	5. 3.1880	66y

DE GARMO

39	Margaret	9.30.1798	80- 6- 0
39	Peter	1.27.1799	44-10- 0

DE GRAW

103	Garret	7. 7.1845	49- 6- 2

DE KEYSER

33	Jane	10.12.1879	85- 5-12
33	John	5.13.1886	17- 4-13
33	Peter	2.22.1879	85- 8-11

DEMAREST

85	Ada W.	4. 6.1878	10- 7-18
7	Agnes DURYEA	10. 4.1830	67- 1-14
86	Ann M.	2.14.1877	63- 4-24
91	Charity	11. 6.1870	78- 7-16
91	Charity	7.20.1852	23- 5- 0
91	David	4.20.1866	75- 3- 0
7	Garret	1.24.1833	76- 0- 0
24	James A.	1.13.1892	69- 1-10
27	Jemima HENNION	9.18.1841	51- 9-29
24	Jemima C.	4. 1.1855	1- 6-10
91	Lavina	9.21.1855	23- 4- 0
26	Martin	7.21.1830	43- 9-27
86	Martin	5.12.1881	73- 2-11
85	Rachel W.	12.18.1852	72- 3-27

DENBOER

46	Elizabeth, Jannetje, & Maria - no dates		

DEVOE

21	Jane	8.12.1865	70- 5-15
48	Letty	3.12.1848	58- 2- 5

DE VOGEL

30	Jemima	12. 3.1884	73- 4- 0

DE VRIES

33	Neeltje	12. 6.1887	

DODD

117	Rebecca LINFORD	8.30.1867	43- 4-25

DOREMUS

51	David D.	2. 7.1856	57- 4-19
85	Eleanor	1. 5.1852	75- 9-27
52	Ella	10.10.1895	37- 7- 0
51	Ellen POST	8.11.1877	75- 8-18

* - see page 328

CEMETERY RECORD

*#		Death	Age
	DOREMUS (con'd)		
98	Evanna	6.17.1870	23- 3-10
37	Maria POST	7.19.1832	22- 8- 5
51	Marselis	4.15.1849	25- 0-25
85	Peter	9.12.1838	70- 6-28
51	Rebecca	7.31.1894	35- 1- 9
51	Samuel	7. 9.1863	24- 5-29
--	Susan	7.25.1896	
	DRUMMOND		
90	Mary	10. 6.1761	0-15- 9
90	Sarah	10.29.1772	4- 9- 4
	DU BOIS		
90	Ezechiel	11.28.1737 or 1757	1- 6- 5
	DUNN		
118	Cornelius E.	7.21.1852	22- 1-21
	DURKIN		
119	John V. R.	9. 6.1862	8-10-13
	ECKHART		
43	Annie	6. 4.1879	42y
43	Georgie	6.12.1892	5- 6-13
	EDSALL		
92	Daniel	8.28.1872	48- 0-14
92	Elizabeth A.	11.28.1875	48-10-15
56	Jane V. W.	6. 3.1870	78y
	EHMAN		
47	Annie	10.31.1865	2- 5- 0
47	Anton	1.26.1871	46-10- 5
47	Christina	3.22.1893	67- 0- 0
48	Denie	8. 4.1883	2- 0-13
48	William	3.27.1873	17-10- 4
	ENNIS		
108	Richard	4.28.1860	89-11-15
	ERSKINE		
33	Hugh	5. 9.1879	42y
	EVERTS		
97	David	6.15.1844	16-10-20
121	Henrietta GLEMMERVEEN	3. 2.1835	55- 0- 0
121	Henry	1.14.1893	93- 5- 5
97	John	4.30.1851	58y
44	John	2. 7.1887	90- 0- 0
34	Matthew	4.24.1814	93y
	FAIRCLOUGH		
36	Cynthia	4.12.1887	40- 0- 0
	FALKNER		
97	Leonard	8.11.1875	32- 6- 2
	FLEMING		
19	Lucinda	3. 6.1861	82- 0-13

* - see page 328

CEMETERY RECORD

Death Age

FOX

		Death	Age
102	G. Clinton	6.30.1873	0- 6-10
102	Paul M.	4.19.1888	13- 0- 0

FRANCIS

41	John	9. 6.1892	25- 0- 0
41	Richard W.	12.12.1891	56- 0- 0

FREDERICK

120	Emma J.	12.15.1854	0- 3- 0
120	Henry	1. 1.1882	55- 3-__
11	Kitty Maria	6.20.1840	8- 9- 0
11	Margaret	9. 1.1856	85- 2-10
120	William	8.28.1857	61- 0- 8
10	William	7.16.1841	37- 7- 0

GARRISON

75	Annie	2. 7.1865	4- 6- 0
--	Elizabeth	4.25.1838	6- 5-16
10	G.	1.11.1737	
10	Garret	11.28.1765	63- 8-18
82	Hannah	2.16.1853	95- 0- 0
--	Henry	7.13.1805	84-11-26
--	Henry H.	10.31.1809	60- 3-29
19	Hiley	2. 9.1799	49- 4-15
--	John H.	3. 9.1817	37- 0- 7
--	Mary VREELAND	11.16.1851	67- 4- 6

GEBHARDT

42	Annie	3.29.1886	26- 5-22
42	Christian M.	3.30.1880	48- 9-22
42	Mary O'NIELL	2.11.1886	52- 0-27

GEHELL

121	Elizabeth	8. 4.1879	27- 3-25

GEIGER

27	Dora HUBER	12.24.1884	56- 2-14
27	Jacob	3.10.1886	65- 2-25

GERREBRANT

35	Ann	10.12.1838	25- 8- 1
57	Cornelia J. VREELAND	10.24.1879	38y
23	Eleanor	12.18.1850	25-10-24
47	John C.	2.28.1830	69- 9-17

GILLHAM

20	Clarissa L.	7.27.1880	0-10-24
20	Robert	12. 1.1866	67- 0- 0
20	Sarah	12.22.1879	26- 4-15

GILLIAM

41	George	11.22.1870	2- 0- 0
37	Maria (R.)	3.22.1879	59- 6- 8

GILLIANS

25	George M.	11. 6.1885	49- 0- 0
26	Joseph W.	8.31.1885	47y

* - see page 328

CEMETERY RECORD

*#		Death	Age
	GLASS		
53	Abraham	3.26.1851	2- 4-21
53	Anna H.	4.22.1859	68- 9- 0
53	Henry	3. 2.1859	73-11- 0
54	John H.	6. 4.1865	51- 8-19
53	Robert	3.24.1851	6-11-17
54	Sarah Ann PAXTON	10.29.1886	68- 8-21
	GOETSCHIUS		
2	Frances	2.14.1845	53- 0- 0
50	Maggie E.		20y
	GREAR		
35	Ruth Jane ASHMEAD	1.29.1881	69- 5-19
	GRIEG		
4	Nana HOBART		
4	Walter R.	3.31.1888	14- 9-16
	HACKETT		
106	Annie	2. 4.1882	0- 8- 0
105	Annie TICE	2.14.1882	8m
105	Fannie E.	11.29.1880	5- 4-22
106	William H.		3- 0- 0
	HAGENS		
70	Jo N.	1893	
	HAMILTON		
85	Mary J.	2.15.1878	34- 9- 3
	HARDTKE		
72	Charles	9. 2.1888	32- 5-17
	HARING		
40	Abraham I.	12.28.1800	33- 5- 0
40	Abraham J.	8. 6.1853	36- 6- 3
40	Ann ELLSWORTH	4. 1.1870	84y
40	Ann Eliza	4. 9.1841	26- 9-16
40	John	10.23.1826	39- 2-10
	HARROW		
69	Mary E.	1. 5.1881	31- 5-14
	HARTLEY		
26	Annie	1.28.1883	1- 5- 0
	HASBROUCK		
50	Willie	11.13.1865	0- 3- 8
	HEDDEN		
73	Jane Gilbert	10.16.1826	26- 7- 5
73	John	12. 2.1855	59- 8-29
73	Margaret VAN RIPER	6. 2.1862	56-11-21
	HELLER		
60	John	3.15.1885	7- 0- 0
60	Paul	7.15.1885	3- 9-10
	HERMAN		
59	Freddie	5.14.1891	2-10-28

* - see page 328

CEMETERY RECORD

*#		Death	Age
	HERTIG		
40	Caspar	3.20.1871	68- 0-17
	HEWLETT		
85	Ann	10.31.1865	55- 9- 0
85	Thomas	2.15.1859	49- 8- 0
	HEYER		
55	Catherine E. OLCOTT	1804-1881	77y
55	John S.	1798-1864	66y
	HOGAN		
20	Martha	6.11.1853	89y
	HOHNHORST		
72	Jamie	10.17.1889	6-11-18
72	Lizzie	10.18.1889	5- 1- 5
	HOLLEY		
73	Jeremiah	6.29.1854	34- 5-29
	HOPPER		
22	Albert C.	6. 5.1871	41- 2-21
28	Albert P.		
95	Catherine	4.27.1860	29- 7-27
89	Cornelius A.	8. 9.1881	84- 0- 7
28	Eliza SPIER	5.21.1869	61- 9-22
90	Elizabeth	12.13.1860	87-11-13
89	Elizabeth	3.22.1878	76-10-17
89	Garret C. H.	12. 1.1863	30- 2-12
91	Jacob G.	2. 3.1832	38- 1-26
20	Jacob H.	1. 5.1883	78- 1-20
28	Julia Ann	12.24.1848	5- 6- 0
90	Keziah	9. 6.1886	84-10-27
90	Kitty VREELAND	2. 9.1832	37- 1-24
20	Rebecca D.	12. 6.1879	68-10-___
	HORNBECK		
64	Sadie	5. 1.1883	1- 1- 2
	HOWARD		
90	Clarissa	5. 2.1845	65- 4-22
58	Leah HENNION	8.24.1884	63- 5-22
58	Lucinda	12.31.1864	21- 4- 4
	HUYLER		
68	Cornelius	4.12.1852	64- 8-18
68	Sarah	8.20.1862	76- 0- 0
	INGRAM		
12	Abigail	1.12.1872	2-11- 0
	JACKSON		
49	Maria	3. 4.1808	0- 8-11
	JACOBS		
116	Abraham	9.15.1843	0- 9-14
116	Abraham L.	7.21.1845	1- 5- 0
116	Anna	9. 9.1852	1- 6- 0
8	Garret P.	10.15.1831	69- 7-19

* - see page 328

CEMETERY RECORD

*#		Death	Age
	JACOBS (con'd)		
116	Harriet L.	9.21.1851	3- 6- 0
116	Henrietta	7.30.1853	1- 0-22
15	Maria	10.11.1824	0-10- 8
8	Mary	3. 5.1834	70- 0- 0
	JAQUES		
72	Rchd W.	3.22.1872	29y
	JENKINS		
99	John	3.17.1881	63-11-27
	JERALEMAN		
86	Catherine	11. 6.1860	67- 3-17
12	Phoebe VREELAND	5.18.1891	78- 5- 6
	JORDAN		
47	James H.	5.23.1846	2- 2- 1
	JURRIANSE		
47	Albert	9.28.1836	17- 1-28
61	Andrew	2.15.1891	48-10-15
48	Catherine	12.30.1853	74-10- 2
55	Catherine	9.10.1850	64- 9- 0
55	Catherine	3.12.1860	34- 0- 0
54	Catherine Ann	9.22.1855	2- 0- 0
109	Charity	8.18.1840	44- 9-22
60	Christopher	3.21.1853	45- 0-21
60	Christopher	11. 7.1865	26- 1-11
45	Clarissa VAN WINKEL	3.12.1895	70- 3-13
47	Elizabeth	9.12.1846	64- 9-26
54	Frederick	1.22.1847	63- 1- 1
54	Frederick	1.11.1864	3- 4- 0
79	Gerrebrant	8. 2.1841	72- 3- 5
54	Gertrude	1.11.1864	6- 7- 0
47	Hannah	1.22.1812	67- 3-20
59	Hannah	9. 7.1854	0- 4- 0
59	Helen Eliza	12.29.1834	1- 4-15
59	Helen Eliza	4.21.1843	4- 3- 1
109	Henry	1.29.1856	66- 5-26
60	Henry H.	4.24.1867	29- 7- 7
61	Henry Z.	11.29.1890	76-11-24
46	Hessel	8.11.1842	79- 0- 0
61	Jane E. VAN VOORHIS	11. 4.1883	47- 5-24
47	Jared	4.15.1835	20- 0-11
47	Jeremiah	6. 8.1845	71- 8- 5
59	John	5.25.1853	17- 7- 5
60	John jr	10. 9.1856	42- 1-25
47	John C.	8. 4.1832	53- 9- 6
67	John H.	12.15.1871	54- 8-__
113	John H.	8. 2.1868	0- 8-23
2	John I.	11.13.1842	58- 0- 0
59	John R.	4. 1.1859	27-11-10
54	Kitty TERHUNE	6.29.1884	65- 1-13
54	Letty Ann	8.16.1852	2- 3- 0
46	Margaret	8.29.1847	77- 0- 0
109	Margaret A.	5.18.1845	3- 1- 6

* - see page 328

CEMETERY RECORD

	Death	Age
JURRIANSE (con'd)		
59 Mary Ann	6. 6.1842	2-11- 8
59 Mary C.	9. 3.1863	31- 9-14
61 Mary E.	12. 3.1848	0- 5-19
67 Peter C.	7. 7.1884	26- 3- 9
59 Richard I.	2.14.1880	76- 0- 0
2 Sarah	1.15.1845	58- 0- 0
61 Sarah A.	4.22.1895	73- 3- 4
KELLY		
66 Mary A.	5.__.1888	75- 1- 0
KEVITT		
44 Cornelia KASTELYN	9.27.1878	73- 5- 2
50 Jacob	1.18.1893	2-11-19
59 Maatje ZEEDYK	3. 5.1885	55- 6-13
39 Nellie	1.24.1890	68-11- 2
39 Nicholas	2.15.1885	65- 5-13
27 Rosa	8.16.1883	17- 3- 7
KIDNEY		
39 Cora	11. 6.1886	8- 7-11
KINGSLAND		
31 Joseph I.	8.31.1891	13- 9-17
KINSEY		
104 Ann SIMMONS	11. 9.1865	55-11- 8
73 Lura	3.16.1879	0- 8- 6
KIP		
3 Ann	8. 5.1889	67- 9- 3
5 Carrie	7.31.1861	0- 4-25
13 Catherine M. ACKERMAN	1825-1895	70y
4 Christina A.	10.12.1856	26y
13 Clara J.	2.13.1874	26- 3- 0
87 Clarissa	10.16.1841	56- 5-22
9 Clarissa	8.11.1839	18- 7-10
4 Cordelia A. ANDRUSS	2.27.1854	31- 6-21
89 Cornelius	10. 3.1813	11-10- 3
20 Cornelius	10.10.1827	14- 7- 1
13 Effie B.	8.31.1885	73y
5 Frank W.	11.12.1871	0- 0-13
5 Frederic H.	4. 5.1860	2- 1-24
9 Hartman	12. 5.1840	0- 4- 5
13 Hartman	5.27.1872	27-10- 5
80 Hendrick	12.10.1796	76- 3- 9
112 Henry I.	9.30.1880	99-10-25
84 Henry P.	2.21.1840	69- 7- 7
13 Henry P.	6.14.1881	68y
21 Jane	8.26.1826	86- 0- 0
14 Jane E.	2.11.1839	1- 0- 1
80 Jany	9.24.1797	76- 1-16
80 Jemima	9.12.1823	72- 4- 0
4 Jennie	4.25.1891	43- 3-13
21 John	3.11.1812	53- 9-13
4 John Wm.	7.19.1853	0- 8-10

* - see page 328

CEMETERY RECORD

*#		Death	Age
	KIP (con'd)		
14	Maria MARSELIS	7. 4.1841	22- 4-14
5	Minnie P.	7.26.1870	1- 2- 3
4	Nana H.	6.__.1892	1m
4	Nicholas J.	10.26.1871	47- 6-27
81	Peter	3. 8.1813	69- 2-10
9	Peter H.	11.14.1845	54- 0- 9
13	Peter P.	2.21.1873	50- 4-__
79	Sally	3.18.1876	78- 0- 0
3	Waling	3.12.1880	61- 4- 0
	KUSANT		
44	Johannie	6.13.1880	25- 6- 0
	LABAUGH		
32	Eliza E.	4.20.1841	1- 8-16
	LANG		
44	Fred	4.21.1886	18- 3-13
	LINCOLN		
30	Luisa	7. 1.1867	29- 0- 0
	LINDEMER		
11	John	10.24.1861	46- 6-25
	LEIGHTON		
55	John	6.10.1875	88- 5-11
55	Margaret TERHUNE	8.28.1850	56- 7- 0
55	Sarah C.	1.28.1883	52-11- 8
	LINFORD		
116	Abraham	4.16.1850	77- 3-21
117	Abraham H.	9.25.1851	45- 2-17
118	Eliza Jane	7.18.1858	40- 7-25
118	Herman	9. 8.1851	81- 2-25
118	Letty	9.27.1848	67- 3-15
117	Mary VAN RIPER	1.28.1854	84- 4-20
18	Sarah SICKLER		
	LOCKWOOD		
1	Helena	11. 4.1890	38- 7-24
	LOGAN		
42	Ellen	5.14.1882	63- 0- 0
42	Henry	8.13.1863	0-15- 0
42	John	2.18.1858	0-15- 0
	LOSEE		
99	William A.	8.17.1861	2y
	LOW		
69	Diana	3.11.1888	80-10-24
69	George V.	5.16.1867	32- 3-__
	LUDLOW		
43	Ann	7.10.1803	0-11-10
1	Elizabeth	5.31.1839	79- 8- 6
49	Elizabeth	7.10.1807	40- 6-23
45	Lena	9. 2.1806	1- 0- 3
1	Richard	11.17.1820	75- 3- 0

* - see page 328

CEMETERY RECORD

*#		Death	Age
59	W. G. M.		
	MARINUS		
90	Ezechiel	11.28.1737 or 1757	1- 6- 5
	MARSELIS		
84	Catherine J.	9.22.1822	3- 5-26
7	Catherine J.	4.13.1864	33- 7-12
9	Clarissa	8.11.1839	18- 7-10
6	Cornelius	12.28.1860	2- 8-24
6	Cornelius I.	11.15.1893	68y
18	Edo	7.13.1813	13- 3-18
22	Edo	9. 9.1845	0- 9- 3
--	Edo G.	1.18.1832	26- 4- 1
1	Edo P.	4. 8.1852	64- 3-18
7	Elizabeth	12.31.1878	75- 0- 9
23	Ellen	5.25.1831	4- 0-29
1	Hetty KIP	7.20.1875	83- 4- 1
2	Hiley Ann	8. 9.1840	0- 7-25
9	Jane VAN RIPER	1. 3.1856	84- 1- 0
86	Jane VAN WINKEL	10. 4.1844	77- 9-22
9	John	9. 7.1841	76-11-20
7	John	9.19.1857	28y
6	Johnny	9.11.1862	6- 6- 0
2	Kitty	1.26.1850	36- 8-10
2	Kitty	7.31.1850	0- 6-19
--	Maria	9.23.1831	5- 3-14
2	Mary	2.15.1867	3- 2-11
2	Mary B.	2.22.1857	0- 6-17
85	Peter	5. 4.1827	67-11-10
1	Peter	2.11.1881	69y
	MARTIN		
30	Harriet L.	1.16.1892	28y
62	Joseph D.	10.16.1856	2- 5-12
62	Richard S. D.	8. 7.1851	0- 8-21
62	Washington I.	5.10.1869	4- 3- 4
	MATHE		
46	Elizabeth May	3.10.1871	3- 2- 5
46	Mary CONKLIN	2.28.1871	31- 1- 8
	MAYNARD		
30	Phoebe Eliza WILBER	1. 7.1868	35- 3-28
	MC CORNAC		
69	Charles	9. 5.1864	30-10-24
69	Harry		
69	John L.	7.31.1858	1- 3- 0
	MC CUNE		
60	William	3.11.1886	52- 6- 0
	MC KEAN		
96	Susannah	6.17.1842	30y
	MC KENZIE		
113	Janet	9. 5.1882	81y

* see page 328

CEMETERY RECORD

*#		Death	Age
	MC PHERSON		
32	Isabelle WHYTE	4.12.1882	66y
32	William	3.31.1891	73y
	MELONEY		
24	Ann	10. 2.1824	74- 0- 0
	MICHELS		
96	Gertrude S.	12. 1.1895	24- 3-22
76	Jeremiah	8. 2.1812	0- 0-12
76	Nancy	7. 6.1807	0- 6- 4
	MOORE		
4	David	7.13.1876	63y
	MORRIS		
15	Jacob	9.19.1799	44- 4- 9
14	Sylvest John	9.25.1819	1-10-25
	MUCHEL		
30	Nancy G.	7. 6.1807	0- 6- 4
	NACKE		
122	John	2. 8.1861	4- 3- 6
	NELSON		
73	Harry	10.25.1893	9m
73	John	1857-1891	34y
	NUTLEY		
70	John	11.23.1868	66- 1-11
	OLDIS		
115	Amos	4. 4.1875	0- 5- 4
81	Garret	7.10.1884	42- 1- 5
	OSBORN		
104	Hazel	12.25.1890	1- 3-26
	OTIS		
50	Ira	7.21.1832	33- 1- 2
	OUTWATER		
68	Annie	5.12.1874	26- 3-16
113	Catherine K.	8.13.1850	67-11-11
112	Henry	1. 6.1887	67- 0- 6
68	John	11.13.1874	30- 3-11
67	John R.	4.28.1885	73- 8- 0
67	Lavinia SPIER	12.25.1891	55- 6-13
113	Mariah VAN WINKEL	7.29.1864	41- 7- 8
68	Mary	8.21.1871	8m
68	Peter R.	12. 4.1871	58- 0- 0
113	Richard	5. 6.1858	81- 2-27
67	Sophia	2. 1.1865	54- 3-__
	OVERBAUGH		
12	Genevieve STEENBERG	4.10.1893	56y
	OWEN		
45	Chester B.	8.29.1882	35- 1- 5

* - see page 328

CEMETERY RECORD

*#		Death	Age
	PALMER		
52	George N.	2.21.1889	67- 3-25
52	Georgie N.	5.22.1886	1- 5-27
52	John A.	4.16.1869	12- 9-12
52	Susan J. AYCRIGG	9.16.1893	59- 6- 2
	PARISH		
120	Johanna SEWARD	3.15.1853	47-11-13
	PATIMOR		
33	Charity A.	9.27.1883	71- 5- 0
	PAULSON		
86	Jane	11. 4.1858	83- 7- 0
86	Peter	3.16.1838	66- 2- 0
	PAXTON		
23	Daniel R.	8.13.1813	77- 0- 0
120	Daniel R.	6. 9.1863	43- 3- 5
23	Elizabeth	4.19.1855	75- 0- 0
120	Elizabeth	8.27.1869	49- 0- 0
50	Henry	9. 4.1865	87- 9-__
23	Mary	8.17.1825	45- 0- 0
	PELL		
53	Benjamin	8. 7.1862	26- 0-25
53	Edward M.	12.25.1863	21- 9-26
53	John B.	12.16.1882	82- 1-26
53	Susan A. AYCRIGG	3.15.1883	77- 4-22
52	Susan A.	5. 3.1837	4- 4- 0
	PETERS		
36	Francis	11.15.1886	80- 0- 0
36	Mary	12. 3.1883	68- 9- 7
	PIER		
34	Mary C.	7.21.1856	24- 2- 0
35	Moses	1.12.1856	64-10- 0
	PIPLING		
101	Aaron	5.23.1892	55y
	POST		
97	Abraham R.	8.23.1870	44- 4- 2
87	Adrian	3. 7.__	30- 2- 7
87	Adrian	2. 3.1781	75- 3-28
87	Adrian	1. 4.1789	82- 7-21
89	Adrian	12.28.1797	85- 4- 3
16	Adrian	6.24.1823	75- 2-17
34	Adrian	8.25.1808	21- 9-15
33	Adrian	8.21.1824	1- 6-24
74	Adrian	1. 4.1874	24- 5- 6
33	Adrian A.	1.11.1806	75- 1- 9
87	Adria- M.	5.25.1829	72- 9-28
37	Agnes	12.24.1884	71- 7- 2
22	Albert	1. 9.1855	0- 5-22
74	Ann ZABRISKIE	6. 8.1854	41- 4-__
98	Ann Eliza	2. 6.1853	4- 3-18
86	Benjamin M.	6.19.1895	58- 7-14

* - see page 328

CEMETERY RECORD

*#		Death	Age
	POST (con'd)		
37	Benjamin Z.	5. 8.1886	50- 0-__
36	Caspar	3.28.1842	75- 4-21
34	Catherine	2. 3.1814	69- 9- 6
72	Clarissa	10.15.1855	70y
35	Cornelius	2. 2.1812	76- 0- 0
37	Cornelius	2.13.1855	77- 7- 4
67	Cornelius	12. 3.1863	70-11- 0
82	Cornelius	12.26.1850	3- 3- 4
21	Cornelius C.	3.27.1856	50- 0-29
75	Cornelius T.	10.17.1884	53- 0- 0
35	Eliza	2. 2.1823	21- 6-16
67	Eliza Ann	9.25.1875	47- 4-16
44	Elizabeth ACKERMAN	5.27.1860	105- 0- 0
88	Elizabeth	11.20.1848	82- 0-12
86	Elizabeth	6.13.1801	19-11- 2
37	Elizabeth	6.28.1811	27- 9-11
66	Elizabeth G.	8.24.1885	84y
73	George	8. 9.1870	30- 6-__
74	George	2.26.1870	23-10-__
88	Hannah	7.14.1825	72- 7-11
21	Hannah VAN HOUTEN	12. 8.1886	7- 0-11
29	Helmich	10.15.1808	6- 6- 5
82	James I.	10.22.1825	52- 8- 8
77	Jane (ACKERMAN)		
33	Jane ACKERMAN	11.15.1835	68- 1-25
82	Jane VAN GIESEN	7.26.1865	58- 4-25
84	Jane	1.22.1881	5- 8-16
98	Jane Ellen	5. 1.1864	34-11- 8
22	Jasper	10.16.1865	20- 1- 2
5	John Aaron	1. 9.1837	9- 0-10
94	John A.	6.19.1814	39- 7- 5
67	John A.	8.17.1858	64- 7-23
72	John A.	12. 2.1864	59- 9-23
24	John G.	8.16.1887	86- 4-12
44	John H.	3. 7.1847	97- 0- 0
121	John R.	10.26.1863	44- 6-2'
96	Josiah	8.12.1870	0- 1-22
75	Julia	2.20.1865	4- 5- 0
33	Kitty	3.15.1820	87- 1- 1
85	Lea Anna	10. 5.1861	7w
45	Margaret GARRISON	10. 2.1880	84- 9-__
36	Maria KONCH	3. 4.1814	75- 4-12
38	Maria	12.30.1848	33- 9-27
45	Maria DEMAREST	2.18.1893	68- 0- 0
89	Marselis	5. 8.1787	81- 0- 0
85	Marselis	8. 7.1845	2-10-26
88	Marselis A.	8.23.1839	50- 9-11
15	Mary	9.29.1821	52-11-24
82	Mary	11.28.1862	69- 8-14
74	Mary VAN RIPER	1.12.1890	79- 8- 2
38	Natia	6. 1.1875	78- 3-10
66	Peter C.	2.19.1895	70- 6- 6
72	Rachel HUYLER	11.14.1852	46y

* - see page 328

CEMETERY RECORD

	Death	Age
POST (con'd)		
38 Richard	4. 1.1861	19-11-18
38&90 Richard A.	5. 3.1843	49- 8-13
84 Richard M.	7.10.1881	30y
24 Sarah J.		45y
48 Sarah J.	1.14.1887	51- 2- 0
36 Sophia PAULSON	5. 3.1859	85- 4- 0
72 Susan Elizabeth	9.22.1855	8- 0-18
74 Theodore	1. 1.1876	68- 6- 2
20 Thomas	1.20.1815	76- 6- 0
63 Tunis C.	2.17.1859	1- 4-22
PRAWL		
56 Aaron	6.23.1875	72-11-23
56 Catherine OLDIS	10.24.1885	81- 7-21
57 Isaac Van Winkel	8.12.1849	12- 7-12
PRENTISE		
26 Ann TERHUNE	7.17.1888	78- 0-10
26 William	12.26.1863	61- 2- 4
26 Willie	9. 1.1871	1- 1-15
PRICE		
36 Ann Amelia	9.25.1838	0- 4- 0
36 Susannah GARRISON	11. 1.1839	27- 0- 0
36 Susannah	8. 8.1832	0- 7- 0
PYE		
3 Pauline DOW	3. 6.1846	44-11- 2
3 Richard Bolton	10.17.1837	1- 5- 5
3 Sarah Eliza	10. 9.1847	7- 8- 2
3 Simon F.	3.24.1845	18- 9-23
RANDOL		
61 Christina	9.20.1880	0- 5-16
61 Clara G.	1.15.1872	0- 0-18
61 Emily L.	6. 7.1873	0- 5-15
61 Isabel G.	9.10.1878	1- 6-15
READER		
29 Louise		
REMIG		
-- Ida May	1.13.1883	1- 1- 2
RETTINGER		
121 Elizabeth R.	9.23.1885	81- 5-17
REYERS		
66 Clarissa	8. 7.1876	63- 1-11
48 Cornelius G.	6.30.1865	25- 6- 5
119 Gerrebrand	1.13.1895	78-11- 6
119 Jane	10.18.1883	68-10-13
-- John V.	1896	
REYNOLDS		
39 Sarah	8.19.1890	80- 2-__
RICE		
70 Frankie		3- 8-__

* - see page 328

```
                    CEMETERY   RECORD
 *#                           Death                    Age
        RICE (con'd)
 73 Meritt E.                 2. 9.1883            32- 6-24
 73 Polly T.                  2.17.1888            63- 9- 7
 70 Samuel W., Prof.          1.14.1882            47- 6-11
        RIKER
 99 Abraham T.                1.22.1867            52- 0- 0
 72 Alfred A.                 8. 8.1864             1- 5- 0
 50 Catherine                 3.12.1846            27-11-22
 47 Eliza Jane                8.26.1840             1- 2- 0
 61 John H.                   1.23.1845             2- 8- 9
 47 John R.                  10.28.1846             0- 8-15
 99 Lucy                      5.14.1869            22-10-22
 49 Margaret                  1.31.1873            61-10-22
 50 Mary                     12.16.1847            63- 0- 0
 31 Mary Ann                  4.29.1890            70- 8- 8
 31 Richard                                        58- 0-23
 50 Thomas                    9.28.1869            82- 6-19
100 William T.                3.10.1862            22- 2-12
        ROMEYN
 87 Auletty ACKERMAN          8.21.1834            43y
 64 Mary BOGARDUS
        ROSE
 43 Adelia                    4.28.1890            74- 0- 0
 43 W. W.                     8.18.1881            66- 0- 9
        SACKETT
 11 Elizabeth                 2. 3.1862            83- 3- 0
        SATTLER
 50 Louis                     2. 5.1892            5y
        SCHENCK
 55 Charles H.               11.21.1889            63- 5-13
 55 George                    6. 1.1876            23- 5- 5
        SCHIERHOLTZ
 59 Frank                     7.21.1885            53- 5- 0
        SCHLEICH
 12 Albert H.                11. 1.1867            51- 0-10
        SCHOONMAKER
 16 Lydia                     5.11.1827            48-11-20
        SCUDDER
  1 Benjamin R.              12. 8.1819            56- 0- 0
 -- Benjamin                 11.22.1829            63- 1- 5
  1 Sarah                    11.22.1829            63- 1- 5
        SEARLE
 47 Frank, Post #7 GAR Dept. N.J.  3.24.1874       38y
        SHELP
 56 Jane E.                   6. 3.1870            78y
 66 Mary A.                   8.24.1890            66- 0-14
        SICKLER
 45 James                    12.14.1804            63- 0- 0

    * - see page 328
```

CEMFTERY RECORD

*#		Death	Age
	SICKLER (con'd)		
44	Mary	2. 6.1802	58- 3- 8
18	Sarah	8.11.1849	77- 4- 0
	SIMMONS		
69	Ann	6. 4.1865	59- 4- 4
69	Anna Matilda	5. 1.1859	16-10-22
73	Anna Matilda	7.13.1864	1- 6-11
56	Henry P.	1896	
69	James	4.16.1880	43- 0- 0
6	Margaret WESTERVELT	3.21.1832	57- 7-30
6	Peter	5.25.1836	78- 1- 2
103	Rachel	10. 8.1853	52- 7- 5
56	Sally	11.18.1877	72- 0- 0
56	Sarah VAN WINKEL	8. 5.1887	69- 0- 0
78	William	10.20.1759	18- 2-12
56	William H.	8.20.1852	1- 7-24
	SIP		
28	Adrian	3.30.1817	66- 6-29
32	Adrian	8.14.1796	10-10- 5
2	Adrian	11. 3.1879	64- 3-19
28	Adrian A.	1. 9.1815	20- 9- 0
58	Adrian I.	7. 3.1895	76-10-29
43	Adrianna MARSELIS	4.19.1842	53- 6- 0
15	Anna	3.23.1855	37- 5-24
41	Annanche	7. 7.1807	91- 8-18
41	Cornelius	8. 9.1825	65-11-16
58	Cornelius	8.23.1872	19- 4-13
15	Cornelius H.	10.25.1853	3- 0-10
3	Edo	8. 3.1856	47- 3-27
5	Eliza J. VAN BLARCOM	2.10.1864	19-10-11
3	Elizabeth VAN HOUTEN	2.14.1883	72- 9- 0
42	Gertrude	2. 7.1822	66- 0- 3
58	Howell Purdy	5.29.1856	6- 3-11
28	Isaac A.	7. 8.1830	41- 3-19
58	Isaac A.	9.15.1861	14- 1-26
38	Jacob	8.23.1839	32- 2- 2
3	Jane VREELAND	5.14.1877	62- 7-16
42	John	11.23.1800	82- 3- 6
42	John	10. 2.1806	58- 5-15
3	John	6.18.1892	84- 2- 1
43	John I.	7. 4.1845	64- 9-16
2	Kitty MARSELIS		
28	Lea	2.15.1815	57- 5-19
58	Lydia H. PURDY	10.16.1865	47- 7-10
41	Maria	1.17.1845	80- 6-16
15	Philip H.	2. 2.1855	1- 0-14
33	Sarah	12.24.1813	0- 5-15
15	Susan PURDY	2.26.1880	59- 7-13
15	Tunis	3.23.1873	51- 8- 3
	SLATER		
88	Charles H.	11.11.1878	28- 3-13
27	James	12.15.1844	40- 5-11

* - see page 328

CEMETERY RECORD

	Death	Age
SLIKER		
117 Harriet LINFORD	3.14.1890	83- 1-14
SLINGERLAND		
41 David	8. 6.1880	16- 3- 0
SLOAT		
68 Agnes A.	5.12.1840	11- 7- 3
68 Catherine	12.15.1856	23- 5- 3
69 Jane	12.21.1836	0- 5-18
68 Peter	5.22.1882	79- 2-12
SMITH		
35 Anna Sophia	2. 2.1877	22- 8-13
53 Augusta H.	12. 4.1884	15- 1- 2
54 Bessie Burrough	10.20.1866	2- 5-22
72 Caspar	8.23.1887	58- 2-12
49 Charles John	6.28.1894	36- 8-10
61 Eleanor E.	8. 4.1864	0- 9-11
49 Elizabeth	8.29.1871	28- 9-20
-- Freddie	5.14.1891	3-11- 2
7 Garret	1.26.1848	0- 7-29
16 Jane	11. 1.1861	30- 8-18
61 Jessie E.	8. 8.1870	1- 1-17
34 Louis	9.19.1892	60- 9-11
35 Louise Frederick	4.18.1876	10- 7- 8
53 M. B., Rev.	9. 1.1882	49- 9-25
61 Norman E.	9.23.1868	0- 3-24
60 Robert B.	1896	
SNEDEN		
7 Rachel	4.10.____	0- 1-24
7 Richard	1.20.1842	27- 8-29
SNYDER		
121 Anna A.	9. 7.1886	4- 5- 1
SOMMER		
12 Clara	4. 3.1871	1- 8- 0
SPIER		
116 Abraham L.	1.26.1860	6y
107 Annie R.	12.28.1893	32- 0-22
93 Charity	3.12.1876	74- 2- 5
28 Eleanor Jane	2.23.1877	59- 7- 6
121 Eliza J. POST	3.14.1889	39- 9- 0
32 Elizabeth TERHUNE	10.14.1843	76- 5-14
115 Elizabeth	1.28.1857	79- 4-27
107 Elizabeth	3. 1.1891	63- 5-20
21 Ella M.	4. 2.1891	30-10- 3
31 Garret	12. 4.1828	75- 2-22
106 Garret Jno.	10.22.1866	84- 0-25
106 Garret R.	3.31.1855	5- 1-10
107 James P.	7.19.1888	81- 5-28
106 Jane	9.20.1856	2- 6-24
30 Jared J.	1.10.1835	17-11-18
31 John	1.22.1818	0- 3-13

* - see page 328

CEMETERY RECORD

*#		Death	Age
	SPIER (con'd)		
93	John I.	5.21.1890	89- 9-26
71	John P.	5. 9.1891	81- 1- 1
31	John T.	6.12.1833	73- 5-21
107	Lea	1.15.1878	60- 8-15
27	Margaret ENNIS	10.12.1816	60-10-22
107	Margaret	2.15.1867	84- 2-25
30	Maria	1. 9.1852	--
110	Mary ALYEA	6.19.1860	67-11- 4
71	Mary Anna	2.16.1869	3- 6-__
31	Nelly	5.31.1795	10- 7- 0
110	Peter A.	7. 6.1881	53- 2-27
107	Peter I.	2.25.1853	73- 3-14
108	Rachel J.	12.25.1867	27- 2-21
107	Ralph G.	12.18.1872	51- 2- 7
108	Richard P.	8.14.1868	0- 7-20
31	Thomas I.	5.15.1836	50-10-15
110	William H.	1.20.1864	26- 6-25
110	William I.	3.16.1860	65- 6- 5
	SPRAGUE		
33	Courtland A.	5. 6.1886	62- 0- 0
	STARK		
60	Neeltje	1.24.1885	7y
60	Philippina	6.21.1885	3- 3- 7
	STEADMAN		
48	Clara Van Blarcom	1884-1886	
	STEARNS		
43	Mary A. ROSE	11.18.1880	36- 6- 6
	STEGG		
14	Catherine VAN RIPER	5.18.1826	48- 8- 5
14	Jacob	11.13.1810	61- 7-13
16	James C.	1.13.1836	59-10-23
16	Lydia	__.11.1827	48-11-20
	STEWART		
114	Jane	8.12.1848	80y
	STONE		
11	William D.	10.30.1853	32- 0- 0
	STRANGE		
44	Emily S.	6.23.1881	24- 6- 8
	STRAYER		
66	Magdalene	2.21.1882	2- 3-17
	STRONG		
54	Cornelia W. HUYER	1826-1893	67y
54	J. Paschel, Rev.	1826-1890	64y
54	Lottie	9.17.1864	0- 0-26
	STROYER		
30	Janey	10. 6.1877	3- 4-28
30	John	9.12.1877	1- 0-12
9	Leonard D.	11.14.1887	29- 2-__

* - see page 328

CEMETERY RECORD

*#		Death	Age
	SWIN		
61	Mary	10. 7.1854	54-11- 0
	TAYLOR		
65	Eleazer C., Capt.	9. 7.1884	71- 6- 1
66	Lillie		
66	Mary F.	5.__.1888	11- 6-21
	TERHUNE		
115	Albert R.	1843-1876	33y
115	Alletta V. D.	1857-1858	1y
4	Ann	8.24.1834	10- 2-24
4	Arianna	9. 1.1857	60- 0-29
8	Carrie	6. 3.1865	4- 4-17
8	Cornelius	10. 6.1852	0-10- 8
92	Cornelius J.	12.15.1894	63- 9-17
9	Elizabeth	12.16.1883	78- 4-__
8	Elizabeth	10.17.1857	4- 1-12
95	Ellen	6.25.1887	53- 0-29
9	Garret, M.D.	7. 2.1886	83- 8-__
115	James H.	1855-1875	20y
4	Jane	8.20.1834	7- 7- 5
5	Jane Ann	7.23.1834	0- 8-11
4	Jane Ann	9. 4.1848	13- 0-18
8	Jane Ann	8.12.1857	0- 9- 5
92	John W.	9. 6.1862	7- 7-16
115	John Z.	1847-1874	24y
--	John Zabriskie	9.17.1837	0- 5-29
92	Letty Ann	2.26.1860	2- 3-17
8	Lillian	9. 6.1863	1- 5- 0
37	Maggie	2.12.1886	0- 0-20
82	Mary B.	4. 8.1820	82- 0- 0
61	Minnie	9. 3.1864	1- 5-23
110	Nicholas	3. 6.1884	79-10- 0
4	Nicholas R.	2.15.1849	57- 1- 1
37	Olive	1.29.1889	16- 1-15
115	Paul	1861-1884	23y
115	Richard	1822-1887	67y
8	Richard	6.21.1865	1- 7- 8
37	Sarah E.	2.25.1886	44y
92	William	6.11.1875	51- 8- 3
	THARP		
48	Nathaniel	2.17.1846	73- 3- 9
	TICKLEMAN		
59	Edward	6.15.1882	18- 2-13
	TOERS		
14	Anna Maria	2.25.1850	0- 8-15
41	David		
	TOMLINSON		
55	George	12.22.1890	52- 4-17
55	George L.	2.20.1893	29y
	TREPPKE		
12	Mary	2.25.1858	31- 5- 0

* - see page 328

CEMETERY RECORD

*#		Death	Age
	TURNER		
71	Charles M.	12.19.1893	41- 7-18
	TYSEN		
105	Eunice	9.10.1862	52y
65	Henry	3.26.1868	88y
106	Henry E.	3. 3.1872	43y
106	John	11.15.1879	72y
65	Mary H.	2.24.1871	85y
72	Phoebe	3.22.1871	68- 8-23
	VAN ALLEN		
10	Elizabeth	5.22.1838	70- 0- 0
	VAN BLARCOM		
49	Adrian	12.18.1891	78-10- 0
49	Elizabeth	5.31.1891	52- 7-__
49	Harriet E.	4.27.1875	5-10-19
49	Phoebe SHELP	9.30.1884	67- 5- 0
48	Sarah	6.24.1875	88- 3-16
	VAN BUSSEN		
109	Cecelia	11. 3.1855	1- 5- 0
28	Eliza Jane	3. 7.1837	25- 4- 7
67	Elizabeth	10.21.1875	63- 6-__
109	Garret D.	10. 1.1888	65- 8- 8
17	Hannah	4.21.1856	79- 5- 0
48	Herman	11.18.1809	24- 2- 7
99	Jane GOETSCHIUS	8. 5.1861	80y
109	Jane	2.18.1895	70- 5- 1
99	John	4. 3.1865	82y
109	Lawrence	7.15.1853	2- 1- 0
18	Peter	1.13.1811	44-11-18
66	Philip P.	2.23.1882	72- 9- 0
109	Rachel L.	9. 7.1857	6m
48	Sietje	3.26.1816	50- 0-10
48	Teunis	9.17.1810	22- 7- 7
	VANDERBAW		
79	Catrana	3.26.1764	9- 5-28
	VAN DER BEEK		
72	Alletta VAN EYDESTYN	1. 5.1861	47- 2-23
72	Catherine Ann	12. 7.1850	9- 0-21
72	Lavinia	8.29.1856	6- 1-20
	VAN EYDESTYN		
9	Agnes	5. 9.1855	38- 1- 5
79	Andrew	11. 5.1858	23- 0- 0
110	Anna A.	5.24.1886	29- 8-18
13	Anny BANTA	12.17.1852	79- 4- 0
79	Catherine Van W.	1787-1861	74y
34	Catherine Jane	10. 9.1875	22- 5- 9
9	David D.	8.27.1852	1- 2-17
79	Eliza	1823-1890	67y
67	Eliza VAN RIPER	11.18.1884	58- 0-15
34	Elizabeth	5.12.1887	75- 5- 4
78	Elizabeth	3.11.1868	33- 6- 0

* - see page 328

CEMETERY RECORD

*#		Death	Age
	VAN EYDESTYN (con'd)		
10	Freddy	12. 7.1870	5- 3-22
95	Gertrude	6.13.1879	72-10-10
95	Gertrude	9.16.1842	1- 7-29
79	Hannah	1820-1896	76y
94	Henry	2. 6.1893	64-10-23
95	Henry P.	4.16.1893	89-10-22
79	Henry T.	2.15.1893	75- 4-17
65	Jennie M. LYON	10. 7.1879	28y
79	John	1769-1840	71y
34	John	1.16.1873	29- 6-29
95	John	11.11.1884	14- 1-27
67	John A.	8.21.1855	1- 9- 2
67	John T.	4.19.1889	70- 7- 6
10	John Wm.	8.31.1867	17- 5-11
95	Mary	4.17.1831	61- 1-29
65	Mary Ann	6.27.1863	22- 5-__
10	Mary J. VAN WINKEL	6.15.1856	30- 6-11
34	Mary J.	10.15.1846	6- 5-14
9	Michael	1.20.1875	59- 0- 0
95	Peter	1.19.1853	87- 0-29
17	Sally	10.10.1823	30- 5-25
34	Theodore	3.31.1877	65- 7-12
34	Theodore	4.24.1870	20- 1-11
13	Tunis	7.24.1828	46- 6- 5
80	Tunis	1810-1840	30y
	VAN GIESEN		
15	Abraham	7.19.1753	86- 8- 6
39	Cornelius	3.31.1797	6- 0-23
48	Elizabeth	2. 5.1816	66- 6- 9
82	Jane	7.26.1865	58- 4-25
10	Susan	8. 7.1839	50- 0- 0
	VAN HEEST		
13	Sadie VAN DEN BURG	1.19.1887	22- 4-21
13	T.		9- 0-12
	VAN HOUTEN		
22	Aaron	3. 4.1884	10- 0- 0
65	Aaron A.	12.17.1858	76- 1-17
64	Aaron C.	9. 7.1883	36- 0- 0
82	Adrian	2. 2.1883	83- 0- 0
18	Adrian	10. 1.1809	1- 7-10
111	Anna POST	12. 4.1858	81- 2- 4
64	Anna Maria	9. 5.1847	2- 5- 0
41	Anny M.	9. 5.1845	2- 4-19
68	Catherine	8.20.1884	62- 8- 5
17	Cornelia VAN NESS	9.15.1824	60- 0- 0
45	Cornelius	9.23.1801	2- 9- 0
69	Cornelius	2. 1.1891	69- 1-22
22	Cornelius	2.14.1884	19- 0- 0
64	Cornelius A.	2. 9.1895	75- 0- 0
--	Ellen Jane	3. 3.1861	4-11-25
17	Garret	8.23.1826	63- 0- 0
65	Hannah	6.20.1875	87- 5- 3

* - see page 328

CEMETERY RECORD

*#		Death	Age
	VAN HOUTEN (con'd)		
25	Henry C.	5.12.1877	92- 9- 8
17	Hester VAN NESS	3.12.1837	36- 1-22
25	Jane VAN WINKEL	3. 6.1822	33-10- 5
64	Jennie	9. 3.1891	38- 0- 0
16	John C.	4.29.1833	61-10-11
16	Maria	2.11.1829	16-11- 8
25	Rachel HARRIS	5. 3.1839	48- 5- 3
	VAN NOSTRAND		
3	Gertrude	1. 6.1841	88- 0- 0
85	Hannah	2.18.1829	75- 2- 0
	VAN ORDEN		
25	Annie M.	7. 2.1870	31- 3-15
25	J. Thomas	2.10.1895	
25	Jacob	12.27.1881	63- 1-18
28	Noah	9. 9.1865	19- 9- 5
	VAN RIPER		
10	A., Capt.	9.16.1880	93- 0- 3
89	Abraham	3.31.1866	83- 6-15
82	Abraham	3.17.1822	26- 9-11
88	Abram W.	6.22.1887	72- 0-19
78	Ann ACKERMAN	4. 5.1859	38- 2-29
27	Anny ALYEA	1.20.1844	25- 9-18
119	Christina	3.27.1874	73- 0-12
88	Clarissa KIP	7.30.1887	71- 9-18
83	Clarissa	9. 3.1841	0-10-29
89	Claushe	12.13.1788	30-10-13
119	Cornelius G.	2.18.1868	75- 5-19
88	Dirk	5.23.1802	66- 6-26
89	Edward	10.24.1872	28- 3- 0
84	Edwin M.	2.26.1847	0- 6-25
78	Eleanor OUTWATER	5.11.1853	52- 9- 5
84	Ellen Jane	1.10.1854	3- 0- 0
78	Garret	11.14.1863	70- 0- 2
81	Garret I.	2.24.1821	82- 0- 0
45	George	8.12.1844	0-11-29
83	George	6. 8.1844	0- 6-15
53	George	receiving vault	
46	Gerrebrant	1.14.1828	21- 9-21
84	Gertrude VAN HOUTEN	1. 6.1870	53- 8-15
45	Jacob	5.15.1807	39- 6-18
83	Jane	5.14.1849	82- 1-28
46	Jane	10.23.1826	49- 9-24
--	Jane	2.14.1838	0- 9- 7
7	John	10.20.1850	0- 2-20
6	John E.	1. 4.1841	87-10-23
84	John E.	9.25.1877	6- 5- 2
6	Lea	9.20.1830	82- 8- 3
81	Lena	9.25.1819	63- 4- 6
88	Lydia KING	12. 8.1873	82- 7- 6
28	Margaret	1.13.1834	4- 2-22
89	Maria	8. 1.1857	72- 0- 0

* - see page 328

CEMETERY RECORD

*#		Death	Age
	VAN RIPER (con'd)		
66	Mary Ann SHELP	8.24.1890	66- 0-14
7	Petrina	10.28.1843	51- 6-24
82	Philip	7.11.1834	79- 6- 3
86	Philip A.	11.24.1882	63- 8- 7
88	Philip I.	8.20.1851	64- 2- 4
89	Silas Canfield	7.27.1854	17- 0- 6
10	Sophrina VAN WINKEL	10.27.1870	73y
57	Waling	10. 7.1873	69- 7-10
11	William H.	2.23.1853	4- 8- 5
	VAN SANT		
2	Eleanor	5.10.1844	51- 9-11
21	Nellie POST	1.24.1858	18- 1- 2
2	Samuel	2. 2.1843	49- 0-27
	VAN VORST		
81	Ellen A.	3.13.1826	51- 5-10
80	Jasper	3.16.1852	82- 6-13
27	John W.	9.20.1842	17- 2- 5
80	Josephine A.	2.22.1880	15- 9-28
80	Rachel	4.11.1853	66-10-12
80	Simon V. B.	5.26.1847	24- 5-11
27	Waling G.	9. 5.1846	59- 7-24
80	William H.	12.22.1888	63- 3- 8
81	William T.	12.19.1854	5- 2-16
	VAN WAGENEN		
80	Garret	3. 2.1804	56- 3-12
80	Herman	10.16.1815	20- 4- 8
80	Ralph	6.13.1816	65- 3-10
56	Sarah	9.23.1841	83- 5- 1
80	Sophia	5. 5.1818	72- 4-23
	VAN WINKEL		
31	Abraham	1.23.1796	85- 0- 0
114	Abraham J.	3.23.1848	0- 0- 3
114	Adolph W.	7.10.1876	63-10-24
114	Adolph W. jr	6.15.1857	46- 2-23
33	Adrian	10.20.1818	24- 0-19
112	Agnes KIP	8.20.1889	84- 6-14
83	Ann	2. 9.1847	81- 0- 3
34	Betsey	8.21.1808	16- 4-20
--	Catherine	4.28.1826	42- 3-15
40	Catherine	9.11.1872	54-11-12
77	Catherine	8.30.1858	49-10- 1
78	Daniel	1.18.1886	69-10-11
114	Edgar B.	8.18.1866	0- 8-10
46	Elcy	4.19.1829	72- 1- 2
115	Eliza OLDIS	4.11.1891	66- 0- 0
24	Elizabeth	12.17.1863	80- 7-21
114	Emeline	9.16.1843	0- 0-11
56	Gaty OLDIS	12.24.1853	66- 7-15
33	Gouy	4.18.1808	21- 6-20
79&85	Hannah VAN NOSTRAND	2.18.1829	75- 2- 0
25	Helmich	5. 5.1822	60-10- 5

* - see page 328

CEMETERY RECORD

*#		Death	Age
	VAN WINKEL (con'd)		
55	Henry V. S.	7.10.1819	22-11-29
56	Henry V. S.	8.25.1859	1- 7-25
77	Hester	1. 3.1854	75-10- 6
77	Isaac	9.14.1848	80- 9- 7
56	Isaac J.	9. 3.1831	45- 4- 4
79	Jacob	8. 5.1834	86- 4-24
36	Jacob A.	12. 4.1814	62- 9-25
86	Jane	10. 4.1844	77- 9-22
17	Jane	5. 5.1824	16- 7-24
43	Jemima		
57	Jeremiah	6.20.1855	33- 0- 0
85	John J.	6.14.1805	32- 9-14
56	John V. S.	6.15.1888	72y
50	Margaret	4. 9.1878	79- 0- 0
50	Marinus	7. 4.1863	76- 5- 0
26	Mary POST	4.13.1821	61- 8- 1
112	Michael	9. 5.1888	87-10-23
--	Nicholas	7. 4.1849	36- 7-17
10	Peter H.	11.14.1853	49- 0-12
114	Petrina	7. 5.1877	58- 7-29
22	Pietertje	1. 1.1846	87- 3-10
48	Rachel	6.25.1803	55- 0-14
18	Richard	4.10.1815	10- 0-13
78	Sarah M.	1. 8.1889	66- 0-16
24	Simon	6.17.1856	72- 8-17
--	Waling	1.17.1832	78- 3-25
18	Waling C.	2.14.1807	32- 2-12
34	Waling H.	9.19.1813	29- 9-17
22	Waling W.	9.29.1832	48- 8-29
114	Waling W.	7.19.1876	9- 1-13
57	Walter Crowell	3.16.1883	2- 0- 0
112	William	2.21.1888	59- 5-28
	VOGT		
43	Elizabeth	12.29.1885	54- 0- 0
	VRELAND		
62	Abraham	5.28.1849	4- 1- 0
118	Abraham H., Rev.	11. 6.1868	56-10-
62	Abraham I.	4.23.1858	69- 5-24
29	Adrian	9. 2.1848	6- 0- 0
28	Adrian E.	12.17.1814	25- 1- 9
29	Ann	1.23.1838	0- 5-18
103	Ann H. JURRIANSE	7.26.1884	69- 8-27
91	Anna	11.29.1875	4-11- 5
65	Anna Margaret	1. 5.1859	3- 4-12
26	Anne	4.27.1816	28- 7- 6
5	Caspar	12.16.1840	23- 7-23
48	Catherine	6.12.1835	69- 0- 0
62	Catherine	4.10.1851	8- 6-20
29	Clarence H.	8.26.1849	0- 9- 0
57	Cornelius J.	10.24.1879	38- 0- 0
62	Daniel A.	12.25.1893	75- 0- 0
80	Dirk	4.23.1786	53- 5-18

* - see page 328

CEMETERY RECORD

*#		Death	Age
	VRELAND (con'd)		
26	Edo	6. 5.1854	71- 3-19
65	Elias A.	10. 9.1871	57- 6- 9
57	Elias E.	10. 1.1892	43- 0- 0
37	Elias J.	5.30.1839	79- 9- 7
--	Elias J.	3. 2.1856	81- 8-12
57	Elias J.	2.22.1895	78- 0- 0
21	Elizabeth	10.18.1827	64- 0-21
83	Elizabeth	1.16.1868	70- 8-10
104	Elizabeth SIMMONS	9. 2.1852	49- 0-13
29	Elizabeth	8.19.1842	1- 6- 0
18	Elizabeth	12.29.1894	3- 8-28
18	Emily M.	12.27.1894	14- 4- 3
23	Enoch	8. 9.1794	1-10- 7
115	Enoch I.	5. 4.1861	62- 7-14
57	Frankie		8- 0- 0
103	George E.	5.15.1891	7- 8- 9
26	Gertrude	8.20.1835	7- 7-26
39	Hannah	5.12.1842	64- 4- 8
39	Herman	10.27.1847	81- 0- 0
91	Ida	12. 2.1875	2- 7- 5
36	Isaac	1.11.1836	90- 0- 0
48	Jacob E.	12. 7.1803	69-11-18
12	Jacob Jon	11. 5.1859	84- 8-11
20	Jane	10.14.1819	86-11-21
1	Jane	11. 5.1889	83- 5- 6
29	Jane	5.15.1849	31-11-21
118	Jane W.	8.28.1883	65-10-22
26	Jemima	7.21.1830	40- 9- 1
91	Jessie	7.16.1878	0-11- 2
5	John	1.15.1850	24- 4- 5
62	John A.	1.22.1873	60- 0-12
79	John E.	6.27.1783	0- 0- 5
19	John El	9.26.1808	78- 0-28
5	John M.	8. 6.1839	8- 3-15
91	Kitty	2. 9.1832	37- 1-24
62	Lydia	10.16.1853	65- 6- 0
37	Margaret	2.14.1854	86- 0- 0
82	Mary (BERTHOLF)	4. 8.1820	82y
32	Michael	9.15.1801	70- 6-13
5	Michael	11. 6.1842	29-10- 8
36	Pemalia	10.17.1821	59- 0- 0
12	Phoebe WALLS	4. 8.1848	69- 1- 8
57	Rachel VAN HOUTEN		
58	Rachel BRINKERHOFF	5. 1.1851	75- 0-20
65	Rachel VAN ORDEN	3.27.1864	42-11-26
19	Richard G.	3. 6.1891	70- 0- 0
57	Ruth	1. 2.1867	60- 9-26
17	Sadie B.	2. 5.1885	3- 9- 1
70	Sarah G.	2.17.1886	57- 2- 6
115	Sophia ACKERMAN	1.25.1892	85- 9-24
	WALDROM		
38	Eliza	5. 6.1851	51- 0- 0
37	Elizabeth	3.16.1827	53- 0- 0

* - see page 328

CEMETERY RECORD

*#		Death	Age	*#		Death	Age
	WANTERS				**WILBUR**		
80	Garret	9.26.1802	56- 2-13	36	Margaret	3.17.1884	78- 8- 5
89	Hannah	5. 2.1791	5- 9-25	36	Moran P.	2. 3.1890	81-10- 3
	WASNIDJE				**WILLIAMS**		
74	Edward	12.25.1865	43-10-13	84	Caroline	12.23.1877	74- 8-19
	WATERS			93	Edmund	6. 3.1862	38- 1- 0
121	John G.	3.13.1857	18- 5-13		**WINIG**		
	WEAVER			49	Henry	12. 7.1807	20-11-25
117	Mary VAN RIPER	5.31.1852	29- 7-10		**WITSCHOF**		
117	Samuel	8.11.1852	0- 3-15	29	My Mother	1.11.1888	62- 1-20
	WEISSERT			29	Annie E.	6. 5.1880	20- 4-22
11	Charles F.	1. 4.1867	1- 1- 0	29	Mina	8.14.1878	0- 8-21
11	Willie G.	10.24.1882	7-10- 1		**WRIGHT**		
	WENTWORTH			67	John W.	8.10.1869	2- 3-15
102	George D.	10.27.1886	5- 0-10		**WUERKER**		
	WESTERVELT			26	Joseph C.	3.30.1887	1- 0-25
83	Albert	4.29.1851	10- 7-25		**YAGER**		
83	David A.	10. 8.1875	78- 0- 2	41	W. A.		
83	Jane	9. 3.1829	2- 7-11		**YALE**		
82	John A.	8. 7.1864	4- 3-11	42	William B.	3.24.1893	33-11-23
83	Rachel	12. 6.1825	0- 9-19		**ZABRISKIE**		
83	Sophia POST	12. 1.1871	64- 4-__	76	Abraham C.	11.16.1849	85- 5-17
	WHARTON			77	Annie	4.29.1891	28- 5-22
102	Abram	5. 4.1891	51- 9-18	63	Edith	8.31.1857	0-10-10
102	Anne	12. 7.1886	23- 5-19	63	Elizabeth	2. 5.1856	2-10- 7
11	Charles	5.10.1858	50- 7- 6	63	Jane M.	4.20.1860	28- 4-15
12	Hannah BUSH	12.30.1884	76- 6- 4	77	John	10.22.1866	0- 8-23
11	Mary A.	12. 6.1878	39- 0- 0	76	Josiah	12.10.1817	1- 8- 9
	WHITE			76	Maria	4.21.1886	87y
11	Bogardus	9. 3.1889	3-11- 0	53	P. M., Dr.	vault of	
11	Johnson	7.26.1894	27- 0- 0	77	Rachel Ann	1.17.1869	38y
	WICKWARE						
18	Malangthon S.						
18	Sarah E.						

* - see page 328

DE KEYSER
  Jane, 334
  John, 334
  Peter, 334

DE LA METER
  Hester, 293

DEMAREST
  Ada, 334
  Ann, 334
  Charity, 334(2)
  David, 301, 304, 319, 320, 322(3),
    323, 324(2), 334
  Elizabeth, 302
  Garret, 306, 325, 334
  Jacob, 307
  James, 327, 334
  Jemima, 334
  John, 307
  Lavina, 334
  Margaret, 303
  Maria, 345
  Martin, 334(2)
  Peter, 302, 321(2), 324(2)
  Rachel, 334

DEMOTT
  Mary, 332

DENBOER
  Elizabeth, 334
  Janet, 334
  Maria, 334

DEUKER
  Henrica, 294

DEVOE
  Hester, 293
  Jane, 334
  Letty, 334

DE VOGEL
  Jemima, 334

DeVoreest - see DE FOREEST

DE VRIES
  Nelly, 334

DeVuu - see DEVOE

Dey - see DAY

Dideriks - see DEDRICK

DIRKSE
  Martje, 296

DITO
  Anna, 294

D"Lameter - see DE LA METER

DODD - 334

DONALD
  Elizabeth, 334

Doremes, Doremis, DOREMUS
  Alida, 298
  Anna, 302, 306
  Cornelius, 295, 310(2), 311, 312(2),
    315(2)
  David, 334
  Eleanor, 334
  Ella, 334
  Evanna, 335
  Henry, 294, 301(2), 304, 306, 318(2),
    319(3), 320(3), 321(3), 322(2),
    323(3), 324(2), 326
  Hessel, 319(2)
  Janet, 296
  John, 294, 302, 306(2), 322, 323,
    324(4), 325(3)
  Joris, 294
  Margaret, 306
  Marselis, 335
  Peter, 305, 323(2), 324, 325, 335
  Rachel, 303
  Ralph, 327
  Rebecca, 335
  Roelof, 302, 306, 321, 322, 323(2),
    324, 325
  Samuel, 335
  Susan, 335
  Thomas, 293, 311(2)

Douwe, DOW
  John, 294
  Pauline, 346

Dreak, DREEK
  Cornelius, 295, 298
  Maria, 298

DRUMMOND
  Mary, 335
  Robert, 315(2)
  Sarah, 335

DU BOIS
  Anna, 299
  Ezechiel, 335
  G., 298(3)
  Gualtherus, 309

DUNN
  Cornelius, 335

Duremus - see DOREMUS

Hendrickse, Hendrickson, HENDRIKSE
  Elizam, 333
  Garret, 295, 311(2)
  Geesje, 293

HENNION, Henniyon
  Abraham, 295
  Anna, 305
  Anthony, 302
  Daniel, 295
  David, 309(2)
  Jemima, 334
  John, 294, 310, 312
  Lea, 338

HERMANS, Hermanusse
  Freddie, 337
  G., 311
  Garret, 309, 310(2), 311(2)

HERRITS
  Elizabeth, 295

Herte - see HARTE

HERTIG
  Caspar, 338

HESSELSE, Hesselzen
  Anna, 294
  Elizabeth, 294
  Gertrude, 295
  Peter, 312
  Rachel, 295
  Vroutje, 294

HEWLETT
  Ann, 338
  Thomas, 338

HEYER
  John, 338

HIBON
  Barent, 296

HOBART
  Nana, 337

HOGAN
  Martha, 338

HOHNHORST
  Jamie, 338
  Lizzie, 338

HOLLEY
  Cornelius, 306
  Jeremiah, 338

HOPPER
  Albert, 338(2)
  Catherine, 338

HOPPER (con'd)
  Cornelius, 338
  Elizabeth, 338(2)
  Garret, 338
  Jacob, 338(2)
  Julia, 338
  Keziah, 338
  Maria, 304
  Rebecca, 338

HORNBECK
  Sadie, 338

HOWARD
  Clarissa, 332, 338
  Lucinda, 338

HUBER
  Dora, 336

Huismans - see HUYSMAN

HUNTER
  Isabelle, 306

HUYER
  Cornelia, 350

HUYLER
  Cornelius, 338
  Rachel, 345
  Sarah, 338

HUYSMAN
  Agnes, 304
  Anna, 298
  Ariantje, 296

INGRAM
  Abigail, 338

JACKSON, Jacson
  Maria, 338
  Nancy, 303
  Peter, 326

JACOBS, Jacobusse
  Abraham, 338(2)
  Anna, 338
  Garret, 338
  Harriet, 339
  Henrietta, 339
  Maria, 306, 339(2)

Jansen - see JOHNSON

JAQUES
  Richard, 339

JENKINS
  John, 339

Jeraalman, JERALEMAN
  Agnes, 331

MARSELIS (con'd)
   Johanna, 342
   John, 327(2), 342(2)
   Kitty, 342(2), 348
   Maria, 341, 342(3)
   Peter, 305, 319, 323(2), 324(2),
     325(2), 342(2)

Martens, MARTIN
   Catlintje, 294
   Harriet, 342
   Joseph, 342
   Richard, 342
   Washington, 342

Marzelissen - see MARSELIS

MATHE
   Elizabeth, 342

Maurusse - see MORRIS

MAYNARD - 342

MC CORNAC
   Charles, 342
   Harry, 342
   John, 342

MC CUNE
   William, 342

MC KEAN
   Susan, 342

MC KENZIE
   Janet, 342

MC LAUGHLIN
   Lena, 302

MC PHERSON
   William 343

MEAD
   Christian, 296
   Elsie, 296
   Giles, 296
   Margaret, 293
   Peter, 296
   Rachel, 305

Meclachlin - see MC LAUGHLIN

Meet - see MEAD

Meloney - see MALONEY

MERREL
   Maria, 293

Mersalus, Merseles, Messeelisse - see
   MARSELIS

MESSEKER
   Maria, 295
   Nelly, 296
   Susan, 305

MEYER(s)
   Cornelius, 303
   H., 299

MICHELS, Michielse
   Catherine, 293
   Gertrude, 343
   Jeremiah, 343
   Nancy, 343

MILLER
   Catlintje, 302

MOFFAT
   John, 304

MONTAINE, Montanje
   Nelly, 303

MONTROSE
   Melissa, 330

MOORE
   David, 343

MORRIS, Mourusse
   Abraham, 301, 302
   Jacob, 343
   Sylvester, 343

MUCHEL
   Nancy, 343

NACKE
   John, 343

Neefjes - see NEVIS

Negro
   Tam, 304

NELSON
   Harry, 343
   John, 343

Neuwkerk - see NEWKERK

NEVIS
   Garret, 298(2)
   John, 295, 309, 310

NEWKERK
   Anna, 298
   Gerritje, 295
   Jemima, 294, 298

NUTLEY
   John, 343

NYS
Susan, 298

OLCOTT
Catherine, 338

Oldes, OLDIS
Amos, 343
Catherine, 346
Eliza, 355
Garret, 343
Gaty, 355
John, 305

OLIVER
Susan, 295
Wyntje, 295

Onderdonck, ONDERDONK
Andrew, 306
Rem, 301, 323(2)

O'NIELL
Mary, 336

OOTHOUD
Margaret, 297

OSBORN
Hazel, 343

OTIS
Ira, 343

Oudewaeter, OUTWATER
Anna, 300, 343
Catherine, 343
Eleanor, 354
Francis, 293
Henry, 343
John, 343(2)
Mary, 343
Peter, 343
Richard, 343
Sophia, 343

OVERBAUGH - 343

OWEN
Chester, 343

Paelding - see PAWLING

PALMER
George, 344(2)
John, 344

PARISH - 344

PATIMOR
Charity, 344

PAULSON, Paulus, Paulusse(n), Pauwelse
Anna, 306

PAULSON (con'd)
Catherine, 304
Christina, 296
Dirk, 293
Echje, 293
Fytje, 306
Jane, 344
John, 313, 314
Kitty, 329
Paul, 300, 316(3), 317(3), 319,
320(2), 321, 326
Peter, 293, 303(2), 313, 314, 315(3),
321, 322, 325, 326, 344
Sophia, 346

PAWLING
Margaret, 296

PAXTON
Daniel, 344(2)
Elizabeth, 344(2)
Henry, 344
Mary, 344
Sarah, 337

PELL
Benjamin, 344
Edward, 344
John, 344
Susan, 344

PETERS(en)
Anna, 298
Ariantje, 296
Catherine, 294
Claasje, 298
Elsie, 293
Frances, 295
Francis, 344
Fryntje, 294
George, 298, 312, 313(2), 314(2),
315(2)
Hessel, 293, 300(2), 308(5), 309(2),
310(3), 311(2), 315(3), 316, 317(3),
318(4), 319, 326
John, 296, 312(3)
Lea, 298
Margaret, 302
Mary, 344
Paul, 297
Peter, 298, 312(2), 314(2)
Rachel, 293

PIER
Teunis Jansen—Anthony, 294
Mary, 344
Moses, 344

Pieterse, Pietersze(n) - see PETERS

REYERS (con'd)
  Gerrebrand, 346
  Gertrude, 297, 302
  Jane, 346
  John, 294, 313(3), 327, 346
  Joris, 294, 309, 321, 322
  Lena, 301, 303
  Maria, 303
  Nancy, 306
  Peter, 305

REYNOLDS
  Sarah, 346

RICE
  Frank, 346
  Meritt, 347
  Polly, 347
  Samuel, 347

RIKER
  Abraham, 303, 347
  Alfred, 347
  Catherine, 347
  Eliza, 347
  John, 347(2)
  Lucy, 347
  Margaret, 347
  Mary, 347(2)
  Peter, 295
  Richard, 347
  Ryck, 298
  Thomas, 347
  Wilhelmina, 298
  William, 347

Roman, ROMEYN
  Jacob, 306
  Maria, 294
  Nicholas, 297
  Peter, 295
  Rachel, 297
  William, 293

ROSE
  Adelia, 347
  Agnes, 332
  Mary, 350
  W. W., 347

ROSET
  David, 294

Rothan, RUTHAN
  Anna, 307
  Daniel, 294

Rycke - see RIKER

Ryerse, Ryerson - see REYERS

Ryker - see RIKER

SACKETT
  Elizabeth, 347

Salomons - see SOLOMONS

SANDERS, Sanderszen
  Egbert, 297

Sandvoort, SANFORD, Santvoort
  Anna, 299
  Dimmi, 293

SATTLER
  Louis, 347

SCHENCK
  Charles, 347
  George, 347

SCHIERHOLTZ
  Frank, 347

SCHLEICH
  Albert, 347

SCHOONMAKE
  Henry, 299, 326
  Jacob, 303
  Lena, 302
  Lydia, 347

SCHOUTEN
  Anna, 294

SCHUYLER
  Aaron, 293
  Anna, 298
  Maria, 298

SCOTT
  William, 328

SCUDDER
  Benjamin, 347(2)
  Sarah, 347
  Susan, 333

SEARLE
  Frank, 347

SEELY
  Samuel, 300

SEWARD
  Johanna, 344

SHELP
  Jane, 347
  Mary, 347, 355
  Phoebe, 352

SHERMAN
  Jacob, 296

GENERAL INDEX for pp 293-358

GENERAL INDEX for pp 293-358